GCSE

Technology

a project approach

GCSE Technology

a project approach

P. WILD
Lecturer in Education,
Loughborough University of Technology

T. CAMBRAY
Head of Technology,
Cirencester Kingshill School

M
MACMILLAN

First published 1990

Published by
MACMILLAN EDUCATION LTD
Houndmills, Basingstoke, Hampshire RG21 2XS
and London
Companies and representatives
throughout the world

Designed by The Design Revolution, Brighton

Typeset by Footnote Graphics,
Warminster, Wilts

Printed in Hong Kong

British Library Cataloguing in Publication Data
Wild, P.
GCSE technology.
1. Technology. Projects – For schools
I. Title II. Cambray, T.
600
ISBN 0–333–43414–5

'from the early days of man, Technology has been one of the four environments in which man has lived – the others being the Cosmic, the Natural and the Social.'

Encyclopaedia Brittanica

'I hear and I forget, I see and I remember, I do and I understand.'

Anon.

Acknowledgements

The authors would like to thank:

Gay, Lizzie and the children for giving us so much help and encouragement in the preparation of the typescript.

Gay for typing the typescript.

Chris Gibson, Advisory teacher for Technology, Gloucestershire, for many useful discussions and project ideas.

Colleagues at Cirencester Kingshill School for providing an environment for curriculum development.

Colleagues at Loughborough University of Technology for providing the facilities and time to complete the manuscript.

The authors and publishers wish to acknowledge, with thanks, the following photographic and illustration sources:

Cyril Bernard page 9; Janet & Colin Bord page 12; British Aerospace page 44 (top centre); British Airways page 62 (bottom right); British Rail page 162; British Tourist Authority pages 8 (bottom right), 44 (top left); British Transport Museum page 97 (top); Jim Brownbill pages 25, 26, 41, 81, 83, 84, 86 (bottom), 87 (bottom), 95, 96, 100, 112, 163; Camera Press pages 8 (bottom left), 10, 32, 54, 77; Cement & Concrete Association page 8 (top left and top right; Central Electricity Generating Board pages 56 (top centre), 112 (left); Charnwood Photographic page 21; Economatics Ltd page 113 (bottom); Department of Energy pages 69, 70; Ford Motor Company page 113 (top); Glacier Metal Company Ltd page 68; Griffin & George Ltd pages 13, 146; Haynes Publishing Group pages 19, 85, 90, 95; The Image Bank (cover); The Keystone Collection page 45 (top); Lotus Cars Ltd page 44 (centre); National Bus Company page 62 (top right); PSC Freyssinet Ltd page 87 (right); Renault Dodge pages 89, 91, 104, 108; RS Components pages 136 (bottom), 144, 150, 151, 152, 154, 155, 158, 159, 166; Schrader Bellows page 120 (top); Townsend Thoresen page 44 (bottom left); University of Washington page 45 (bottom) page 59; Heath Robinson cartoon on page 20 by kind permission of Gerald Duckworth & Company Ltd General Publishers; Figure 3.68, page 98, taken from Watson: *Understanding Your Car* (1976) and reproduced by kind permission of the author.

Every effort has been made to trace all the copyright holders, but if any have been inadvertently omitted the publishers will be pleased to make the necessary arrangements at the first opportunity.

Illustrations by Taurus Graphics, Ian Foulis & Associates, Brian Walker.

contents

introduction

TO THE PUPIL AND TEACHER

Any technology course should aim to develop problem-solving and design skills but it should also aim to encourage curiosity, an enjoyment of applying science and design to a problem and the scope to allow individual pupils to develop ideas. The gathering of knowledge from many sources should be used alongside experimentation and practical application. The skills and knowledge gained by the pupil can then be communicated in a relevant form to demonstrate a solution to a problem.

GCSE Technology provides information on the scientific aspects of school technology courses and covers the material needed for GCSE courses in Technology and CDT: Technology. It is not, however, the full story of technology. There will always be a need to refer to other sources of information as no single source will ever be completely satisfactory. This is because technology is a process involving many areas of science, design and craft, and the finding of relevant information is a basic skill of the technology process.

A wide range of projects is presented so that the learning of the scientific aspects, problem-solving skills and communication techniques can occur in a technological environment. Some projects will need more guidance than others; this will depend upon the pupil. Too much teacher guidance would remove the need for pupils to plan and develop their own solutions. With this type of approach it is important for the pupil to use the teacher as another resource for information and for the pupils to learn by *doing* rather than by the teacher teaching. The learning process then becomes much more active and creative. Problem-solving skills will then develop. The relationship between technological problems, their solution, the environment, industry and society are complicated but need to be considered when developing solutions. Most technology syllabuses put some stress on knowledge and understanding of current topics and issues. No text-book can ever remain up to date, so current periodicals and newspapers are a good source of relevant information.

Solutions to a problem are usually communicated through notes, reasoned drawings and sketches. Important aspects of drawing standards are given in Appendix 4, but it must be emphasised that clarity is of the utmost importance. The use of specific British Standards is not required at this level but communication with others is improved if British Standard symbols are used. Examination papers will use British Standards but candidates will not be penalised for failing to use them. Make sure that symbols in diagrams are labelled so that the meaning is clear.

Many aspects of a technology syllabus are covered in books which are already available in schools. Physics, electronics, metalwork, woodwork, graphic communication and more general CDT textbooks are useful to have around in a technology room for reference. Manufacturers and suppliers catalogues are also an important resource. Pupils are encouraged to use all possible reference material positively in the early stages of any project and throughout a technology course.

The book is divided into a Projects section and a further three information chapters on Structures, Mechanisms (mechanical, pneumatic and electrical) and Electricity and Electronics, with aspects of materials included where relevant. The three chapters are intended for information retrieval in the problem-solving process rather than to be read in isolation. The contents listing, keywords (Appendix 8) and index should be used to trace information. At the end of each of the information chapters is a section on investigations. These are aimed at reinforcing understanding and gaining background knowledge. The investigations should be carried out in a similar way to projects using the design cycle shown in Figure 1.1. The solutions might not be as open-ended as they are in the projects.

Some general information is included in the appendices.

1

p r o j e c t s

1:1 THE DESIGN PROCESS AND PROJECT REPORTS

This chapter contains many projects which can be used to develop the essential problem-solving skills of technology while covering the basic topics and concepts of a GCSE Technology and CDT Technology courses. You are not expected to know all the facts and knowledge required to solve the problems before you start but it is essential that you quickly learn the important skill of being able to decide which information you need for a particular project, look up that information and make relevant notes. You will save time later if you also keep a careful note of the source of information, even if it came from your teacher.

You need to be well organised and a useful way of keeping all your information would be in a diary format. One way of doing this is shown later in the sample project report in Figure 1.2.

Once you have found all the necessary information you need, sketch your various ideas of how to solve the problem using clear drawings. Some of these projects will only be taken to the prototype stage using kits or construction sets, although some of them will require the use of odd bits and pieces. Some projects will be taken beyond the prototype stage using relevant materials and workshop skills. Remember to keep careful notes: you might have to submit them to the examination board for assessment towards your final examination grade. A photograph of your final product will be useful for your report and might be essential for the examination board.

The design process used in these projects will possibly follow the flow chart shown in Figure 1.1. The exact process will depend very much on the problem or project. A careful and logical approach is important. Designing is an active and continuous process of trying ideas, testing, changing designs, redrawing, remaking and retesting.

Looking carefully at Figure 1.1 the design process can be examined in more detail.

Defining the problem is the first stage. In industry a designer is given the design brief by a firm which wants something designed. This might be an item to be made for sale, such as a new style of telephone, or a way of improving the flow of materials through a factory in order to improve efficiency. The exact specification is important: if the designer is not briefed properly then the final design is unlikely to do the job properly.

Researching ideas involves looking through books and magazines, looking at materials available and talking to other people. You might have to take measurements of distances or of forces that can be applied by people. For example, a toy for a child which was too big for little hands or which required a large force to work it would not be a very good design. It is important that good notes are kept of your findings and discussions, summarising your ideas as they arise in words and sketches. Keep a note of where you get ideas from which you think might be useful so that you can refer back to them later.

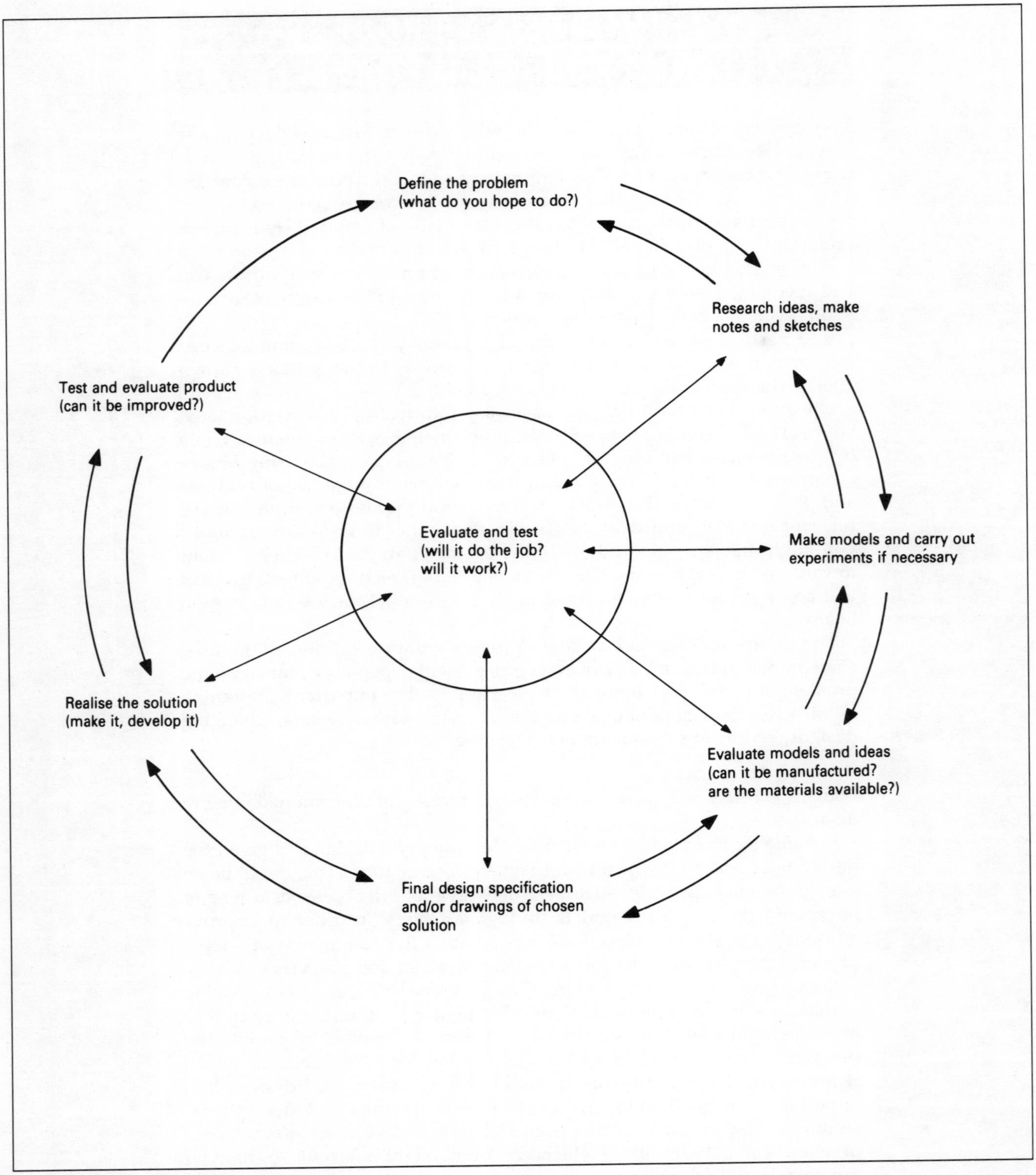

Figure 1.1 *The process of designing*

Making models and carrying out experiments can sometimes help your own understanding of whether an idea might work. This should involve only quick testing of ideas at this stage, so use modelling systems, such as Meccano or Fischertechnik. Electrical circuit testing would usually be done on some form of prototype board as described in Appendix 2.

Evaluating your ideas in terms of the original problem needs to be done at all stages. This is central to designing and is therefore given the central position in Figure 1.1. There are also specific stages at which certain aspects should be evaluated. Converting the models and experimental work into a final product will need some real materials: could the model actually be made with the materials available?

Final design specification will be a collection of all your best ideas into one final design. Sketch your final design and discuss your reasoning with friends and teachers. Shaping, materials, type of surface finishing all need to be considered. Will it really do the job specified in the original design brief? Can it be made with the tools and materials available? Any reasoning and explanation for your design should be written briefly with your final sketches. When you are satisfied that your design is the best you can do in the time available, you must then produce the working drawings and materials lists to make your solution. An outline of drawing techniques is shown in Appendix 4.

Realising the solution might not be as straightforward as you thought. Evaluating and modification should still be possible if you find problems in the manufacture of your design.

Test and evaluate your final product. Does it do the job? Does its appearance look right or could some further modification make it a more pleasing object to look at? Could a small change make the production easier and cheaper without affecting its use? If you think that changes are needed then you need to *define the problem* and find your solution.

To develop a successful solution to a design problem you will need to consider:

1. time available
2. function — does it do the job? Is it easy to use?
3. aesthetics — size, shape and general appearance
4. availability of materials
5. construction — is it possible to make?
6. environment — does it cause pollution? does it fit its surroundings?
7. safety in making and using the final object
8. reliability and service life
9. efficiency in making and using — can the use of energy be reduced?
10. need and cost — will the final product sell?

The use of materials to make your project will sometimes be fixed by what is available within your school. This is not really any different from working in industry where similar constraints always exist.

Some projects, although based mainly in a particular topic area, will cross the boundaries used to separate technology into 'chapters' or 'modules'. This is because, in real life, technology cannot be partitioned into separate topics.

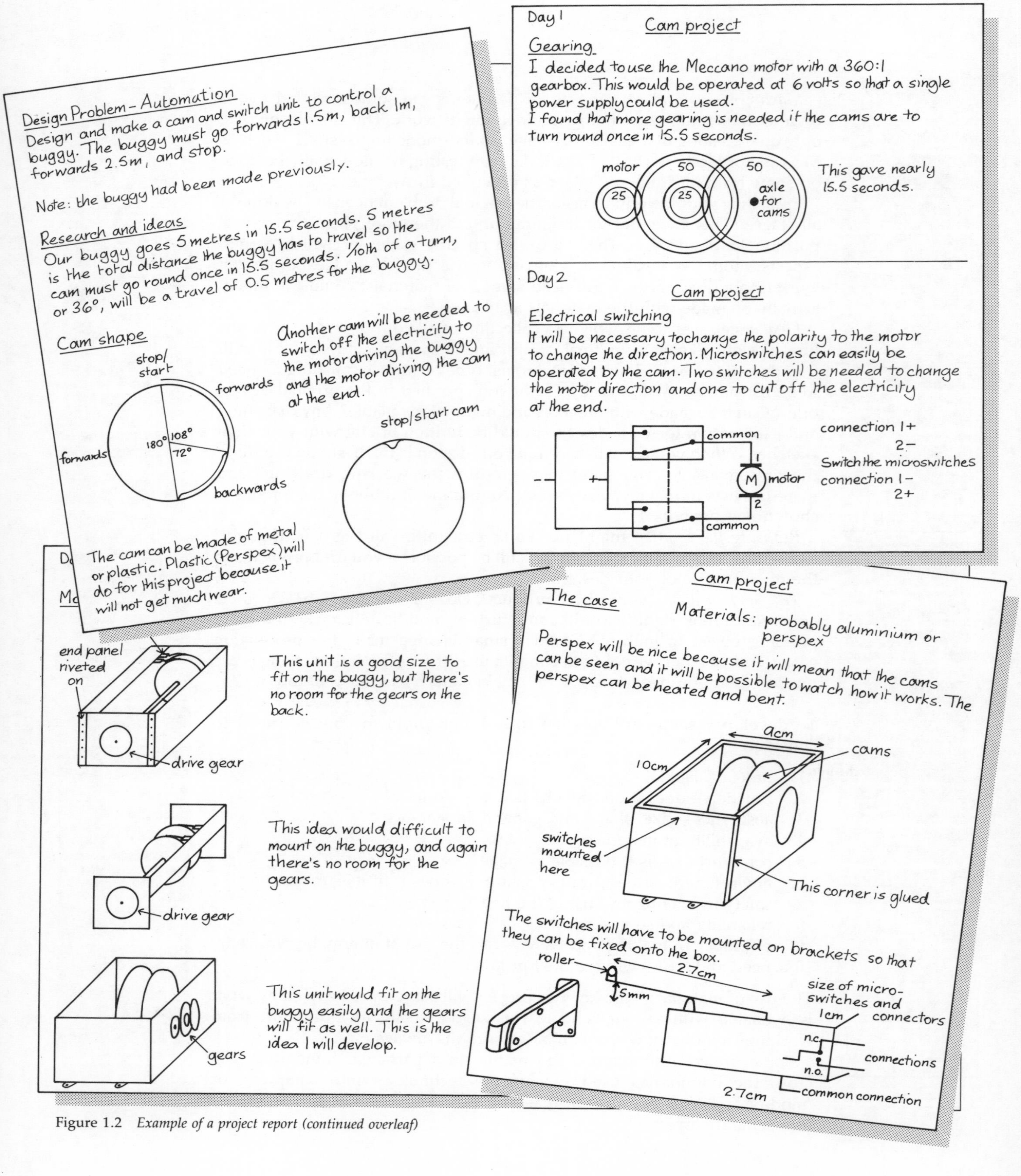

Design Problem – Automation

Design and make a cam and switch unit to control a buggy. The buggy must go forwards 1.5m, back 1m, forwards 2.5m, and stop.

Note: the buggy had been made previously.

Research and ideas

Our buggy goes 5 metres in 15.5 seconds. 5 metres is the total distance the buggy has to travel so the cam must go round once in 15.5 seconds. 1/10th of a turn, or 36°, will be a travel of 0.5 metres for the buggy.

Cam shape

Another cam will be needed to switch off the electricity to the motor driving the buggy and the motor driving the cam at the end.

The cam can be made of metal or plastic. Plastic (Perspex) will do for this project because it will not get much wear.

Day 1

Cam project

Gearing

I decided to use the Meccano motor with a 360:1 gearbox. This would be operated at 6 volts so that a single power supply could be used.
I found that more gearing is needed if the cams are to turn round once in 15.5 seconds.

This gave nearly 15.5 seconds.

Day 2

Cam project

Electrical switching

It will be necessary to change the polarity to the motor to change the direction. Microswitches can easily be operated by the cam. Two switches will be needed to change the motor direction and one to cut off the electricity at the end.

connection 1+
2–
Switch the microswitches
connection 1–
2+

This unit is a good size to fit on the buggy, but there's no room for the gears on the back.

This idea would difficult to mount on the buggy, and again there's no room for the gears.

This unit would fit on the buggy easily and the gears will fit as well. This is the idea I will develop.

Cam project

The case

Materials: probably aluminium or perspex

Perspex will be nice because it will mean that the cams can be seen and it will be possible to watch how it works. The perspex can be heated and bent.

The switches will have to be mounted on brackets so that they can be fixed onto the box.

Figure 1.2 *Example of a project report (continued overleaf)*

Day 4

Cam project

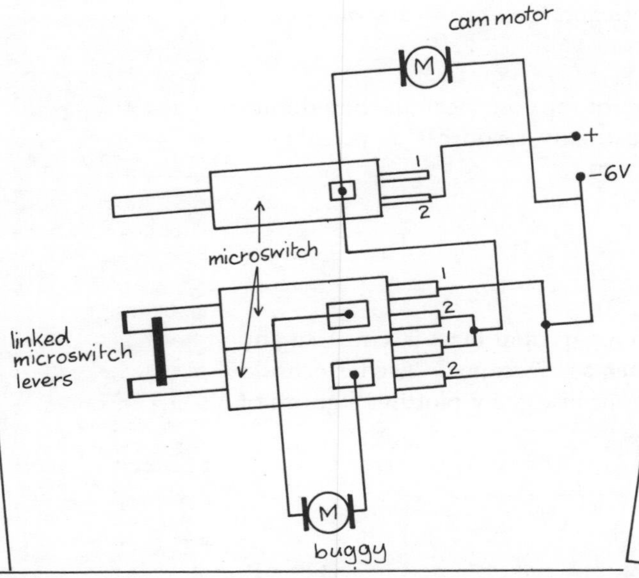

Day 4

Working Drawing

Cam project

SIDE VIEW

Scale

END VIEW

TOP VIEW

CUTTING LIST

Day 5-11 were spent making the final design

PHOTOGRAPH OF FINAL PRODUCT

Day 12

Cam project

Evaluation

There was a problem with gears not meshing properly but this was solved by adjustment. The total distance travelled was 4m 96cm which is not bad when using off-the-shelf gears. The cam box was nice looking, with all the working parts visible. The external cogs would probably have to be covered in a machine because of safety. It fitted onto the Fischertechnik buggy very easily with bolts. The mounting plate holes had to be made into longer slots to line up with the slots in the buggy.

Working Drawing

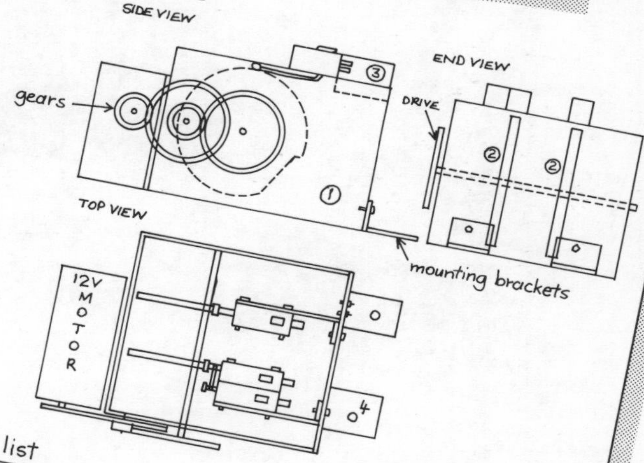

Cutting list

Part	Description	No. of pieces	Length	W	T	Material
1	Box	1	400mm	80mm	2mm	Clear perspex
2	Cam	2	60mm	disc	3mm	Perspex
3	Switch bracket	2	50mm	16mm	2mm	Perspex
4	Mounting bracket	2	30mm	20mm	2mm	Perspex

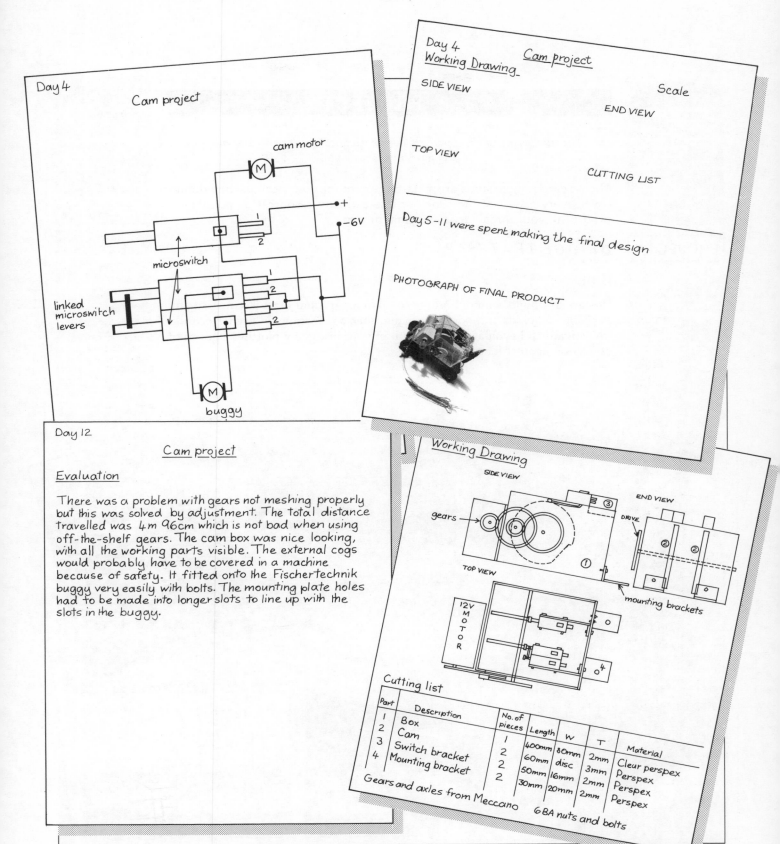

Gears and axles from Meccano 6BA nuts and bolts

1:2 PROJECTS

The numbering of these projects does not indicate any particular order: it is for convenience only.

The research suggestions are a starting-point for your design; they do not cover every aspect of the projects. Use as many resources as possible in producing your initial ideas and final design.

PROJECT 1

BRIDGE THAT GAP

BRIEF

Design and build a model bridge to span a gap of at least 50 cm. Use any available materials or modelling system such as Meccano or Fischertechnik. Investigate and evaluate the strength of your bridge by plotting a graph of deflection against load.

RESEARCH

Bridges have become a common sight because of the need to cross rivers, ravines, roads and railways as the demand for a better transport system emerged in the 18th and 19th centuries.

What shapes produce strong structures?

How can beams be strengthened without too much increase in weight?

SPECIFIC REFERENCES: SECTIONS 2:1 2:2 2:3 2:4 2:10

PROJECT 2

THE YOUNG GYMNASTS

BRIEF

Design and build a model of a climbing frame for children up to 12 years old. Show clearly estimates and calculations on static and dynamic forces and the factor of safety. Carry out some market research on its appeal to the prospective users (children) and purchasers (adults).

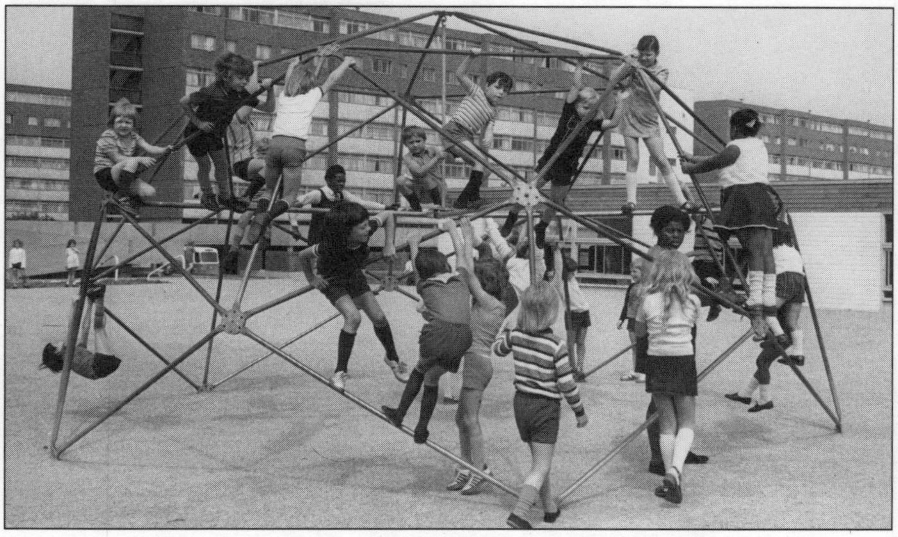

RESEARCH

Your initial investigations will require looking up how to find the static and dynamic forces (Section 2:7). Estimate the weight (in newtons) of a 12-year-old child.

What materials can be used?

What can children do of interest on the frame?

How will you carry out the market research?

How can you estimate the price for prospective purchasers?

SPECIFIC REFERENCES: SECTIONS 2:4 2:7 2:14 2:15

PROJECT 3

AN ABSORBING CRASH

BRIEF

Design a car body which will absorb as much energy as possible on collision. Use A4 cartridge paper and glue.

RESEARCH

Cars are made out of sheet materials strengthened and stiffened by bending. The figure shows what can happen in an accident. Much of the energy from the collision is safely absorbed by the bending of the metal. Decide on a standard testing method to find the greatest force which your model can withstand in an accident. Test to destruction. Suggest how the shape of the body might be altered to increase the safety of the occupants. Think about energy being absorbed as the material bends. You might need to experiment with a few ideas before deciding on your final design.

SPECIFIC REFERENCES: SECTION 2:10

PROJECT 4

Will It Stand?

Brief

Using a single sheet of A4 paper (80 gsm), design and build a tower, at least 18 cm tall, to withstand a downward load of 10 newtons and a sideways pull on the load of 0.5 newtons at the top.

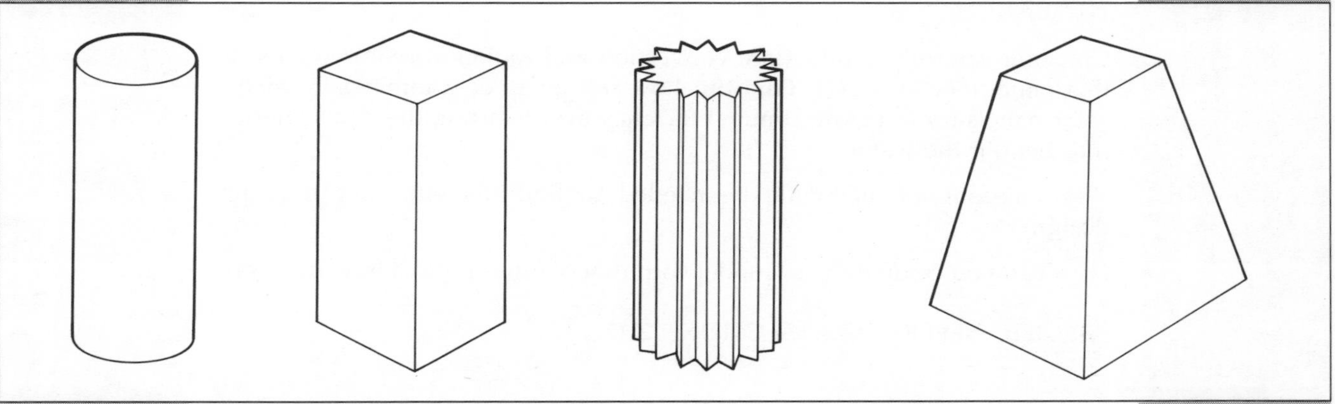

Research

The sideways pull might represent the force of the wind on a bridge support.

What shapes are best at supporting vertical forces?

How can you support the structure against the sideways forces?

You are allowed to use glue to stick the paper where necessary.

SPECIFIC REFERENCES: SECTIONS 2:3 2:5 2:7

PROJECT 5

The Winner Takes . . . What?

Brief

Design an appropriate trophy to be awarded to the winner of a tournament of your choice. Your trophy should use a mixture of metal, wood and plastic suitably joined together, be aesthetically pleasing and represent the type of tournament.

Research

What tournament are you going to choose?

What shape of trophy would fit the tournament?

What joining methods can be used and how will this affect the design?

SPECIFIC REFERENCES: SECTIONS 2:11 2:15

PROJECT 6

HOT STUFF

BRIEF

Design and build a small model solar panel which relies on gravity circulation to heat a tank of water. If possible, compare the efficiency of your design with that of others.

RESEARCH

Consider carefully conduction, convection and radiation requirements of this panel (Section 2:17). Find out how designers of commercially made solar panels try to get maximum efficiency in converting the sun's energy into heat in the water.

What measurements would be needed to find the efficiency of your design?

How can you compare your model with that of other groups in your class?

SPECIFIC REFERENCES: SECTION 2:17

PROJECT 7

HOW DID THEY DO IT?

BRIEF

Design and build a mobile framework to lift a mass of 2 kg (20 N force) when the mass is hung below the highest point of the structure. The strength should be developed by the design of the framework and not through excessive use of materials.

RESEARCH

We are still not sure how the pyramids or Stonehenge were built, but we do know the problems involved. How to convert human power into lifting power is a very old preoccupation. The problems don't stop at how to apply a force capable of lifting a particular mass. You also have to provide a support which is not only strong but also capable of being moved into the right position to put the mass down again.

You will need to consider the shape of your framework to give maximum strength and should try to achieve the best result with the least possible material.

What mechanism will be suitable for lifting the load?

SPECIFIC REFERENCES: SECTIONS 2:3 2:4 2:6 2:10 3:7

PROJECT 8

THE STRENGTH TESTER

BRIEF

Design and build a tensile testing machine to test metals in the form of wires. Your machine should be capable of comparing metal wires of the same diameter and finding the tensile strength of a particular metal.

Safety: use eye protection when using your machine.

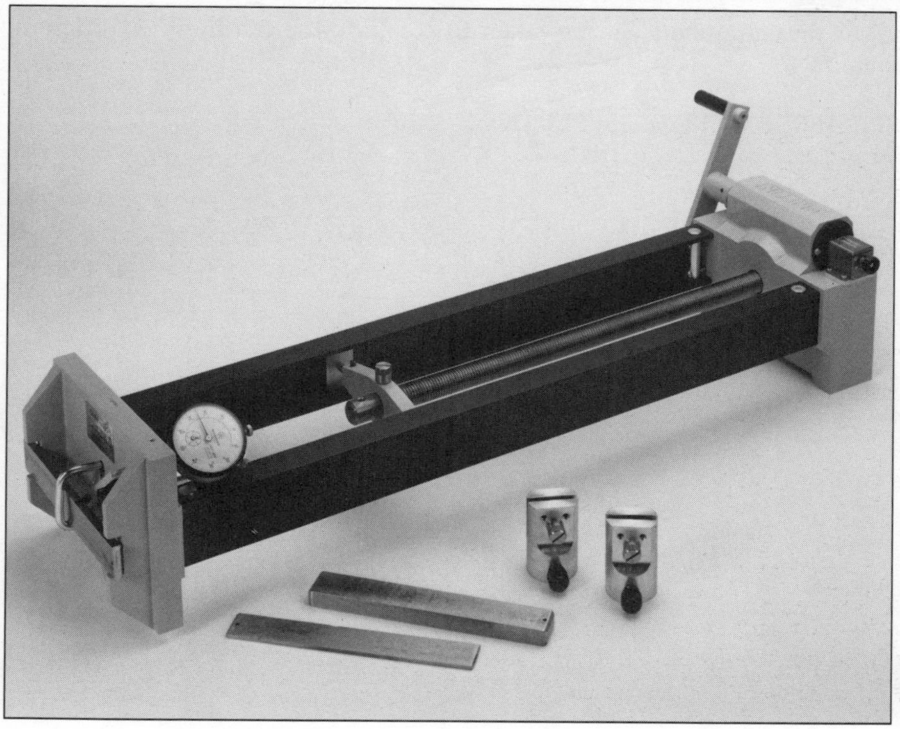

Research

Many structures use metals to provide strength under tension. Engineers and designers often need to know the forces that a metal can withstand without breaking. Tensile strength testing machines are used to find the stress at which a material will break. The stress is normally given in terms of newtons per square metre. The materials tested will normally be in the form of wires or specially prepared samples and the measurement is converted into the standard unit for comparison between materials. Your machine will have to measure the force in newtons.

You will need to look up the meaning of *tensile strength, stress* and *strain* as a starting-point.

What type of mechanism can be used to apply the force?

SPECIFIC REFERENCES: SECTIONS 2:12 2:13 3:4 3:5

PROJECT 9

Hard and Soft

Brief

Design and build a testing machine to compare the hardness of metals and woods.

Research

Look up the meaning of *hardness* to start your research.

What measurements can be taken to compare the hardness of different materials?

SPECIFIC REFERENCES: SECTION 2:10

PROJECT 10

HANG IT

BRIEF

Design and build a bracket for a hanging flower basket.

RESEARCH

In designing your bracket you might make use of the following information:

Tensile strengths: mild steel 2400 MN/m^2
wood (spruce) 100 MN/m^2
plastic (rigid PVC) 60 MN/m^2
Maximum weight of basket (freshly watered): 200 N

The bracket is to be fixed to a strong wall and will need to include a tie and a strut.

The forces in the frame can be calculated using the triangle of forces method or by experimenting with various thicknesses of materials which are available to use. You will need to consider strength in tension and compression.

The final product should be as cheap as possible but *safe*.

You will need to find out about:

triangular structures

ties and struts

triangle of forces

factor of safety

SPECIFIC REFERENCES: SECTIONS 2:3 2:6 2:7 2:9 2:14

PROJECT 11

THE BIG SQUEEZE

BRIEF

Design and build a device to test the compressive strength of mortar (cement and sand) cubes.

RESEARCH

Mortar is used to bond bricks together in many buildings. The mortar at the bottom must be under a lot of compression force. What force can it withstand? You will need to make up some small cubes of mortar to test. Try to get an idea of the size of force which you will need to consider by finding the weight of bricks above a point at the bottom of a house wall.

How will you apply a large force to your samples?

What mechanisms will be needed?

SPECIFIC REFERENCES: SECTIONS 2:5 2:7 2:10

PROJECT 12

DING DONG BELL

BRIEF

Design and build a door chime which gives two different notes.

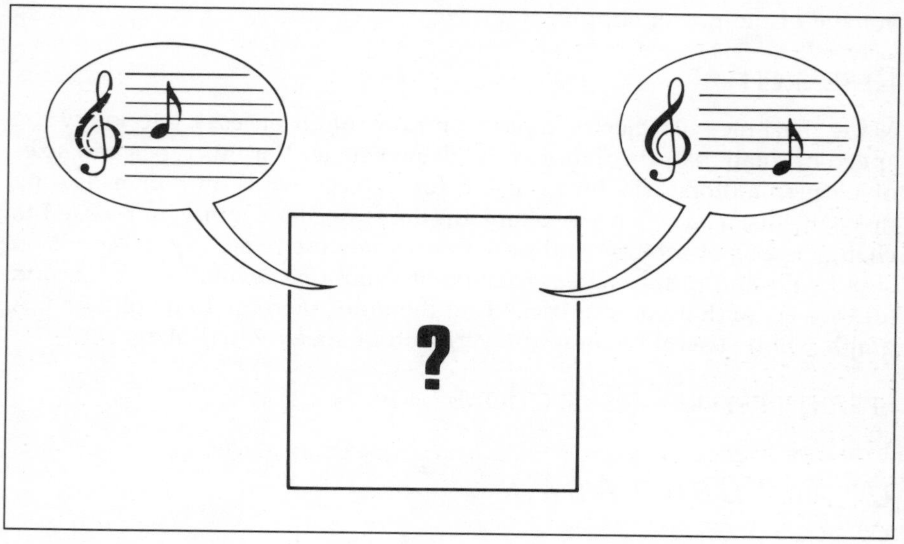

RESEARCH

Your research will need to consider:

Where will it be used?

How can it be operated?

What materials give ringing noises?

Size? Structure? Materials?

Electrical or mechanical operation?

Safety (operation in wet weather)?

You should be able to see from the above questions that a possible solution to the problem will need to consider information from all three areas of basic technology covered in Chapters 2–4.

SPECIFIC REFERENCES: SECTIONS 2:10 2:15 3:5 3:19 4:2 4:9

PROJECT 13

Many Happy (Re)turns

Brief

Design and build a gear system to enable you to measure the speed of an electric motor. Investigate how the speed of the motor depends on the voltage of the power supply.

Research

Many machines use electric motors and it is often necessary to know the speed of rotation of the motor at the design stage. Various types and sizes of electric motors will be available for project work and investigating mechanisms. You will need to look up the way gear chains can be used to change speed of rotation and how to calculate the overall gear ratio. You should aim to produce a gear rotating at about one revolution per second (or slower) so that you can easily find the time taken for 10 revolutions. A graph will be useful to show the variation of speed with voltage.

SPECIFIC REFERENCES: SECTIONS 3:19 4:4

PROJECT 14

Up and Down Again

Brief

Design and build a buggy to go up a 10% (1 in 10) slope at 2 cm/s. When it gets to the top it should automatically reverse. Measure the input and output power of your buggy when carrying a 1 kg mass. Hence work out the efficiency of your buggy.

Research

Many machines involve automatic processes which occur without anybody taking any action. This buggy is a simple example of such an automatic process. The ideas in Project 13 will be needed to set the speed of your buggy.

How will the speed depend on wheel size and gearing?

What do you need to measure to find the input power?

What do you need to measure to find the output power?

The efficiency of a machine is given by:

Efficiency = mechanical advantage/velocity ratio

or

Efficiency = output power/input power

How well do your values for the efficiency agree? Remember that the motors are not very efficient.

You could also find out how to measure the torque created at the rim of the drive wheels.

SPECIFIC REFERENCES: SECTIONS 3:12 3:17 3:19 4:4 4:7

PROJECT 15

Fast and Slow

Brief

Design and make a two-speed gearbox using a suitable modelling system to give velocity reductions 1/3 and 1/2 between the engine end (driver gear) and gearbox output (driven gear).

Research

Many vehicles and machines propelled by engines or motors require a gearbox. This is because the engines and motors operate best within quite a small speed range, the effect being far more important with engines. A gearbox enables the speed of the machine to be varied a lot while the speed of the motor remains within its speed limits.

What size gears will give the speed ratios?

How can the gears be moved in and out of mesh to give the gear change?

SPECIFIC REFERENCES: SECTION 3:17

PROJECT 16

A Free-For-All

Brief

Using as many different mechanisms as possible, design and build your own Heath-Robinson-type system to 'do something'. Your mechanism can be operated either from a small electric motor or a falling 1 kg mass.

RESEARCH

Heath-Robinson is famous for outrageously complicated mechanical systems which were designed to do relatively simple jobs. The picture shows a typical example. Your research will consist of finding out how to link as many different types of mechanisms as possible so that they all have a part to play in your own design. Try to keep the aim of the device as simple as possible.

PROJECT 17

FUN FOR ALL

BRIEF

Design and build a model fairground ride which would provide that stimulating 'fun of the fair' using a selection of levers, gears, cams and eccentrics, cranks and pulleys. A small electric motor can be used to power your ride. Your design should include decoration to help attract the crowds.

RESEARCH

Have you ever looked at the number of different mechanisms used at a fairground? All those exciting rides depend on the types of mechanisms available in any mechanism modelling kit. You will need to find out how to use the mechanisms to give the feeling of excitement and thrill which attracts the people.

Which fairground rides are popular?

What type of motion is involved?

PROJECT 18

AUTOMATIC TURN ON

BRIEF

Using an electric motor, gears as necessary and a cam made by yourself, produce a mechanism which will turn a light bulb on for 10 seconds, off for 5 seconds, on for 5 seconds, off for 10 seconds for each rotation of the cam.

RESEARCH

Rotating cams are often used as a method of producing time intervals in automatic processes. The control units of many washing machines and dishwashers are common examples. The speed of the cam is determined by the speed of the motor and the gear system. You will find it useful to do Project 13 if you have not already done so.

What circuit will be needed to light the bulb?

What type of switch can be operated by the cam?

SPECIFIC REFERENCES: SECTION 3:10

PROJECT 19

CREEPY-CRAWLY

BRIEF

Design and make a creepy-crawly type of mechanism which will automatically release a marble to fall onto a target. The creepy-crawly must travel at least 4 metres along strings and once started must not need any further help.

RESEARCH

Automatic control systems are now commonplace at home and at work: automatic kettles switch themselves off; cookers switch themselves on and off; tape recorders stop and some even eject the tape when it reaches the end. These processes are designed to make life easier. Automatic processes in industry are designed to increase efficiency and improve competitiveness in the world market-place.

In this project you will need to develop a drive mechanism which will grip the string(s) to move the creepy-crawly along. Gearing will be important if you use an electric motor as the power source.

SPECIFIC REFERENCES: SECTIONS 2:3 3:17

PROJECT 20

SLOW CRAWL WITH A GAME WHILE WAITING

BRIEF

1. Design and build a small vehicle propelled by 'elastic-band power' to go as far as possible as slowly as possible. Use any materials available.
2. Design and build an elastic-powered marble-pushing machine with a distance calibration. Use your machines to have a game of marbles to evaluate their usefulness.

RESEARCH

Elastic materials store potential energy which can be changed into kinetic energy. The potential energy can be in the form of twisting or stretching. The control of the energy change will decide how well your design will work.

Will gearing help to control the energy change in the vehicle?

What happens to a marble if it is hit too hard at the wrong angle?

Remember that your marble pusher will have to move around and be adjusted for distance without touching the marble.

SPECIFIC REFERENCES: SECTION 3:3

PROJECT 21

Bin It

Brief

Design and make a model mechanism that will open the lid of a rubbish bin with one press of a pedal and close it with a second press. Use a modelling system such as Lego, Fischertechnik or Meccano and any other materials generally available.

Research

Many pedal bins are foot-operated but you have to keep your foot on the pedal to keep the lid up. This is sometimes inconvenient and the consequences of moving your foot at the wrong time can be very unpleasant. You will need to work out how the foot pedal can latch the lid up on the first press and release the latch when pressed a second time.

PROJECT 22

The Big Lift

Brief

Design and build a screw jack to lift a load of about 50 N with an effort of less than 5 N. Find the efficiency of the mechanism.

Research

Screw mechanisms are often used to lift heavy objects such as cars. These are called 'screw jacks', which are an example of a simple machine based on the inclined plane. The effort needed to move the load is reduced but the distance that the effort will have to move is increased. You will need to look up the meaning of the terms *mechanical advantage*, *velocity ratio* and *efficiency*. Friction will reduce the efficiency of your jack, so make sure you allow for it.

SPECIFIC REFERENCES: SECTION 3:13

PROJECT 23

A PROBLEM OF BALANCE

BRIEF

Design and build a simple balance for measuring up to 1 kg and calibrate it.

RESEARCH

This is based on the balancing of turning moments summarised by the Principle of Moments.

SPECIFIC REFERENCES: SECTION 3:4

PROJECT 24

JEWELS FROM THE BEACH

BRIEF

1. Design and make a device to polish pebbles.
2. Using a polished pebble as the centre piece, design and make a brooch or necklace.

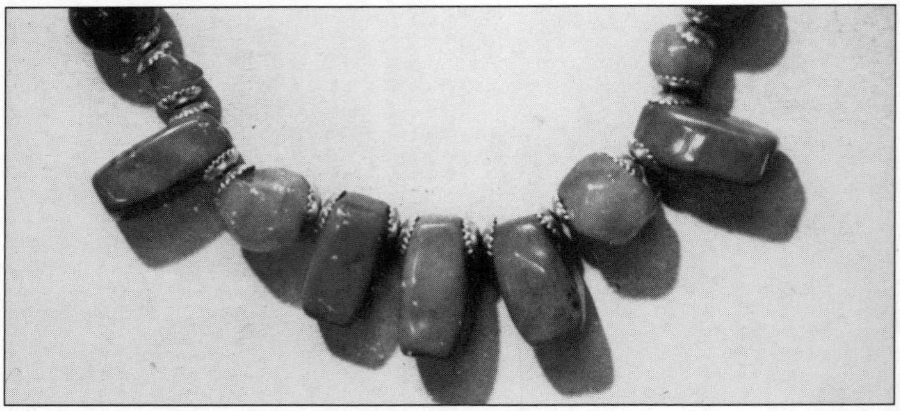

RESEARCH

Attractive and inexpensive jewellery can be made from polished pebbles, a process called 'lapidary'. This type of jewellery is particularly evident in the souvenir shops at the seaside. It is possible to polish your own by putting them in a device similar to a very small tumble drier with carborundum powder and water. Carborundum is a fine abrasive powder which can be bought in various grades. Course grades are used first, followed by finer grades to achieve the final polish. The drum should rotate quite slowly so some gearing will be necessary. A windmill could be used to power your machine.

How will you mount your polished pebble into a setting for a brooch or necklace?

SPECIFIC REFERENCES: SECTIONS 3:7 3:8 3:17 3:19

PROJECT 25

DIP IT

BRIEF

Design and make a model of a pneumatic system which might be used for cleaning large metal structures (such as car bodies and washing-machine bodies) before painting, by lowering them into large vats of caustic solution. The body must go into the solution slowly to prevent splashes but could be lifted out faster to reduce costs.

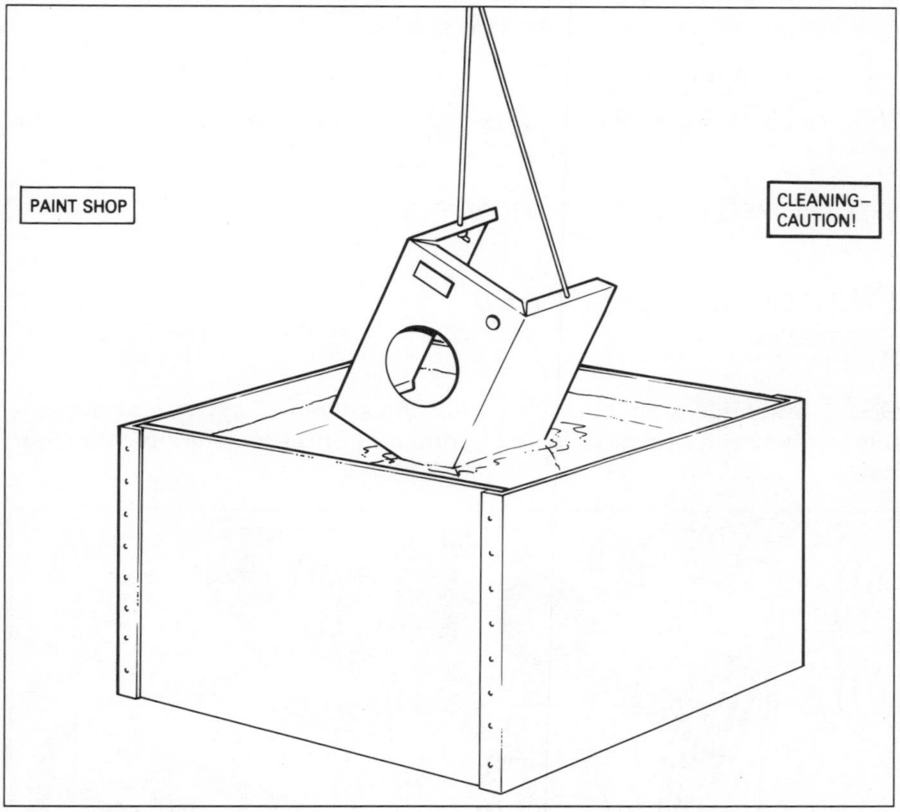

RESEARCH

Pneumatic systems are often used in automation. The forces which can be developed are high and the speeds can be easily regulated. You will need to consider how to lift the body, how to swing it over the vat and how to lower it.

SPECIFIC REFERENCES: SECTION 3:20

PROJECT 26

The Little and Large Force

Brief

Design and build a calibrated pneumatic system to have a game of marbles or to test a bow after it has been re-strung.

Research

Pneumatic cylinders can be used to punch metal sheets into various shapes. It is often necessary to know the exact force developed by a cylinder and to provide a calibration system.

What is meant by calibration?

How can you work out the expected force produced by a pneumatic cylinder?

SPECIFIC REFERENCES: SECTION 3:20

PROJECT 27

Exposing the Thread

Brief

Design and build a pneumatic wear-testing system. Carry out a comparative test between carpets or fabrics of different prices to determine the 'best buy'.

Research

A new fabric or carpet material should be wear-tested to ensure that it will provide customer satisfaction. A reciprocating pneumatic system can be used to give a wear test by persistently scraping something like a shoe over a piece of carpet. It is possible to set up counters in pneumatic systems but, if a speed control is used, a time measurement can provide a comparison between different materials.

SPECIFIC REFERENCES: SECTION 3:20

PROJECT 28

JUICY FORCES

BRIEF

Design and build a pneumatic press to extract the juice from pieces of apple. Make sure that everything is absolutely clean if you intend to drink your apple juice.

RESEARCH

The forces developed by pneumatic cylinders make them ideal for presses for cider making. The force provided by the press needs to be controlled because apples vary in their firmness.

How will you collect the juice from the apples?

What will you put on the end of the piston to press on the apples?

SPECIFIC REFERENCES: SECTION 3:20

PROJECT 29

Phew! It's Hot in Here!

Brief

Design and build an electronic and pneumatic circuit to open the windows of a greenhouse in hot weather.

Research

Large greenhouses need a lot of ventilation in hot weather. The big vents or windows can be operated by pneumatic systems. A solenoid valve connected to an electronic temperature sensor will be needed. The solenoid valve can be operated via a relay from a temperature-sensitive transistor switch.

How will your circuit be adjusted for different opening temperatures?

SPECIFIC REFERENCES: SECTIONS 3:20 4:17

PROJECT 30

No Hands Make Light Work

Brief

Design and build a light-sensitive switch on veroboard. Your circuit should be adjustable so that it switches on a light bulb at dusk.

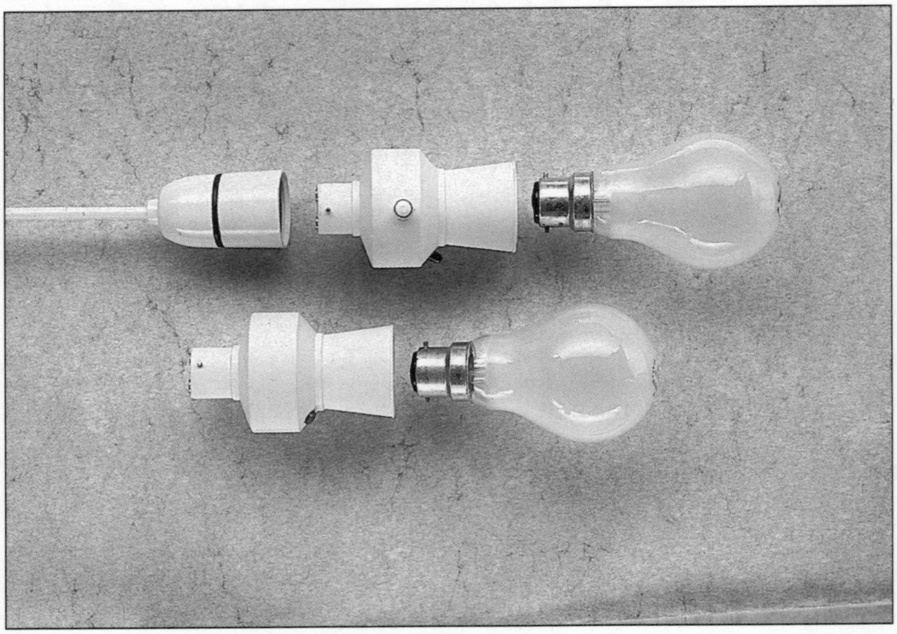

Research

Many street lights are now controlled by light-sensitive switches which can be seen on top of the lamp casing. Similar control is available for porch lights and internal lights which are being marketed as security devices.

How is a circuit diagram converted into a veroboard diagram?

How can the switch-on light level be controlled?

SPECIFIC REFERENCES: SECTION 4:17 Appendix 2

PROJECT 31

AC/DC

Brief

Design and build a full-wave rectifier circuit on matrix board. The circuit should be designed to give about 5 volts DC output at a maximum load of 1 amp. The input AC should be taken from a laboratory power supply. Use an oscilloscope to investigate the operation of the circuit.

Research

Full-wave rectifier circuits are very common in electronic equipment such as radios, video players and televisions. The electronic circuitry works from direct-current electricity but only alternating-current electricity is available from the mains. The rectifier circuit changes AC into DC using diodes.

How do you find out what current can safely pass through a diode?

What is matrix board?

How is a circuit diagram converted to a matrix-board circuit?

SPECIFIC REFERENCES: SECTION 4:14 Appendix 2

PROJECT 32

Computers in Control?

Brief

Design a printed circuit board and build a computer output buffer circuit. The circuit should use a 6 V low current (up to 1 amp) light bulb to indicate an output from the computer. Test your circuit by connecting it to a suitable output port on a computer.

Research

Many automatic processes are now controlled by computers and warning lights and buzzers are often used to attract an operator's attention if problems occur. The warning devices are operated by the computer through a buffer circuit so that the low-power output from the computer can switch on high-power circuits. A similar type of circuit can be used to

operate the computerised electronic score boards seen at many sports events.

You will need to find out how to convert a circuit diagram into a printed circuit board design.

Program the computer to switch the bulb on and off and then switch up to eight of these circuits on and off in turn.

SPECIFIC REFERENCES: SECTION 4:24 Appendix 2

PROJECT 33

Where Is It, Miss?

Brief

Design and build a piece of apparatus which can be used to demonstrate the switching action of a transistor to a class of 30 pupils.

Research

The switching action of transistors is very important in modern automated control systems but the transistor is small and difficult to see. Some teachers still teach by demonstrating everything to pupils before the pupils are allowed to touch the equipment. The pupils find it rather boring watching demonstrations they cannot see.

How can a large demonstration system be set up so that everyone can see what the teacher is talking about?

You will need to find out how the transistor works as a switch and what measurements are needed to show the switching action.

SPECIFIC REFERENCES: SECTION 4:17

PROJECT 34

FLEXIBLE ENERGY

BRIEF

Design and build a simple DC electric motor and then:

1. use it to generate electricity
2. alter it as needed and calibrate it to measure an electric current.

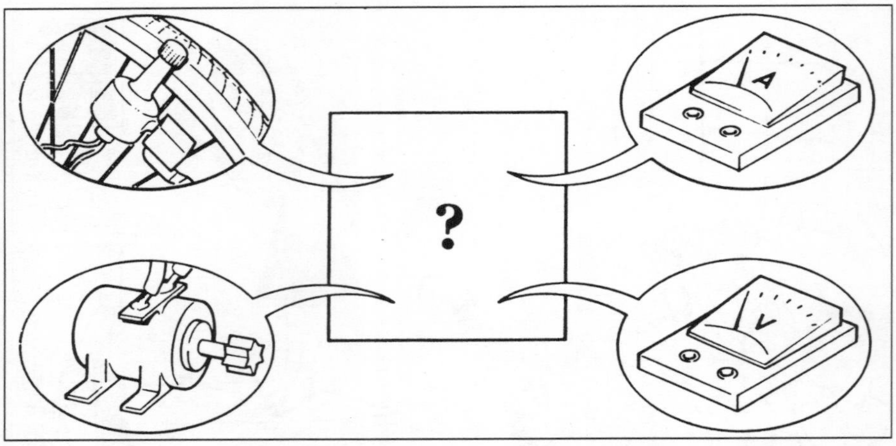

RESEARCH

Many devices work on the same principle as that used in electric motors: a wire carrying electric current will try to move out of a magnetic field. The energy change can be reversed so that a wire made to move in a magnetic field can be used to produce electric current. Your first step will be to find out how electric motors work.

SPECIFIC REFERENCES: SECTIONS 3:19 4:9 4:10

PROJECT 35

HOW FAR IS IT?

BRIEF

Design a system using a lamp and a light-dependent resistor to measure distances.

RESEARCH

The intensity of a light beam reduces as you move away from the source of light. This reduction can be used to vary the current in an electric circuit.

What component is needed?

What will show the change in current?

How can the change in current be used to show a distance?

SPECIFIC REFERENCES: SECTIONS 4:4 4:17

PROJECT 36

Hello Over There!

Brief

Using bulbs, wires and a battery, design and build a simple circuit to send a message across the room using the ASCII computer code.

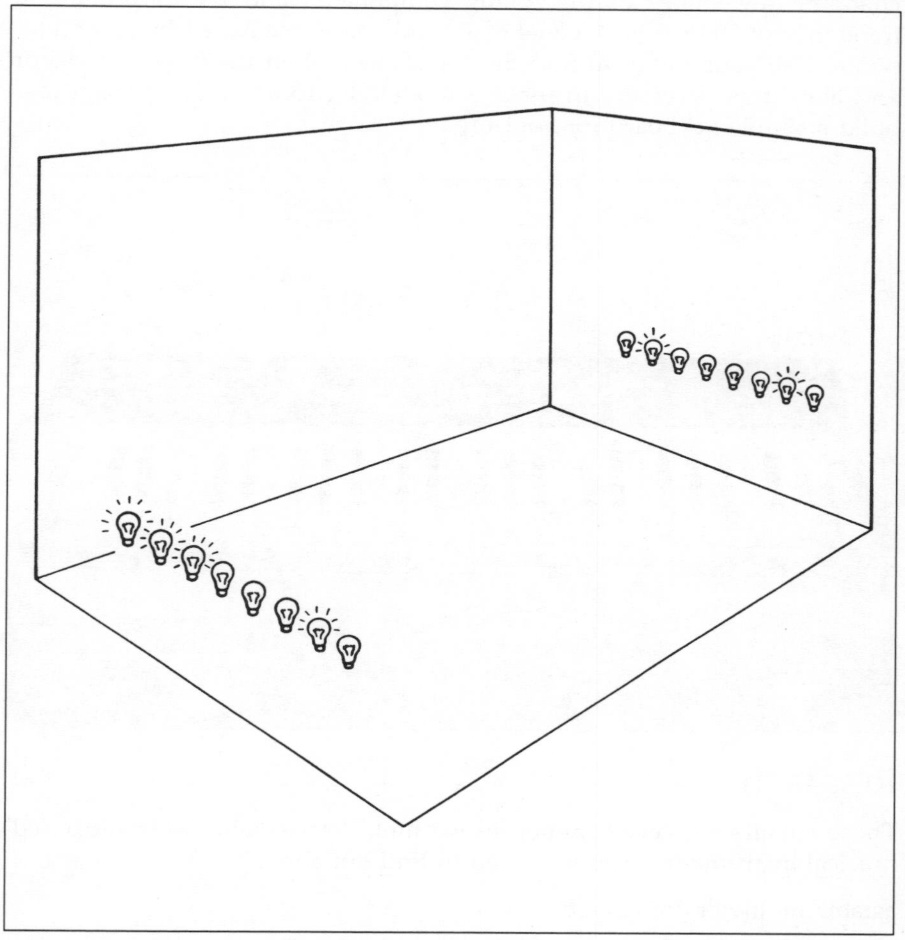

Research

Messages have been passed by means of lights for many years. The Morse Code is often used: it consists of combinations of long and short intervals to represent different characters (letters, numbers, space). Computers work using digital systems which can only recognise 'on' or 'off', so other codes have been developed. One of these is the ASCII code which is used in most modern computers.

What does *ASCII* stand for?

How many bulbs will be needed in your code transmitter?

SPECIFIC REFERENCES: SECTION 4:24

PROJECT 37

Musical Maestro

Brief

Design and build an astable multivibrator with audible output, choosing timing components to give a frequency of 1 Hz. Investigate the effect of changing the values of the timing components and try to produce a frequency of 100 Hz, with equal mark and space, measured by an oscilloscope. Use your circuit to find the capacitance of an unmarked capacitor and alter it as necessary to make a model electronic organ. Design and build a simple keyboard for your organ.

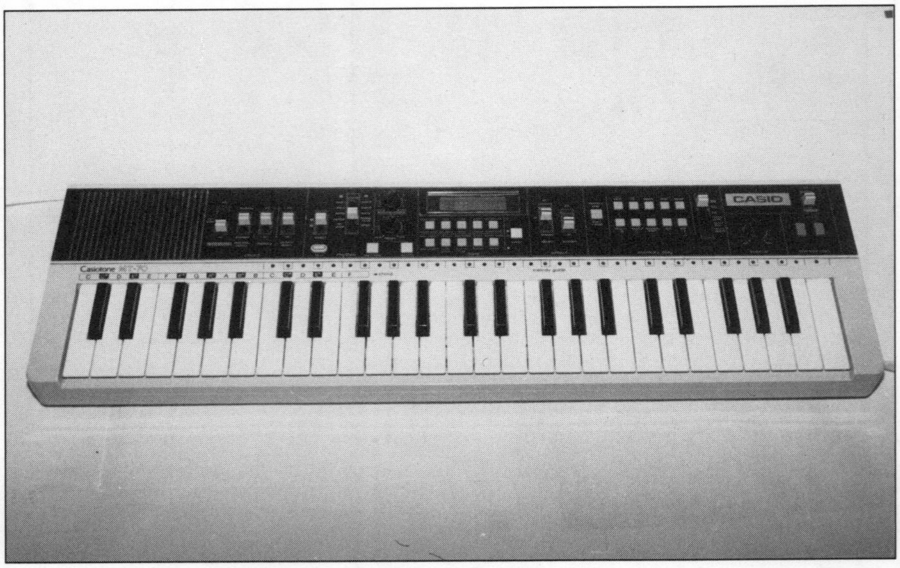

Research

These circuits are very common in warning devices and electronic-based musical instruments. You will need to find out about:

astable multivibrator circuits

the importance of $C \times R$ in capacitor circuits

using an oscilloscope to measure frequency.

SPECIFIC REFERENCES: SECTIONS 4:11 4:20

PROJECT 38

5–4–3–2–1

Brief

Design and build an electronic egg timer or darkroom timer.

Research

Timer circuits are used extensively in modern automated processes and computerised equipment. This project will involve:

timer applications

variable timing components

the operation of monostable multivibrator circuits

a relay, if you are designing a darkroom timer.

SPECIFIC REFERENCES: SECTION 4:20

PROJECT 39

Raising the Alarm

Brief

Design and build a logic circuit for a combined fire and burglar alarm which automatically activates alarms at the police station and/or fire station as required. The burglar alarm should be activated by detectors of movement or light.

Research

You will need to look up the way logic circuits can be used to provide different switching functions. This project is concerned mainly with the logic circuit design but try to outline a design for the detectors which would be used.

SPECIFIC REFERENCES: SECTION 4:21

PROJECT 40

WHO PUT TEA IN MY COFFEE?

BRIEF

Design a model of a hot-drinks machine using two-, three- and four-input OR gates. Decide on the combinations of drinks your machine will provide. Each drink must require one single-pole switch. Assume that a logical 1 output from the gates switches on the ingredient dispenser. Outline the requirements and possible design of dispensers for milk, sugar, tea, coffee and water.

RESEARCH

You will need to use four-input OR gates for the logic function and find out about solenoids for the dispenser design.

SPECIFIC REFERENCES: SECTIONS 3:19 4:17 4:21

PROJECT 41

BETTER CONTROL SAVES MONEY

BRIEF

Design and build a logic circuit for a central heating control unit which takes inputs from six different areas of a house. Your design should use AND and OR functions.

RESEARCH

With the supply of such energy sources as oil and gas starting to run out, costs will rise. Efficient operation of central heating units can reduce the use of energy by as much as 50%. This will require much more sophisticated control units than are currently used in most homes.

What does a central heating control unit do?

What conditions would turn on the boiler?

What would turn off the boiler?

Look up the truth tables for AND and OR logic circuits.

SPECIFIC REFERENCES: SECTION 4:21

PROJECT 42

THE MISER BOX

BRIEF

Design and build a circuit, mounted in a suitable box, to test the basic operation of an npn transistor as a switch. A light-emitting diode (LED) should be used to indicate a 'good' transistor. Your design should include an easy method of inserting different shapes and sizes of transistors into the circuit.

RESEARCH

Transistors are quite sensitive to harsh treatment and fault finding will involve testing transistors. A simple device which easily shows whether or not a transistor works would be very useful.

Find out about different transistor packages, light-emitting diodes and transistor switch circuits to start off your research.

SPECIFIC REFERENCES: SECTIONS 4:17 4:18

PROJECT 43 ANOTHER MISER BOX

BRIEF

Design and build a circuit, mounted in a suitable box, to test the operation of semiconductor diodes and light-emitting diodes. Your design should include a quick method of connecting the suspect components. You will need to include a resistor to limit the current through the diode under test or you will blow the diodes while testing them!

RESEARCH

'Time is money' is a favourite saying of some people in industry. Quick ways of testing electronic components is an important part of their production. Make sure that you understand how diodes are supposed to work so that you can work out how to test them. What can be used to indicate that the diode is working correctly?

SPECIFIC REFERENCES: SECTIONS 4:3 4:14

PROJECT 44 SOLAR HEATING EQUALS SMALLER BILLS?

BRIEF

1. Design and build a complete model solar panel and storage tank to get maximum efficiency.
2. Design and build the control unit based on a 741 operational amplifier (or equivalent).

RESEARCH

Solar water heating can be an economical way of reducing heating bills if the panels and control unit are own-made. The panels can be used on radiators painted matt black with insulation to prevent heat loss to the surrounding air. The control unit needs to switch on a pump when the temperature of the panel is about 3 °C higher than the water temperature in the tank. Testing and evaluating are very important to ensure that the design does its job properly.

Information sources:

physics textbooks

electronics books which include operational amplifiers

RS components catalogue

RS data sheet 3992 July 1983 'The 590 kH Temperature Sensor'

Heating and Ventilating Contractors Association, ESCA House, Palace Courts, London W2 4JG.

SPECIFIC REFERENCES: SECTIONS 2:17 3:19 4:26

PROJECT 45

STOP THAT THIEF!

BRIEF

Design and build a simple burglar alarm. The alarm should be battery-operated and the alarm should be activated by breaking the circuit.

RESEARCH

Burglar alarms can be expensive to buy but contain quite basic circuits to:

detect a movement, e.g. window switch or tread mat switch

activate a circuit

cause a noise.

Window and door switches can be made from reed relays. How can the circuit be set to sound the alarm when the circuit is broken?

SPECIFIC REFERENCES: SECTIONS 4:17 4:20

PROJECT 46

Sweet Sweet Music

Brief

Design a synchronisation method and produce a short musical piece for two computers.

Research

Computer-generated music can be very pleasant and easy to produce. It is not too difficult to program one computer to play a piece of music and by synchronising computers it is possible to extend the musical potential. One computer will have to look for a signal from the other computer for the correct time to start. The user port lines can be used for this signal. If the internal clocks of the computers are running at the same speed then no more signals will be needed. If the internal clocks are very different more synchronising signals will be needed.

SPECIFIC REFERENCES: SECTION 4:24

1:3 OTHER PROJECT IDEAS

1. A cam-operated control unit to control a buggy, e.g. move forwards 1.0 m, stop for 2 s, move back 0.5 m.
2. Front-wheel-steering model to allow a three-point turn in a 0.75 m square.
3. A body for a buggy.
4. A railway signal with fail safe, operated by air pressure or electricity.
5. A solenoid door bolt with a coded electronic combination keypad to operate it.

6. An automatic server for table tennis.
7. A computer controlled buggy/turtle.
8. Boat hull design (computer software from Academic Software, Sourby Old Farm, Timble Otley, Yorkshire LS21 2PW).
9. A portable wheelchair ramp for kerbs.
10. A tortoise-detecting mechanism for the garden.
11. A robot arm.
12. A bottle opener.
13. A bird scarer.
14. A pneumatically-operated coded door lock.
15. A canned drinks dispenser.
16. A mechanism to rotate slowly a rotatable washing line.
17. A rain detector with audible warning.
18. A car trailer anti-theft device.
19. An electronic metronome.
20. A bicycle alarm.
21. A humidity-controlled switch.
22. An electronic weather station: temperature, wind speed, rainfall.
23. A computer database to catalogue Technology stock.
24. A burglar alarm with automatic camera facilities.
25. A wind-powered vehicle.
26. Automatic watering system for plants in a greenhouse.

2
s t r u c t u r e s

2:1 WHAT IS A STRUCTURE?

All the photographs in Figure 2.1 show structures. Structures surround us. Some are natural, such as trees, and some are produced by humans, such as buildings. A structure is designed and built to carry a load or force and this load or force must be held in the correct position without the structure collapsing. The structure might also be designed to protect something inside it as in a house or garage.

Looking at structures will help you to understand the need for manufactured structures, which can also often make use of natural structures.

Figure 2.1 *Examples of structures*

2:2 STRUCTURAL FAILURE

As we know, both natural and manufactured structures often fail dramatically (Figure 2.2). Though often exciting to watch, failures are dangerous and obviously best avoided.

The reason for all failures could be described by the words 'poor design', but we really need to look beyond this simple explanation. What is 'poor design'? A lot of design is based on a scientific and general knowledge of the properties and strengths of materials. If a structure is designed to withstand about four times the known load it will actually have to support we might expect it to be strong enough. (The factor of 4 is called the 'safety factor'.)

So why do structures fail? One reason is that scientific knowledge is never complete; another is that the loads applied to the structures may be greater than the original designers expected. The early motorways and motorway bridges are typical examples of these failures: the number of cars and lorries and the size of lorries have all increased more than expected. The forces on the road surfaces and bridge supports are therefore greater than anticipated and the flexible joints in some of the early bridges are collapsing, partly because the designers could not know how the materials used would stand up to future loads.

Figure 2.2 *Examples of structural failures*

Certain structures can have key members that provide support for other members. The failure of one key member can be catastrophic. However, such a failure is not always the fault of the designers. An explosion, for instance, is beyond their control.

To prevent catastrophic failures a designer needs to:

(a) allow a high enough factor of safety in the strengths of the members of a structure
(b) have as few key members as possible
(c) try to anticipate the worst possible cause of failure and reduce its effect.

2:3 STABILITY OF STRUCTURES

All structures have a **centre of gravity**. This is the point from which the weight of the structure may be considered to act. The centre of gravity is the balance point. The position of the centre of gravity decides whether a structure is stable (Figure 2.3).

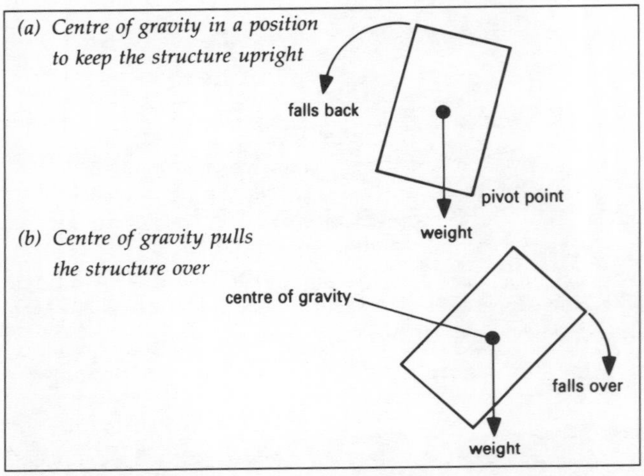

Figure 2.3 *Stability and the centre of gravity*

The way a structure is used will determine the design for stability. For example, the centre of gravity of a road bridge must always be within the supports, even if one side of the road has many 38-tonne vehicles on it and the other side of the road has no vehicles at all. The centre of gravity therefore depends on both the structure itself and the use to which it is put. The use of the structure adds external forces which must be taken into account in the design.

2:4 WEIGHT, MASS AND FORCE

All substances or materials have **mass**. Mass is measured in units of kilograms. If a substance is being pulled by **gravity**, as it is when it is near a large body like the earth, then the substance will also have a **weight**. Weight is the amount of **force** on a substance due to gravity and is measured in units of newtons. On earth, a mass of 1 kilogram has a weight of 10 newtons (see Figure 2.4).

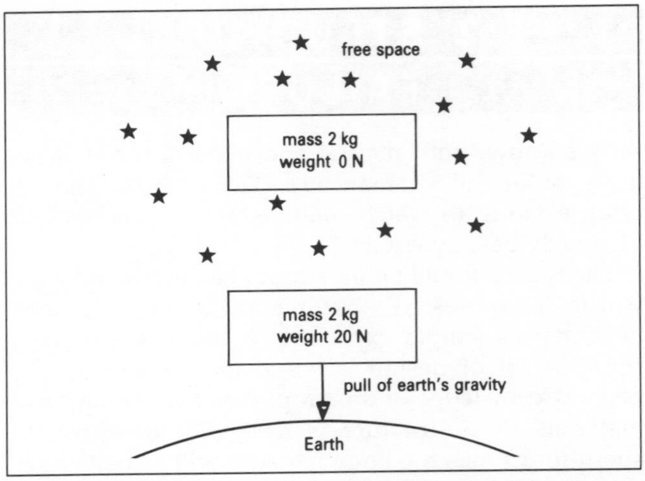

Figure 2.4 *Defining mass and weight: substances in 'free space' have no weight*

2:5 MEASURING FORCES

Forces are measured in units of newtons with a newtonmeter. Most newtonmeters (Figure 2.5) rely on the linear stretching of a spring. Linear means that equal increases in load will give equal increases in the length. Within certain limits most springs will obey this rule which is known as **Hooke's Law**. Figure 2.6 shows a schematic diagram of a newtonmeter and a graph of expected results. The spring must be chosen so that it remains within the straight (linear) part of the graph so that it always returns to its original length (zero extension) when the load is removed.

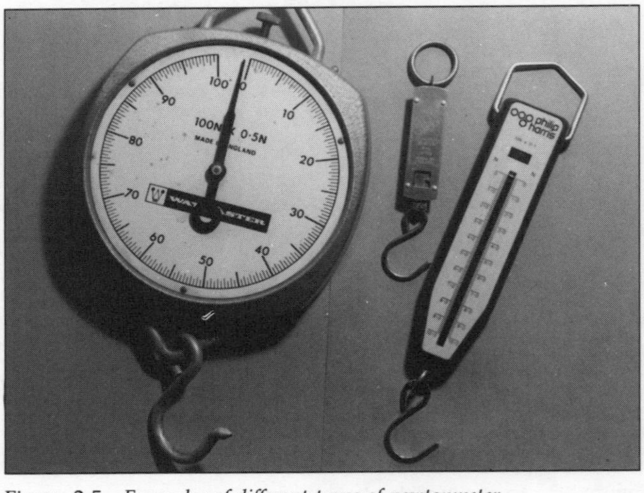

Figure 2.5 *Examples of different types of newtonmeter*

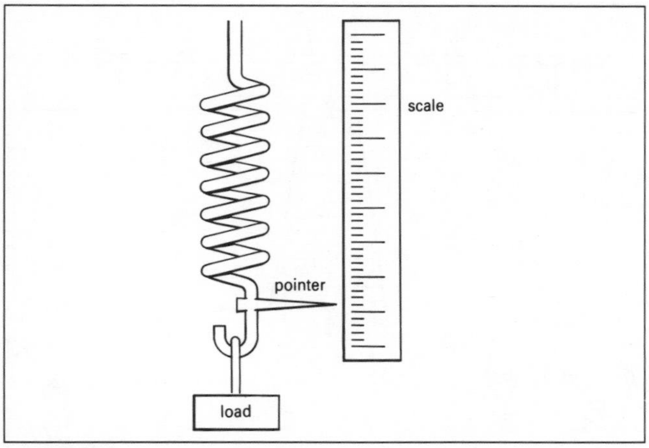

Figure 2.6 *(a) A newtonmeter*

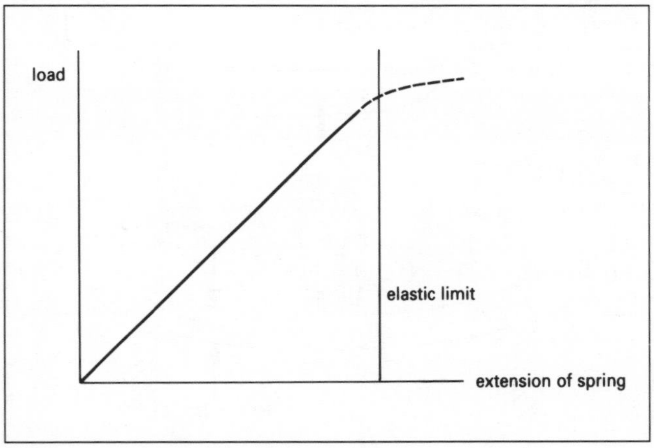

Figure 2.6 *(b) Linear action of a newtonmeter*

2:6 TURNING FORCES

The forces which affect stability are known as **turning forces**. Think back to your days playing on see-saws. You will probably have worked out that heavier people need to sit nearer the pivot to balance lighter people sitting further from the pivot. This is summarised by the principle of moments:

force (weight) × the distance from a pivot

is called the **moment of a force**. The pivot point is often called the **fulcrum**.

A structure (sometimes called a body) will be stable if the total clockwise moment is equal to the total anticlockwise moment (Figure 2.7):

weight W × distance Z = weight V × distance Y

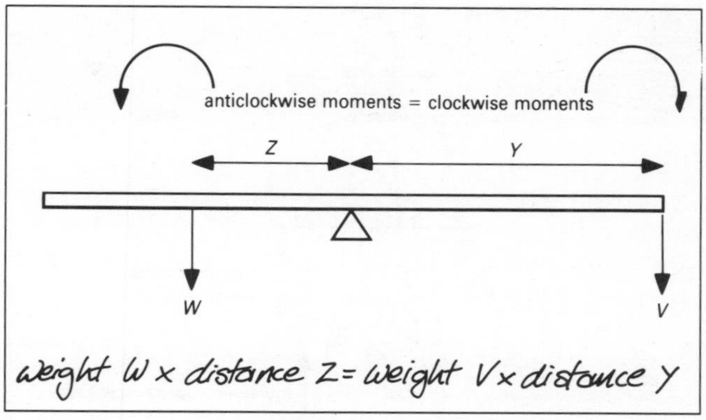

Figure 2.7 *Conditions for stability*

Example In Figure 2.7:

if distance $Z = 3\,\text{m}$
and distance $Y = 6\,\text{m}$

then a 20 kg child at position V will balance a 40 kg child at position W because

$$20 \times 6 = 40 \times 3$$

A stable or balanced structure is sometimes described by the term stable **equilibrium**.

Cantilever bridges and tower cranes need careful stability testing during the design process. The wind is a variable external force which can seriously affect stability and structures have to be designed to withstand the worst possible case. In practice, design against the elements can never be one hundred per cent complete. The Building Regulations allow drainage systems to be designed to take water from a 'once-in-20-year rainstorm'. This means that, on average, once in every 20 years the drains will not cope with a rainstorm. The Building Regulations also specify sizes of structural members needed to withstand forces from wind. The calculations have to include the highest likely wind speed, but who knows what the highest wind speed is going to be?

2:7 EXTERNAL FORCES

A structure must be built to withstand the external forces applied to it. The external forces include any loading of the structure and any reactions on supporting foundations. The reactions include the structures own weight. Figure 2.8 summarises the external

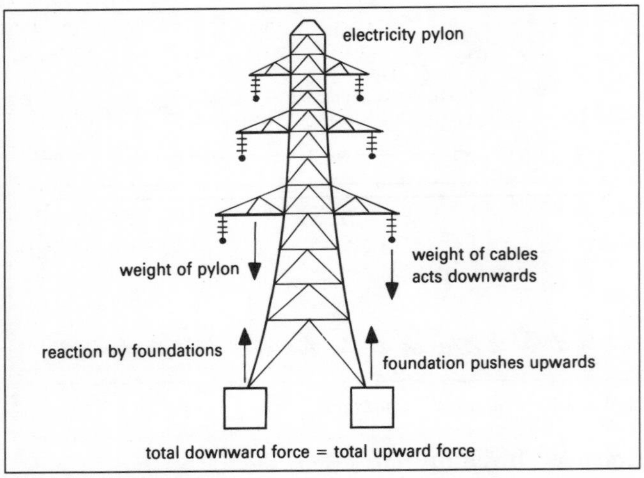

Figure 2.8 *External forces on a structure*

forces. Note that the structure's weight acts from the centre of gravity. External forces cause instability by moving the centre of gravity.

External forces can cause the centre of gravity to move. The turning moments will then change and could cause toppling. If the external forces are too high for the materials and structure to support then the structure will collpase.

Types of External Force

Five types of external forces (illustrated in Figure 2.9) can act on a structure. These are:

(a) compression (pushing)
(b) tension (pulling)
(c) bending
(d) torsion (or twisting)
(e) shear (slicing).

Compression forces are pushing forces. They try to squeeze the structure, as in Figure 2.9(a). A **strut** will be in compression.

Tension forces are pulling forces. They try to stretch the structure. A **tie** will be in tension, as shown in Figure 2.9(b).

Bending forces occur in beams. They set up compression and tension within the structure, as shown in Figure 2.9(c).

Torsion forces are twisting forces, as shown in Figure 2.9(d).

Shear forces are cutting forces. They try to make one part of a structure slide past another part, as Figure 2.9(e) illustrates.

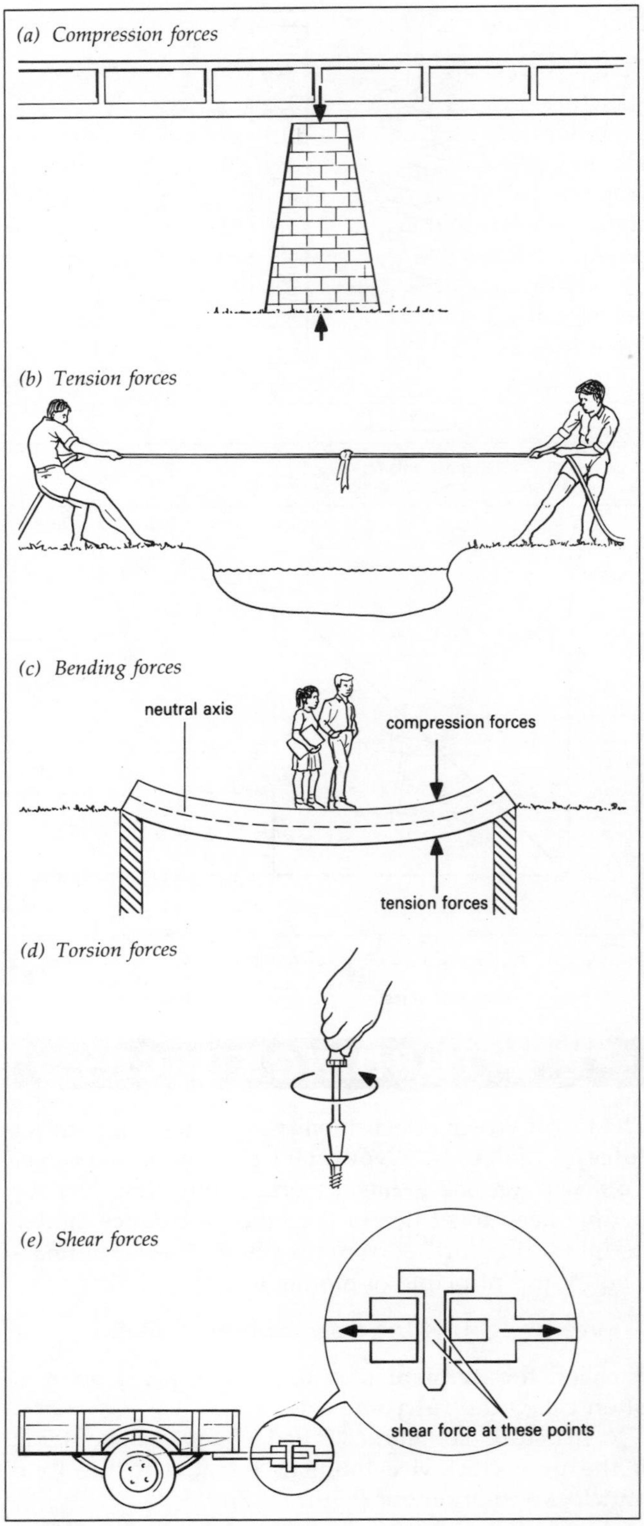

Figure 2.9 *Different external forces*

Static and Dynamic Forces

Static forces are the result of the weight of the structure and any stationary load on it.

Dynamic forces are caused by movement. When a moving object increases or decreases in speed a force is needed. This force can be much greater than the static weight of the object itself. For example, if a person of mass 50 kg and weight of 500 N sits down quickly on to a stool, the person's speed is 3 m/s just before sitting down and the stool stops the movement in 0.2 s.

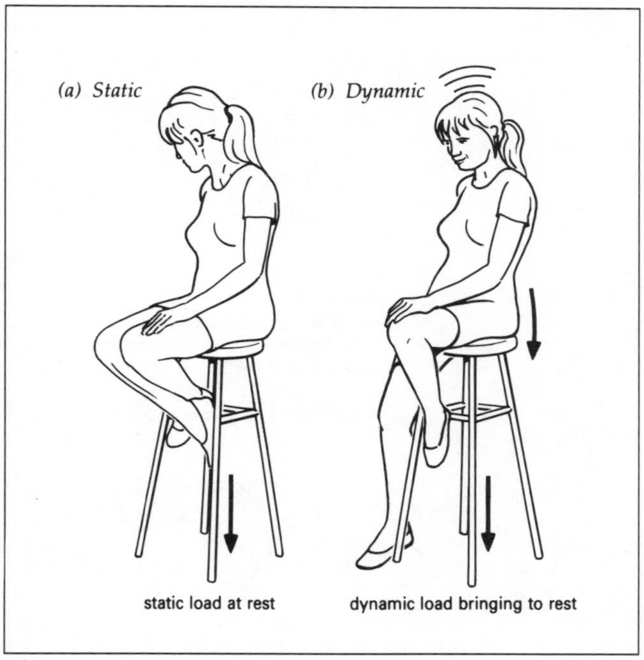

Figure 2.10 *Forces on a stool*

One of Newton's Laws tells us that:

force = mass × acceleration

and the rules of motion tell us that:

$$\text{acceleration} = \frac{\text{change in speed}}{\text{time taken for change}}$$

In this example:

$$\text{acceleration} = \frac{3}{0.2} = 15\,\text{m/s}^2$$

The force needed to stop the person is therefore:

force = 50 × 15 = 750 N

This force has to be applied by the person on the stool, so the stool would have to withstand a downward force of 750 N.

In fact, a factor of safety is always added and if the maximum load is 750 N, then the design load would be four times this. The design load would therefore be 3000 N. The static load, once the person has settled, would be the same as the person's weight, i.e. 500 N.

Newton's Laws

Newton's Laws state that:

(1) an object remains at rest or moves at constant speed in a straight line unless a force is applied to the object
(2) force = mass × acceleration
(3) action and reaction are equal and opposite.

In the example above, the stool pushes up on the person by the same force as the person pushes down on the floor. This is what the third law tells us. The forces must be equal in size but opposite in direction otherwise the stool would move.

It is difficult to test the first law fully without the object being in 'free space', in other words without gravity or frictional force acting. These laws were used in the navigational calculations for the control of space craft to the moon and beyond, so they have been well tested.

2:8 INTERNAL FORCES

Internal forces oppose the external forces applied to structural members. The forces between the molecules and atoms which make up the materials in use provide this opposing force. When a member breaks or fractures the internal forces have been overcome. On a microscopic scale the molecules and atoms have been dragged apart.

A shear failure is caused by the atoms sliding over each other. This generally takes less energy than a tension failure where the atoms are being pulled apart. Compression causes the atoms and molecules to be pushed closer together. This will have the effect of reducing the volume. When the external pushing force exceeds the internal force keeping the molecules apart the molecules try to move into each other, so causing the structural member to bulge outwards.

Bending forces cause a combination of compression and tension within the structural member as shown in Figure 2.11. Buckling or deformation can result on the compression side and fractures occur on the tension side (Figure 2.12). Torsion forces produce a combination of tension and shearing forces on the molecules. Fractures due to torsion occur in such components as axles and drive shafts, which are used in rotary mechanisms.

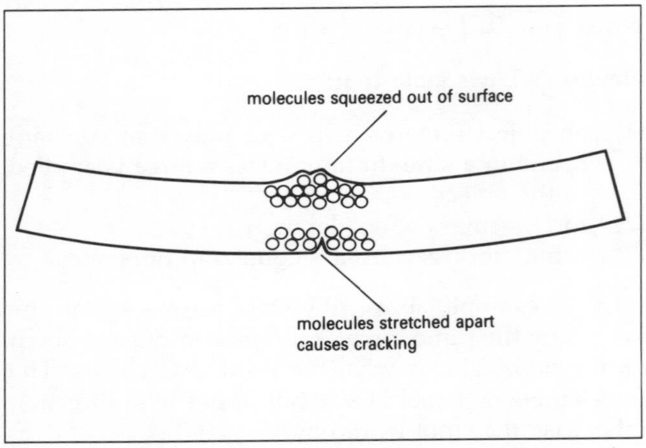

Figure 2.11 *Internal forces in a bent beam*

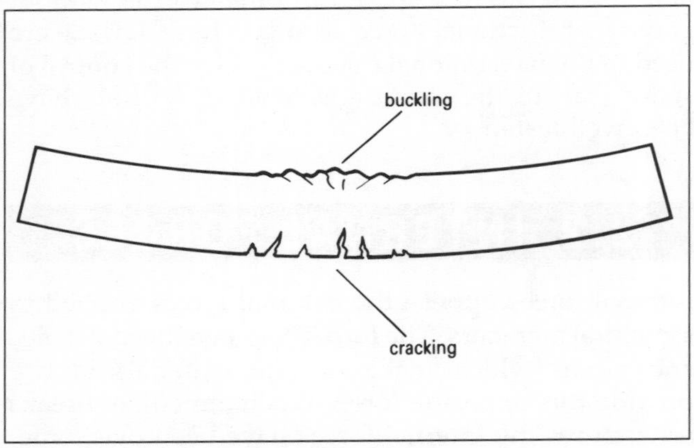

Figure 2.12 *Bending and fractures in a beam*

2:9 DRAWING FORCES

Simple Examples

Forces can be drawn using straight lines. The length of the line is used to represent the size of the force. The direction of the line is used to represent the direction of the force (Figure 2.13).

Values which have both size and direction are called **vectors**. Examples are force and velocity. Values which only have size, such as mass, speed and time are called **scalars**.

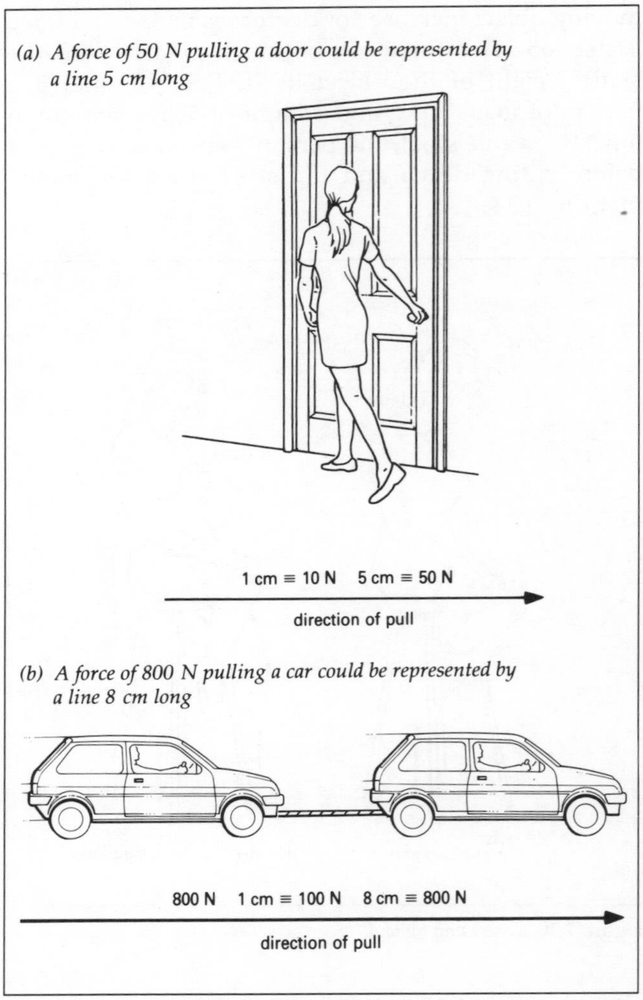

Figure 2.13 *Examples of drawing forces*

Combining Forces

At any particular place in a structure there will be several forces acting. If several forces are acting at the same time along the same line, the net force resulting can be easily worked out.

If the forces are in the same direction then the forces are added together. The net force is called the **resultant force**. If the forces are in opposite directions then the resultant force is the difference between the forces.

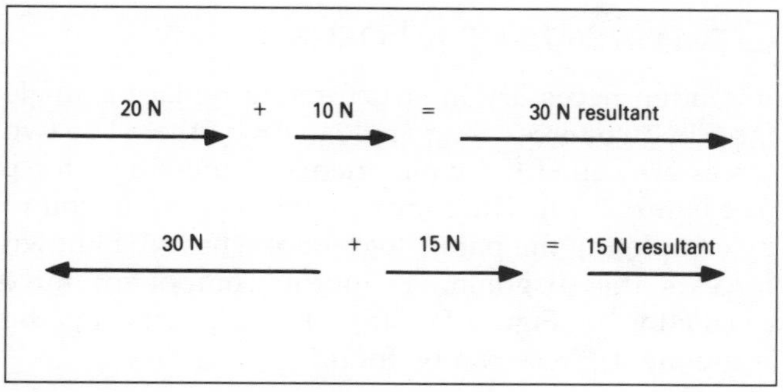

Figure 2.14 *Examples of combining forces*

Forces acting at an angle to each other are added together as shown in Figure 2.15. The diagonal of the parallelogram completed from the two forces gives the direction and size of the resultant. This method of finding the resultant force is called the parallelogram of forces. The lines should be drawn to scale so that the size of the resultant can be found by measuring the length of the line.

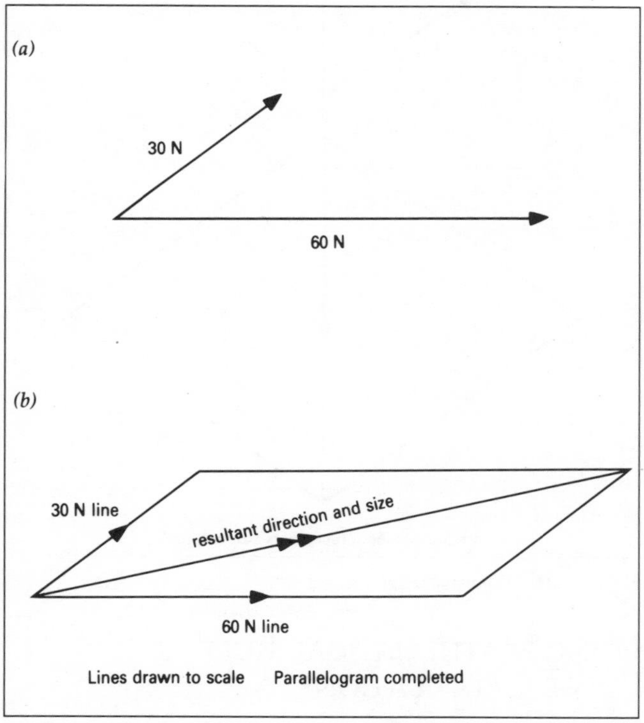

Figure 2.15 *(a) Forces at an angle; (b) using the parallelogram of forces*

Example Two people are pulling on a cart. One pulls with a force of 200 N, the other with a force of 300 N. The angle between each force is 60°. Figure 2.16 shows how the resultant force is calculated.

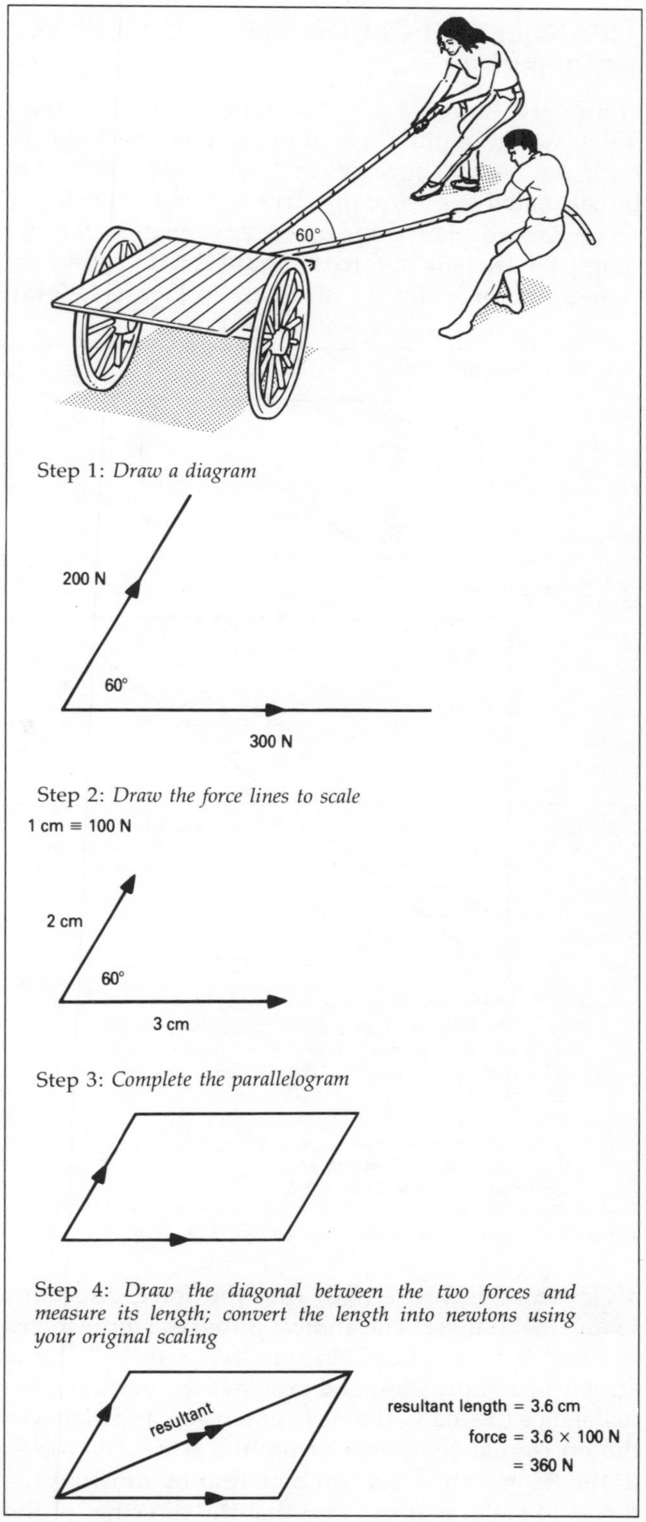

Figure 2.16 *The force calculations for two forces*

Triangle of Forces: Three Forces in Equilibrium

Figure 2.17 shows a common type of structure used when wall-mounting a sign or in some mechanisms such as a crane. The forces in the tie and strut need to be calculated to ensure the structure will not collapse when loaded. Three forces are involved so this requires the triangle of forces. Figure 2.17(b) shows the triangle of forces for the structure in Figure 2.17 (a).

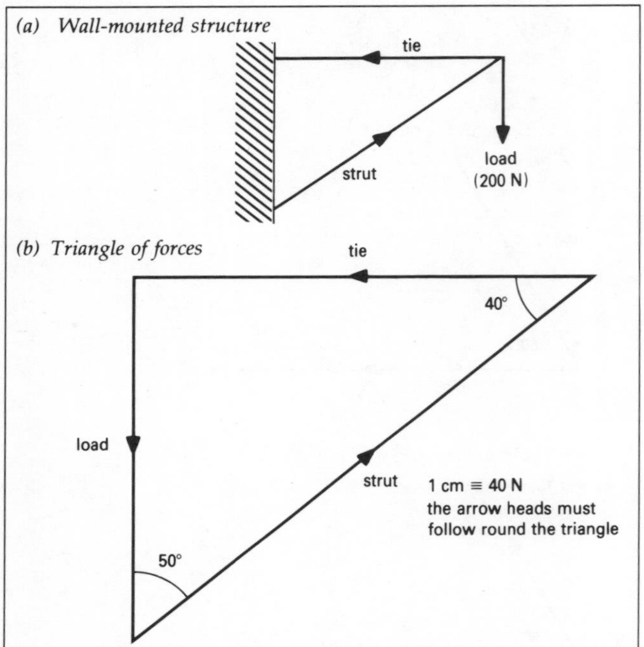

Step 1: *Draw the load to scale 1 cm = 40 N*
Step 2: *Draw the strut force at the correct angle to the load*
Step 3: *Draw the tie force at the correct angle to the load*
Step 4: *Measure the length of the unknown lines*
strut = 7.8 cm
tie = 6.0 cm
Step 5: *Convert back to Force using the scaling*
tie force = 6.0 × 40 = 240 N
strut force = 7.8 × 40 = 312 N

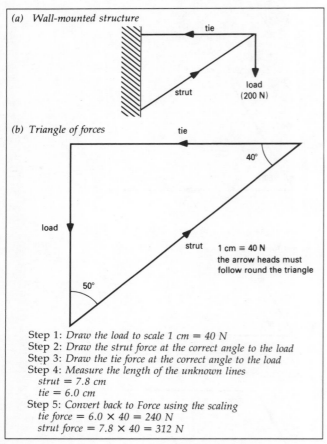

Figure 2.17 *Common structure used for wall-mounting*

Notice in Figure 2.17(b) that the force directions follow the triangle. This indicates that the three forces combine to form an equilibrium. In Figure 2.17(a), the strut is in compression and provides the vertical force to balance the load. The tie is in tension and balances the horizontal component from the strut. The forces in the tie and the strut can be found by drawing the forces to scale, making sure that the direction of the forces is maintained.

Components of a Force

It is often necessary in structures to replace a single force by two forces at an angle to each other. The two forces are called the components of the single force (see Figure 2.18). The component forces can be found by completing the parallelogram of which the known force is the diagonal, as in the component force calculation of Figure 2.18(b). By scale drawing the component forces can be found.

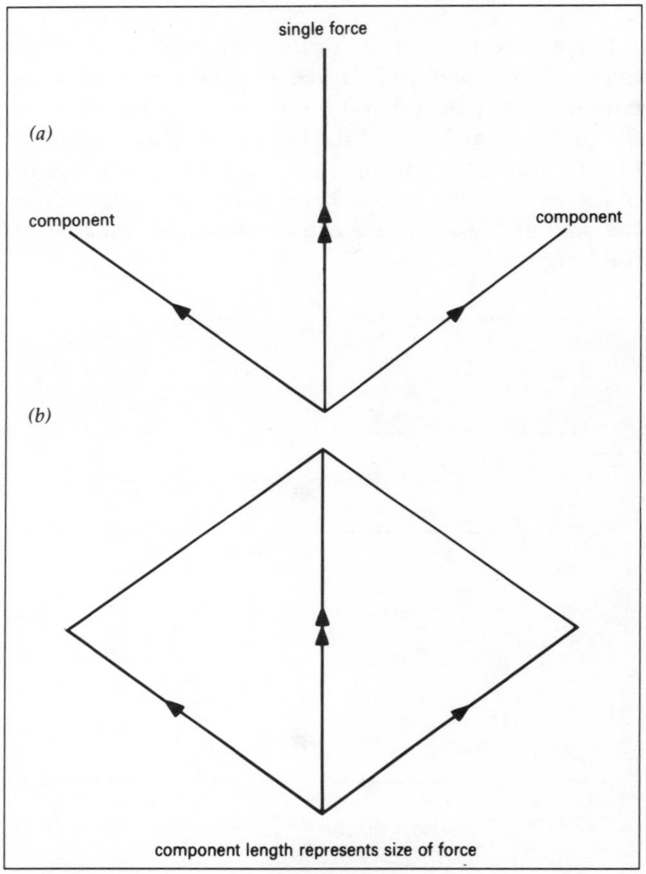

Figure 2.18 *Components of a single force*

Using Mathematical Rules in Force Calculations

Sine, cosine and tangent rules can be used with a right-angled triangle, instead of scale drawing. More complicated rules are needed for other triangles. The use of drawings help to understand the way forces combine. Figure 2.19 shows the example used in Figure 2.17(a) and (b).

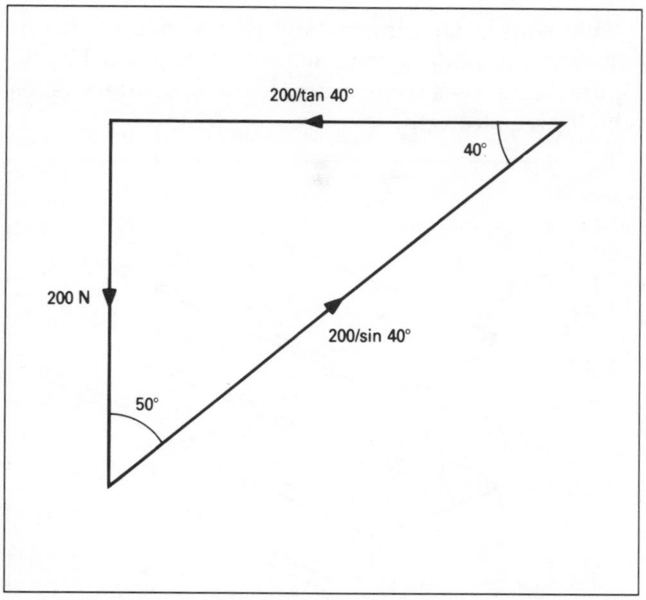

Figure 2.19 *Using mathematical rules in force calculations*

2:10 THE STRENGTH OF STRUCTURES

The overall strength of a structure depends on:

(a) the materials used in the structure
(b) the shape of the members of the structure
(c) the shape of the structure
(d) the jointing between members of the structure.

Strength means the ability to resist a force without breaking.

MATERIALS AND THEIR PROPERTIES

There are four properties of materials which need to be considered when deciding on a suitable material to do a specific job:

(a) strength
(b) elasticity
(c) hardness
(d) toughness.

The strength of a material is its ability to resist the external forces mentioned in Section 2:7, without breaking.

If a material returns to its original shape after being deformed then it is said to have elastic properties. Elasticity is important in structures such as springs.

Structures are liable to wear when surfaces move over each other. The materials used must be hard to prevent such wear. Hardness is important in structures such as engines, gearboxes and bearings, and such tools as drill bits would be made out of hardened steel.

A material which can absorb a lot of energy without breaking is said to be tough. Toughness should not be confused with strength. Brittle materials tend to fracture easily and are not tough but, in contrast, ductile materials, such as copper, are tough but cannot always be classed as strong.

All materials have all these properties to a greater or lesser extent. Which properties are important depends on the use to which the material is put. Some examples are shown in Figure 2.20.

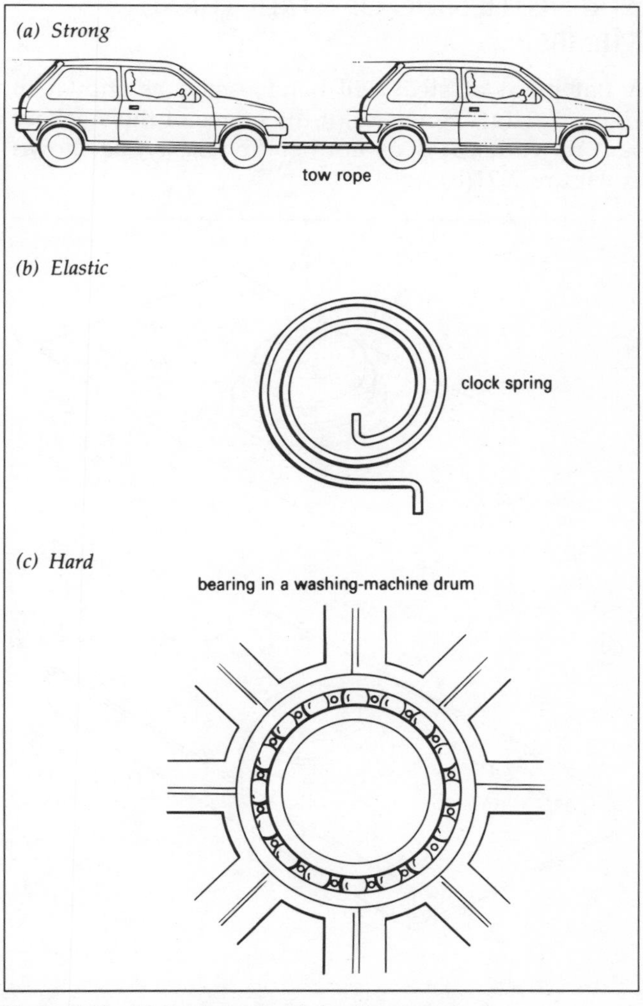

Figure 2.20 *Materials for the job (continued overleaf)*

Figure 2.20 *(continued) (d) Tough*

Strengthening of Structural Members

A flat piece of steel will bend easily, as shown in Figure 2.21(a). However, if the edges of the steel are bent upwards, it does not bend so easily, as shown by Figure 2.21(b).

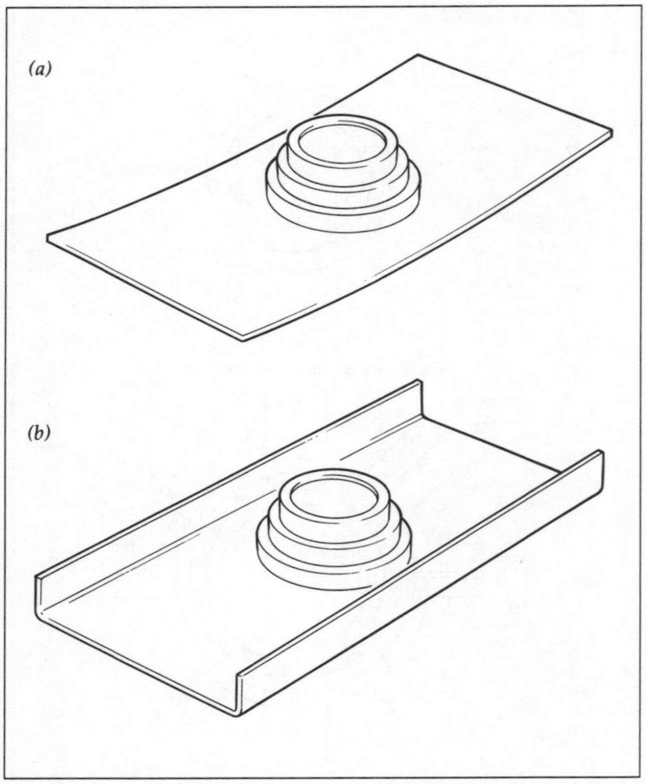

Figure 2.21 *Simple structural shaping*

This simple shaping means that structural members can be made strong without being too heavy. Figure 2.22 shows some examples of structural shapes which give strength.

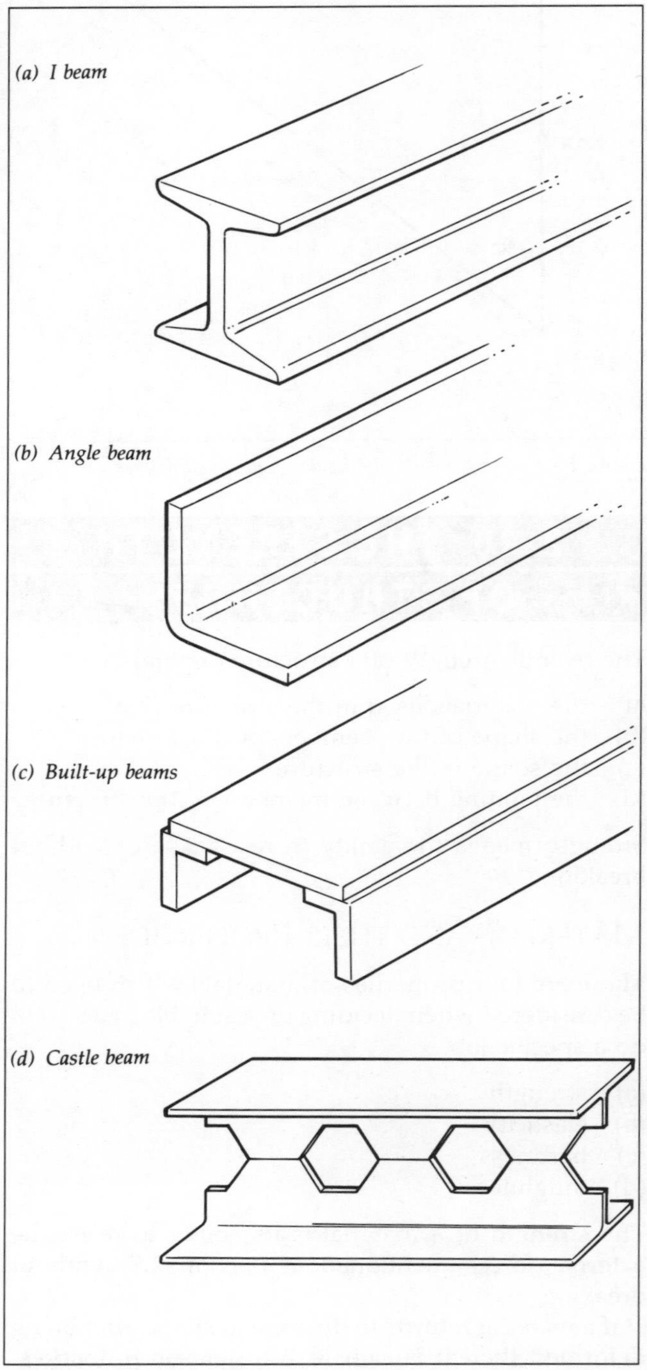

Figure 2.22 *Strength through shaping of structural members*

REINFORCING

Brittle materials, such as concrete, can be reinforced so that they can be used in a greater range of structures. Concrete is weak under tensile forces but steel wires, which are strong in tension, can be used to reinforce concrete, as Figure 2.23 shows.

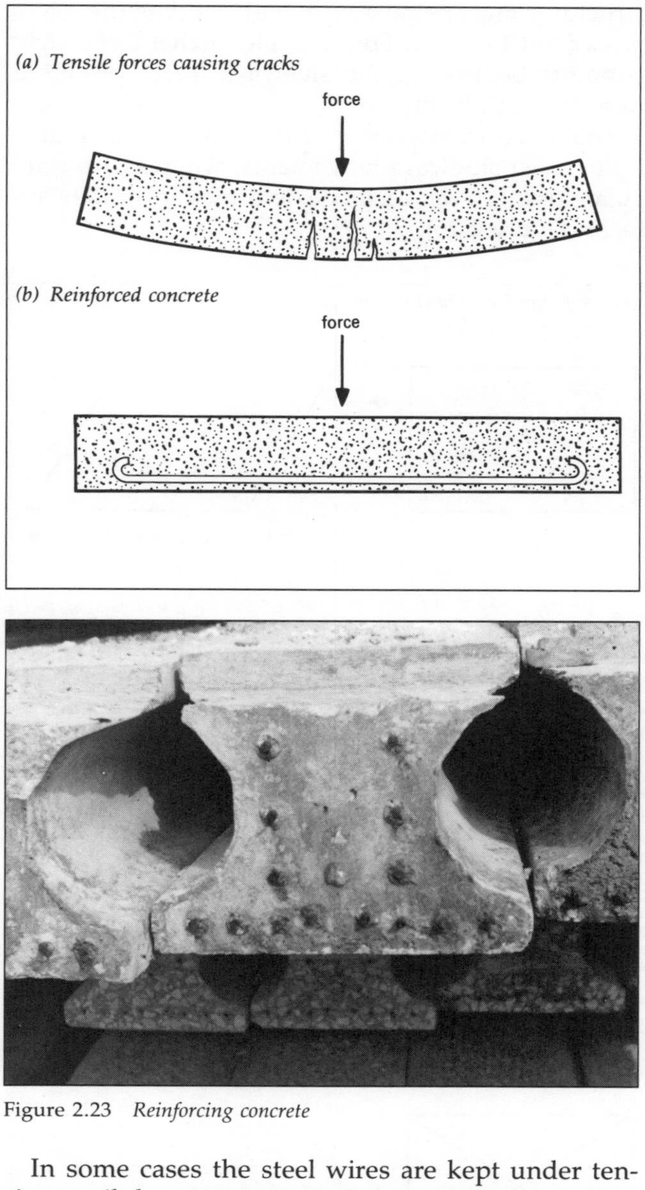

Figure 2.23 *Reinforcing concrete*

In some cases the steel wires are kept under tension until the concrete sets. Releasing the wires then puts the concrete into compression. This provides a beam which, without increasing the size or weight, can take even greater loads.

Other examples of reinforcing include glass-reinforced polyester, sometimes called fibre-glass or GRP, which is described in Section 2:15. Mixing straw with mud was a technique used by ancient civilisations and is still used today in Third World countries to make flat sheets for building houses. Before plasterboard was developed, horsehair was mixed with mortar to bind it together for wall finishing.

LAMINATING

Certain materials can be strengthened by the technique of laminating. For example, although wood is a useful building material and large beams can be made from solid timbers, because of defects such as knots the strength is non-uniform. Very large beams can be built up by laminating a large number of thin pieces and glueing them together with the grain of successive pieces in different directions (Figure 2.24). Beams formed in this way can be shaped to produce very strong and large roof structures. Plywood is an example of a commonly used laminated material. Laminated timber does not warp (bend) as easily as single planks because of the overlapping grain in successive sheets.

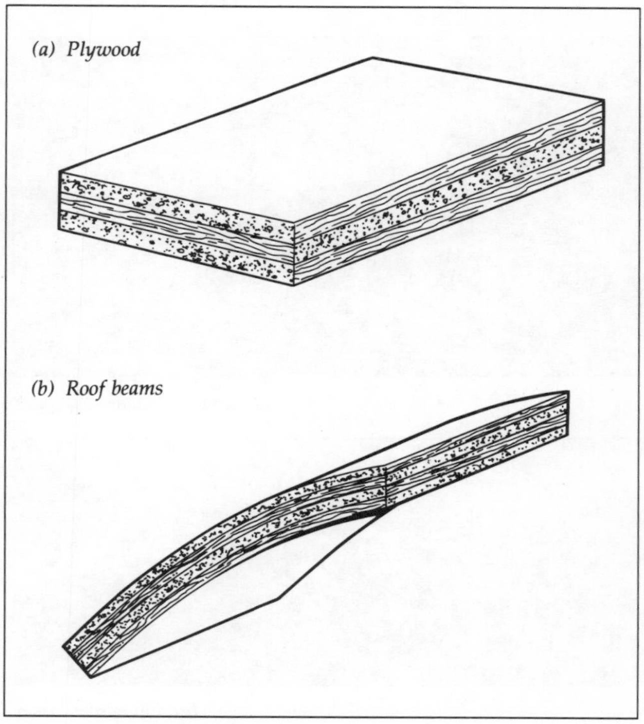

Figure 2.24 *Laminated timber*

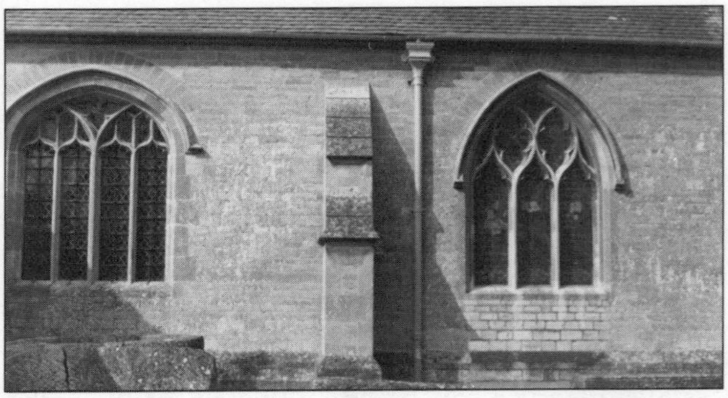

(a) Stone arches

(b) Triangular frameworks

(c) Stone arch with keystone

(d) Box girder bridge

Figure 2.25 *Strength through structural shaping*

Structural Shaping

The shaped laminated wooden roof beam shown in Figure 2.24(b) is an example of structural shaping. Other examples are shown in Figure 2.25.

The correct shaping of structures provides strength and rigidity; downward forces and sideways forces are resisted. The foundations or other supports to the structures must be capable of withstanding the forces passed on to them. For example, arches need rigid supports because of the sideways forces produced from the arch itself.

Triangular frameworks are rigid through their ability to resist sideways movements, whereas a rectangular structure can easily be deformed by a sideways force (Figure 2.26).

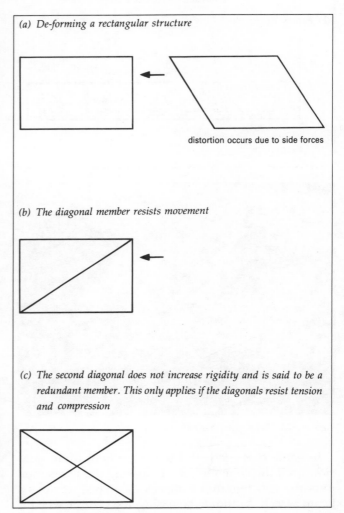

(a) De-forming a rectangular structure

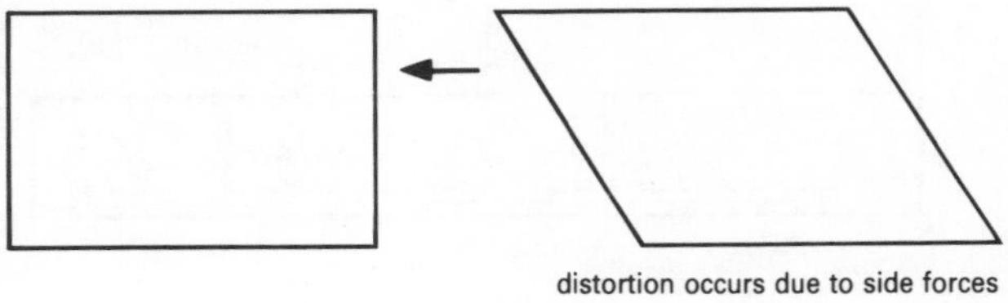

(b) The diagonal member resists movement

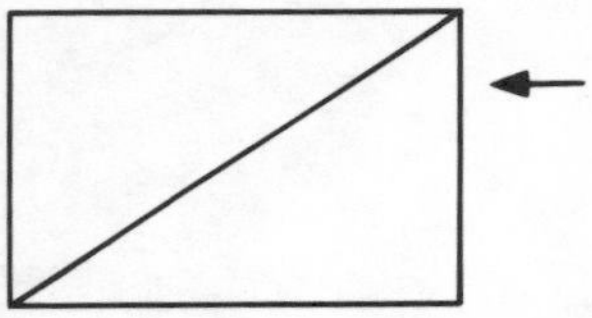

(c) The second diagonal does not increase rigidity and is said to be a redundant member. This only applies if the diagonals resist tension and compression

Figure 2.26 *Triangular rigidity*

2:11 JOINTING IN STRUCTURES

The methods used for jointing depend on the materials in use and the forces which the joint has to withstand. A well-designed joint distributes any force or forces throughout the structure without overloading it at any particular point. Many structures are satisfactorily joined using conventional techniques. Riveting, screwing and bolting are often sufficient for joining similar or dissimilar materials. Over the last few years there has been a growth in the use of chemical jointing or 'bonding'. Bonding is now often used where the drilling of holes for rivets or bolts causes too much weakening, as in modern aircraft. A drilled hole is a source of uneven stress in the material at which continual flexing could cause failures through cracking. Bonding allows the forces at the joints to be spread over a much larger area. Figure 2.27 illustrates jointing methods for different situations and materials.

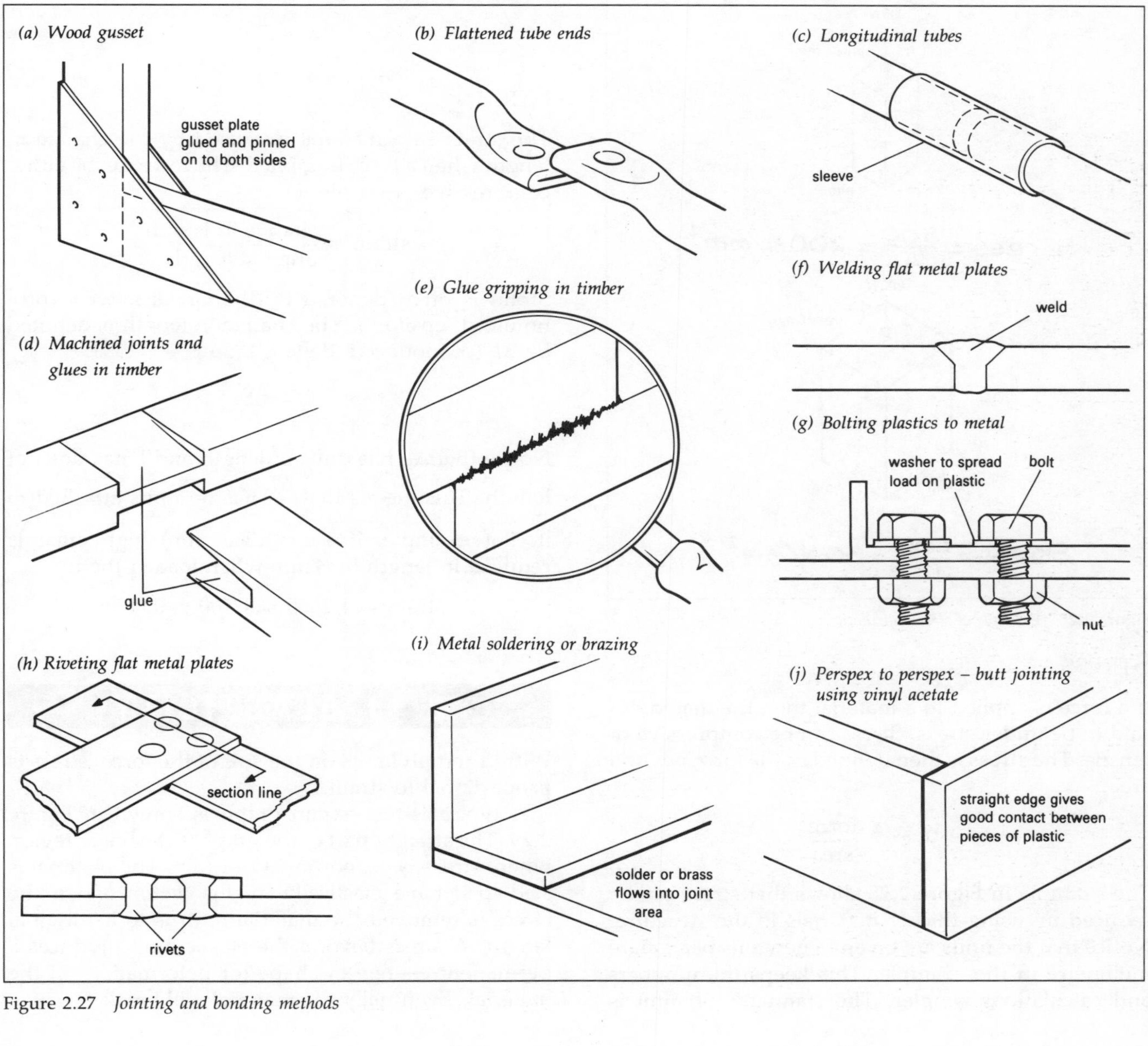

Figure 2.27 *Jointing and bonding methods*

2:12 STRESS AND STRAIN

The choice of material for a particular job depends on many factors and it is sometimes necessary to compare the properties of different materials. This usually requires some kind of measurement on the material to give a scale for comparison. Two measurements often taken are of the **stress** and **strain** applied to the material.

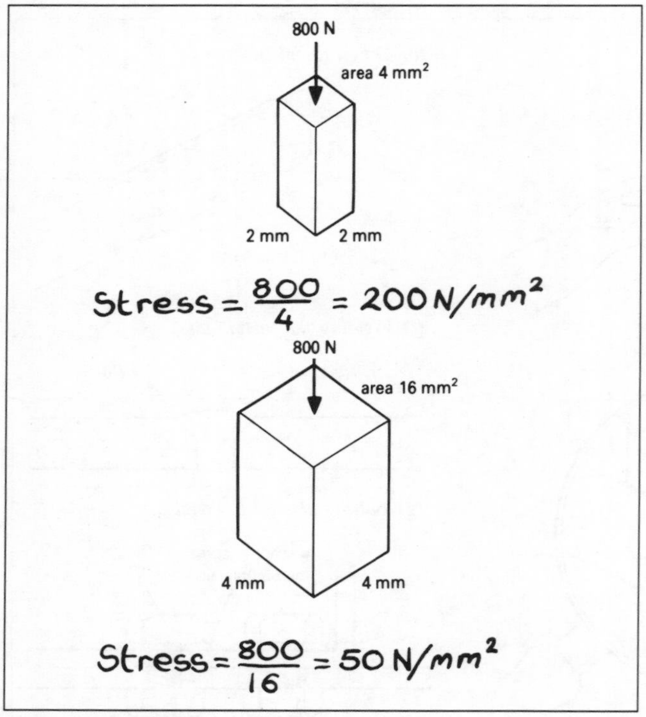

Figure 2.28 *Example of stress calculation*

Stress

If a force is applied to a material then the material is said to be under stress. Stress can be compressive or tensile. The stress is then defined as the force per unit area:

$$\text{stress} = \frac{\text{force}}{\text{area}}$$

The example in Figure 2.28 shows that stress can be reduced by using thicker materials in the structure. Notice that the units are given in newtons per square millimetre in the example. This keeps the numbers and calculations simpler. The standard (SI) unit is newtons per square metre N/m^2 which makes calculations more difficult. In some situations the unit used is MN/m^2 (meganewtons per square metre).

The unit conversions between MN/m^2 and N/mm^2 are:

$$\begin{aligned} 1 \text{ meganewton} &= 1000\,000 \text{ newtons} \\ 1 \text{ square metre} &= 1000\,000 \text{ mm}^2 \\ \text{So} \quad 1 \text{ MN/m}^2 &= 1 \text{ N/mm}^2 \\ 8 \text{ MN/m}^2 &= 8 \text{ N/mm}^2 \text{ etc.} \end{aligned}$$

Stress is often denoted by the Greek letter σ (pronounced 'sigma'), so:

$$\sigma = F/A$$

Strain

The strain in a material is caused by the change in length when a force is applied. The force can be either compressive or tensile, i.e.:

$$\text{strain} = \frac{\text{change in length}}{\text{original length}}$$

Strain is often denoted by the Greek letter ϵ (pronounced 'epsilon'). The change in length is denoted by ΔL (pronounced 'delta L'). So

$$\epsilon = \frac{\Delta L}{L}$$

Notice that ΔL has units of length and L has units of length. This means that $\frac{\Delta L}{L}$ has no units attached to it. For example, if a 2 m (2000 mm) high pillar is reduced in length by 4 mm when loaded then:

$$\text{strain} = 4/2000 = 1/500 = 0.002$$

2:13 ELASTICITY

Within certain limits on the size of the force, stress is proportional to strain.

A typical stress–strain graph is shown in Figure 2.29. The straight part of the graph is the linear region where stress is proportional to strain. The material is said to behave elastically in this region and if the stress is removed the material returns to its original length. A stress beyond the elastic limit produces a permanent change in shape (or deformation) in the material. Eventually the material will break.

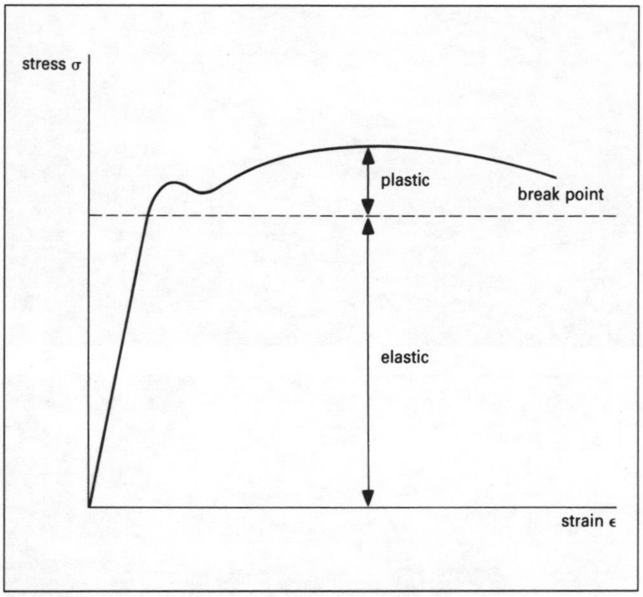

Figure 2.29 *Typical stress–strain behaviour*

Structural designers will usually make sure that the materials are loaded so that only the lower part of the elastic line is used. In this region

$$\frac{\text{stress}}{\text{strain}} = \text{constant}$$

The constant is called the **modulus of elasticity** or Young's modulus:

$$\text{modulus of elasticity } E = \frac{\text{stress}}{\text{strain}} = \frac{\sigma}{\epsilon}$$

The highest stress on the curve in Figure 2.29 is called the ultimate stress.

2:14 FACTOR OF SAFETY

The ultimate stress can be measured for any structural material. Designers will always ensure that the working stress of the material is well below the ultimate stress and a **factor of safety** is always allowed (Figure 2.30). A factor of safety of 4 is common:

$$\text{working stress} = \frac{\text{ultimate stress}}{4}$$

Too high a factor of safety means unnecessary expense; too low a factor of safety means possible failures of a structure.

From the working stress it is possible to work back through the relationship stress = F/A to find the cross-sectional area of the material to withstand the required force. Table 2.1 shows the ultimate stress (compressive and tensile) and modulus of elasticity figures for some common materials.

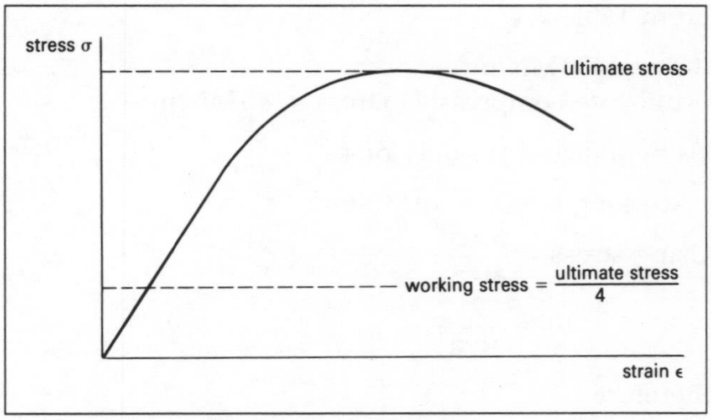

Figure 2.30 *Factor of safety and working stress*

Table 2.1 Approximate strength and modulus of elasticity for some common materials

Material	*Young's modulus (MN/m²)*	*Typical tensile strength (MN/m²)*
aluminium	70 000	90–150
copper	130 000	150 (cast) 300 (rolled)
cast iron	150 000	100–230
gold	78 000	–
silver	83 000	–
brass	100 000	–
zinc	110 000	125
mild steel	200 000	430–490
ash	16 000	60–110
oak	11 000	60–110
pitch pine	16 000	60–110
deal	–	40–80
yellow pine	16 000	30–70
silk fibre	–	20–50
fused quartz	73 000	260
crown glass	71 000	1000
nylon	1000–3000	60–100
polypropylene	1100–1600	30–40
polyethylene	400–1300	21–35
polystyrene	2700–4200	34–52
glass reinforced polyester (GRP)	20 000	400
concrete	14 000	40 (compressive)

NB: wood measurements are along the grain

Example A concrete pillar is to be designed to support a compressive load of 2 MN (2 million newtons). Find the required cross-sectional area for the pillar and the maximum change in length of a 10 m tall pillar. Comment on the factor of safety and the change in length.

From Table 2.1

$E = 1400\,\text{MN/m}^2$
ultimate compressive stress $= 40\,\text{MN/m}^2$

Using a factor of safety of 4

working stress $= 10\,\text{MN/m}^2$

Using stress $= \dfrac{\text{force}}{\text{area}}$

$$10 = \frac{2}{\text{area}}$$

therefore

$$\text{area} = \frac{1}{5}\,\text{m}^2 = 0.2\,\text{m}^2$$

Using $E = \dfrac{\text{stress}}{\text{strain}}$

$$1400 = \frac{10}{\text{strain}}$$

therefore

$$\text{strain} = \frac{10}{1400} = \frac{1}{140}$$

Change in length is therefore $\dfrac{1}{140}$ m for every metre.

$$\text{Total change in length} = \frac{10}{140}\,\text{m} = \frac{1}{14}\,\text{m}$$

A factor of safety of 4 is a 'rule of thumb' minimum value. If the change in length is too great, the area will have to be increased to give a smaller length change. This means a higher factor of safety at greater expense.

2:15 COMMON STRUCTURAL MATERIALS

The overall form or shape of a structure is often determined by the materials used as well as the function (or job) for which the structure is designed (Figure 2.31).

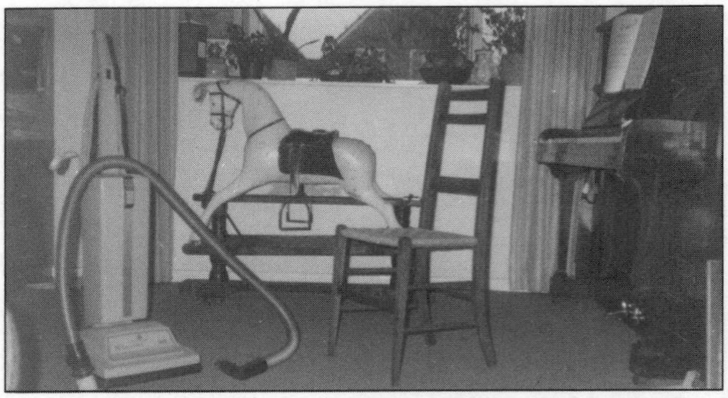

Figure 2.31 *Examples of materials in structures*

WOOD

Wood has been used in structures for many thousands of years. It is strong for its weight and can be shaped using even crude tools. When forests covered most of the northern hemisphere it was also very easily available. Today most buildings and fittings contain some wood.

These days different woods for use in buildings are graded for strength and durability and the Building Regulations specify the sizes to be used for particular jobs such as roof members or floor joists. The Building Regulations are a legal document produced by the Department of the Environment and approved by Parliament. In some areas, local by-laws also specify treatment against wood-boring insects.

The strength of wood is determined by the grain. Close-grained woods such as oak are stronger than wider-grained timbers such as pine. The close grain means that the tree takes longer to grow and so is more expensive. The designer needs to ensure that the correct wood is used for each job. The builder needs to ensure that the wood does not have any major defects such as large knots.

The use of solid wood has now largely been replaced by blockboard, plywood and chipboard, especially for large boards (Figure 2.32). Large sheets of these wood products can be produced at a lower cost and are less prone to warping, which occurs during the drying process of the timber as a result of the uneven forces caused by the grain.

Chipboard, made from chips of wood bonded together with resin glues, is extensively used in floors and modern furniture. Decorative coverings of veneers, melamine or formica make chipboard very flexible in its applications. The disadvantage of chipboard is its great weight due to the resins used in bonding. Manufactured boards are less prone to attack by wood-boring beetles because of these resins but can still rot, especially in damp conditions.

Blockboard is often used for shelving. It is cheaper than plywood and stronger than chipboard. Edging strips are usually added for decorative purposes.

Plywood tends to be more expensive than both chipboard or blockboard but is lighter and can be made in a greater range of thicknesses. It is useful for panels in furniture and larger panels where low weight and decorative finish are important.

Large buildings now use wooden beams more often as a result of developments in timber engineering, which allow decoratively appealing curved beams to be produced. Laminated timber beams are bent during production by the application of hot steam while applying the bending forces.

METAL

Metals have advantages over wood in some situations, especially where some shaping is involved. They are used in many structural forms, such as girder bridges, metal frames of large buildings, cars and domestic equipment. Steel is the most common metal used in structures, but many other metals, such as copper and aluminium, and **alloys** are also used where the structure requires different properties. Steel is of greatest importance because of its relative ease of extraction from iron ore which is mined from the ground. The properties of iron are modified by adding a small amount of carbon to produce the steel. However, the disadvantage of steel is that water and oxygen, both readily available in the atmosphere and rivers, cause corrosion in the form of rust.

Alloys are made by mixing or chemically combining different metals. Aluminium and copper alloys can be

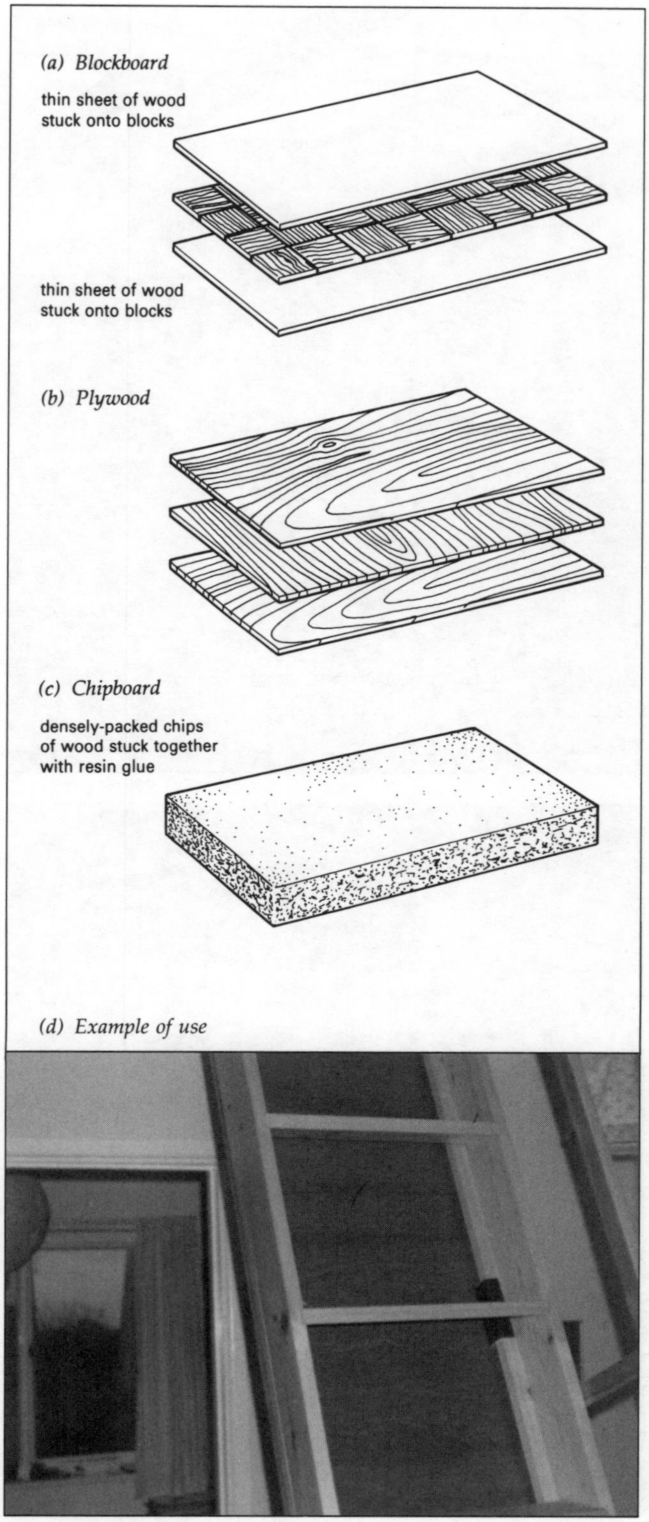

Figure 2.32 *Manufactured timber boards*

made which are as strong as mild steel but which are much lighter and not subject to the same corrosion problems. However, they cost much more to produce than mild steel since the metals used to make them must be highly refined. Five times more energy is needed to produce the refined metal than is required for steel so alloys are used in large structures only in very special circumstances.

Figure 2.33 *Use of steel in structures*

Figure 2.34 *Use of alloys in structures*

Some alloys are specially made to have low melting-points for use in soldering and brazing. These are based on lead, tin and copper. Other important alloys found in modern structures include: magnox (magnesium and aluminium), used in nuclear reactors and aircraft; stainless steel (steel and chromium), used in cutlery and sink units; and cupronickel (copper and nickel), used for minesweeper hulls because of its non-magnetic property.

Table 2.2 summarises different metals and their strengths. Compare these with those materials listed in Table 2.1. Mild steel is generally used in large structures. Figures 2.33 and 2.34 show examples of the use of steels and alloys. Alloy steels which contain up to 6% of other metals have strengths up to 1500 MN/m^2 and are typically used in bearings, high-strength bolts, and engine crankshafts.

Table 2.2 Metals and their strengths

Metal	*Carbon content*	*Young's modulus*	*Tensile strength*
Mild steel	up to 0.25%	200 000	400
Medium carbon steel	0.25–0.5%	200 000	500
High carbon steel	0.5–1.5%	200 000	600
Cast iron	2.0–4.5%	150 000	150
Aluminium	–	70 000	100
Copper	–	120 000	300
Magnesium	–	45 000	180
Lead	–	16 000	12
Brass	–	100 000	230
Phosphor bronze	–	110 000	800
Tin	–	50 000	25

Bricks and Concrete

In early times really solid houses could only be built where local stone was available. Gradually it was discovered that softer substances like clay, sand, and even cow dung, could be made into blocks and substituted for solid rock.

Clay is used to make bricks. The finished bricks are bonded together using a substance called mortar. Mortar is a **particle composite** consisting of sand, lime and cement. When water is added to this combination of particles the lime and cement form crystals which bind the sand particles together.

Concrete, another example of a composite, is basically made from sand, stone and cement. In recent years, the use of concrete blocks has been replacing bricks. They are lighter and therefore can be made bigger, enabling buildings to be constructed faster with reduced costs. Another advantage is the many different types of concrete blocks available for different jobs. Exterior walls use quite dense concrete made with fine sand. Interior walls do not need the same weatherproof properties and so can be made with a much more open and, hence, lighter structure. Air pockets can be left inside the blocks to improve thermal insulation as shown in Figure 2.35. This type of block will not carry large loads and would usually be used in walls in between metal girders or in non-supporting walls which do not carry any upper-floor loads. Concrete blocks are bonded together with mortar in the same way as bricks.

Figure 2.35 *Concrete building blocks with air cavities for thermal insulation*

Concrete can also be used in much larger structures where brickwork or blockwork would not be self-supporting. It is made up from sand, stones and cement. The stones, usually called aggregate, will normally be between 1 cm and 3 cm across, depending on the structure. The sand fills the gaps between the stones and the cement binds everything together through crystallisation (a chemical process) after being mixed with water (Figure 2.36). The strength depends on the ratio of aggregate:sand:cement. A typical example would be 3 parts aggregate:2 parts sand:1 part cement. Excessive water weakens concrete because evaporation leaves small holes throughout the concrete.

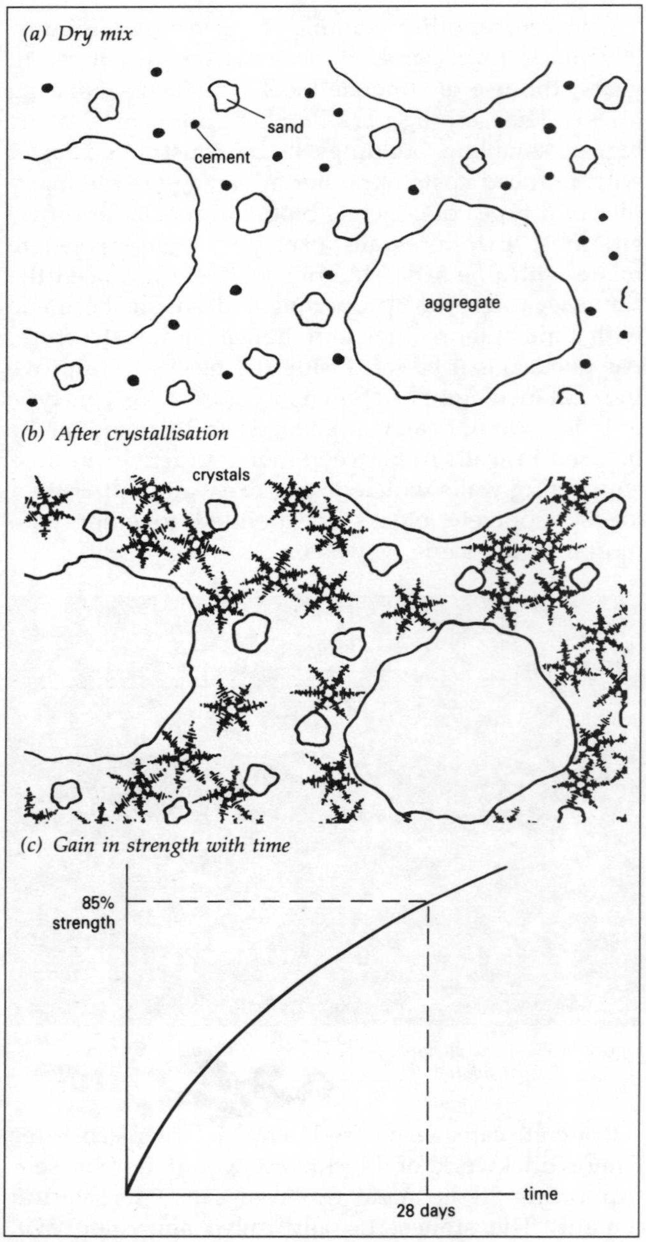

Figure 2.36 *Crystallisation of cement in concrete*

Concrete is very strong under compression. Tensile and bending forces are better resisted by reinforcing with steel rods (Figure 2.37). However, steel rods can corrode through rusting if they come into contact with water. The rust takes up more space than the steel so the concrete can be forced apart. In order to prevent such damage in this way, the rods need to be more than 25 mm from any surface.

Figure 2.37 *Reinforcing rods in concrete*

PLASTICS

Plastics refers to a group of materials which have certain properties in common, just as the terms 'wood' and 'metal' refer to groups of materials. Plastics are so useful because they are:

(a) resistant to rot (biological decay)
(b) resistant to corrosion (chemical decay)
(c) electrical and thermal insulators
(d) easily moulded into almost any shape
(e) reproducible in almost any colour
(f) low in cost.

Their strength-to-weight ratio is also very high compared to woods and metals.

Plastics are synthetic. They are made from chemicals which come from oil or coal. The molecules are formed into long chains which are called polymers. Within the plastics group are two sub-groups called **thermoplastic** and **thermosets** (Table 2.3).

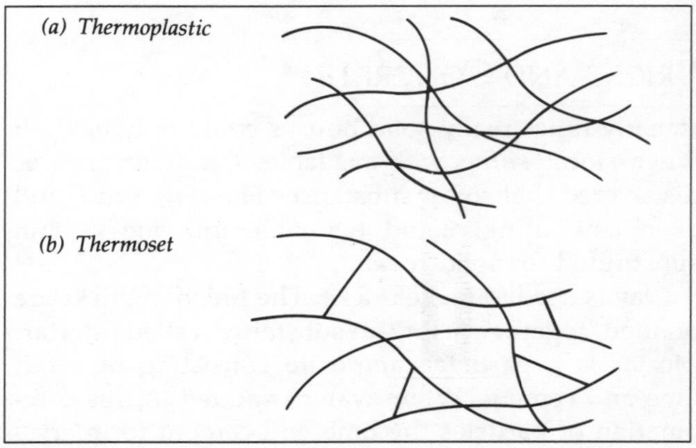

Figure 2.38 *Polymer chain structure of plastics*

Table 2.3 The plastics sub-groups

Sub-group	*Properties*	*Examples*
Thermoplastic	Soften on heating Poor heat resistance Polymer chains intertwined Can be rigid or flexible (Figure 2.38a)	Polyethylene (Polythene) Polystyrene Polyvinyl chloride (PVC) Nylon
Thermoset	Remain hard on heating Good heat resistance Polymer chains interwined and cross-links formed Rigid when set (Figure 2.38b)	Bakelite Melamine formaldehyde (Formica) Glass-reinforced polyester (GRP) Phenolic resins Epoxy resins

Various methods are used to shape plastics into different types of product.

Extrusion is used to shape plastics into long lengths to make objects such as curtain rails, drainpipes and narrow, flat sheets.

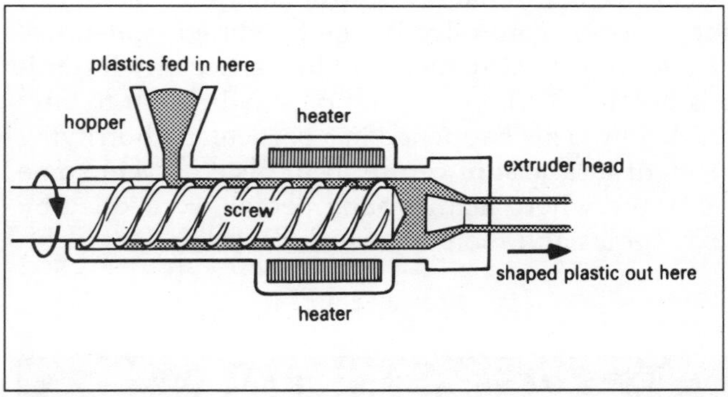

Figure 2.39 *Extrusion*

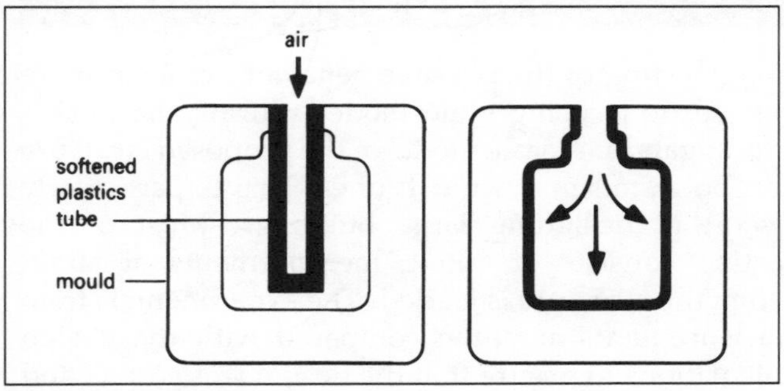

Figure 2.40 *Blow moulding*

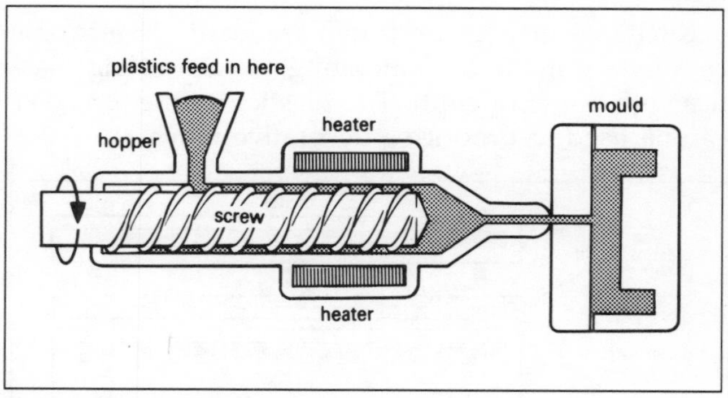

Figure 2.41 *Injection moulding*

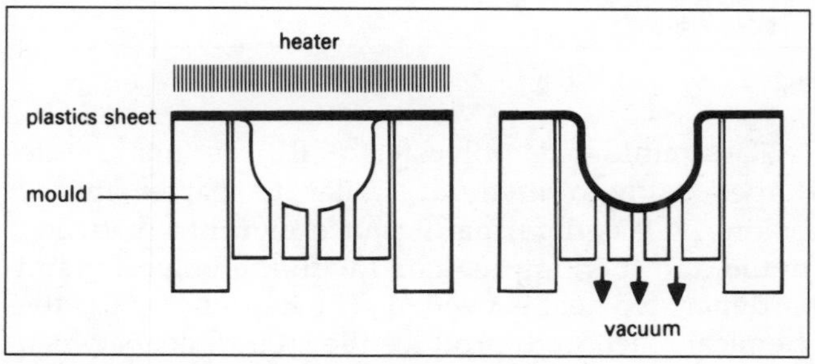

Figure 2.42 *Vacuum forming*

Hollow objects such as plastic bottles are made by blow moulding, in which the plastics material is blown into the shape of the mould.

Washing-up bowls, dustbins and model kits are made by injection moulding, in which the molten plastic is squeezed into a mould.

Thin plastic mouldings, such as refrigerator liners and chocolate trays, are produced by vacuum forming. The plastics sheet is softened and a reduced pressure is produced under the plastics sheet, causing it to be pushed into the mould by atmospheric pressure.

Thermosetting plastics are shaped by compression moulding. The plastics raw material is placed in a mould and heated. The second half of the mould then squeezes the plastics into shape, which then hardens.

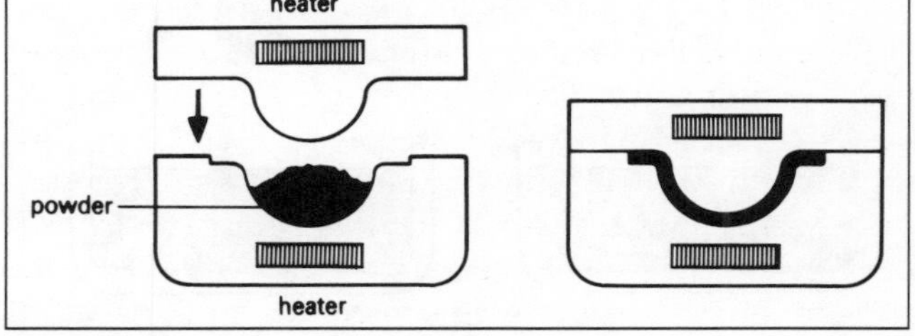

Figure 2.43 *Compression moulding*

Kitchen worktops and the baseboard of electronic circuits are made by laminating thermosetting plastics with paper or cloth. The plastics on the top layer can be used to produce a decorative finish.

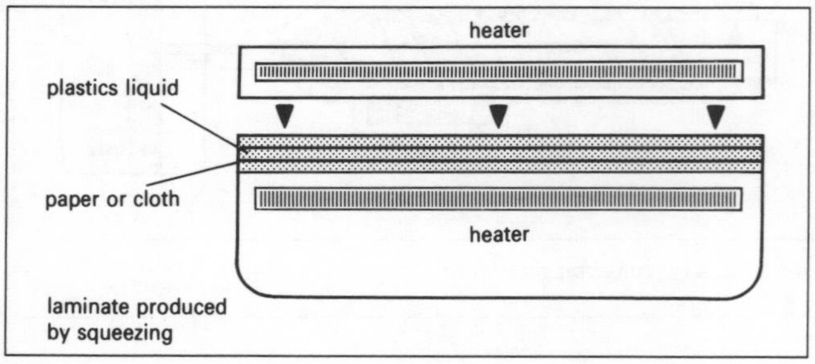

Figure 2.44 *Laminating*

Glass-reinforced polyester (GRP) is made into shapes using a method similar to papier mâché making. Glass-fibre mat is put down into or over a mould and then impregnated with the polyester and hardener. No heat is needed. The hardener starts the chemical reaction to produce the cross-links between the polymer chains.

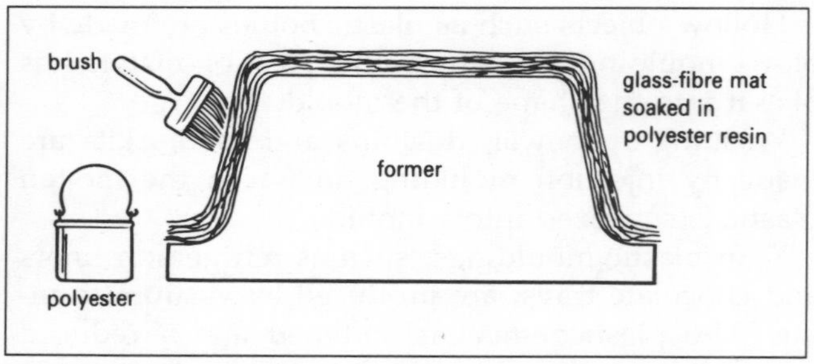

Figure 2.45 *GRP laying*

'Rubber' gloves and plastic boots are formed by dip moulding. A shaped mould is dipped into the molten plastics, pulled out and then left to dry.

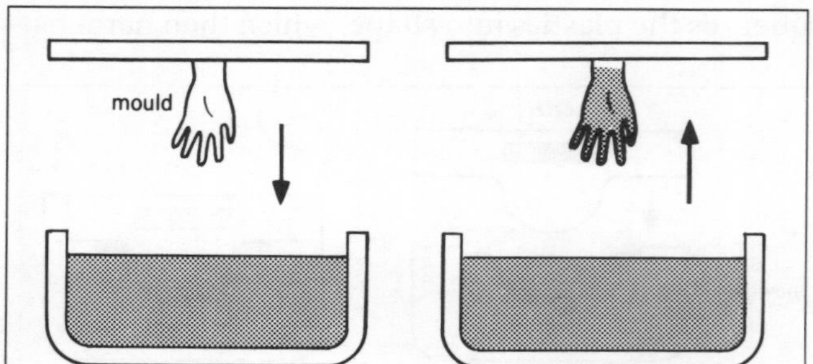

Figure 2.46 *Dip moulding*

Two further methods for shaping plastics are rotational casting, for hollow objects such as footballs in which the plastics need to be evenly spread, and calendering which produces thin sheets as used in plastic bags.

The modulus of elasticity and tensile strength of some plastics are shown in Table 2.1. The tensile strength of plastics is comparable with that for wood but the modulus of elasticity is generally much lower for plastics. The exception to this is glass-reinforced polyester, a particularly strong form of plastics material where the fibres of glass act as reinforcement in a similar way to steel bars in concrete. GRP is commonly used in sailing dinghies and motor cruisers because of its very high strength-to-weight ratio and its resistance to corrosion and rotting.

The problem of corrosion in cars can be overcome by the use of GRP. However, moulding and joining GRP is much more labour-intensive than using pressed steel, so the cars tend to be more expensive. Minesweepers also use GRP for their hulls because of its non-magnetic properties.

The main disadvantage of plastics is the ease with which they burn. Thermoplastics ignite relatively easily and give off toxic fumes when burning, so the use of plastics in habitable structures such as houses and offices is controlled by the Building Regulations. Plastics in roof structures can be particularly hazardous because molten burning plastic drips on to anyone below. This happened in a particularly horrifying incident at a leisure centre in the Isle of Man some years ago where many young people were killed by toxic fumes and molten plastics materials.

2:16 TESTING STRUCTURES

Some testing of the possible behaviour of a structure can be done using scale models during the design investigation. A scale model of the proposed structure can be tested in a wind tunnel. This is particularly useful in designing large buildings. Most of the testing consists of taking measurements of strain when the structure is loaded. The experimental strain measurements are then compared with the design calculations to ensure that the design was correct and complies with safety specifications.

MEASURING STRAIN

Figure 2.47 shows two types of gauge. The dial gauge measures movement of a structural member directly but is limited to situations where it can be easily seen and rigidly supported independently of the test piece. If the test piece is loaded then the dial gauge indicates bending or change in length. Strain gauges are much more flexible in their use and are used for detailed investigation of the strain in structures. The strain gauge is bonded onto the structure and the wires connected to a special strain gauge amplifier which measures the increase in length of the strain wire. This is possible because the resistance of the strain wire increases when it is stretched. The increase in resistance results in a small reduction of the current which can be measured using an amplifier and a meter.

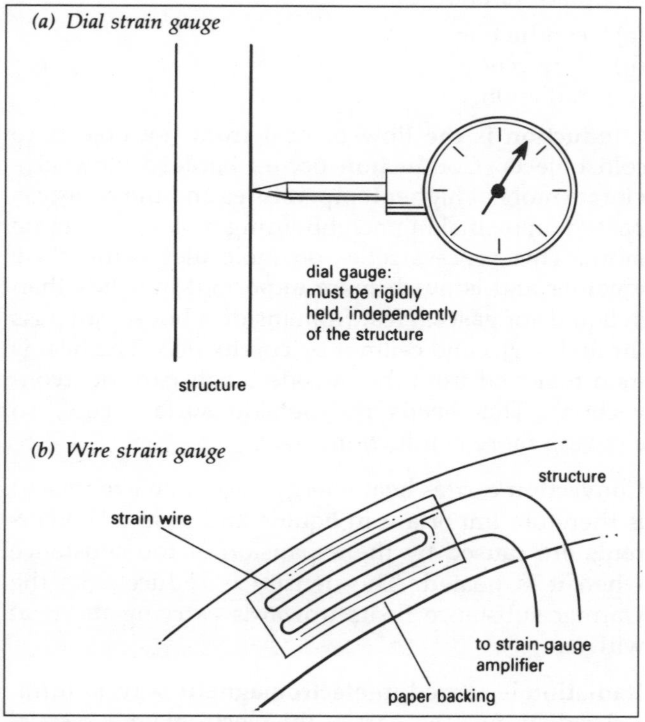

Figure 2.47 *Types of strain gauge*

The strain gauge should always be connected to the test piece so that it will measure the maximum change in the length of the wires. The **active axis** and **passive axis** of a practical strain gauge are shown in Figure 2.48. Strain gauges can be used in places where access is limited. For example, the strain on internal girders of aeroplane wings can be measured when the aeroplane is actually flying: the amplifier and meter would be inside the cabin enabling the engineer to take readings from a number of strain gauges fixed to the aeroplane.

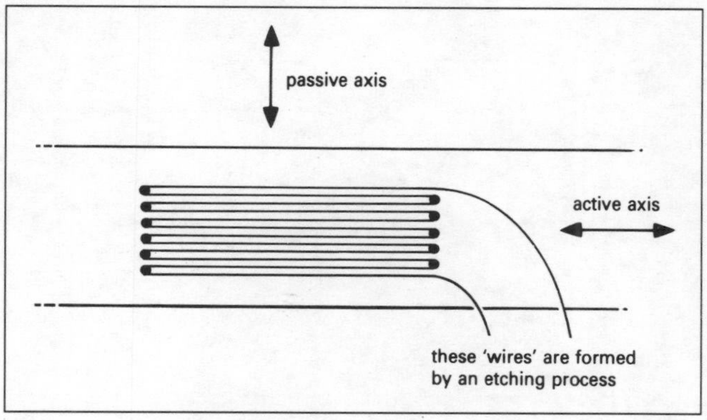

Figure 2.48 *A practical strain gauge*

PHOTOELASTICITY

Photoelasticity uses polarised light to analyse the stress in structural pieces used in buildings and machines. The light is passed through polaroid material as shown in Figure 2.49(a) which gives the basic layout of a **polariscope**. Models of the test piece are made from perspex or epoxy resin (Araldite). The model is then put under stress in the polariscope. The stress affects the way the light passes through the plastic and patterns are produced, examples of which are shown in Figure 2.49(b). The scientific term for this effect is 'birefringence', meaning doubly refracted. The double refractions enable the patterns to show areas of excess stress when the model is loaded in a similar way to the real object in a structure.

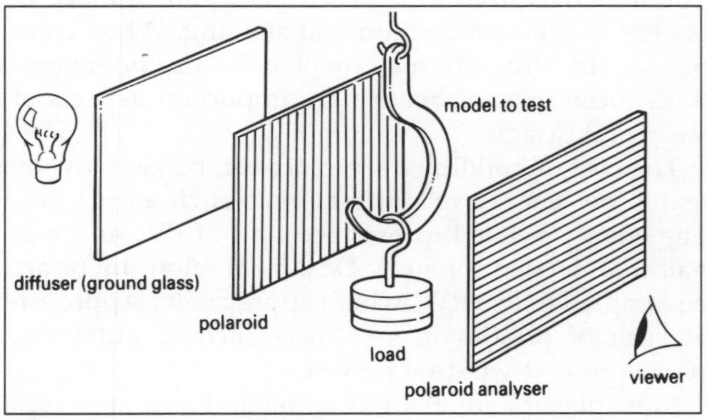

Figure 2.49 *(a) A polariscope*

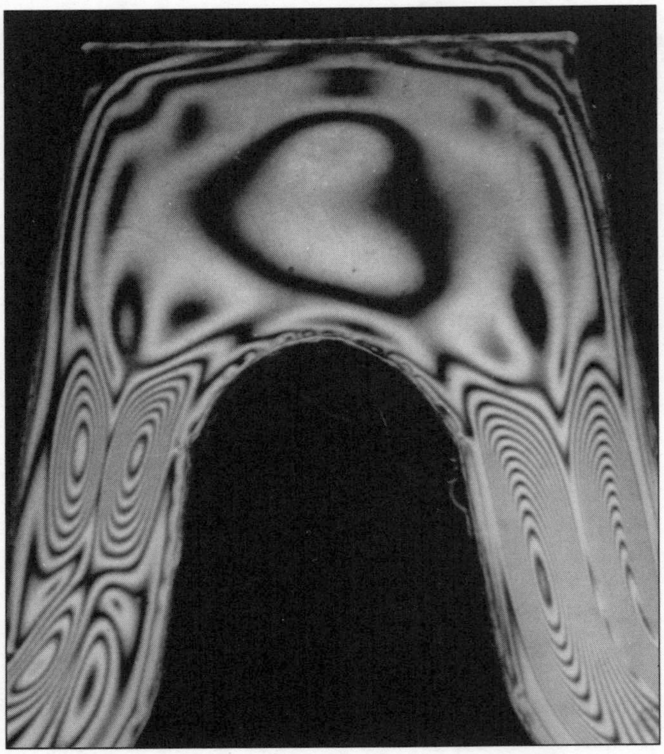

Figure 2.49 *(b) Example of birefringences*

2:17 ENERGY CONSIDERATIONS IN STRUCTURES

General Issues

The materials used in a structure require the use of energy in their production and shaping. When completed, the structure may involve the use of energy. Both these uses of energy are important aspects of structural design.

The cost of building a structure can be kept low by using low energy reliant materials such as plastics. The energy needed to produce 1 m^3 of PVC is about half that needed for steel. Designers might therefore be tempted to use PVC where appropriate. Appropriate use of plastics in structures include guttering, pipework and window frames.

Most plastics are made from oil and as oil reserves diminish over the next 50 years the cost of plastic will increase. This might mean that plastics will become less appropriate.

Other materials used in structures might also become more expensive. Cement is made from gypsum, which is a mined substance. As the reserves of gypsum are used up, the cost of extraction increases and, since the remaining gypsum will be in more inaccessible areas, more energy will be used in the process of extraction. There might come a time when new materials will have to be developed to replace much of what is presently used.

The energy used in using a structure can be demonstrated by looking at how heat is lost from a house and how the loss can be reduced.

Processes of Heat Loss

Energy is lost by three processes of heat transfer from one place to another:

(a) conduction
(b) convection
(c) radiation.

Conduction is the flow of heat from hot objects to cold objects. Conduction occurs because molecules vibrate more at higher temperatures and the energy is passed on by making neighbouring molecules vibrate more. This process relies on molecules being close together and is much more important in solids than in liquids or gases. Heat from inside a house can pass through walls and ceilings by conduction. The heat is then removed from the outside by air currents (convection). This keeps the outside surface cool, so allowing more conduction.

Convection carries heat energy away in currents and is therefore important in liquids and gases. The currents are caused by the expansion of the substance when it is heated. The density is reduced, so the warmer substance floats upwards carrying the heat with it.

Radiation is carried in **electromagnetic waves**. Infra-red radiation is the part of the electromagnetic spectrum which 'feels' hot. Figure 2.50 shows the full range of waves in the electromagnetic spectrum. All the energy which the earth receives from the sun travels as electromagnetic waves. The infra-red waves are absorbed best by matt black surfaces but these surfaces also emit radiation best. White or shiny surfaces absorb radiation least and are poor emitters of radiation.

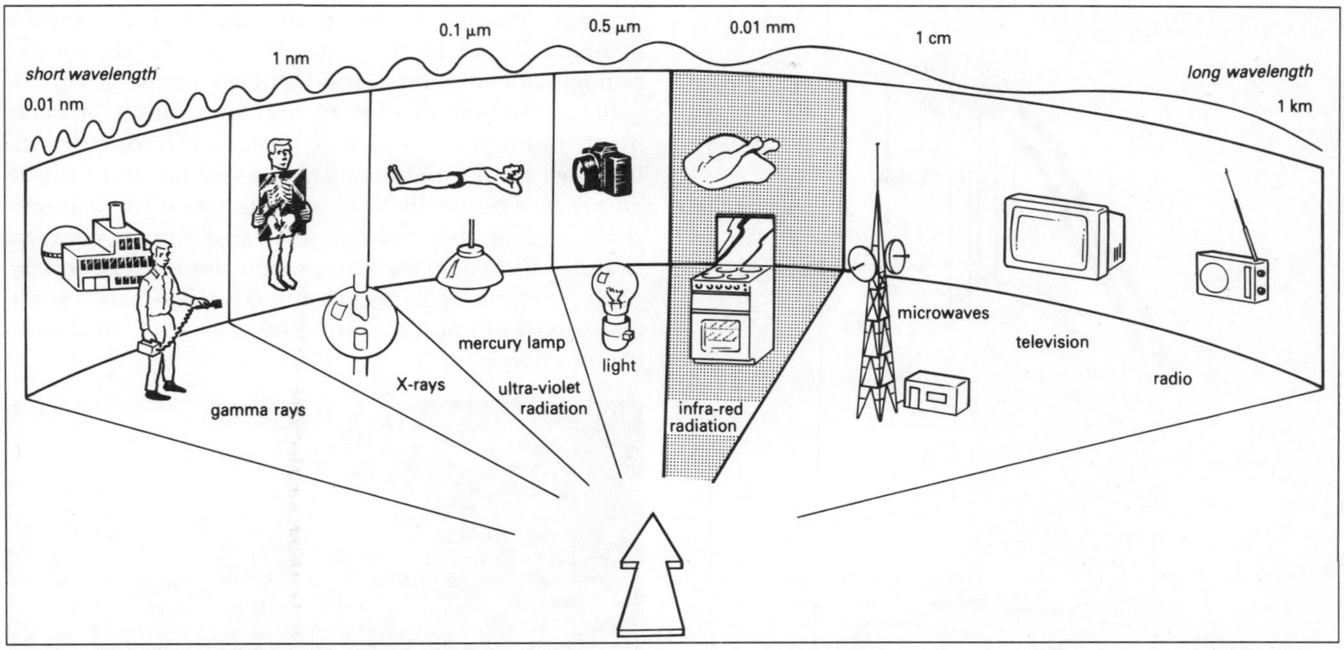

Figure 2.50 *The electromagnetic spectrum*

INSULATION METHODS

Insulation is designed to reduce conduction, convection and radiation. Fibre-glass wool and expanded polystyrene prevent convection currents because air is trapped in the fibres. Air is a poor conductor of heat because the molecules are too far apart. The standard methods of insulation are illustrated in Figure 2.51.

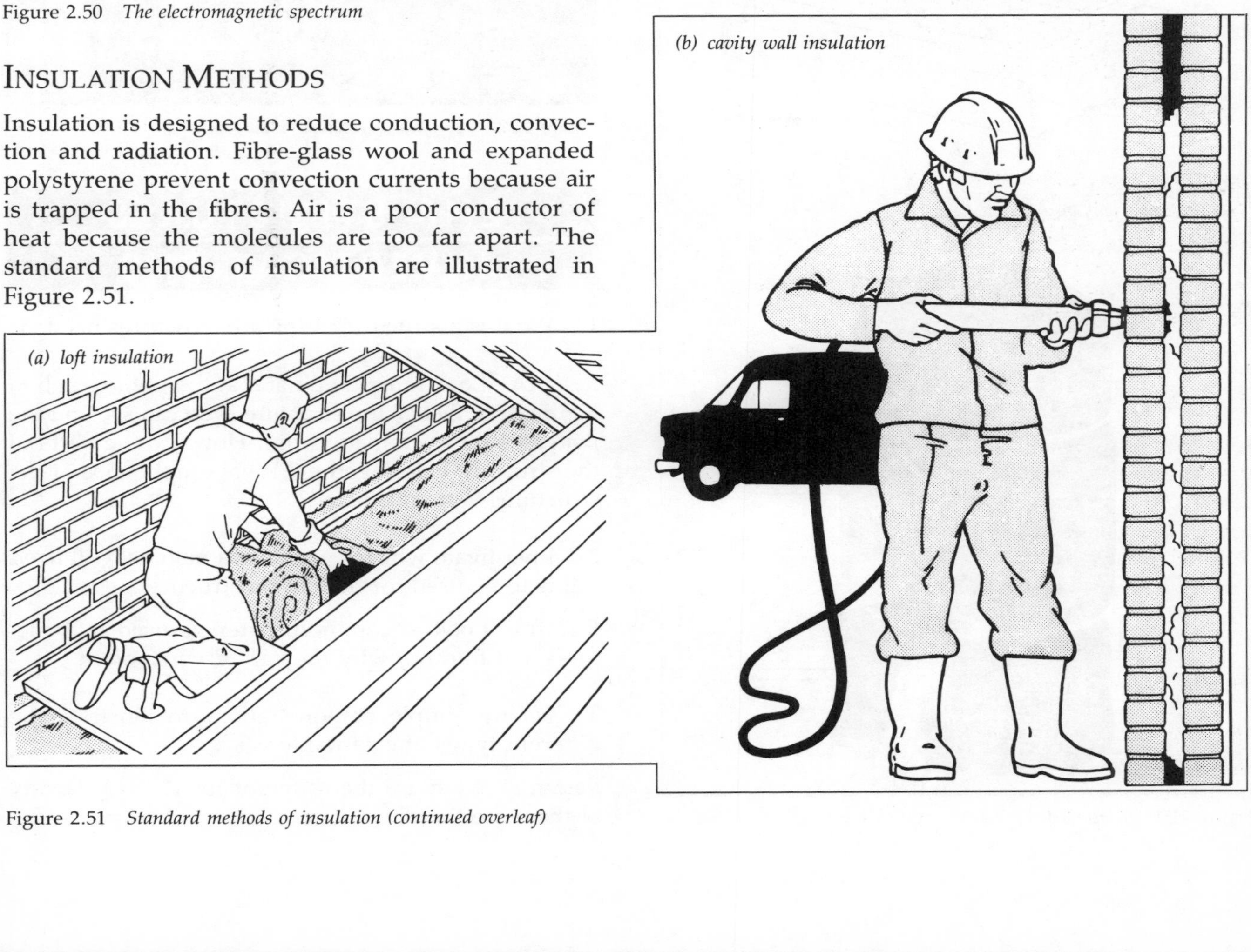

Figure 2.51 *Standard methods of insulation (continued overleaf)*

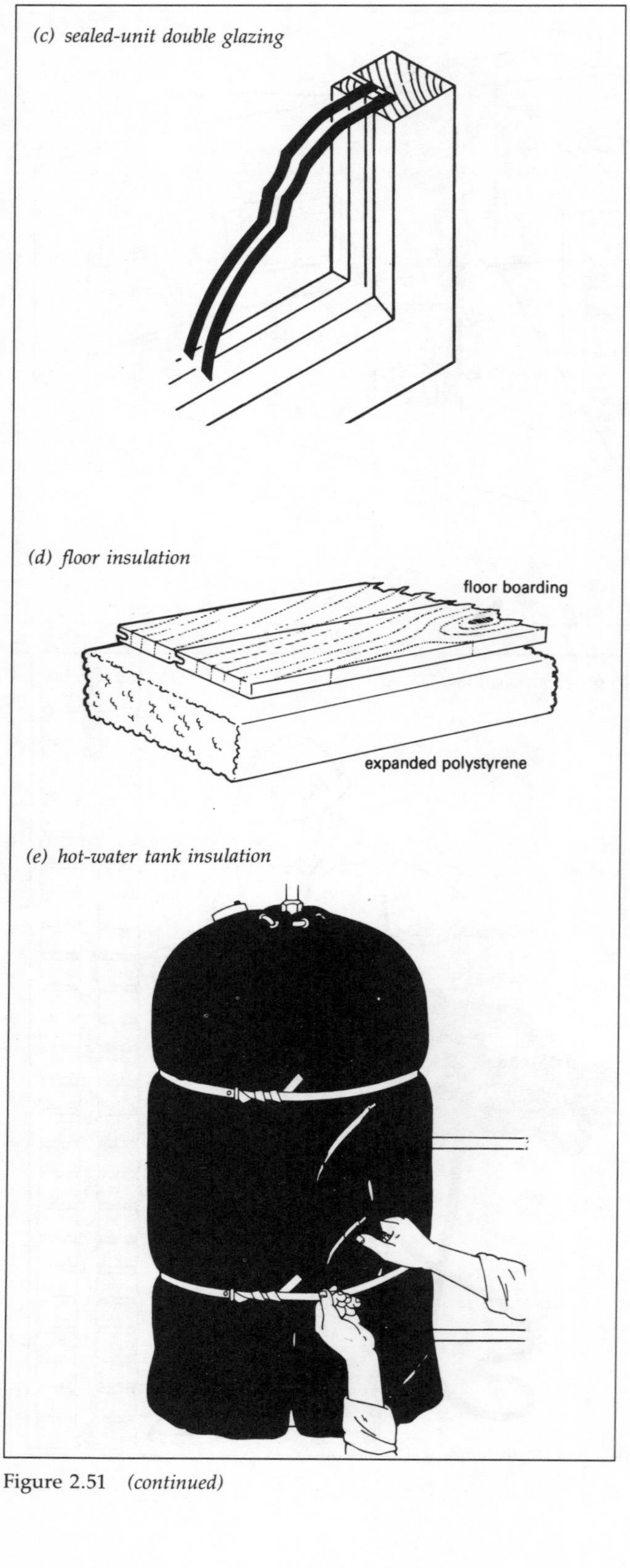

Figure 2.51 *(continued)*

Modern building regulations are much stricter on insulation than in the past. Figure 2.52 shows expanded polystyrene being installed in the cavity as walls are being built. Some other countries have been much more successful than Britain in reducing the heat lost from buildings. The energy needed to heat an average house in Norway or Sweden for example is about half that needed to heat a similar average house in Britain, even though their climate is generally colder. Triple glazing, insulated floors and well-insulated walls and roofs are the reason for this lower use of energy.

Figure 2.52 *Expanded polystyrene in the cavity*

2:18 STRUCTURES INVESTIGATIONS

1. What is a structure? Why are structures needed?

Research Look around you and at the photograph in Figure 2.53. List all the structures you can see and the materials they are made from. How are the parts of the structure held together? What are the jobs of the structures you have listed?

2. Investigate which properties a material will need if it is to be used for building a structure.

Research Look at common materials used in structures and find out why they are used so often.

3. Set up simple demonstrations to illustrate the different types of external forces.

Research What are the different forces? How many of them are there?

Figure 2.53 *Various structures*

Figure 2.54 *A triangular structure*

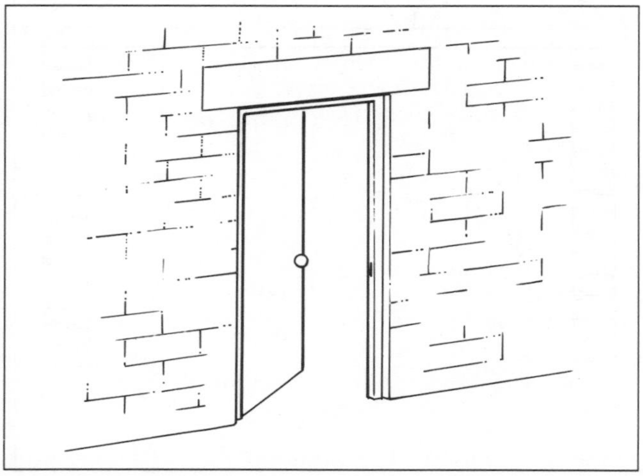

Figure 2.55 *Lintel over a door*

4. Figure 2.54 shows a triangular structure. Investigate why triangles form stable structures.

Research Use Meccano or something similar to compare triangular structures with other shapes. Draw diagrams showing examples of structures and how they are liable to collapse.

5. Beams have many uses – see, for example, Figure 2.55. Why are they used so often?

Research What different types of beams are there? Which materials can be used for beams? How does a beam transfer the load on it to the beam supports? What is a reaction? How can they be calculated? Where are compressive and tensile forces acting on the beam? What is a neutral axis?

6. Make and calibrate a newtonmeter.

Research How does a newtonmeter work? Find out about Robert Hooke and his law concerning springs. What does calibration mean? One newtonmeter cannot measure all forces. What range of forces might you want to measure?

7. Describe how you would design a new bridge.

Research What is the bridge going to carry? Where is it going to go? The gap the bridge will span is also important. Some types of bridges can only be used for small gaps and others are too expensive to use for anything but large gaps. What is the ground like? Soft? Hard? Marshy?

8. Find out how much material goes into a structure. Use this to find how heavy structures are.

Research Calculating volumes will be necessary. To find the quantity of material, the density of each material is needed:

mass of material (kg)
= volume (m^3) × density (kg/m^3)

Do materials have different densities? How does this affect the load on the foundations?

9. Investigate how a roof truss reacts to different loads.

Research Build a simple roof truss (Figure 2.56) (Meccano or similar building kits can be used for this). Load the truss using a newtonmeter and/or weights to test for deflection. If more members are added to the frame, how much deflection occurs when the frame is loaded? How does the load taken by each part of the frame change? Calculations by triangle of forces are needed.

10. Investigate the best ratio of cement, sand, aggregate and water in a concrete mix.

Research Make different mixes of concrete and cast them into cubes. You will need to build a mould and find a way to test varying strengths of the cubes. How do you stop the concrete from sticking to the moulds?

11. Concrete is strong in compression but weak in tension. Where is the best place to put steel reinforcing rods into a beam to stop beams failing in tension?

Research Where are beams in compression and tension? Why are steel rods used? If steel rusts, does this matter? What happens if the beam expands and contracts?

12. Trusses and beams are supported by walls at either end. Investigate using models how much load each support wall carries due to the load on the frame or beam (Figure 2.57).

Research How are loads measured? What are 're-actions'?

13. Investigate how the centre of gravity determines the stability of structures.

Research What is stability? What are the three types of equilibrium? Does centre of gravity have an effect on stability? What is centre of gravity? How does the centre of gravity of a structure change when it is loaded?

14. Compare the bonding properties of epoxy resin, polyvinyl acetate (PVA) and vinyl acetate.

Research Which materials will the glues stick? Look at various metals, woods, plastics, ceramics, rubber and cloths. Are all the joins the same strength? A means of testing join strength is needed. Can the strength of the bond be improved by preparing the surface of the material?

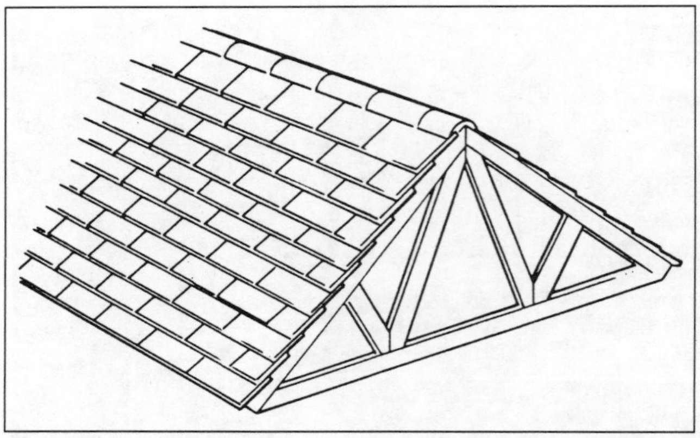

Figure 2.56 *A loaded roof truss*

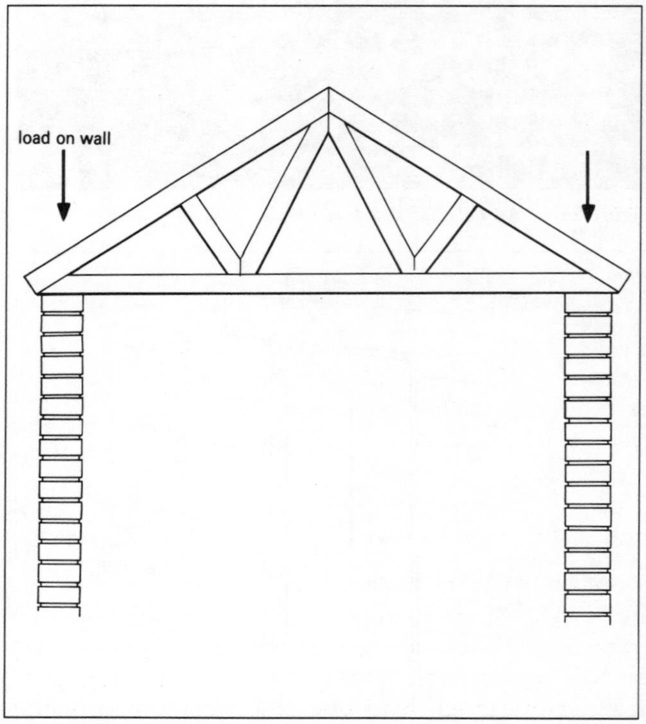

Figure 2.57 *Reactions on roof trusses and beams*

15. Investigate the stress and strain on a wire when it is loaded. Compare the effects of stress and strain on different materials (Figure 2.58).

Research What are stress and strain? How can they be measured? What is a stress–strain graph? Are they the same for all materials? How can the graphs show if a material deforms plastically or elastically or is brittle or ductile?

16. Design and build a strain gauge.

Research What is strain? How can it be measured? What is a strain gauge? How does something electrical measure something mechanical? The type of wire, how long it should be, the diameter of the wire and how it is fixed to the structure need careful thought.

17. Investigate how well a layer of trapped air reduces heat loss.

Research What is heat? How could you measure the flow of heat? How does the structure and the materials used effect heat flow?

18. A roof truss often contains many members. Draw diagrams to show the possible methods available to join the members together.

Research How is wood joined? What methods are best in different circumstances?

19. Investigate how much force is needed to open a door.

Research What is a turning force? Does the force change as it moves away from the hinge?

20. Investigate the differences between dynamic and static forces.

Research What is meant by dynamic and static force? Build a pair of identical structures out of rolled newspaper. Compare putting weights carefully onto and dropping weights onto the structures (Figure 2.59). How much load does the structure support? Why is there a difference?

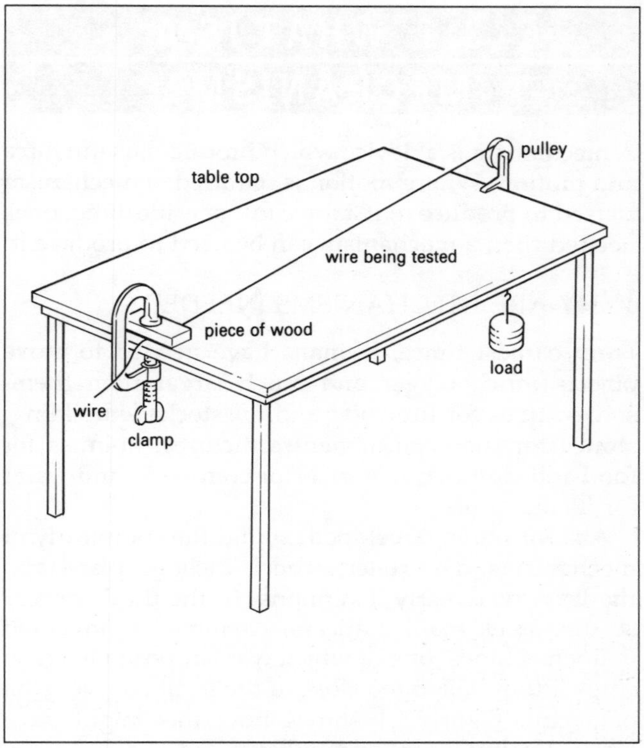

Figure 2.58 *Apparatus for stress–strain measurements on wires*

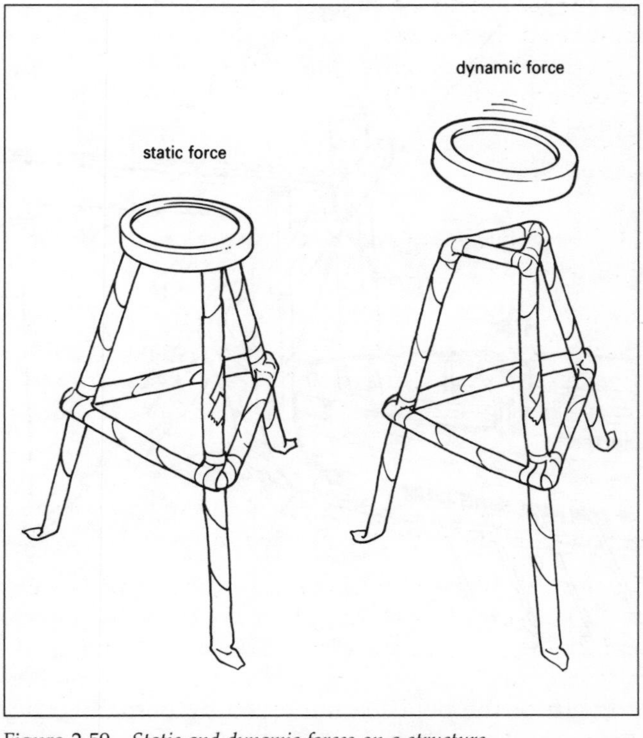

Figure 2.59 *Static and dynamic forces on a structure*

3

m e c h a n i s m s

3:1 WHAT IS A MECHANISM?

A **mechanism** is a device which produces useful force and motion. Where motion is required, a mechanism is used to produce it; if a force in a specific direction is needed then a mechanism can be used to produce it.

WHY ARE MECHANISMS NEEDED?

From earliest times, humans have needed to move objects much bigger and much larger than themselves: trees for firewood and for stockade building; stones for more permanent structures; animals for food and clothing; materials for craftwork, and water for its many uses.

As civilisation developed, so did the complexity of mechanisms. The roller, wheel, inclined plane and the lever were early inventions. In the third century BC the Greek mathematician, Archimedes, invented many machines, one of which was supposed to crush ships if they sailed too close to the fortified river wall of a city. Figure 3.1 shows how this might have worked using levers and pulleys.

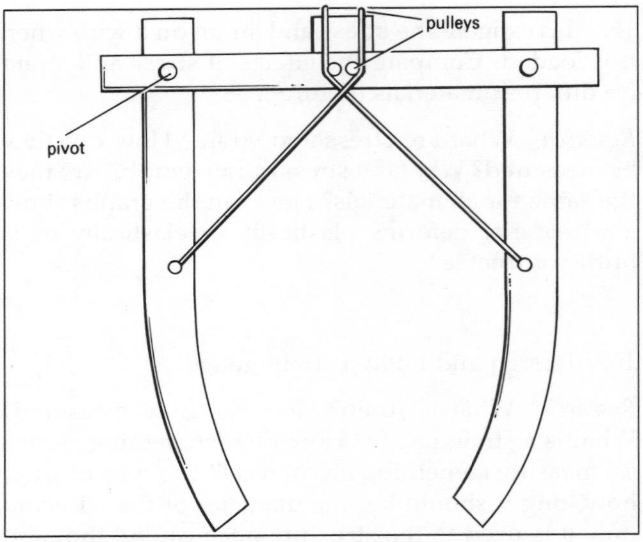

Figure 3.1 *Archimedes' ship crusher: (a) end view*

At the battle for Masada in 73 AD it was a Roman engineer who broke the stalemate by some ingenious problem solving. The problem was how to get the Roman legions up 65 metres to the castle walls and so invade the fortress against which there was no other means of attack (see Figure 3.2).

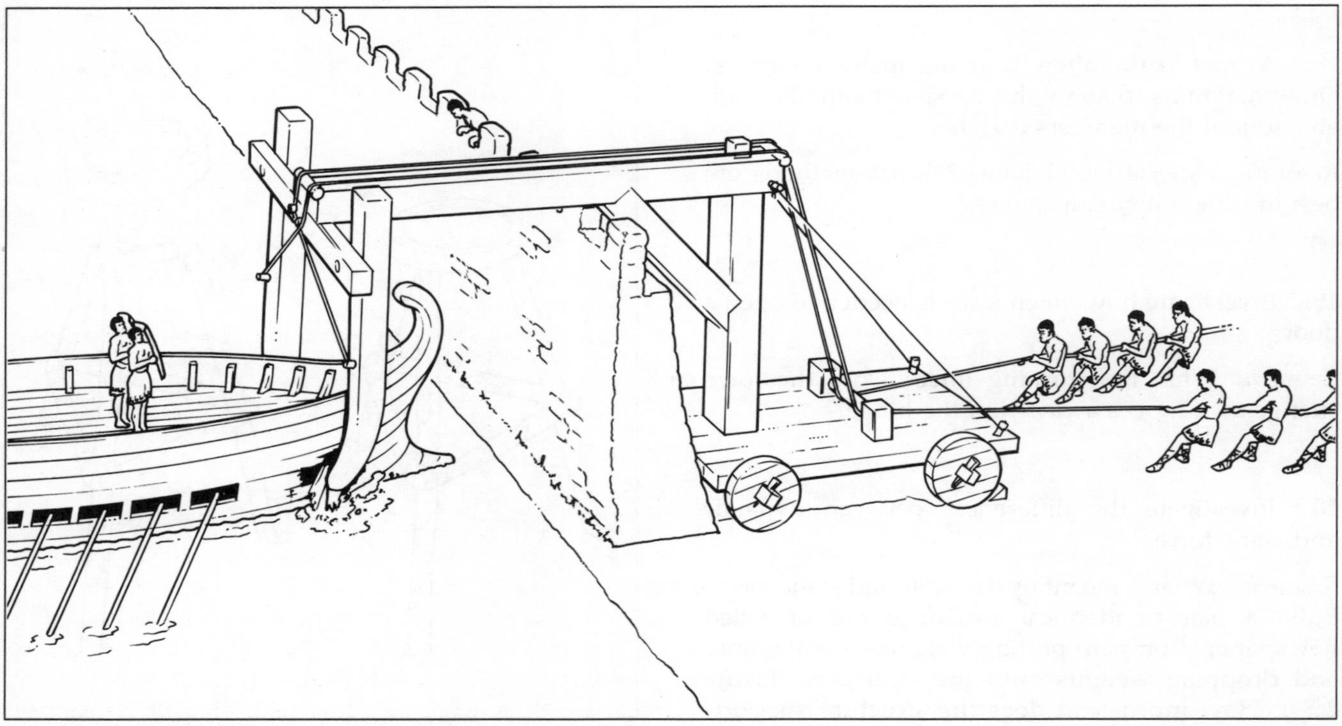

Figure 3.1 *Archimedes' ship crusher: (b) side view*

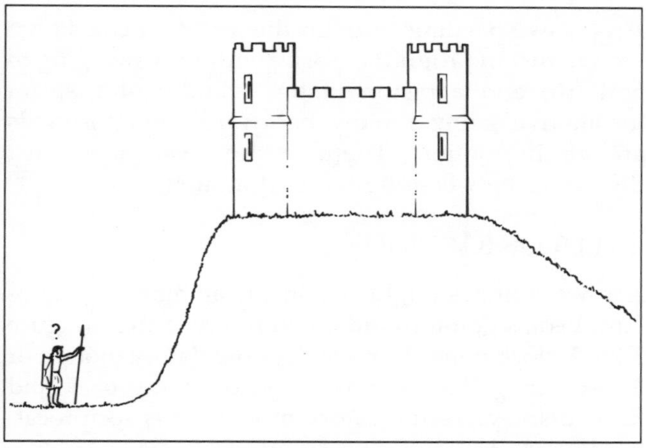

Figure 3.2 *How do you capture this castle?*

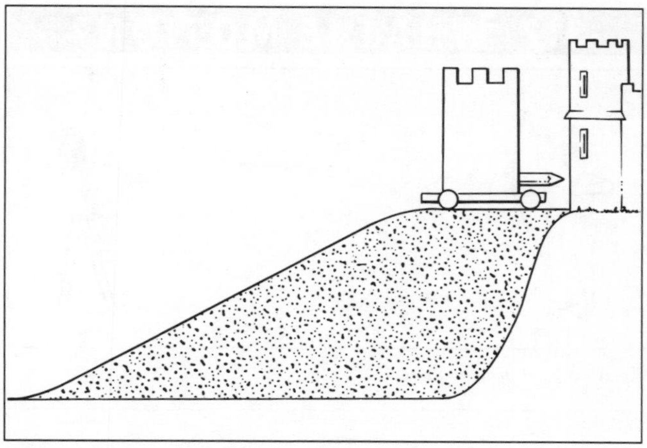

Figure 3.4 *Using a slope*

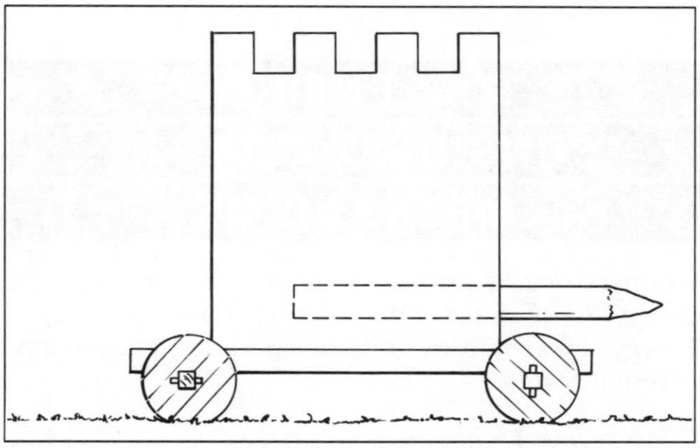

Figure 3.3 *Battering ram in a small, movable fort*

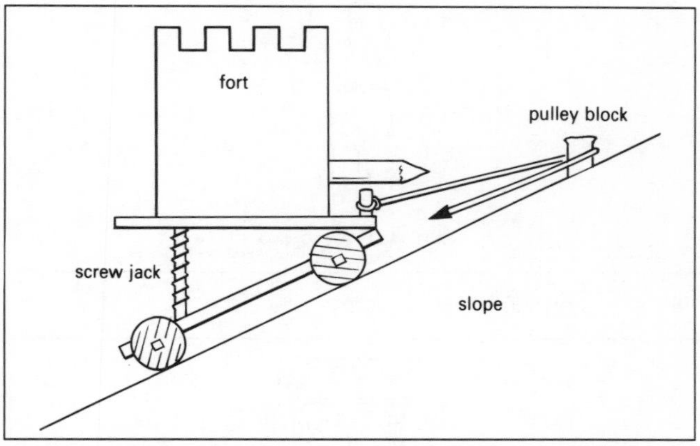

Figure 3.5 *Getting the fort up the slope*

He first considered what was needed to break down the walls (see Figure 3.3) and then how to get it near the walls (see Figure 3.4). But two difficulties remained: the portable battering ram was likely to tip over on the slope; also, how could it be hauled up a steep slope without the defenders shooting and killing anybody pulling the ram?

Mechanisms solved the problems. The solution was to jack up the back of the fort holding the ram so that the chassis of the fort moved up the slope in a horizontal position and to use pulleys set in the side of the slope to pull the fort from the bottom (Figure 3.5). The engineer made success possible using mechanisms.

There are many modern examples of mechanisms. If a milk float is to be driven up a slope at 20 km/h, the mass of the float, the effect of the slope on the driving force and how the float is to move must be known. Milk floats are often powered by electric motors but electric motors will stall (stop turning) at low speeds of rotation. By introducing a gear system the motor can work effectively and produce the required speed of wheel rotation.

Another example is the internal combustion engine used in cars. By using a crank and slider mechanism (in the form of a piston and cylinder), the chemical energy in petrol and diesel can be released to produce a turning force sufficient to move cars, coaches and lorries.

Mechanisms make it possible to dictate exactly what force and movement is produced by a machine. Mechanisms can alter the size of forces and the distance over which they act. Those that increase the size of the force being put into a machine are called **force magnifiers**. Those that increase the size of the distance over which the force acts are called **distance magnifiers**.

3:2 WHAT IS MOTION?

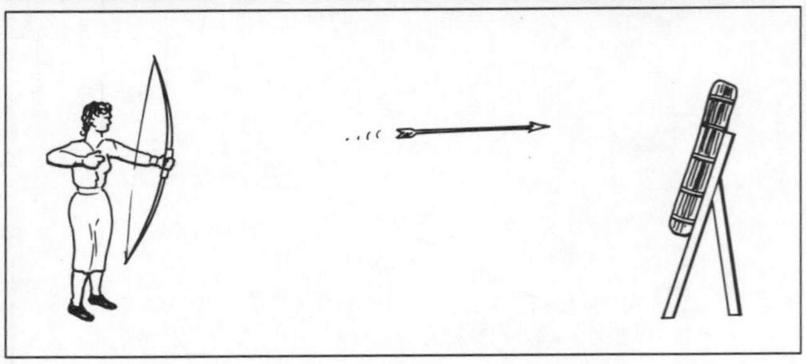
Figure 3.6 *Linear motion*

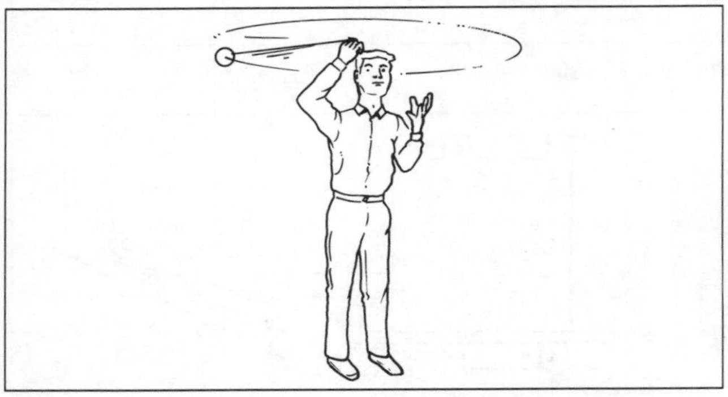
Figure 3.7 *Rotary motion*

Figure 3.8 *Oscillatory motion*

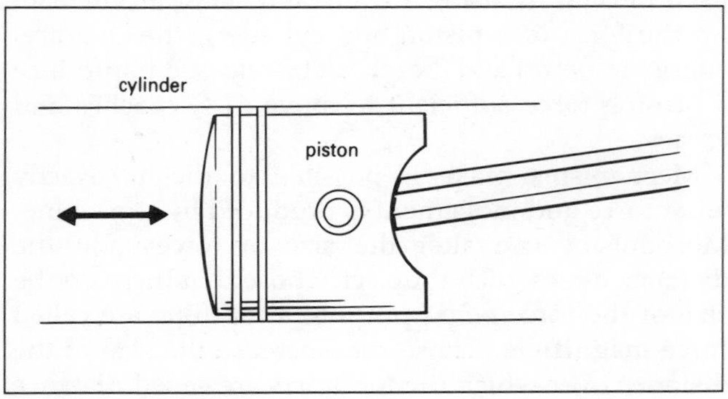

Figure 3.9 *Reciprocatory motion*

An arrow speeding through the air; the pedals on a bicycle turning round; a clock pendulum swinging to and fro; and a piston in the cylinder of a steam locomotive going rapidly backwards and forwards are all in motion. There is, however, a distinct difference between the types of motion.

Types of Motion

Arrows going straight are in linear motion (Figure 3.6). Pedals going round are in rotary motion (Figure 3.7). A clock pendulum displays oscillatory motion or is oscillating (Figure 3.8). A piston going back and forth displays reciprocatory motion or is reciprocating (Figure 3.9).

3:3 ENERGY CONSIDERATIONS IN MECHANISMS

When a force is applied to something one form of energy is changed into another form of energy. Energy, measured in units called joules, takes many different forms.

Forms of Energy

Energy can only be changed from one form to another. A mechanism provides the method for this change. Figure 3.10 shows the energy changes which take place in the various mechanisms of a power station to produce electricity. The most common forms of energy are:

heat	kinetic
light	potential
electrical	chemical
nuclear.	

Kinetic energy is the energy of movement and so is particularly important in mechanisms. It is calculated as:

$$\text{kinetic energy} = 1/2 \times \text{mass} \times \text{velocity} \times \text{velocity}$$
$$\text{K.E.} = 1/2\,mv^2$$

The velocity is the speed of an object in a specific direction.

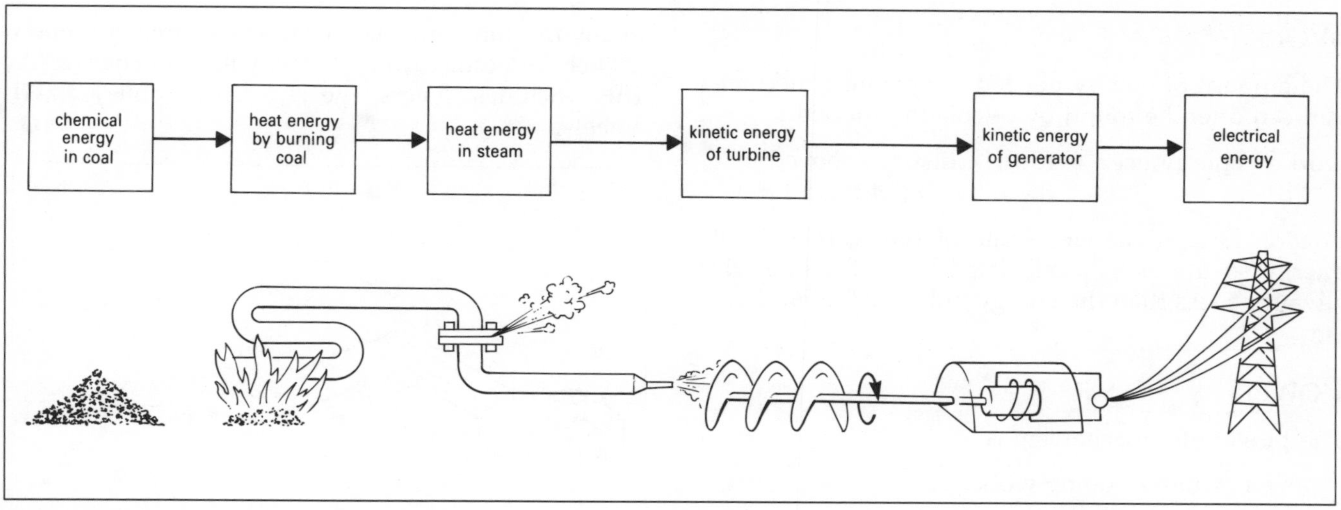

Figure 3.10 *Energy changes in a power station*

Potential energy is stored energy due to the position or condition of the object. The spring in a clock stores potential energy in the compression of the spring (condition). An object above the earth has gravitational potential energy due to gravity pulling on it (position).

Gravitational potential energy is calculated from:

potential energy = mass × acceleration due to gravity × height

P.E. = mgh joules

g, the acceleration due to gravity, can normally be taken as $10\,\text{m/s}^2$. As an object falls the potential energy is changed into kinetic energy as the speed increases (Figure 3.11).

Figure 3.11 *Potential energy changing to kinetic energy*

Figure 3.12 shows chemical energy being changed to kinetic energy by applying a force to an object. Some of the energy would also be changed to heat energy.

Energy sources for mechanisms include:

(a) electrical energy being converted into kinetic energy by an electric motor or solenoid
(b) potential energy being converted to kinetic energy by a spring or falling weight
(c) chemical energy from a person being changed into kinetic energy by movement of an arm.

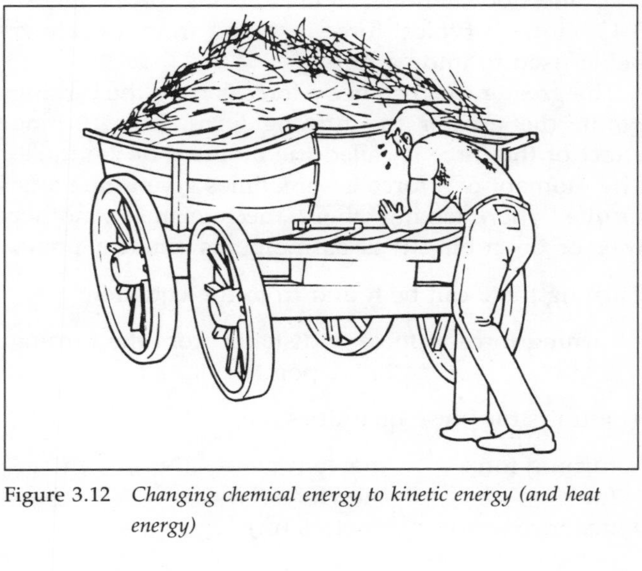

Figure 3.12 *Changing chemical energy to kinetic energy (and heat energy)*

Work

The amount of energy needed to operate a mechanism can often be found by calculating the **work**.

work = energy used = force × distance moved in the direction of the force

Friction always changes some of the work to heat energy so the energy calculated from this rule will always be less than the energy put in to the mechanism.

Power

The **power** of a mechanism is:

$$\text{power} = \text{rate of doing work} = \frac{\text{work done}}{\text{time taken (seconds)}} \text{ joules/second}$$

The unit of joules per second is called the watt, after the engineer James Watt who designed the early steam engines. It is often useful to remember that 1 watt = 1 joule per second.

3:4 TURNING FORCES

A force which causes movement in a circular direction is a **turning force**. Screwdrivers, spanners, wrenches and door handles all use turning forces. Figure 3.13 shows a typical force resulting from a spanner being used to undo a nut.

The greater the distance a force is from the turning point, the greater the turning force. This turning effect of the force is called the **moment** of the force. The moment of a force is sometimes given the name **torque** when talking about mechanisms. Another way of describing it is as moments about a point.

Turning force can be found from the equation:

turning force = force × distance from the turning point

The units for these quantities are:

turning force	newton metres (Nm)
force	newtons (N)
distance	metres (m)

In any machine or mechanism where circular motion is likely to occur turning forces will be encountered. This includes levers, gears, cams, pulleys and wheels.

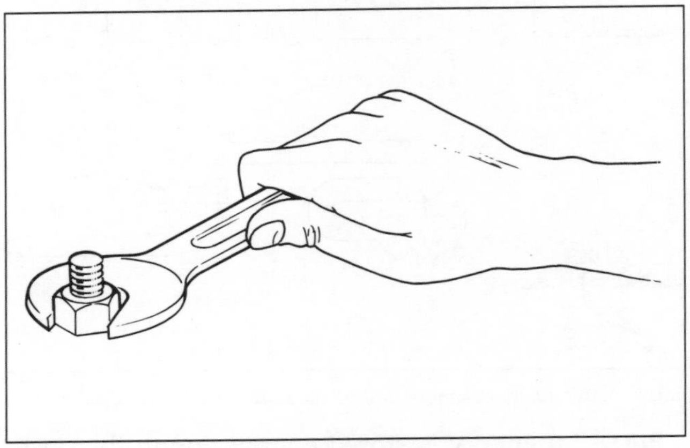

Figure 3.13 *A spanner turning a nut*

3:5 LEVERS

The **lever** is a common mechanism. The human skeleton makes substantial use of levers. Figure 3.14 shows some of the many examples of levers. The important parts of a lever are:

(a) effort – the force applied to the lever
(b) load – the force to be moved by the lever
(c) pivot or fulcrum – the point around which the lever turns.

These three parts can be placed in three different orders:

effort	pivot	load, e.g. scissors, a see-saw
pivot	load	effort, e.g. wheelbarrow, nutcrackers
pivot	effort	load, e.g. tweezers, sugar tongs

Levers owe their effectiveness to turning forces and this can be expressed in the Law of the Lever (see Figure 3.15) which states that:

turning force of effort = turning force of load

or:

clockwise moment of force = anticlockwise moment of force

This is the same rule as stated in the principle of moments described in the structures chapter, Section 2:6.

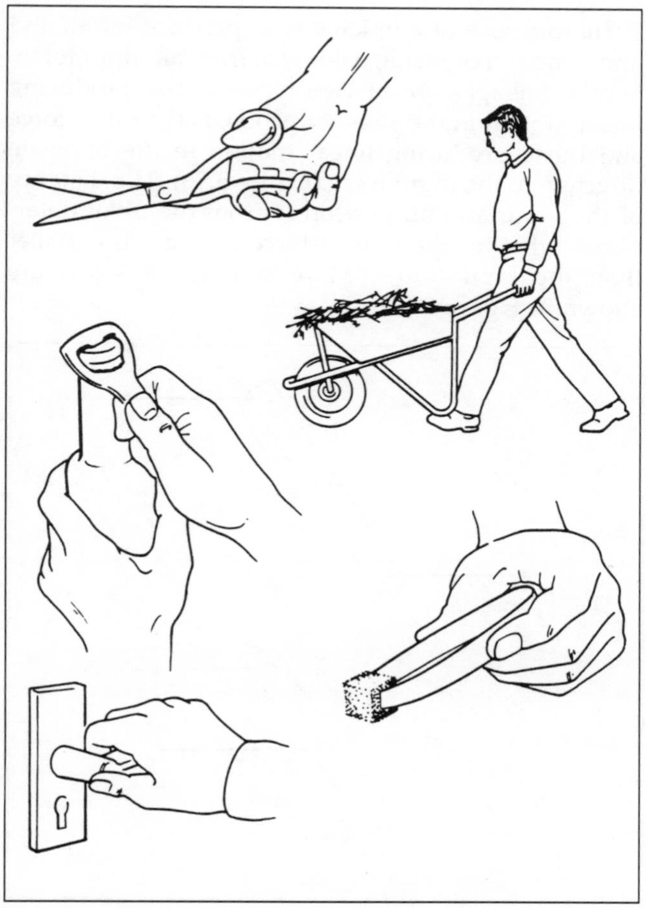

Figure 3.14 *Levers*

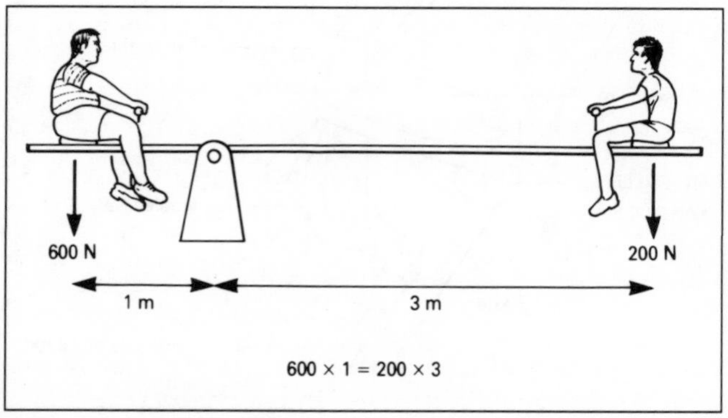

Figure 3.15 *The law of the lever*

Example A manufacturer of wheelbarrows wants to know how much weight a new design of wheelbarrow will lift. The design allows for the load to be placed 0.25 m from the wheel. A 200 N force is applied on the handles 1 m from the wheel as shown in Figure 3.16. To find how much weight is lifted, the manufacturer will do these calculations:

$$\text{weight} \times \text{distance} = \text{effort to lift} \times \text{distance}$$
$$? \times 0.25 = 200\ \text{N} \times 1$$
$$? = 800\ \text{N}$$

The barrow will lift 800 N. Now the manufacturer can decide if this fits the job that a wheelbarrow has to do and what the best materials are for the barrow based upon their strengths.

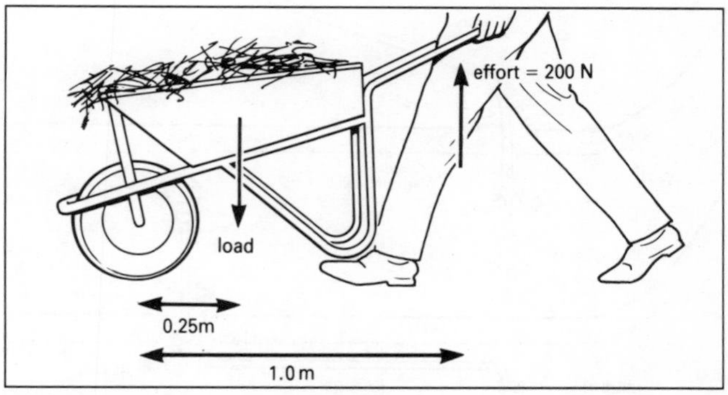

Figure 3.16 *A design of wheelbarrow*

A very useful type of lever is the bell crank lever, which allows levers to work round through 90° (a right angle). It is found on many old houses where servants answered the door. Before the advent of electrical doorbells, a means of alerting the servant was achieved using a bell-pull linked to a bell in the servants' quarters (Figure 3.17).

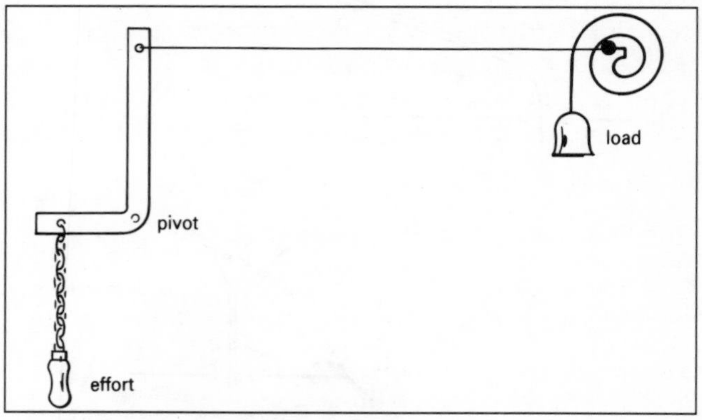

Figure 3.17 *A bell crank lever system*

3:6 LINKAGES

The usefulness of levers can be shown most effectively in **linkages**. A comparison between the gearsticks of a 1969 and a 1985 Mini car show this (Figure 3.18). The action of the gearstick lever is brought closer to the driver. What is more important is that the movement of the gearstick is greatly reduced and made a lot more convenient (see Figure 3.19).

The purpose of a linkage is to produce forces and linear motion of manageable size from an input force. Simple linkages are of two types: those producing linear motion in the same direction as the input force and those producing linear motion in the opposite direction to the input force (Figure 3.20). The distance of the input and output forces from the pivot determines whether the output force is larger or smaller than the input force. More complex linkages are shown in Figure 3.21.

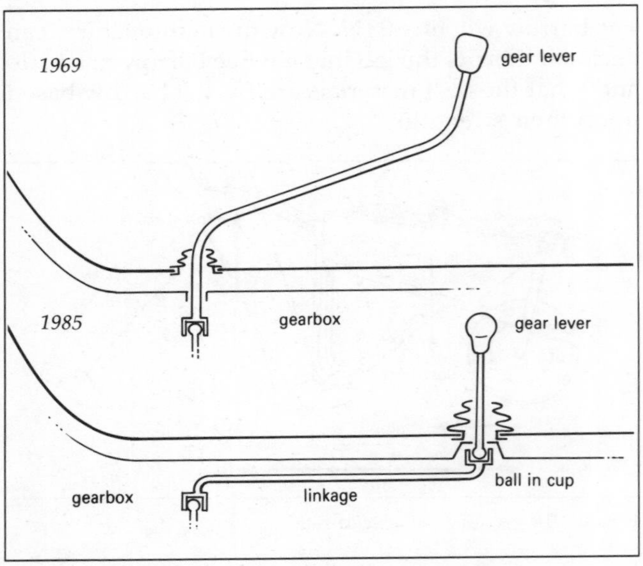

Figure 3.18 *Gearsticks of a 1969 and a 1985 Mini*

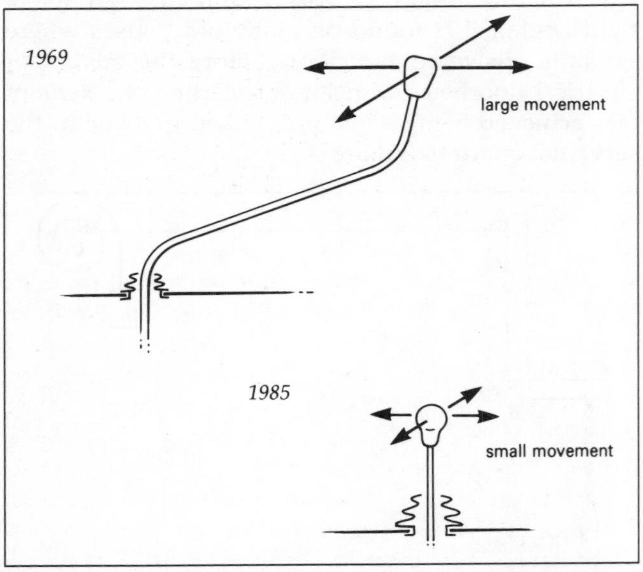

Figure 3.19 *Comparison of the movement of the Mini gearsticks*

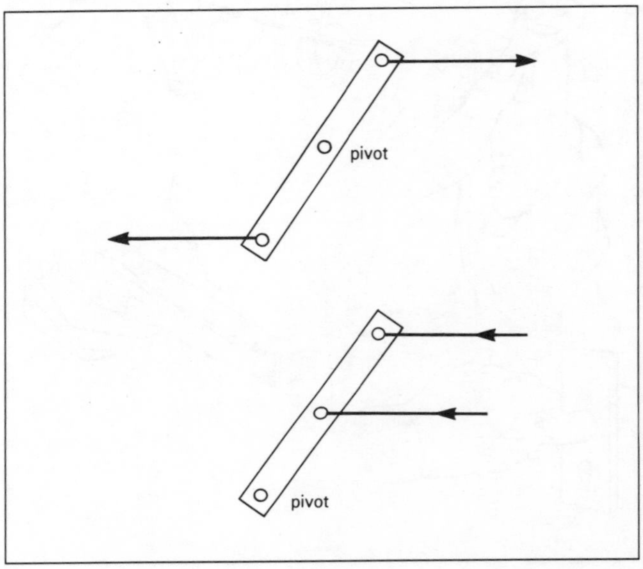

Figure 3.20 *Two simple types of linkage*

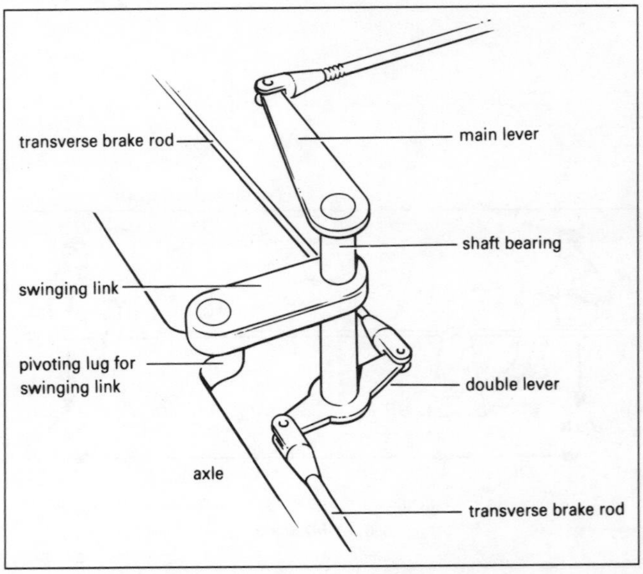

Figure 3.21 *Linkages: (a) as used in mechanical vehicle brake systems*

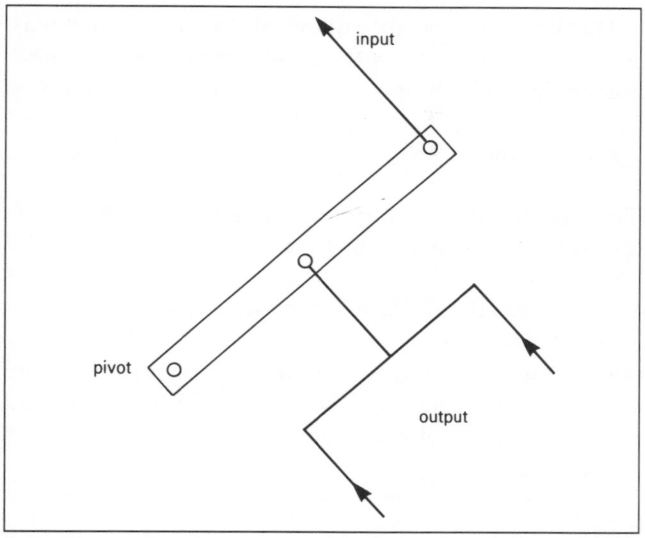

Figure 3.21 *(b) Equalising*

Figure 3.21 *(c) Parallel*

Figure 3.22 *Crane using a pulley system*

3:7 PULLEYS

SIMPLE PULLEYS

Pulleys are used to lift large loads or to change a speed of rotation. Dock-side and building-site cranes use them to enable large quantities of materials to be moved with ease. Their great advantage is that the force produced to lift a large load is much greater than the force produced by the engine, motor or person driving the pulley system. Consequently, pulley systems are very good force magnifiers. Figure 3.22 shows a pulley system in action.

The workings of pulley systems are shown in Figure 3.23. The size of the load that can be lifted increases as the number of pulley wheels increases, without changing the size of the effort needed to lift the load. As the number of pulleys increases, so does the force needed to overcome **friction**. The more pulleys that are included in a pulley system, the greater is the energy loss in overcoming friction and the lower the **efficiency** of the pulley system. This effect can be seen from the graph in Figure 3.24 based upon a student's experimental results.

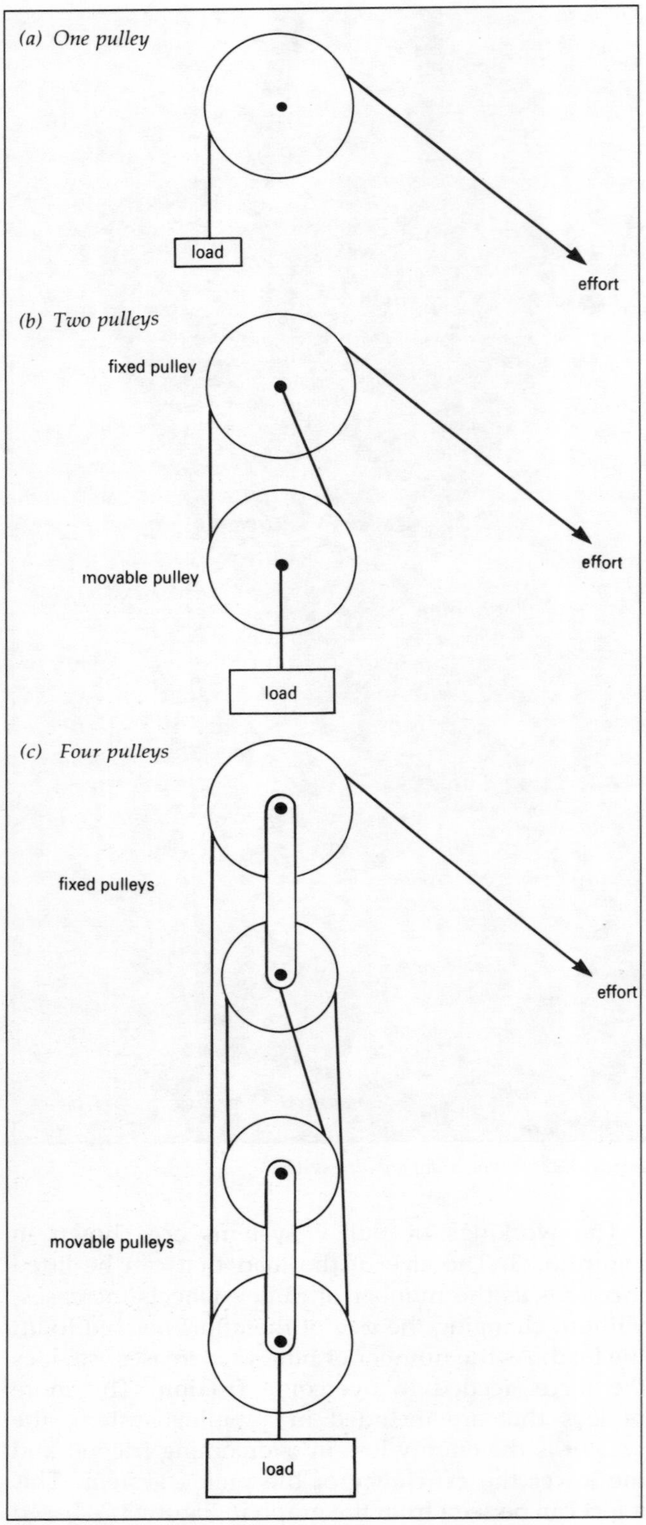

Figure 3.23 *Simple pulley systems*

The correct type of pulley system to do a job is chosen by determining their **velocity ratios** and their **mechanical advantage**. These are given as follows:

$$\text{velocity ratio (VR)} = \frac{\text{distance moved by effort}}{\text{distance moved by load}}$$

(For a pulley system the velocity ratio is also given by the number of pulleys in most cases.)

$$\text{mechanical advantage (MA)} = \frac{\text{load}}{\text{effort}}$$

where the load and effort are forces measured in newtons. Note that both MA and VR have no units.

The efficiency of a pulley system is:

$$\text{efficiency} = \frac{\text{MA}}{\text{VR}} \times 100$$

efficiency is always quoted as a percentage (%).

The disadvantage of pulley systems is that the effort force must move further than the load is lifted or moved. This is linked to the velocity ratio. If the velocity ratio of the pulley system is 4, it means that for every 1 m the load is lifted, the effort will have to move 4 m. For a large crane with a pulley system whose velocity ratio is 20, for every 1 m the load is lifted, 20 m of cable will need to be winched in by the crane engine.

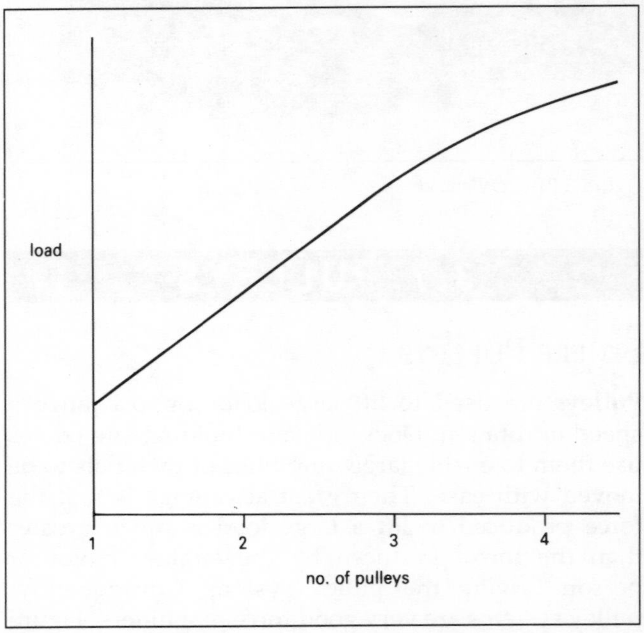

Figure 3.24 *Load against number of pulleys for a set effort*

Wheel and Axle

This very common mechanism provides a mechanical advantage by making use of a large-radius wheel and a small-radius axle. Figure 3.25 shows a typical arrangement, where the wheel is fixed to the axle. Common examples include the car steering-wheel, the train wheel and axle, and gears and shafts in machinery.

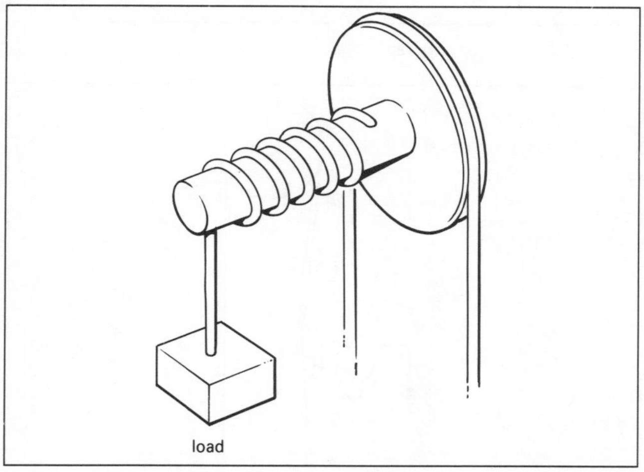

Figure 3.25 *Wheel and axle*

On a wheel and axle the effort pulling on the rope round the wheel is able to lift a large load connected to the axle rope. The wheel and axle idea is used in the windlass (Figure 3.26).

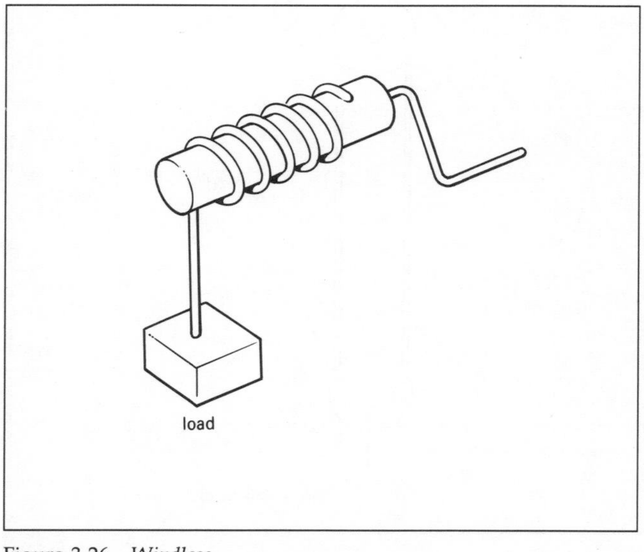

Figure 3.26 *Windlass*

The turning forces in a wheel and axle are given by:

load $\times\ r$ = effort $\times\ R$

where r is the radius of the axle and R is the radius of the wheel. The mechanical advantage (MA) of a wheel and axle is given by:

$$\text{MA} = \frac{\text{load}}{\text{effort}} = \frac{R}{r} = \frac{\text{radius of effort wheel}}{\text{radius of axle}}$$

The velocity ratio (VR) is found using:

$$\text{VR} = \frac{\text{circumference of wheel}}{\text{circumference of axle}} = \frac{2 \times \pi \times R}{2 \times \pi \times r} = \frac{R}{r}$$

This implies the efficiency (MA/VR) of the wheel and axle is 100%. In practice, the effort will be higher than expected because inertia and friction will need to be overcome before the wheel will start turning. Friction will occur where the axle is mounted into its supports.

Belts and Pulleys

These mechanisms are a development of pulleys but are used in a similar way to gears. Their main use is to transmit circular motion from a **driving shaft** to a **driven shaft** over greater distances than is possible with gears. Typical uses are drive belts on washing machines and vacuum cleaners and the fan belts on cars, lorries and coaches. Figure 3.27 shows typical examples.

Figure 3.27 *Belts and chains in use: (a) Belt and pulley, motion in the same direction*

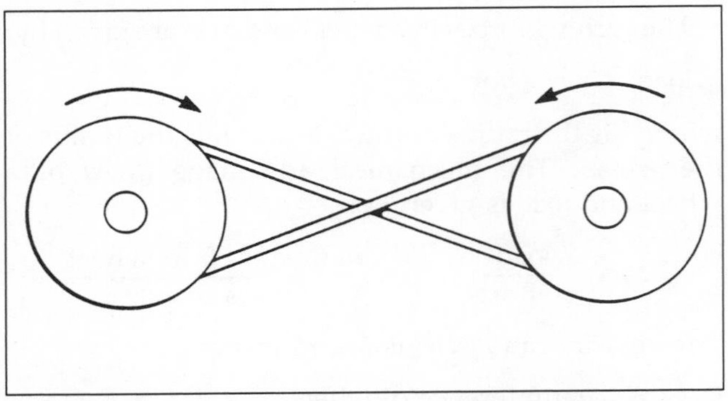

Figure 3.27 *(b) Crossed belt and pulley, motion in the opposite direction*

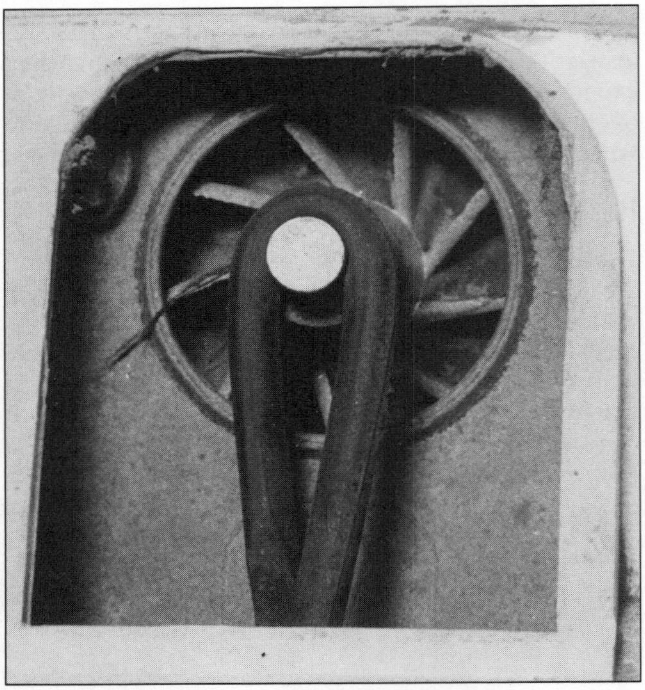

Figure 3.27 *(c) Belt and pulley on a vacuum cleaner*

Belts can stretch in use causing energy to be lost in the system and the machines to become inefficient. There is also a tendency for belts to slip. Also, if the belt is too tight there is a risk of it breaking. Belts are generally only used where small forces need to be transmitted or where space is at a premium and use of gears would be too awkward. For a belt system:

$$VR = \frac{\text{radius of the driven pulley}}{\text{radius of the driving pulley}}$$

Belts can be kept at the correct tension by using a jockey pulley. This is a pulley over which the belt runs. The jockey is adjustable so that it pushes on the

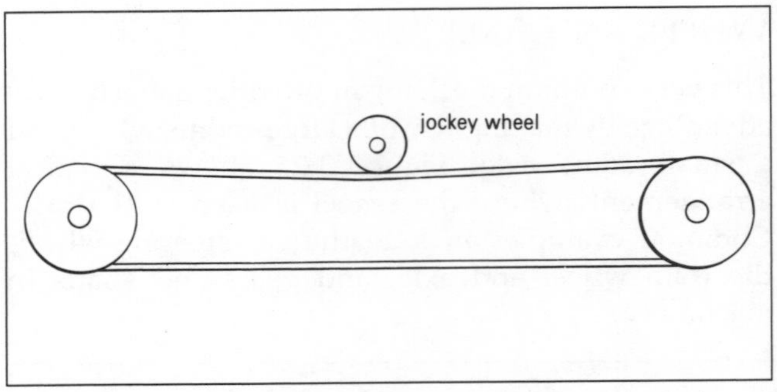

Figure 3.28 *Use of a jockey wheel*

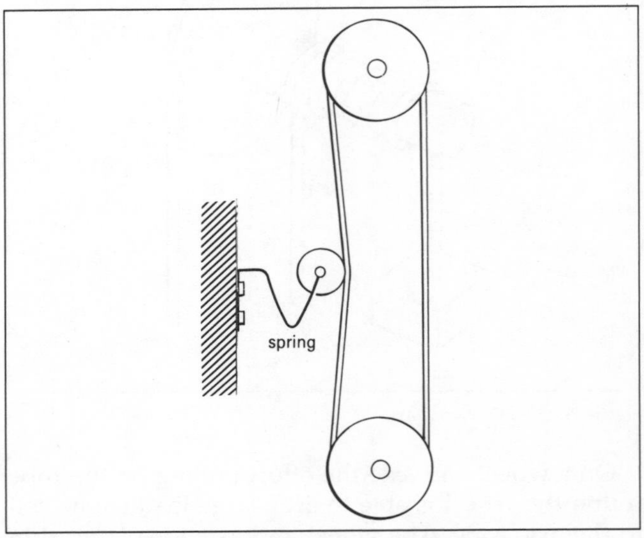

Figure 3.29 *Automatic adjusting jockey and pulley*

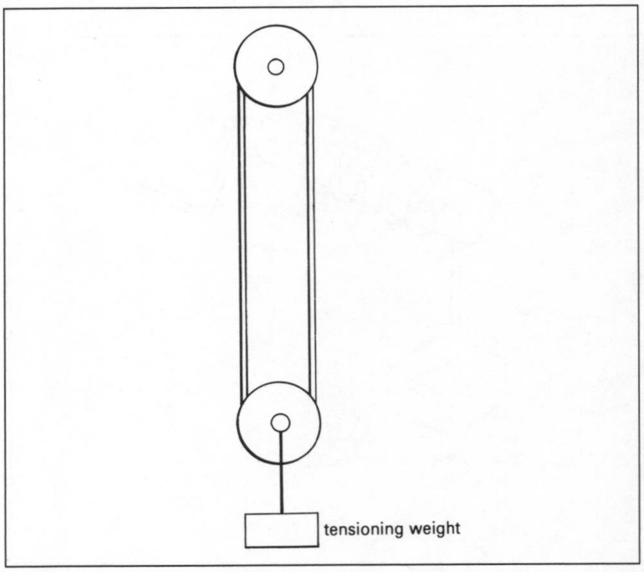

Figure 3.30 *Keeping tension in a belt using a weight*

belt to keep it tight. Figure 3.28 shows a typical application. On some jockey wheel systems the adjustment is spring loaded and therefore is automatic (Figure 3.29).

Another way to take up any slack on the belt or chain is to weigh down the lower of the two drive pulleys, shown in Figure 3.30. Belts can be kept tight by sliding one of the pulleys to one side until the belt is tight and fixing the pulley in position. If the belt does become slack through use, pushing the pulley over further takes up the slack again. Figure 3.31 shows how this is done on car alternators.

For low load applications, round belt and grooved pulleys are used. Vacuum cleaners, sewing machines and food mixers use this type, which is shown in Figure 3.32. The low torque means that the pulley can be fixed to the shaft by a small screw located on a 'flat' on the shaft.

For higher torque applications, such as car fan belts and drive to vertical drilling machines, vee belts and pulleys are used. On coaches and lorries, these are often 'stacked' to transmit even higher torques from the engine to the alternator (see Figure 3.33). As torques are higher, the pulleys are fitted to the shafts using tapered keys which fit into a groove on the shaft and a slot on the pulley. This prevents the pulley from slipping round the shaft.

Figure 3.31 *(a) Taking up the slack on a car fan belt*

Figure 3.31 *(b) The tightening adjustment (© Haynes Publishing Group, 1981)*

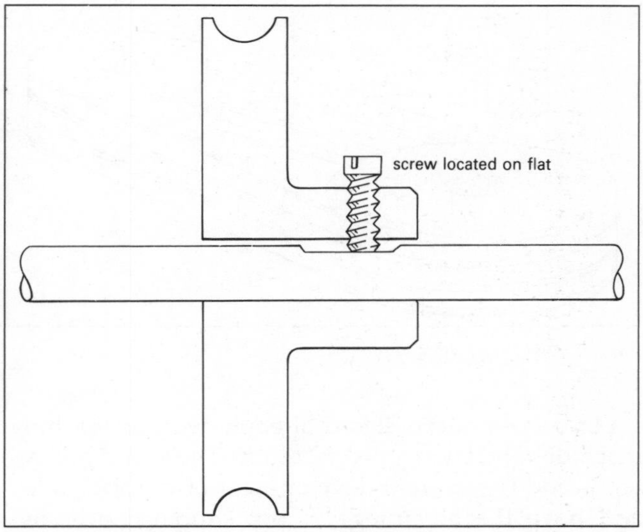

Figure 3.32 Round belts and grooved pulleys: *(a) Fixing to the shaft*

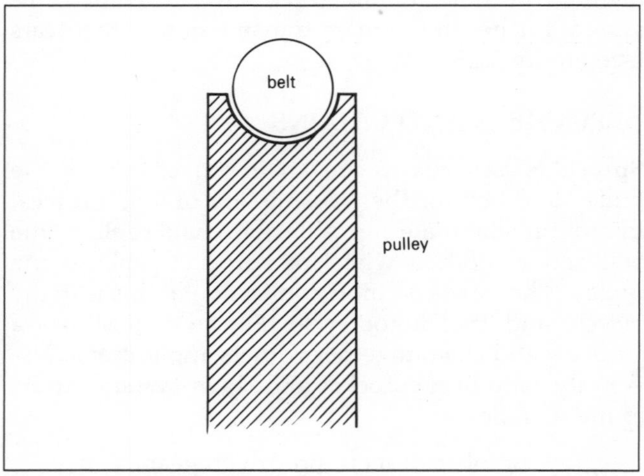

Figure 3.32 *(b) Belt and pulley*

On old farming equipment, flat belts and pulleys were used. They were effective in transmitting power from a steam traction engine or stationary boiler to such equipment as grinders requiring rotary motion. Figure 3.34 shows this belt and an application. Flat belts were actually slightly barrel-shaped to keep them riding on the centre of the pulley.

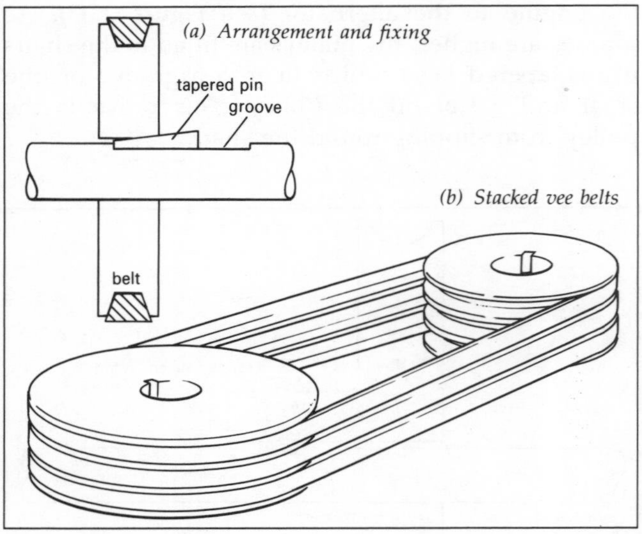

Figure 3.33 *Vee belts and pulleys*

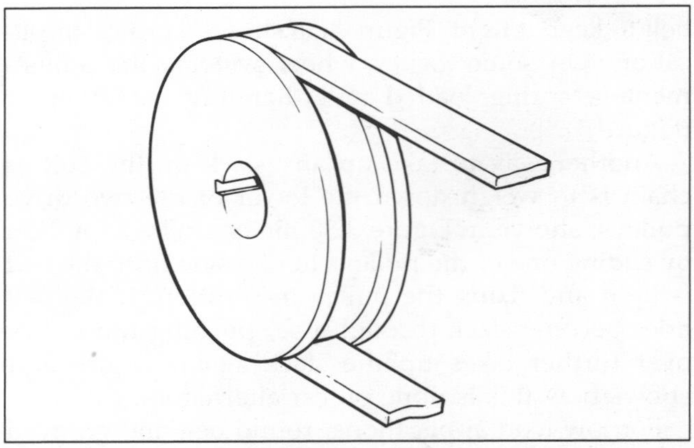

Figure 3.34 *Flat belts and pulleys: (a) A general arrangement*

Figure 3.34 *(b) On farm equipment*

On such modern electrical equipment as washing machines and lawn mowers, toothed belts and pulleys are used. These are a development of the flat pulley and have the advantage of not slipping so easily. Higher speeds and torques are also possible. The car manufacturers DAF and Volvo have developed this system further in the main transmission of their cars (see Figure 3.35b).

Sprockets and Chains

Sprockets and chains are an improvement on the pulley and belt for the transmission of larger forces. In order to eliminate slip, a flexible chain replaces the belt and a toothed wheel or sprocket replaces the pulley. The most common application of this is in the bicycle and the motor cycle. Figure 3.36 shows a sprocket and chain together with its applications. The velocity ratio of a sprocket and chain system can be found as follows:

$$VR = \frac{\text{number of teeth on driven gear}}{\text{number of teeth on driving gear}}$$

Figure 3.35 *Toothed belts and pulleys: (a) On a lawn mower*

Figure 3.35 *(b) On the main transmission of cars*

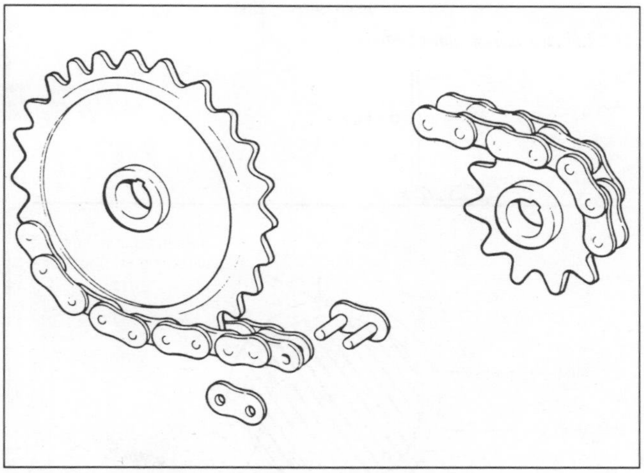

Figure 3.36 *Sprocket and chain: (a) Detail of the chain and how it fits over the sprocket*

Figure 3.36 *(b) On a bicycle*

3:8 BEARINGS

Bearings are used to reduce friction when one surface is moving over another surface. There are three kinds: flat, journal and thrust bearings. All can be plain, ball or roller type, depending on the speed of movement and the direction and size of the force. Lubrication is very important and most bearings are provided with a constant supply of oil or grease in assembly and operation.

FLAT BEARINGS

Where one flat surface slides over another, a flat bearing is used. They are found on the tool post and top slide of a metalwork lathe and allow for expansion in bridge supports (Figure 3.37). As the speed of movement is generally very low, friction is not a serious consideration. Where forces are high, as in bridge supports, rollers are sometimes used.

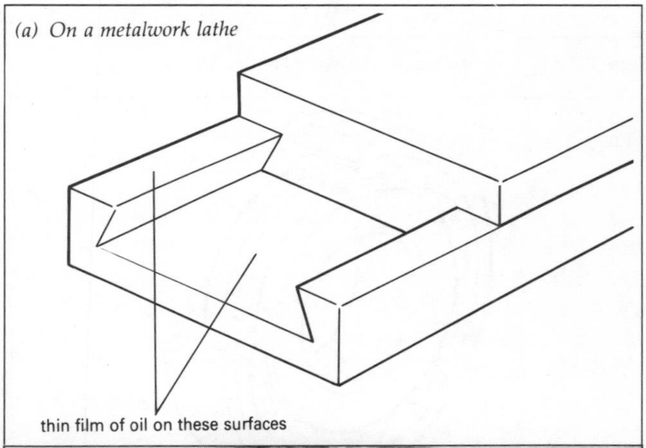

Figure 3.37 *Flat bearings: (b) On a bridge*

Journal Bearings

These are designed to take loads at right angles to the shaft or **radial loads**. The main bearing of a washing machine, which supports the drum, takes a radial load as clothes are being washed (Figure 3.38). Roller bearings would be used for greater loads (Figure 3.39).

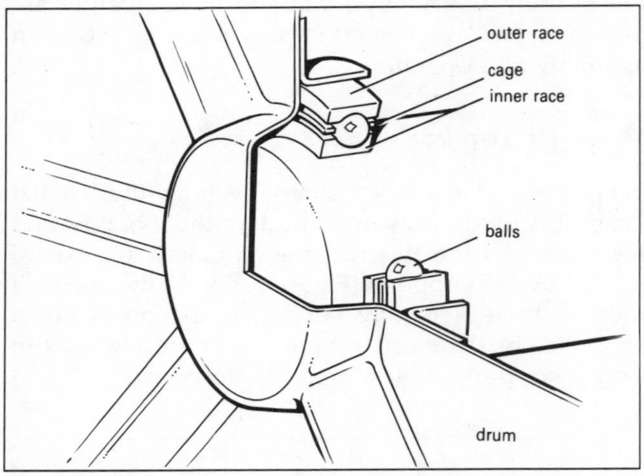

Figure 3.38 *Ball bearing of a washing-machine drum*

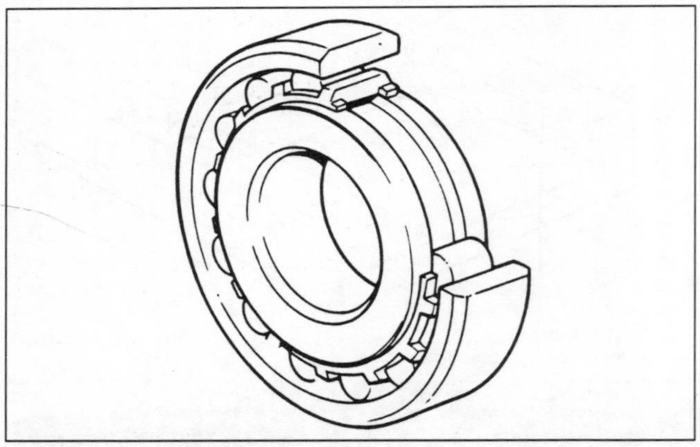

Figure 3.39 *Roller bearings used for greater radial loads*

For lower speeds, plain bearings are used where a shaft passes through a hole made in a mounting. In most cases a sleeve, usually called a **bush**, is fitted tightly into the hole for the shaft to turn in (Figure 3.40a). The bush would be made of a softer material than the shaft so that the bush wears out first and can be replaced instead of the more expensive shaft. Plain bearings made of metal usually have a lubrication hole so that a film of oil can be maintained around the shaft (Figure 3.40b).

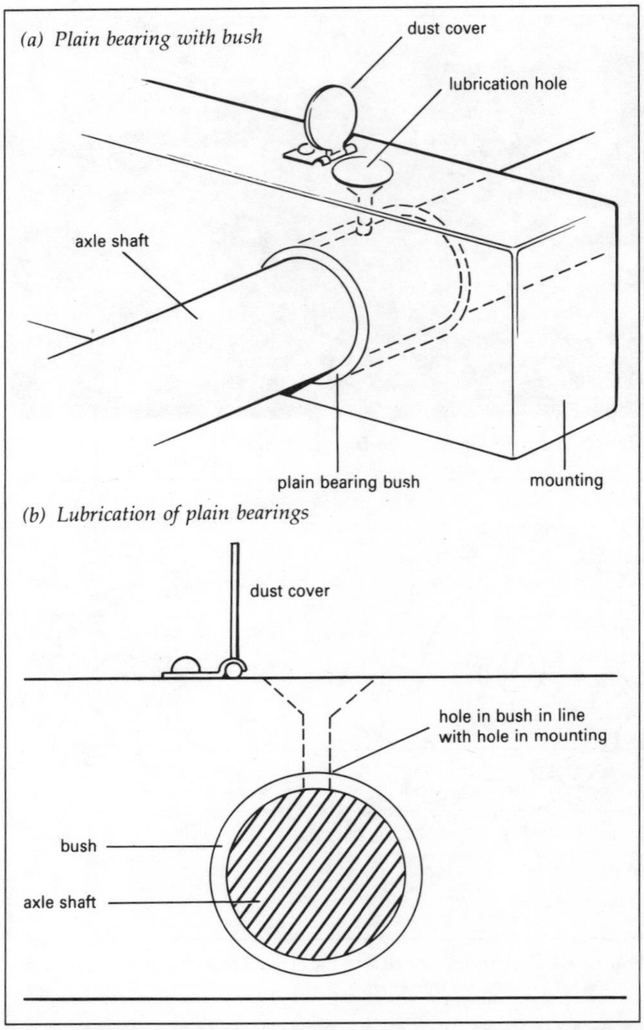

Figure 3.40 *Bearings*

Bushes are often made from plastics such as nylon or PTFE (poly-tetra-fluoro-ethylene), as in some small children's bicycles, but other materials used include bronze, white metal (an alloy based on tin) and cast iron.

Thrust Bearings

Loads imposed along the shaft of an axle or **axial loads** are carried by thrust bearings. The lower bearing in the front fork (steering) of a bicycle is a common example of a ball type thrust bearing (Figure 3.41), although a plain nylon thrust bearing is sometimes used on cheaper bicycles (Figure 3.42).

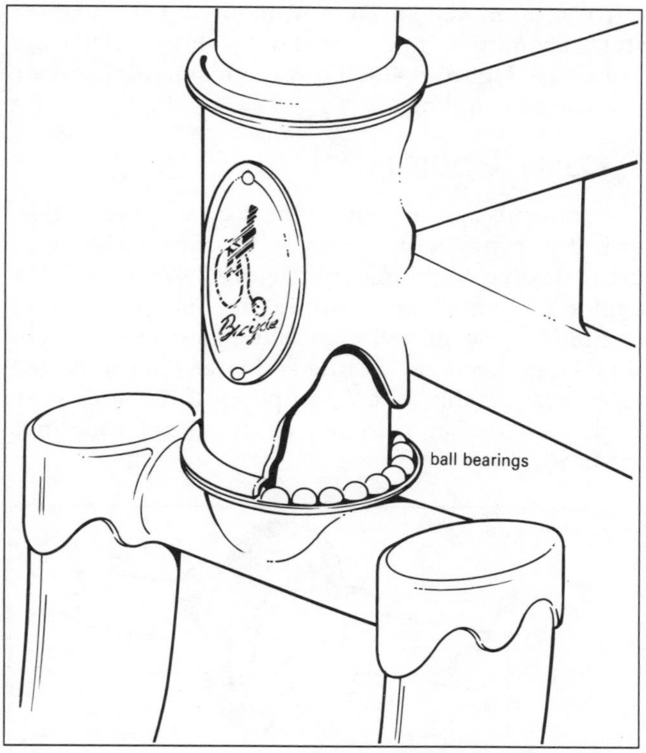

Figure 3.41 *Ball type thrust bearing in bicycle steering*

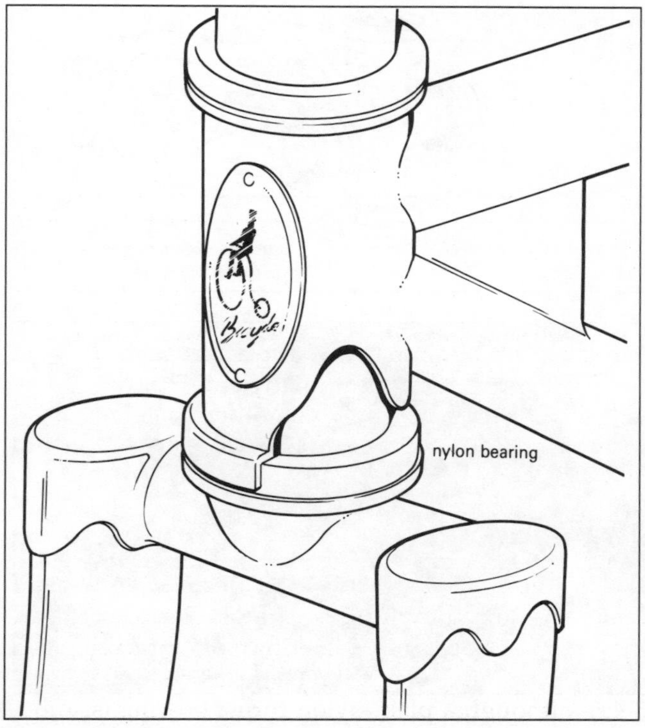

Figure 3.42 *Plain type nylon thrust bearing*

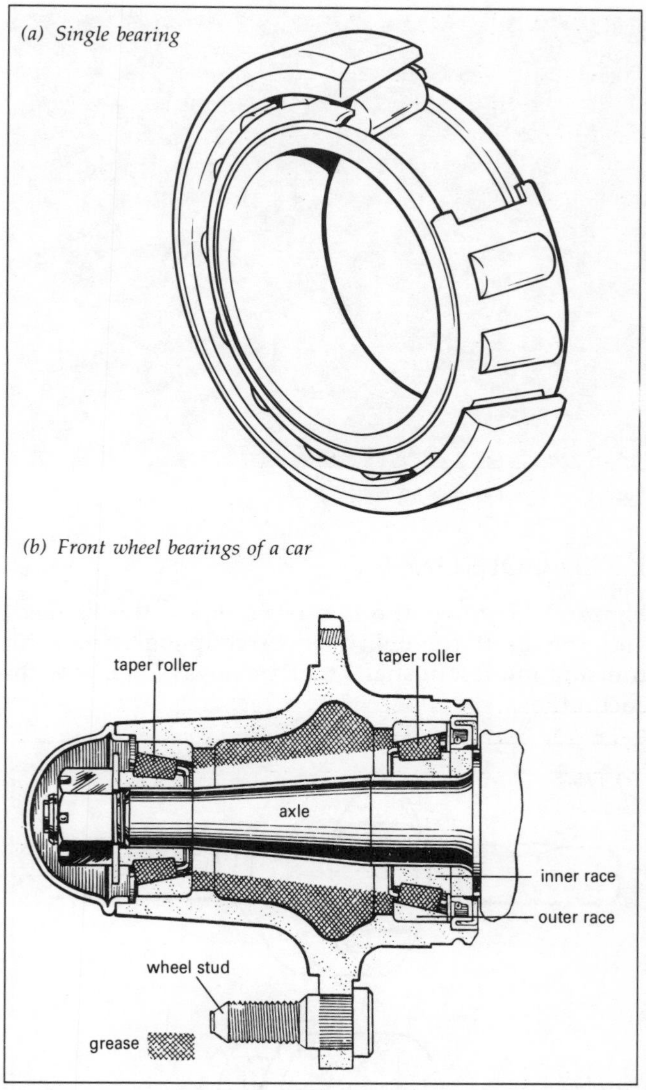

Figure 3.43 *Tapered roller bearings for large axial and radial loads*

Tapered roller bearings are used in pairs to support larger axial and radial loads, as in motor vehicle axle bearings. Slackness and wear can be adjusted by moving the bearings closer together (Figure 3.43).

3:9 COUPLINGS

Couplings can be either rigid or flexible but the principle of transmitting motion from one shaft to another is the same in both cases. Figure 3.44 shows a selection of couplings available for project work in technology.

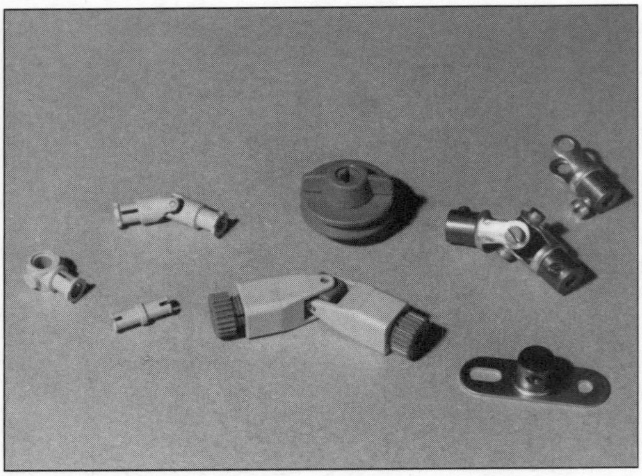

Figure 3.44 *Couplings for project work*

Rigid Couplings

Figure 3.45 shows the two basic types, the flanged and the muff (or split sleeve) couplings, used to transmit motion in shafts that are always in line with each other.

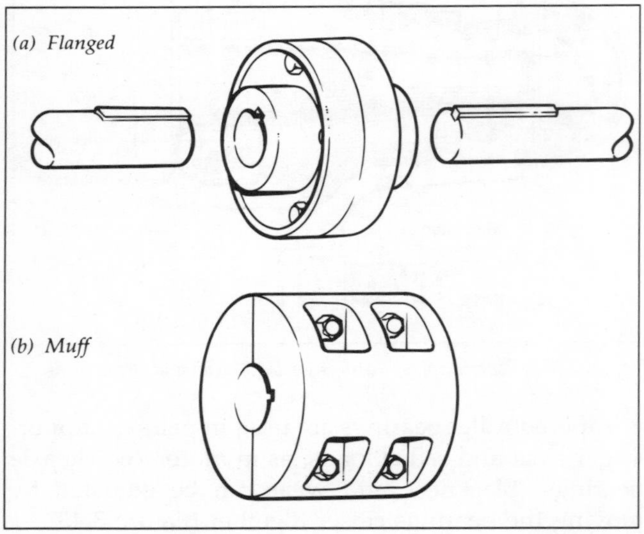

Figure 3.45 *Rigid couplings*

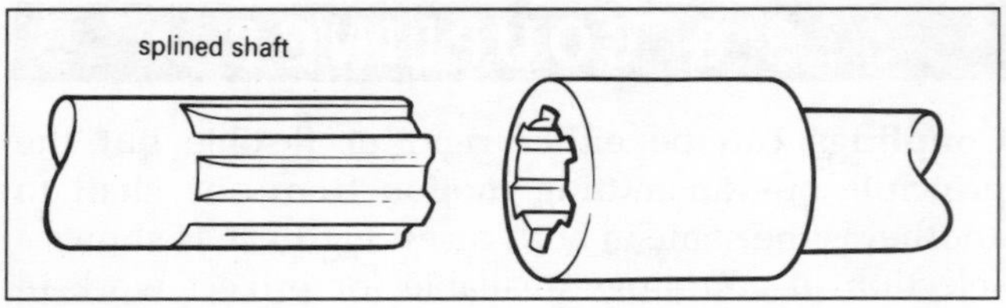

Figure 3.46 *Splined shaft*

To accommodate axial movement of a shaft whilst still transmitting rotary motion, splined shafts are used (see Figure 3.46). Power transmission in cars uses these couplings.

Flexible Couplings

The transmission of motion through varying angles, as in the prop shaft of cars and lorries, is achieved using flexible couplings (see Figure 3.47). Where the angles are small and mainly due to vibration of equipment, flexible disc couplings are used to join shafts together. Car steering and large floor-mounted machines use this type of coupling. If the angles are large then rubber trunnion or doughnut couplings are used.

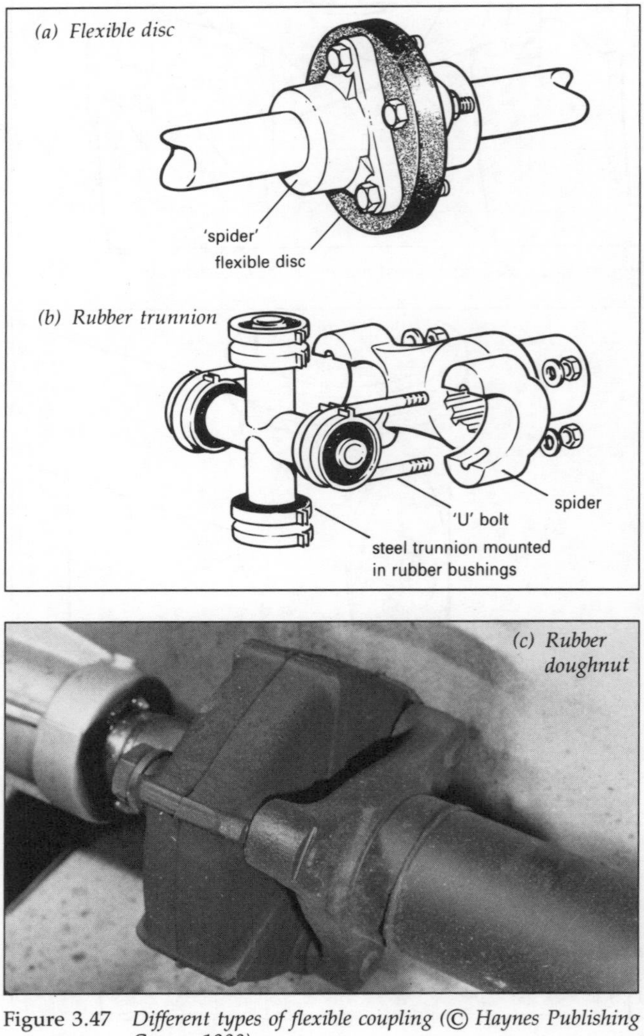

Figure 3.47 *Different types of flexible coupling (© Haynes Publishing Group, 1988)*

If the angle between the shafts changes continually and a high torque is transmitted through that angle, universal joints and constant velocity joints are used. These can be used for a change in direction of 20° between the connected drive shafts but only for medium torques. The amount of torque can be increased if the angle does not exceed about 10° and even more if the angle is smaller. Figure 3.48 shows some examples of universal joints.

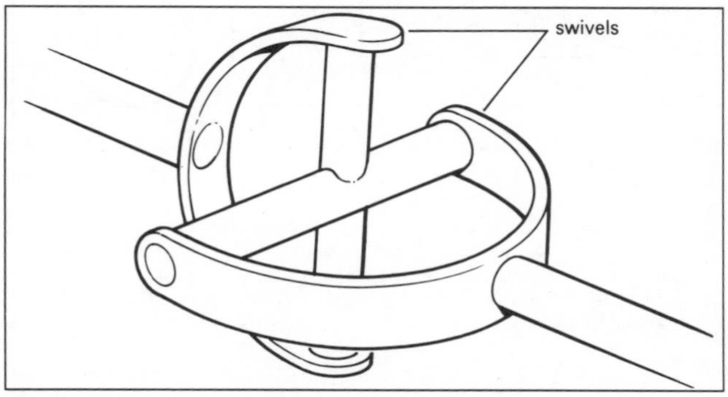

Figure 3.48 *Universal joints: (a) Hooke's joint*

The steering wheel linkage in some cars also uses a universal joint to change the angle of the steering wheel and to give the correct angle for connection to the wheel-turning mechanism. On some cars it is possible to change the angle of the steering wheel. This is achieved by including another universal joint just under the dashboard (see Figure 3.49).

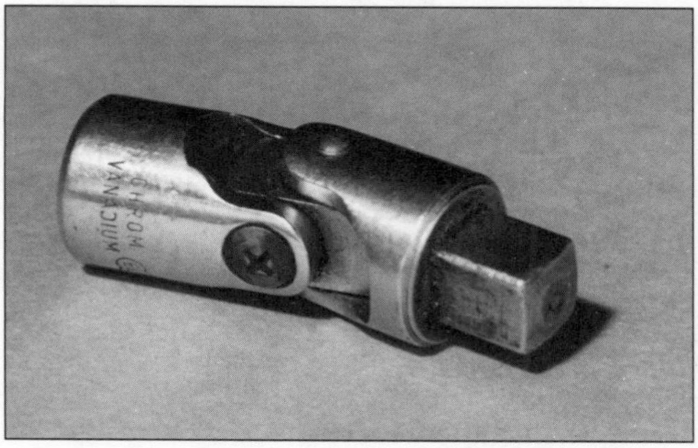

Figure 3.48 *Universal joints: (b) In a socket spanner set*

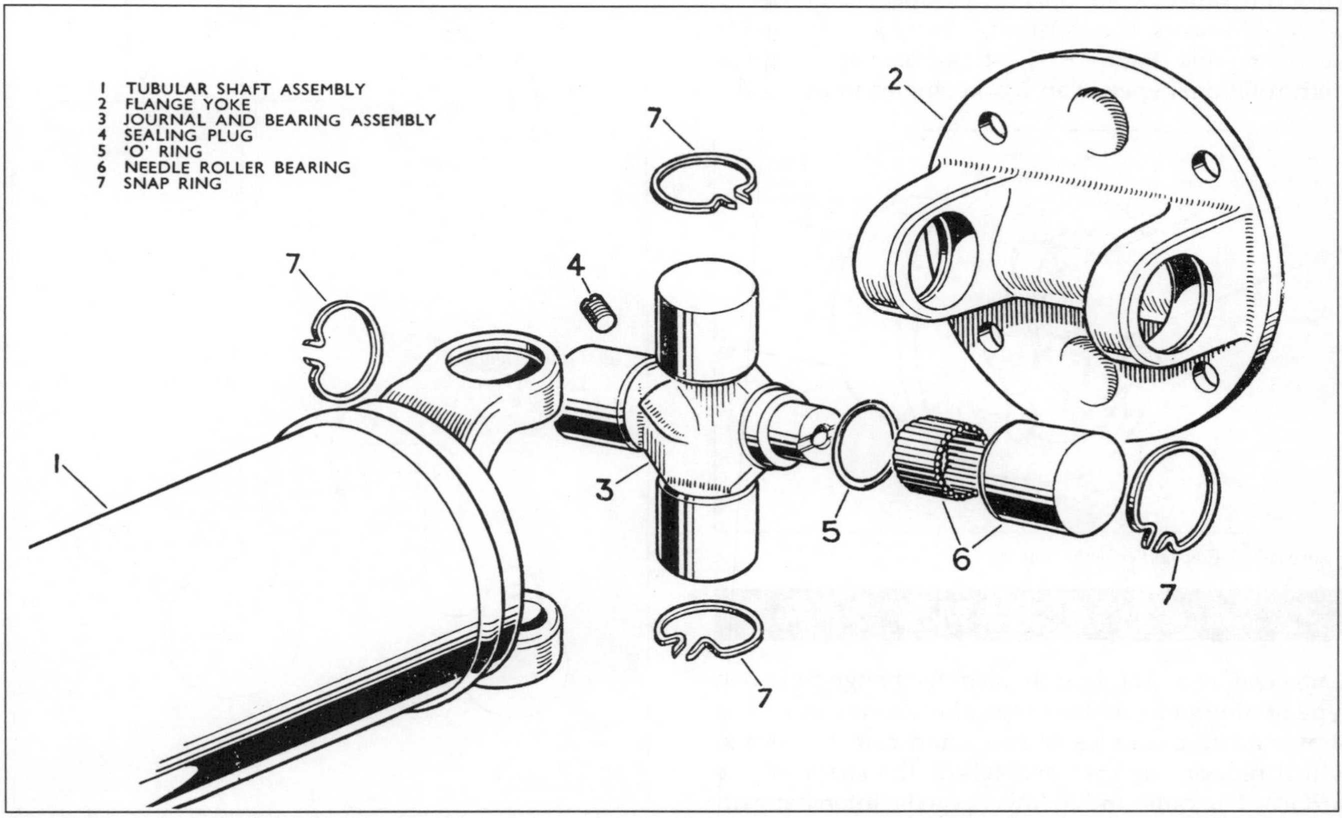

Figure 3.48 *Universal joints: (c) In a car prop shaft*

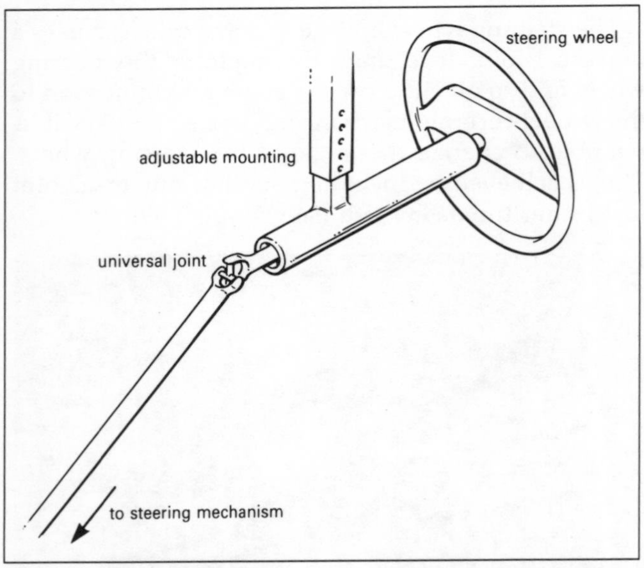

Figure 3.49 *Using a universal joint to change the steering wheel angle*

The rotational speed of the shafts varies on successive quarter turns when universal joints are used. This can cause vibration at high speeds. On front-wheel drive cars, the constant velocity joint is used to overcome this (Figure 3.50). It enables large torques, high rotational speeds and large angles to be used.

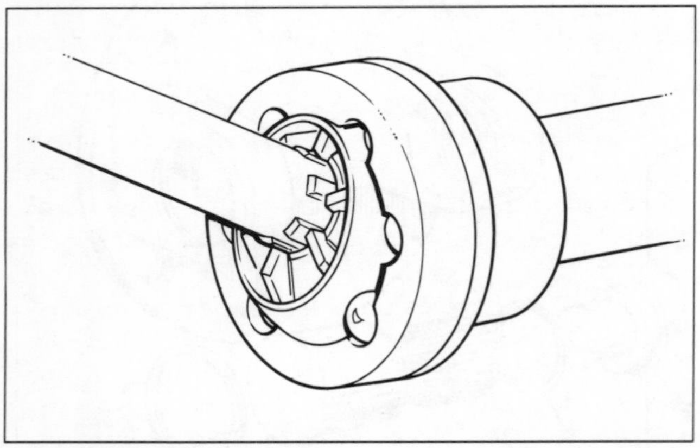

Figure 3.50 *Constant velocity joint*

3:10 CAMS

Cams can be a useful mechanism to change from one type of motion to another type of motion. Figure 3.51 shows some examples of cams and **cam followers**, which rest on the cam and follow the shape of the surface. The cams and followers can be interchanged, depending on the application.

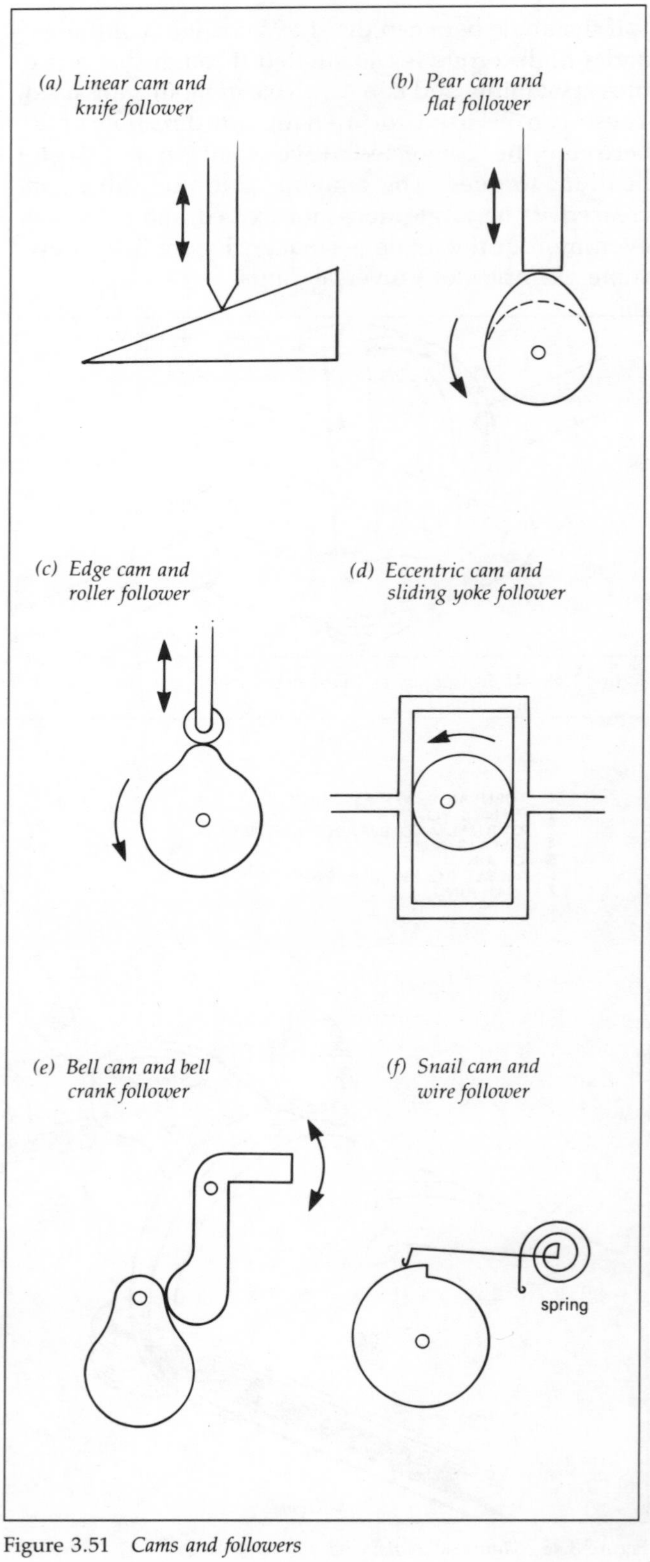

Figure 3.51 *Cams and followers*

The shape of a cam will depend on the application. For example, if a pear-shaped cam operates a switch at every rotation and a light needs to flash once a second, the speed of rotation of the cam must be one revolution per second or 60 revolutions per minute. This could also be done by using a cam which rotates at 30 revolutions a minute and having two lumps on the cam or 20 revolutions a minute and three lumps on the cam. It is then a matter of sorting out angles on the cam and setting the speed of the cam correctly (see Figure 3.52).

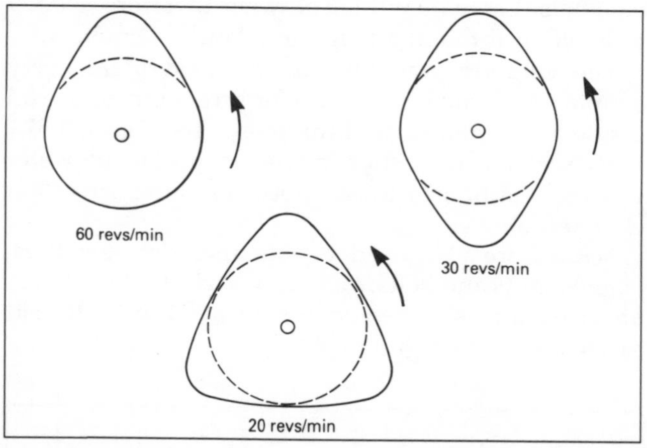

Figure 3.52 *Designing a pear-shaped cam for different speeds of rotation*

3:11 RATCHET AND PAWL

The ratchet and pawl is common in clock and crane mechanisms and washing machine controls. It allows circular motion in one direction only. The ratchet and pawl on crane winches allow the motor to wind in the cable but the pawl prevents the winch from going back again (see Figure 3.53).

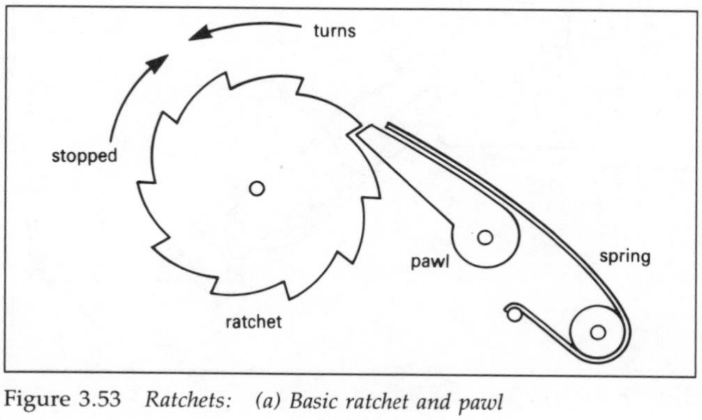

Figure 3.53 *Ratchets: (a) Basic ratchet and pawl*

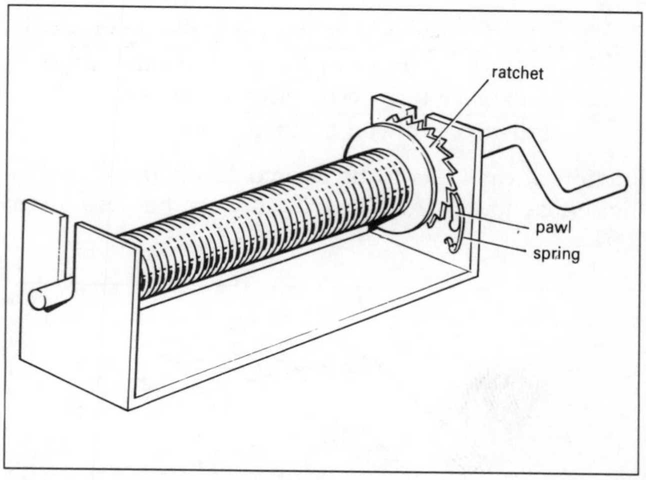

Figure 3.53 *(b) On winches and cranes*

3:12 THE INCLINED PLANE

Lorry manufacturers have always faced a difficult design problem: how to get goods and materials from ground level on to their vehicles and off again, especially if the goods are very heavy or are awkwardly shaped. This is especially true of furniture and removal vans.

One solution to this problem has been to build lorries with a large closing flap which can be let down to form an inclined plane. This mechanism has a long history and it is suggested that the ancient Egyptians used the inclined plane to build the pyramids. Figure 3.54 shows the ancient and modern use of this mechanism. A more common name for an inclined plane is, of course, a slope.

Inclined planes have many other uses; some obvious, some less so. In multi-storey car parks the most effective way to get cars to the higher storeys is to use the inclined plane. The person who sells logs for firewood also uses an inclined plane in the form of a wedge to split large diameter logs into more manageable sizes. Some wood- and metal-working tools such as the lathe tool and chisel rely on the inclined plane to be effective.

The load and effort are not at right angles to each other on the inclined plane. The mechanical advantage (MA) and velocity ratio (VR) can be found from the measurements shown in Figure 3.55.

$$MA = \frac{\text{load}}{\text{effort}} = \frac{\text{weight acting vertically downwards}}{\text{force of the push up the slope}}$$

$$VR = \frac{\text{distance moved by effort}}{\text{distance moved by load}} = \frac{s}{h}$$

Friction always has to be overcome on the slope so the efficiency (MA/VR) will always be less than 100%.

Figure 3.54 *The inclined plane in use: building pyramids and in the back of removal vans*

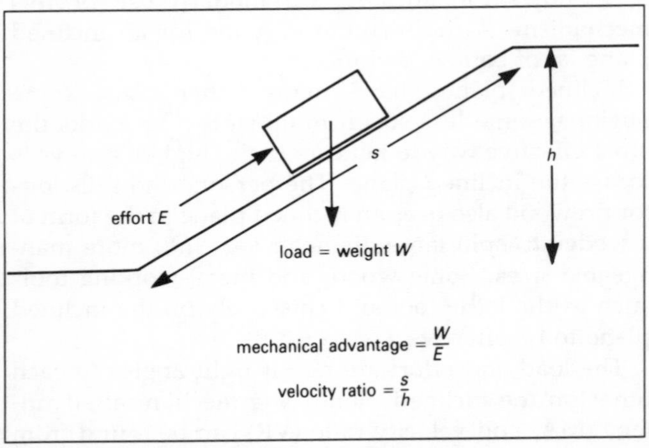

Figure 3.55 *Finding MA and VR for an inclined plane*

3:13 THE SCREW THREAD

If an inclined plane triangle is wrapped around a rod, a **screw thread** is produced (see Figure 3.56).

The screw thread has an ancient heritage. The Archimedes screw was developed several hundred years before the birth of Christ, when Archimedes developed it to answer a water supply problem in fields around the area of Greece where he lived. The summers were so hot that the river water used to irrigate the fields fell below the level of the irrigation channels. Large quantities of water therefore needed to be lifted through a height of about 1–2 metres.

The solution was, like many good ideas, very simple. Archimedes enclosed a screw-threaded rod inside a tube and rotated the screw (see Figure 3.57). Each screw thread then carried a pocket of water upwards until it was dropped into the irrigation channels above.

Screws are also used to join materials together. Screws, nuts and bolts, and screw jacks for lifting cars are all examples of the very widely used screw-thread mechanism (see Figure 3.58).

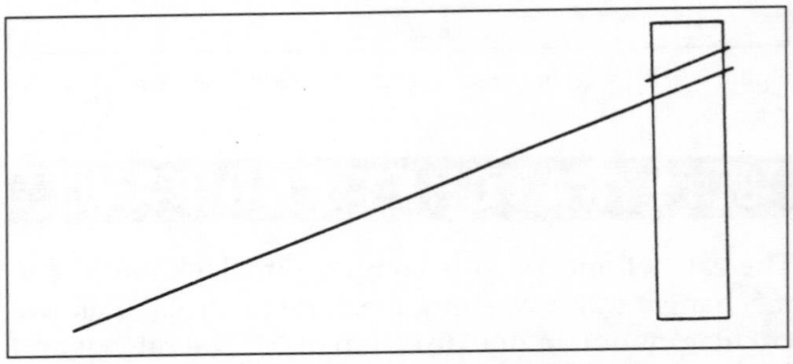

Figure 3.56 *Inclined plane developed into a screw thread*

Figure 3.57 *The Archimedes water pump*

Different screw threads have been developed for certain applications. The two main types, v-thread and square thread, are shown in Figure 3.59 together with the terms used for describing threads. Table 3.1 gives the details of thread forms together with their applications. The most common thread now is the International Organization for Standardization (ISO) metric thread which has replaced a large range of old imperial threads. These are quoted in M sizes which gives the outside diameter of the screw thread in millimetres.

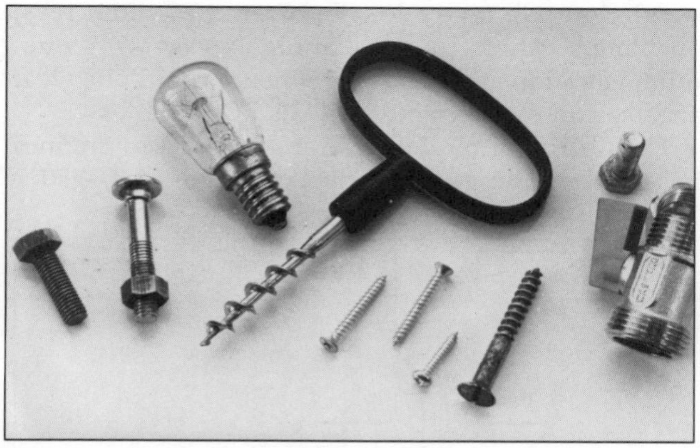

Figure 3.58 *Uses of the screw thread*

Table 3.1 Forms of screw thread

Name	Shape	Uses
ISO/Metric	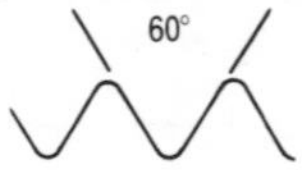 60°	General use, nuts and bolts. Has replaced most other types of V-threads.
Square	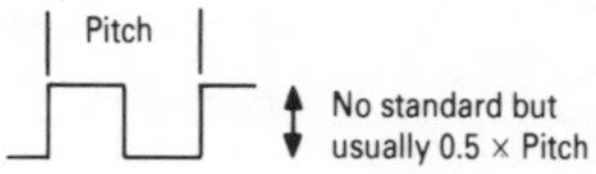 Pitch; No standard but usually 0.5 × Pitch	Machines and transmission of large forces. G Clamps, vices, car jacks.
Acme	 0.5 pitch	Replacing square in many situations. Easier to cut.
Buttress	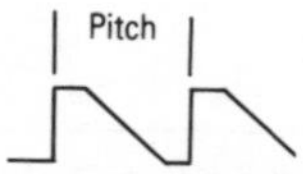 Pitch	Used for quick release mechanisms such as used on vices.

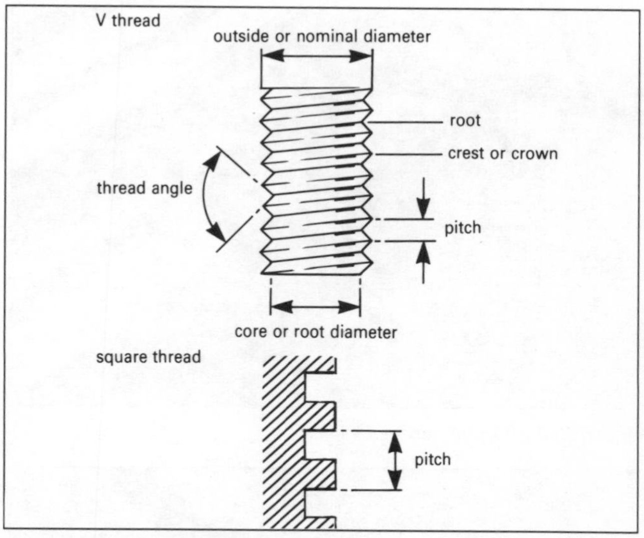

Figure 3.59 *Terms for describing screw thread*

3:14 CRANKS AND SLIDERS

The **crank** is a means of applying torque (turning force) to a shaft. Figure 3.60 shows the layout of a crank and how it can be used.

A **slider** connected to a crank can be used to change circular motion into linear motion or linear motion into circular motion. In some cases, cranks and sliders are used in pairs so that the cranks are balanced on a shaft. This device is used in motor vehicle engines: the pistons are the sliders and the cranks become the crankshaft. Figure 3.61 shows the basic crank and slider mechanism, with the applications to engines shown in Figures 3.62 and 3.63.

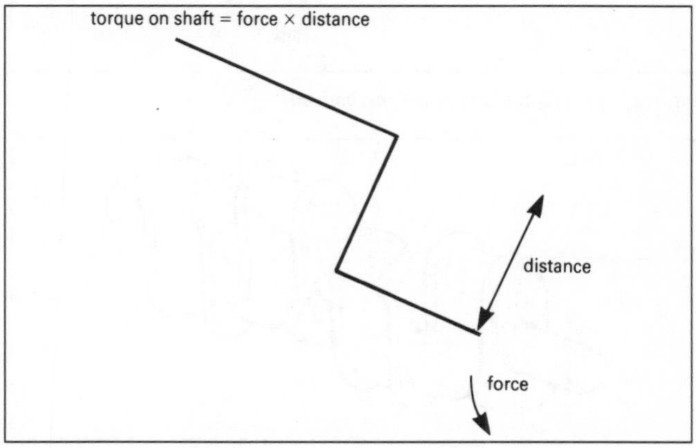

Figure 3.60 *Cranks and their uses: (a) A crank*

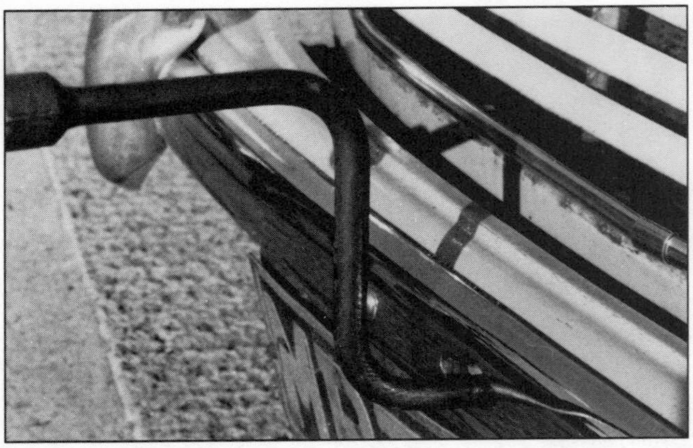

Figure 3.60 *(b) Car starting handle*

Figure 3.60 *(c) Hand food mixer*

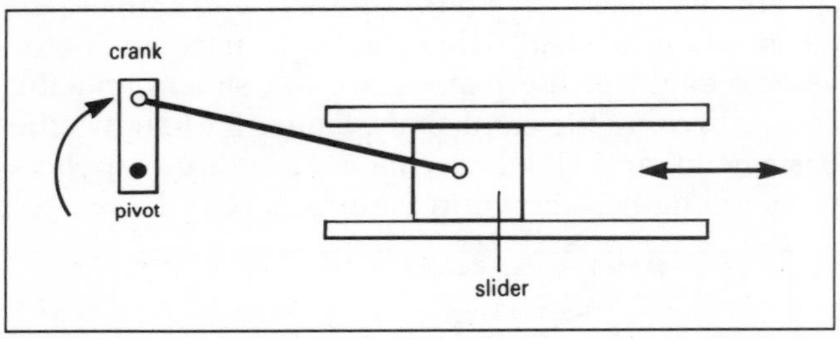

Figure 3.61 *Crank and slider mechanism*

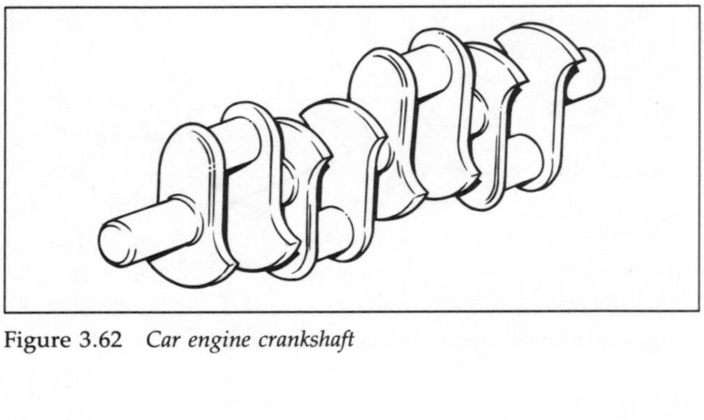

Figure 3.62 *Car engine crankshaft*

The total travel of the slider is given by the distance of the crank from the centre around which it turns:

slider travel = 2 × crank to centre distance

The slider travel is important because it determines the characteristics of an engine: the speed at which the piston and crank moves, the ability of the engine to speed up and slow down and the power developed. Figure 3.64 shows how the slider travel is linked with the offset of the crank. If the piston travel is small, the engine will accelerate and decelerate well. If the piston travel is long, the engine will pick up speed slowly but will give a lot of power at medium revs, enabling a vehicle to cruise at high speed with minimum vibration and good fuel consumption. The wear and tear on such engines will also be a lot less.

The design of modern car and motorbike engines has reflected these ideas. The motorbikes of 50–250 cc

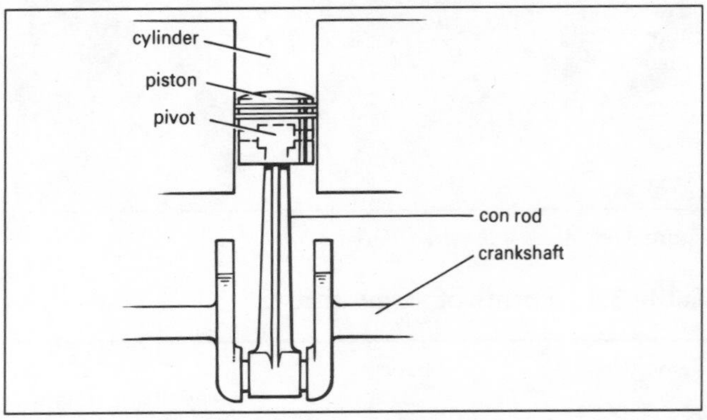

Figure 3.63 *Piston attached to a crankshaft*

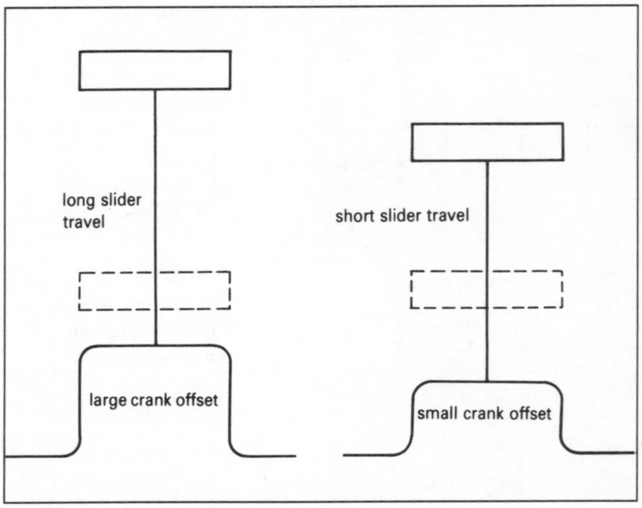

Figure 3.64 *Comparison of short and long slider travels*

Figure 3.65 *(a) Driving crank of a railway steam locomotive*

(b) Steam engine

(c) Spinning wheel

have a lot of acceleration due to their short piston travel but, for long-distance driving, the bigger bikes with their longer-travelling pistons give a much smoother ride at higher speeds. The same is true in motor cars. In general, the difference in engine abilities will be determined by the difference in piston travel.

Other applications of cranks and sliders can be seen on old steam engines and railway steam locomotives. Here, the crank transfers force from the piston and cylinder to turn a wheel, as shown in Figure 3.65. The slider is not always so obvious, as in the case of a treadle-operated spinning wheel (Figure 3.65c), where the link from the end of the treadle to the crank is acting as the slider.

3:15 CLUTCHES

A **clutch** is a removable connection between a driving mechanism, such as a car engine or electric motor, and the driven mechanism. For example, to enable a car engine to pull a car up hills as well as enabling it to cruise at high speed on a motorway, every car needs a gear box. When selecting the gear required, the engine must be disconnected from the drive shaft and then reconnected afterwards. This is the job of the clutch, of which there are two main types: positive and friction.

Positive Clutches

Positive clutches are used where both driven and driving shafts can be stopped before the clutch is disengaged, a gear change can be made and the clutch re-engaged. Lawnmowers and many metalwork machines have these types of clutches. Figure 3.66 shows a dog clutch, which is the most common type of positive clutch.

Friction Clutches

The principle of a friction clutch can be demonstrated by a simple model. Put a sanding disc onto an electric drill and then mount a circular piece of wood on an axle. The drill can represent the car's engine and the wood, the flywheel and drive shaft of the car. Switching on the drill and bringing the sanding disc in contact with the wood will make the wood rotate at the same speed as the drill (Figure 3.67).

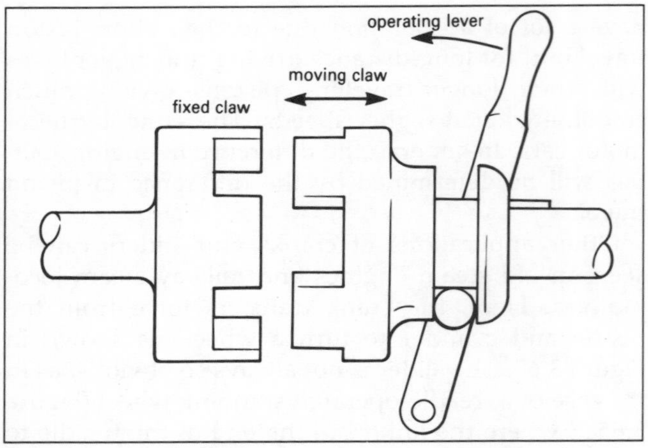

Figure 3.66 *A dog clutch*

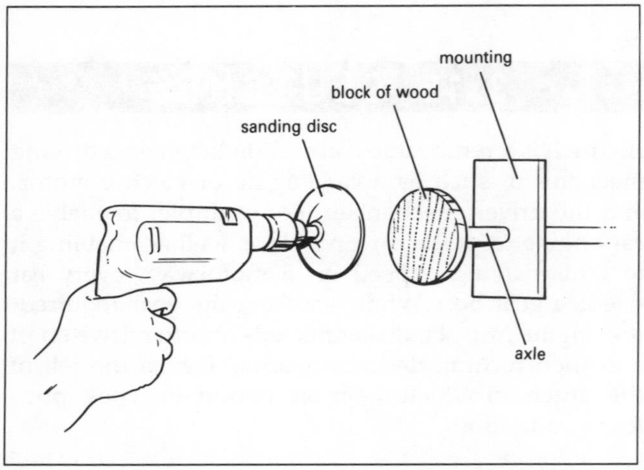

Figure 3.67 *Using an electric drill to show how a friction clutch works*

If the sanding disc is brought roughly in contact with the wood, the drill tends to be thrown to one side. This is due to the inertia of the wood. A similar effect is achieved if the clutch of a car is engaged sharply when the car is stationary. Scratch marks on the wood indicate why clutches treated like this wear out so rapidly. If, however, the sanding disc is brought gradually into contact with the wood, the wood has time to speed up to the sanding disc and wear is significantly reduced. In a car, gentle starts are achieved in this way and one of the first lessons a learner driver has concerns clutch control!

Once the clutch plates are in contact it is important they remain so, for the load on the engine and wheels of a car will vary according to road conditions. If the contact is not good, the clutch will slip and wear will rapidly increase. Transmission of force from the

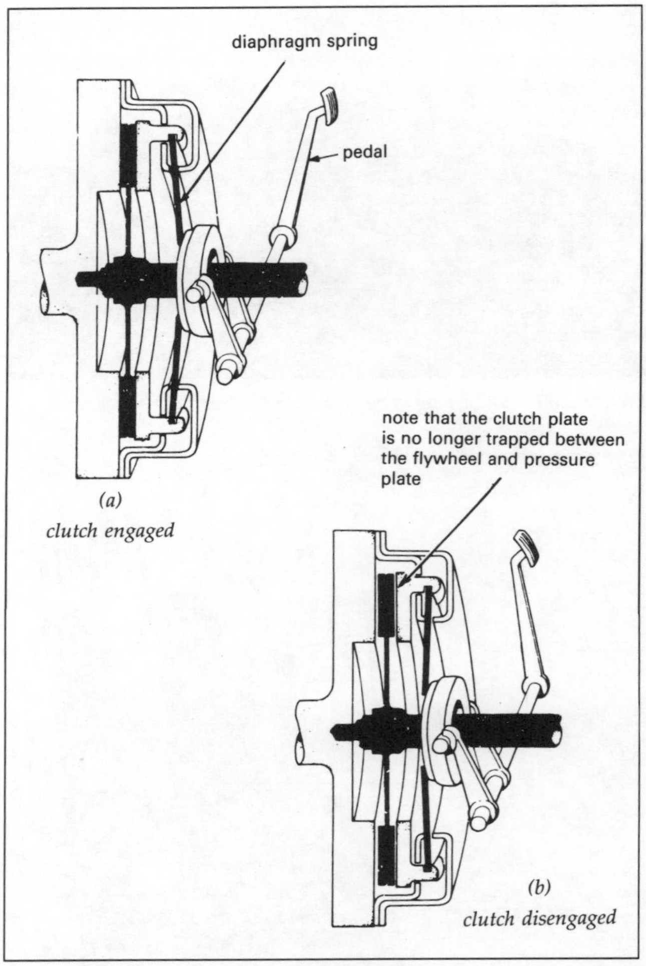

Figure 3.68 *Typical single-plate clutch*

engine to the wheels is also much reduced. Clutch plates are therefore made from a very hard and wear-resistant material with good frictional properties to improve grip. It should also have good heat resistance to withstand the heat produced when the clutch plates are separated and brought back together. A typical single-plate clutch, as might be used in a family car, is shown in Figure 3.68.

For more hard-wearing applications and higher loads, multi-plate clutches are used. Lorries and racing cars have this type of clutch (see Figure 3.69). As they are small assemblies, motor bikes also use them.

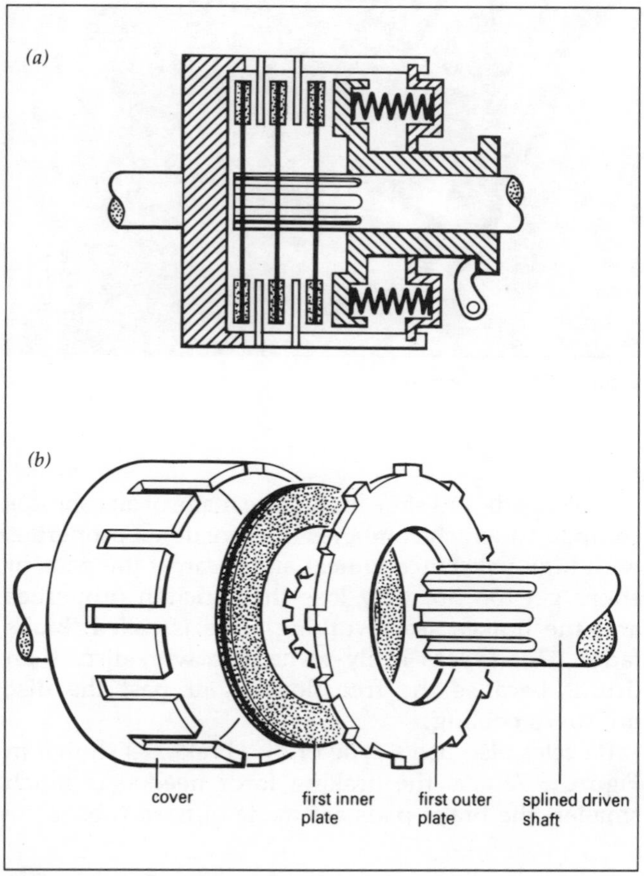

Figure 3.69 *Multi-plate clutch*

Vehicles with automatic gear change have centrifugal clutches. When the drive shaft reaches a certain speed, the clutch plates are flung out against the driven shaft (see Figure 3.70). Cars with such transmission only have two pedals: accelerator and brake.

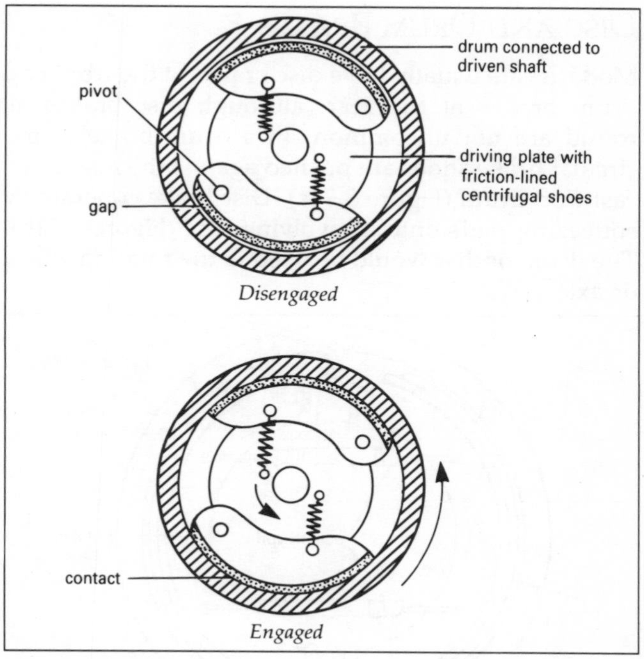

Figure 3.70 *Centrifugal clutch*

Operation of Clutches

Clutches can be operated by linkages or by hydraulics. A rod and lever system was commonly used in old vehicles but was superseded by a cable system. The rods did not allow for vibrations and movement of the transmission in relation to the vehicle body. Many modern cars use a cable system which is cheap to install and easy to maintain, with most now being self-adjusting to take up slack as the clutch plate wears. An alternative hydraulic system is used in some cars which is also self-adjusting and requires very little maintenance. Hydraulic systems are described further in Section 3:16.

3:16 BRAKES

Brakes, like vehicle clutches, are a type of mechanism which relies on friction to work. In stopping a moving object the energy of movement (kinetic energy) is changed into heat energy by the brakes. The heat produced when stopping a car going at 40 miles per hour in 20 seconds is about the same as having eight electric fire bars on for 20 seconds (160 kilowatts of power). There are two basic types of brake: drum and disc.

Disc and Drum Brakes

Modern cars usually have disc brakes at the front and drum brakes at the rear, although disc brakes all round are not uncommon. In a drum brake, semi-circular brake shoes are pushed against the inside of a cast-iron drum (Figure 3.71a). Disc brakes operate by squeezing pads onto a revolving disc (Figure 3.71b). The drum or disc would be fixed to the rotating wheel or axle.

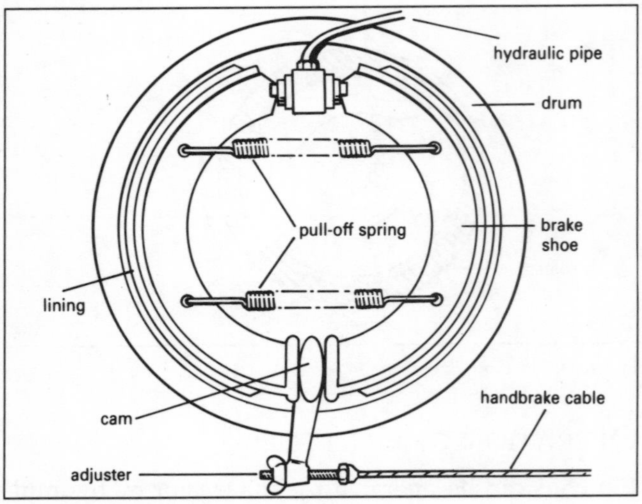

Figure 3.71 *(a) Drum brake*

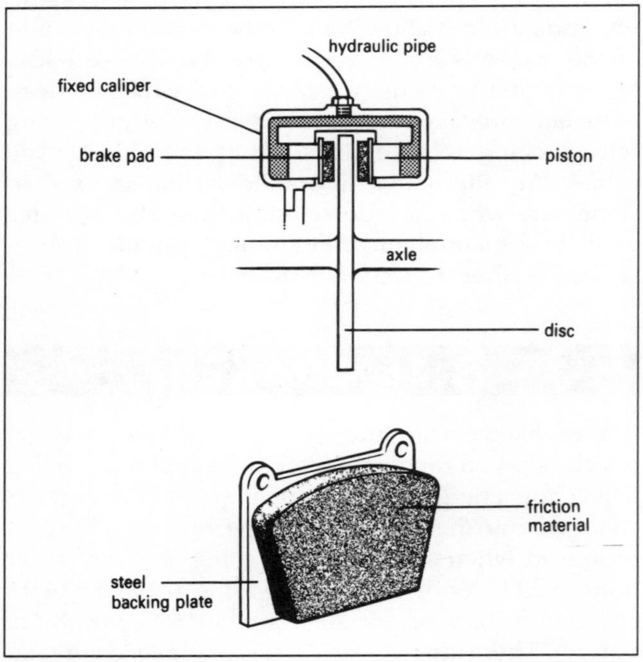

Figure 3.71 *(b) Disc brake*

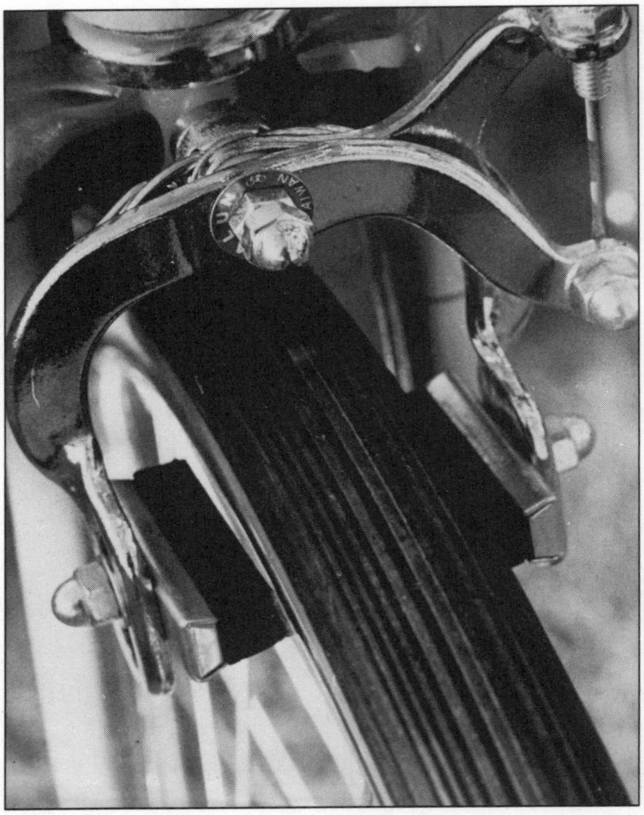

Figure 3.72 *Bicycle brakes*

Brake pads and shoe linings are made of an asbestos compound which combines high frictional properties with high resistance to heat and wear. If the pads or shoes get too hot they lose their friction properties and the brakes stop working. This is called 'brake fade'. This is less likely to happen with discs than drums because the free flow of air past the disc improves cooling.

Bicycles also use a type of disc brake, as shown in Figure 3.72. As the braking force needed is much smaller, the brake pads are made of hard rubber.

Mechanical and Hydraulic Linkages

As with clutches, the force can be transmitted to the brakes by using linkage cables or hydraulic systems. Cables are only used for small braking forces, such as on bicycles, and for the handbrake or parking brake on motor vehicles, which by law has to be independent of the main braking system.

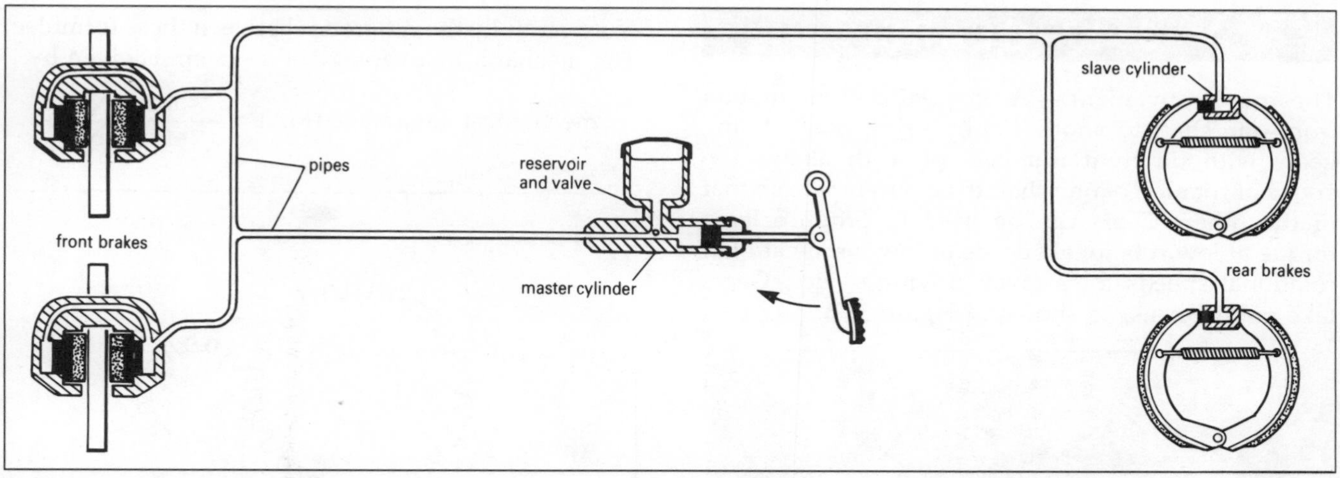

Figure 3.73 *Hydraulic brake system*

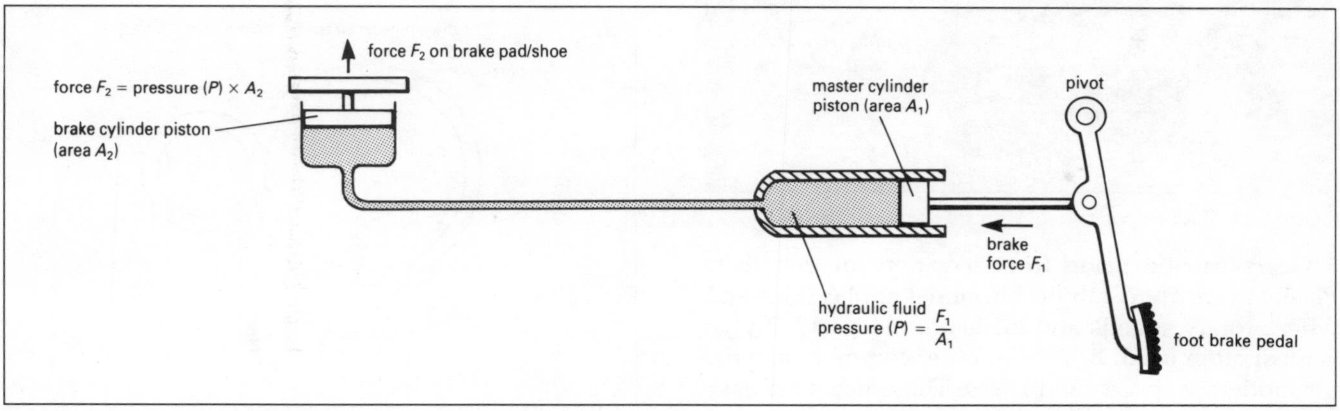

Figure 3.74 *Model of a brake system*

The principle behind the hydraulic system (Figure 3.73) is that liquids cannot be compressed so they transmit force very easily. A great advantage hydraulics have over cable and linkage systems is that hydraulic systems are very good force magnifiers. The model in Figure 3.74 demonstrates how this works.

For the force in a brake system:

force on brakes (N) = pressure in brake fluid (N/m^2) × area of brake piston (m^2)

or

$$F = P \times A$$

As the pressure throughout the brake fluid is the same, the greater the area of the brake piston the greater the braking force. To achieve this greater braking force, the distance travelled by the footbrake pedal is much larger than the distance travelled by the brake piston. The footbrake pedal is used as a lever to give a large mechanical advantage.

Hydraulic systems use a fluid based on vegetable oil. This oil transmits the force very well, does not change viscosity (see flow properties, Section 3:18) significantly over a wide temperature range, has a low freezing-point, lubricates the system and prevents corrosion.

An alternative fluid used in brake systems is compressed air. Air at atmospheric pressure is useless, since applying the brakes will merely compress the air in the brake system. By compressing the air first it becomes a very effective means of force transmission especially useful in lorries and coaches. This type of system is usually called a pneumatic system, more details of which can be found in Section 3:20.

3:17 GEARS

The most convenient way to pass circular motion from one shaft to another is by using **gears**. Using gears with different numbers of teeth allows the speed of rotation of one shaft to be different from that of the other. Gears can be used to produce large torque at low rotational speeds or low torque at high rotational speeds for a given driving device. Gears take many forms, as shown in Figure 3.75.

Figure 3.75 *Various gears*

Gears can be made from a variety of materials. Plastic gears are common for model applications and where rotary speeds and loads are moderate. Nylon is most often used. Brass is another common material for moderate speeds and loads. These gears are easy to make accurately by extrusion (Section 2:15) and will tend to harden with use. No lubricant is needed for brass or plastic gears, which increases their usefulness. Mild steel, hardened steel and cast iron are used for larger gears, especially those with heavy engineering use. Mild steel is often case-hardened to increase the wear-resisting properties of the gear.

Gear Ratios and Mechanical Advantage

Where shafts linked by a gear system are turning at different speeds, the **gear ratio** is used to work out the different speeds (see Figure 3.76). The gear ratio will give the same result as the velocity ratio defined in Section 3:7.

$$\text{gear ratio} = \frac{\text{number of teeth on driven gear}}{\text{number of teeth on driving gear}} = \frac{\text{speed of rotation of driving gear}}{\text{speed of rotation of driven gear}}$$

Note carefully the difference between these formulae. The mechanical advantage of a system is given by:

$$\text{mechanical advantage (MA)} = \frac{\text{load (N)}}{\text{effort (N)}}$$

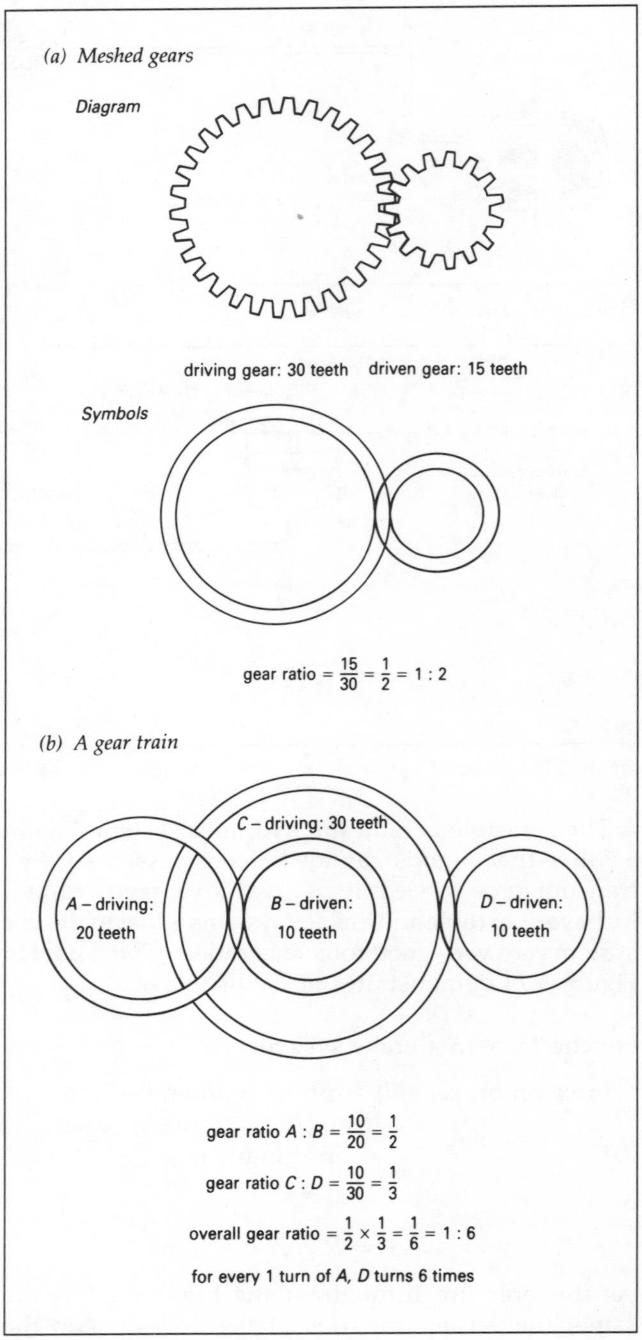

Figure 3.76 *Finding the gear ratios*

In the case of gears, the load and effort are the turning forces at the outside edge of the gear so:

$$MA = \frac{\text{load torque}}{\text{effort torque}}$$

Torque at the outside rim of a gear is given by force × radius and the size of the force applied at the rim of each gear must be the same (Newton's Third Law, Section 2:7).

Referring to Figure 3.76, this gives:

$$MA = \frac{F \times R}{F \times r} = \frac{R}{r}$$

The number of teeth on the gears will depend directly on the radius of the gear, so this means that:

$$MA = \frac{\text{number of teeth on driven gear}}{\text{number of teeth on driving gear}}$$

Spur Gears

The teeth of spur gears are cut into the edge of the gear. When two spur gears mesh, rotary motion is transferred from one shaft to a parallel one. Figure 3.77 shows typical spur gears. Spur gears are very common and can often be found in the 'engines' of model cars (Figure 3.78a). A third gear is sometimes positioned between the driving and driven gears. This is called an idler gear; it is used to make the driving and driven gear rotate in the same direction (Figure 3.78b).

Figure 3.77 *Spur gears*

Figure 3.78 *(a) Spur gears in models*

Figure 3.78 *(b) Use of idler gear*

Bevel and Mitre Gears

These will also turn motion through a right angle having their teeth cut at a 45° angle to the edge of the gear. Bevel gears always have different-sized driving and driven gears, so they change the rotary speed between one shaft and the other. Mitre gears are always the same size and are used where no change in rotary speed is required (see Figure 3.79).

A special form of bevel gear is used where high torque and rotational speeds together with quiet operation are needed. These are known as spiral bevel gears and a typical application is in the differential gearing of the drive wheels of cars, where they are called the 'crown wheel and pinion' (Figure 3.80).

Figure 3.79 *(a) Bevel gears*

Figure 3.79 *(b) Mitre gears*

Figure 3.80 *Spiral bevel gears: (a) Crown wheel and pinion in car differential (© Haynes Publishing Group, 1981)*

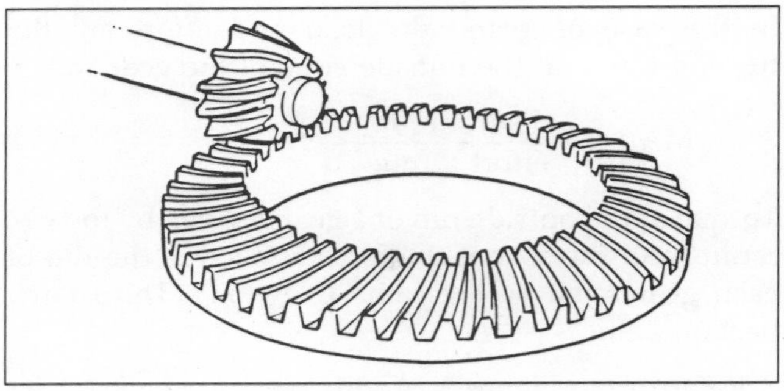

Figure 3.80 *(b) A set of spiral bevel gears*

Figure 3.81 *Helical gears in a gear box*

Helical Gears

Where large torque is to be transferred between shafts which are either parallel or at right angles, helical gears can be used. These are similar to plain gears but the teeth are set at an angle around the edge; they also curve very slightly (see Figure 3.81). Helical gears are used where gears have to slide in and out of mesh. The change is much smoother and actually encouraged by the shape of the gears.

Worm and Wormwheel

For very high gear ratios, the worm and wormwheel can be used. The classic use for these gears was on traction engine steering (Figure 3.82a). They are now often used on the output shaft from electric motors to convert the high-speed, low-torque output to a much lower speed but much higher torque for driving machinery or models. As the worm has only one tooth:

gear ratio = number of teeth on driven gear

Figure 3.82 *Worm and wormwheel gears: (a) a model set; (b) on traction engine steering*

Rack and Pinion

To convert circular motion to linear motion, a rack and pinion set is used. Lathes and car steering systems use these gears. Examples are shown in Figure 3.83.

Gear ratios do not apply to rack and pinion gears but the movement of the rack will have to be calculated in any design process:

$$\text{movement of rack} = \frac{\text{number of teeth on pinion} \times \text{number of times pinion turns}}{\text{number of teeth per metre on rack}}$$

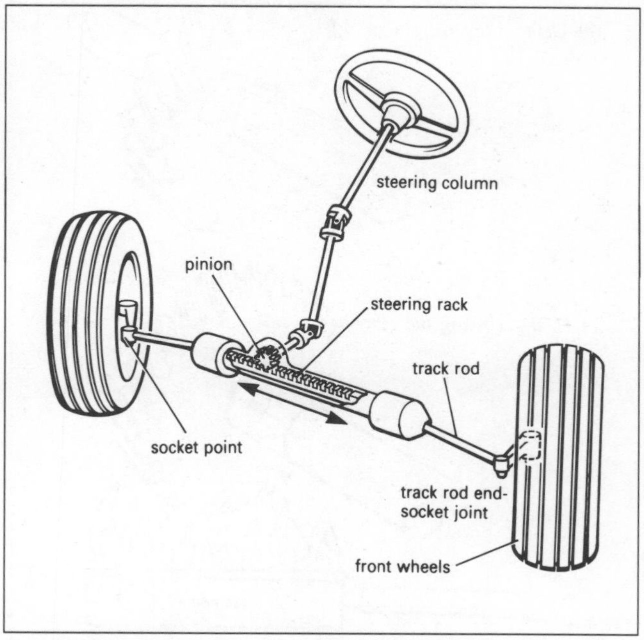

Figure 3.83 *Rack and pinion gears: (a) From Fischertechnik; (b) In car steering systems*

Fixing Gears to Shafts

For smaller gears, a grub screw is tightened through the collar of the gear onto the shaft. If the grub screw slips round the shaft then the shaft can be flattened slightly to give the screw a better grip. For higher torques, a tapered pin is placed in a slot in the shaft and pushed into a slot in the gear. For very high torques, the gears are heat shrunk onto the axle. This is done by machining a hole in the gear slightly smaller than the shaft diameter. The gear is then heated so that it expands and can then be slipped on to the shaft. After the gear has cooled and contracted, the gear grips the shaft very tightly. Gears fitted to railway vehicle axles are fitted this way (see Figure 3.84).

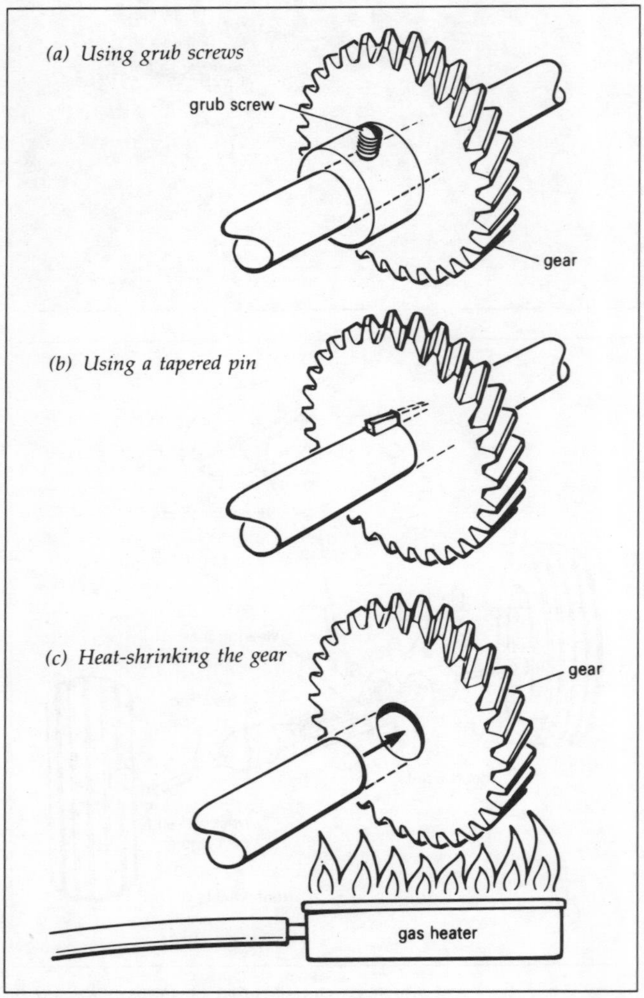

Figure 3.84 *Fixing gears to a shaft*

3:18 LUBRICATION

Friction can often be a problem in a mechanism but it can never be completely eliminated. However, its effects can be reduced through using lubrication. Friction occurs whenever two surfaces rub together. By putting a **lubricant**, such as oil, between the rubbing surfaces the frictional force is reduced. Figure 3.85 shows a microscopic view of a pair of surfaces before and after lubrication. The oil fills in the bumps on each surface and forms a layer of oil molecules between the two surfaces which acts like a layer of ball bearings.

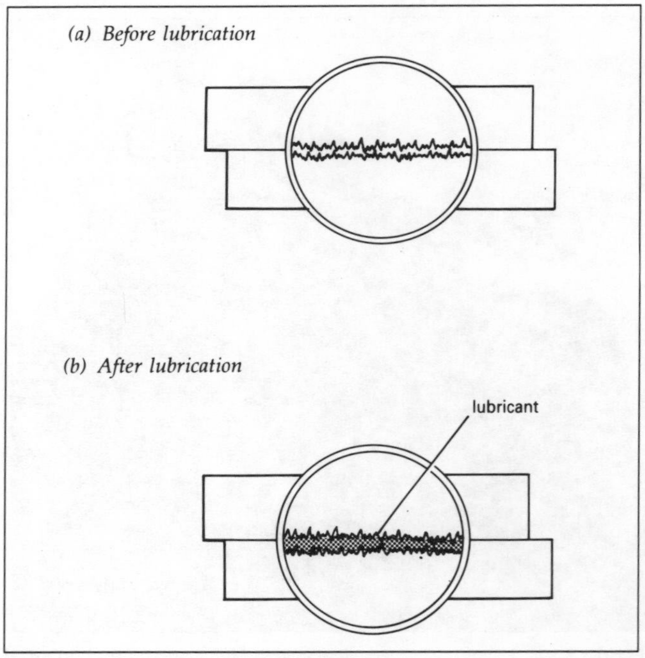

Figure 3.85 How lubrication works

Viscosity and SAE Numbers

There are many different types of lubricants, designed to meet different needs. Before the advent of multigrade oils for cars, motorists had to change oils at certain times during the year. This was due to the change in **viscosity** of the oil resulting from a rise in temperature. The hotter it is, the thinner the oil becomes but car engines run much hotter in the summer than in winter when, even in mild weather, engines only run warm. So, to maintain the right viscosity of oil throughout the year and keep the engine well lubricated, a thick oil was needed in the summer and a thin oil in the winter. Multigrade oils have now been developed which make this change unnecessary because they keep their lubrication properties through a bigger range of temperatures.

Recent developments have indicated that petrol consumption of cars is greatly increased with thicker oils and research by oil companies has produced oils of lower viscosity which provide the necessary lubrication without the consequent extra wear associated with thinner oils.

Mineral lubricating oil is given an SAE (Society of Automotive Engineers) number depending upon its viscosity at 99 °C. The lower the number, the lower the viscosity or the thinner the oil. The number is the time it takes for a certain amount of oil to drip through a certain size hole. Table 3.2 shows the different SAE numbers.

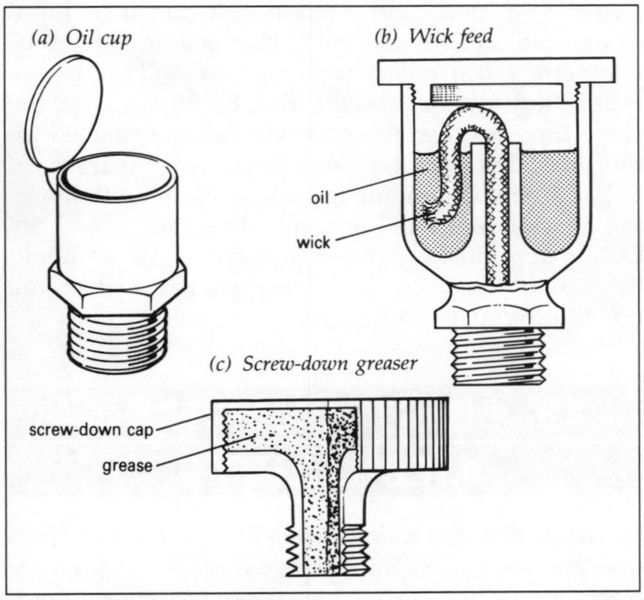

Figure 3.86 *Three types of lubricator*

Table 3.2 A table of oil SAE numbers

SAE number	*Oil thickness*	*Uses*
10–20	Extra light–light	Low load applications, small bearings, models, typewriters
30–50	Medium–heavy	General lubrication, large bearings, engines
60–250+	Extra heavy/very heavy	For high-pressure uses, gearboxes, differentials

Other lubricants are available but their uses are usually specific to the job. Water is used where there is no risk of freezing, boiling or corrosion; graphite where low atmospheric pressure (air pressure) allows oil to evaporate; and vegetable oils where heat is limited and will not cause the oil to burn and 'carbonise' such as in hydraulic brakes.

Additives

Additives are used to enable lubricants to withstand variety of testing conditions without losing their lubrication properties. Some types of additives are listed in Table 3.3.

Methods of Lubrication

There are three ways to introduce oil to bearing surfaces: gravity feed, splash feed and force feed.

Devices called **lubricators** allow oil to fall, because of gravity, on to the bearing surface. Care should be taken to limit dust entering them, as the flow of oil would be markedly reduced. Figure 3.86 shows three types of lubricator.

Table 3.3 Oil additives

Additive	*Function*
Anti-foaming agents	to reduce the gas absorption of the oil and so reduce foaming
Oxidisation inhibitors	to reduce the effects of burning and oxidisation of the oil at higher temperatures
Detergents	have the same effect on dirt in oil as they do on dirt in washing: they keep dirt particles in suspension and prevent coagulation into larger lumps which could then block small oil pathways
Thickening agents	are added to keep the viscosity up when the oil is running at high temperatures; also used to form grease which is a self-supporting lubricant for use where normal oils would run out
Emulsifiers	limit the corrosive effects of water getting into the oil by keeping the water mixed with the oil and not allowing it to collect at the bottom of the sump

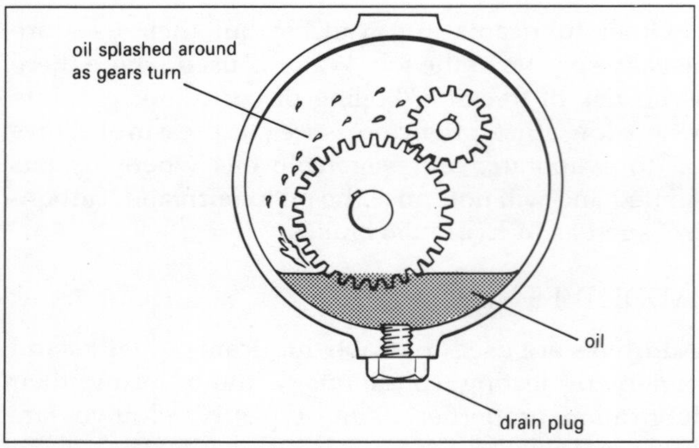

Figure 3.87 *Splash lubrication*

Splash feed is achieved by allowing bearing surfaces to dip into an oil supply and spread the oil around as they move. Gearboxes and differentials on cars use this method (see Figure 3.87).

For more complex machines such as vehicle engines it is necessary to force feed the oil using oil pumps (Figure 3.88). Only then can oil be guaranteed to be reaching all bearing surfaces.

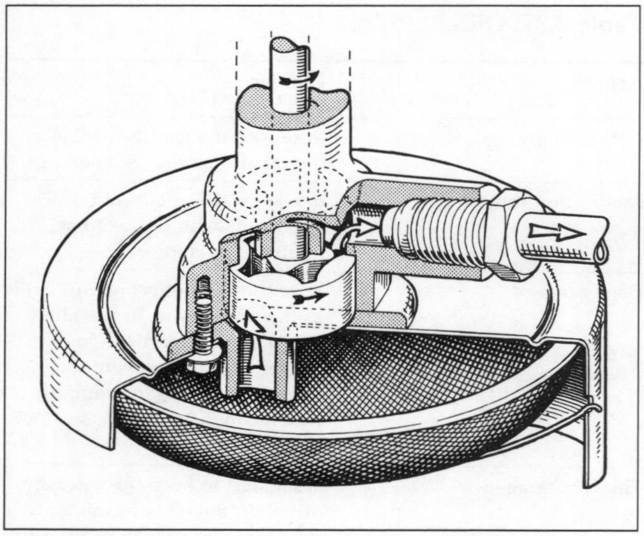
Figure 3.88 *An oil pump*

For applying grease, nipples are used. These have grease forced into them by grease guns at regular intervals. The pressure of the grease and the movement of the surfaces carry the grease to the areas in which it is needed. Figure 3.89 shows a grease nipple used to lubricate a plain bearing.

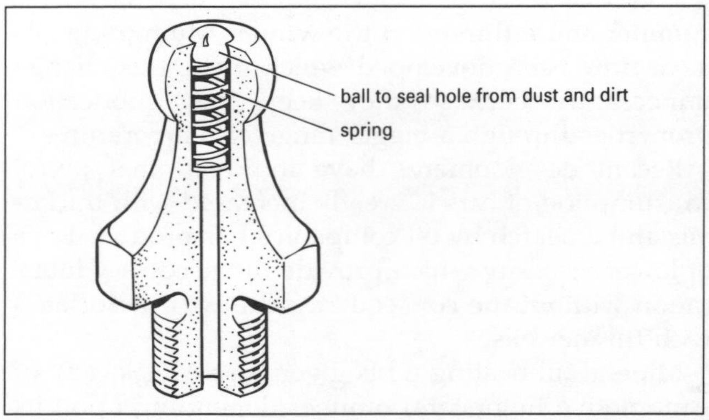

Figure 3.89 *A grease nipple*

Life of Lubricants

All lubricants must be changed after a while because they can become contaminated with chemicals and particles of metal and dirt, so reducing their lubricating qualities. In cars oil is changed at about 8000 kilometre (5000 miles) intervals. Any filters in the lubrication system should also be changed at the same time because these slowly become clogged up with particles of carbon and metal. A comparison of old and new car engine oil will show the difference, the blackness in old engine oil being caused by carbon deposits from the engine. Oil or grease should be regularly applied to any moving parts which are not continuously lubricated.

3:19 ELECTROMECHANICAL MECHANISMS

Electromechanical mechanisms use electricity to produce motion or, in some cases, use motion to produce electricity. When electricity is passed through a wire, a magnetic field is produced around the wire. It is this magnetic field, together with magnetic metals, which is used to produce motion.

Electric Motors

Electric motors are used to produce circular motion. Fischertechnik and Meccano motors are ideal for project work but many other small motors are also available. It is worth hunting through the electronics catalogues to find motors which meet a project's requirements. A selection of motors is shown in Figure 3.90.

There are two basic types of motor: those which use alternating current (AC) and those which use direct current (DC). To distinguish them, DC motors have brushes and commutators whereas AC motors have slip rings (see Figure 3.91). Most small motors are DC.

Another useful type of motor is a stepper motor. These turn through a certain angle (e.g. 7.5°) every time the motor is turned on. Such motors are used in robotics. They are quite expensive and require an equally expensive driver circuit. Figure 3.92 shows a typical specification from a supplier's catalogue.

Figure 3.90 *Typical motors used for technology projects*

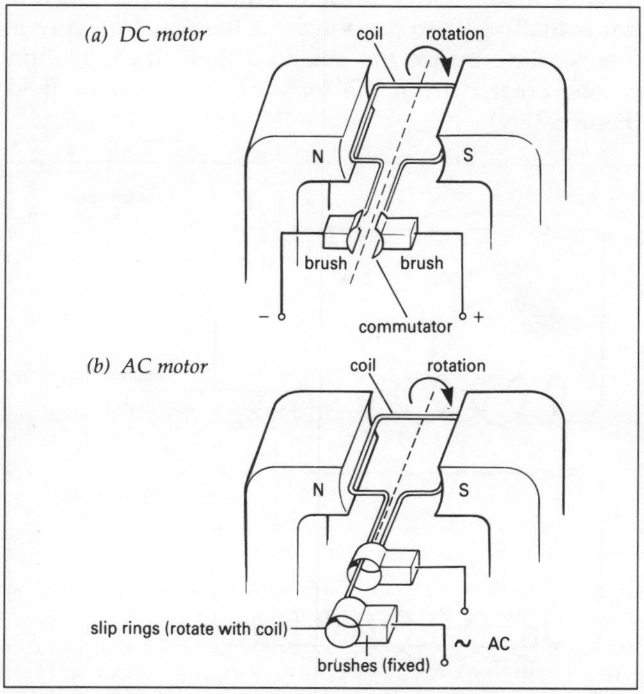

Figure 3.91 *Difference between AC and DC motors*

size 1

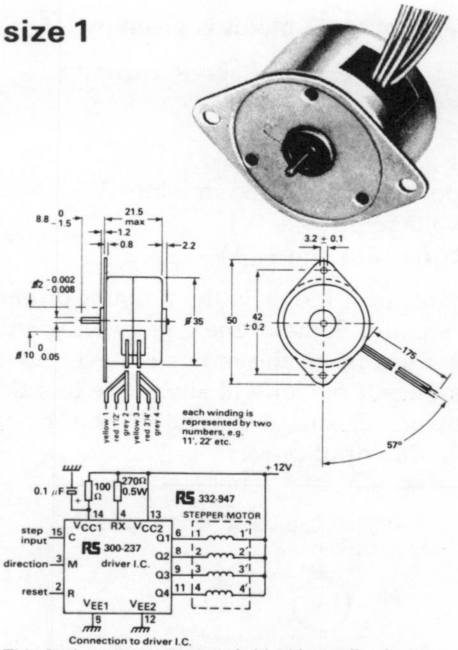

This 4-phase stepper motor is ideal in applications requiring low torque drive and low power consumption. In addition to direct drive applications this motor can be fitted to the **RS** range of synchronous gearboxes, 336–400, etc., to provide reduced step angles and higher torque capability. The output step angle for each gearbox when used with the motor at 7·5°/step is given below. These angles are halved if the motor step angle is halved.

gearbox	*output step angle*	*gearbox*	*output step angle*
332–868	1·8°	336–422	0·06°
336–450	0·6°	336–416	0·03°
336–444	0·3°	336–400	0·03′
336–438	0·15°		

Note: Typical gearbox backlash is 2° and this should be allowed for when positional accuracy is critical.

This motor is supplied with 175 mm long colour-coded double-insulated flying leads.

technical specification

Step angle	7·5°
Step angle tolerance	±40′, non-cumulative
Working torque, max.	6 mNm
Holding torque	10 mNm
Pull-in rate, max.**	350 steps/s
Phase (coil) resistance at 20 °C	120 Ω/phase
Phase (coil) inductance at 200 step/s	160 mH/phase
Current per coil	100 mA
Ambient temperature range	−20 °C to +70 °C
Max. motor temperature	120 °C
Rotor inertia	2·6 g cm²
Nominal voltage	12 V d.c.
Power consumption	2 W

** Max. pull-in rate is the maximum speed at which an unloaded motor can start without losing steps.

Figure 3.92 *Typical specifications of stepper motors*

Power and Torque of Electric Motors

The power input to a motor is given by:

$$\text{power} = \text{voltage} \times \text{current}$$

or

$$P = V \times I$$

where power is measured in watts (W)
voltage in volts (V)
current in amps (A).

The power of a motor is the amount of energy it uses per second. Some of the energy will be used to overcome friction, so the motor is never 100% efficient; the output power will always be less than the input power. Figure 3.93 shows the circuit for measuring the input power.

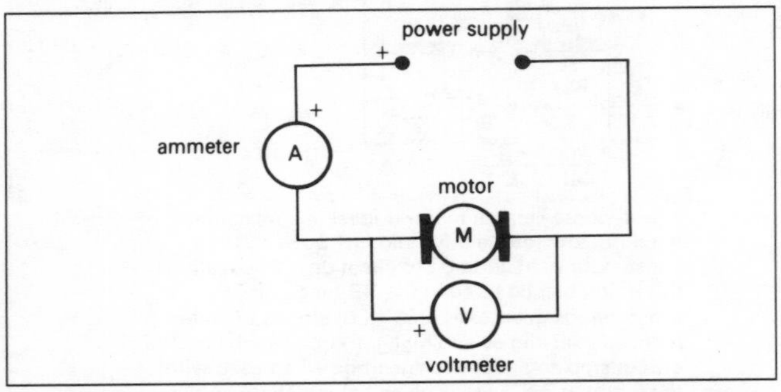

Figure 3.93 *Circuit for measuring the voltage and current for a motor*

The theoretical maximum torque of a motor can be found from:

$$\text{torque} = \text{power} \times \text{time motor is operating}$$

where torque is measured in newton metres (Nm)
time in seconds (s)
power in watts (W)

The torque found from this rule is a theoretical maximum value for a 100% efficient motor. It does not allow for friction or other energy losses. The actual working torque can be found experimentally using newtonmeters or by lifting weights.

The maximum force applied by the teeth of the gear attached to the drive shaft of the motor can be found from:

$$\text{force} = \frac{\text{torque}}{\text{radius of gear}}$$

where force is measured in newtons (N)
gear radius in metres (m)

Measuring the Speed of Motors

The speed of a motor is often needed in design work, and can be found by using a gear train.

Attach a small gear to the motor and match it with a much larger gear on a separate axle. Mark the larger gear with a radius line and time how long the larger gear takes to do, say, ten turns. The motor speed can be worked out from the following relationship:

$$\text{motor speed} = \frac{\text{rotations of larger gear} \times \text{gear ratio}}{\text{time taken for number of rotations}}$$

To increase accuracy for a fast motor the gear train can be extended until the final gear is going slow enough to count the turns.

Solenoids

When electricity is passed through it, a coil of wire can produce a strong magnetic field. A coil with many turns of wire is called a **solenoid**. The magnetic field can be concentrated more in the centre of the solenoid if the wire is wrapped round a core of magnetic material. Steel could be used but this becomes permanently magnetised. In many cases the core must lose its magnetism when the current is switched off. In this case a material called **soft iron** is used. The *soft* refers to the magnetic properties; it is not actually soft to the touch. If the soft iron core is free to slide inside the solenoid then linear motion can be created from the force of the magnetic field (Figure 3.94).

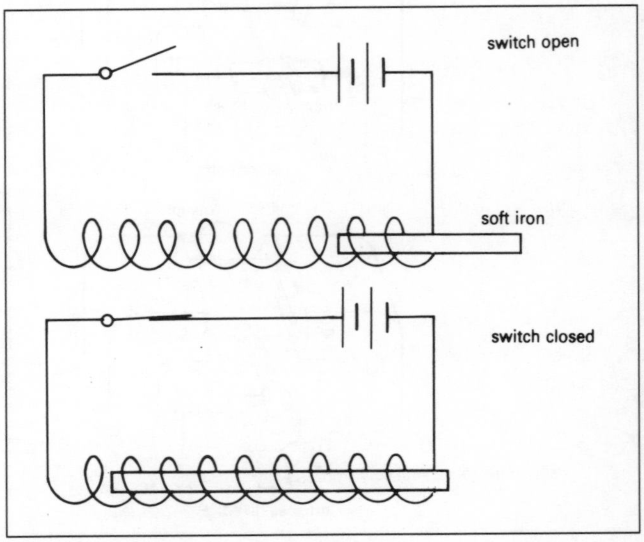

Figure 3.94 *A solenoid and soft iron core*

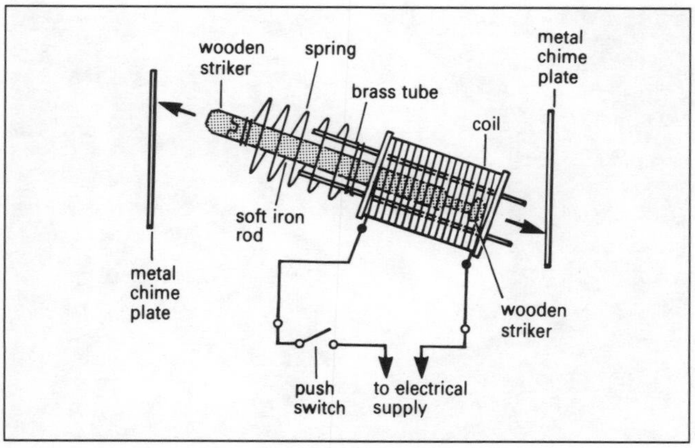

Figure 3.95 *A two-tone door chime*

Solenoids have a variety of uses, a common one being in doorbell chimes. The distinct 'ding-dong' is produced by the soft iron core in a solenoid first moving one way and hitting the first chime then being returned by a spring, to hit the other chime (see Figure 3.95).

Solenoids will be found in switches, car starting circuits and applications where a small linear movement is required from an electrical current. Figure 3.96 shows the solenoid switch in a car's starting circuit. The current drawn by the starter motor can be as high as 300 A. This would quickly burn away the contacts which could be operated by a key. The key is used to turn on a low current through the solenoid which causes the soft iron core to connect the high current circuit. This is an example of a simple relay but in this case it is usually known simply as a solenoid. (Details of relays are given in Section 4:17.)

The force produced by the coil depends on the current passing through it and the number of turns on the coil. The approximate force can be found from:

$$\text{force} = \frac{12.5 \times \text{number of turns} \times (\text{current})^2}{1000}$$

or

$$F = \frac{12.5 \times N \times I^2}{1000}$$

where F is force measured in newtons (N)
N is number of turns on the coil
I is the current measured in amps (A).

To get from a solenoid a force of a reasonable size, a large number of turns and a large current are needed.

Electricity Generators

The link between electricity and magnetism was discovered by a Danish scientist, Hans Oersted, in 1820. Soon afterwards the British scientist Michael Faraday used the link to make an electric motor. While working on this he found that, by moving a coil of wire through a magnetic field, he could produce electricity (see Figure 3.97). This effect forms the basis of the electrical generator.

Whenever a wire passes through a magnetic field electricity is produced. Modern power stations (see Figure 3.98) use this effect to produce electricity, although they have modified the arrangement so that the magnets revolve inside the coil of wire. AC electricity is produced in the power station generator. Such generators are more generally known as alternators.

Electricity is a very convenient form of energy. Its use is so widespread that it is difficult to imagine life without it.

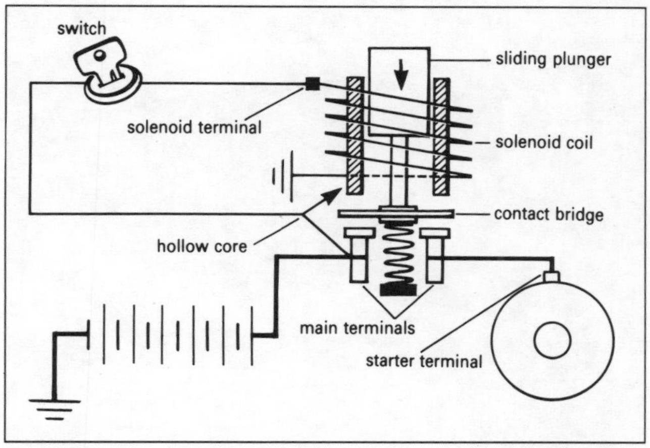

Figure 3.96 *A car solenoid switch*

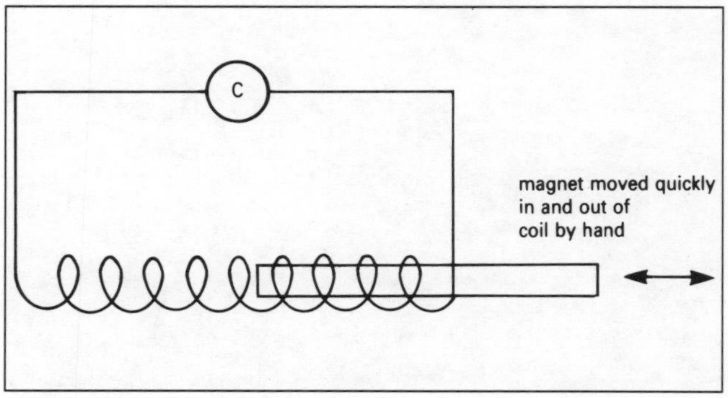

Figure 3.97 *Faraday's coil and magnet experiment*

All motor vehicles require electricity for the lights, fans, windscreen wipers and ignition system. This is supplied by a generator system; the **alternator** or **dynamo** are used and these are run from the engine via the fan belt (see Figure 3.99). The AC output from an alternator is converted to DC using a diode rectifier circuit (Section 4:14).

In most cases, the construction of alternators and dynamos is identical to that of electric motors. The only difference is that in a motor, electricity is used to produce a rotary motion, whereas in a generator rotary motion is used to produce electricity. Generators producing AC have slip rings; those producing DC have brushes and a commutator.

For projects requiring the production of electricity, it is worth considering the bicycle dynamo. Motion is produced by making the wheels of the bicycle rotate. Two types of bicycle dynamo are available, as shown in Figure 3.100.

Figure 3.99 *Driving the alternator from a vehicle engine*

Figure 3.98 *The generator in a power station*

Figure 3.100 *Bicycle dynamos: (a) rubbing against the wheel tyre; (b) mounted in the hub of the wheel*

3:20 PNEUMATIC MECHANISMS

The production of movement using compressed air is called **pneumatics** and pneumatic control mechanisms are widely used in industry (see Figure 3.101). Large forces can be produced to press metal sheets into various shapes or to operate powerful guillotines. The absence of electricity in pneumatic tools makes them ideal in medical treatment; the dentist's drill probably being the best-known example. Many automated factories use pneumatic systems to move components to the next stage of production.

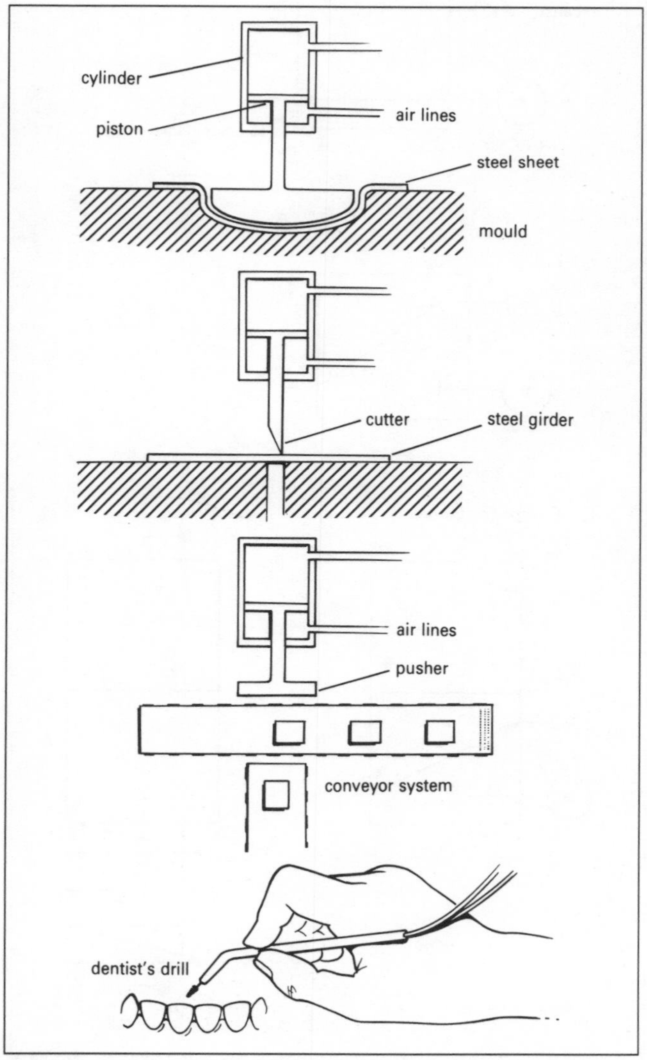

Figure 3.101 *Pneumatic mechanisms in use*

Figure 3.101 *Pneumatic mechanism on a car production line*

Figure 3.102 *(a) Typical compressor*

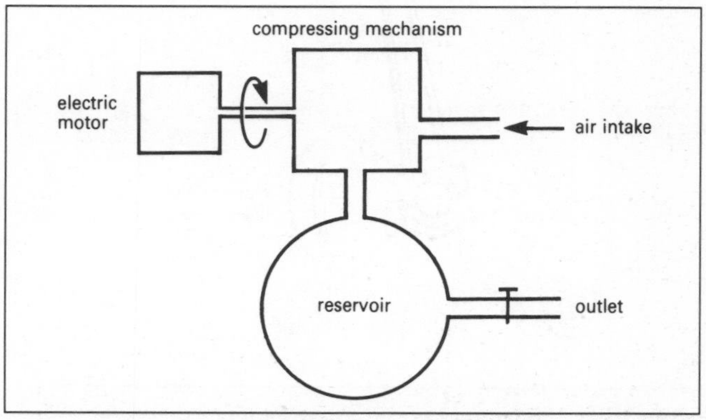

Figure 3.102 *(b) Schematic layout of a compressor*

Producing a Supply of Compressed Air

The supply of compressed air necessary for pneumatic systems is produced by a **compressor**. Compressors vary in design but the basic principle is the same in all of them. Figure 3.102 (page 113) shows a typical compressor.

A single-acting reciprocating compressor consists of an electric motor driving a crank shaft with a piston going up and down in a cylinder which pumps air into a receiver tank. Every time the piston goes up it pushes air past a non-return valve in the tank. This closes as the piston goes down, causing a second valve to open and allow more air to be drawn into the cylinder. As the piston goes up again, air is pushed past the first non-return valve and the cycle repeats itself. Figure 3.103 shows the main parts of a compressor. It is important to remember that, because compressed air produces so much force, it is potentially very dangerous.

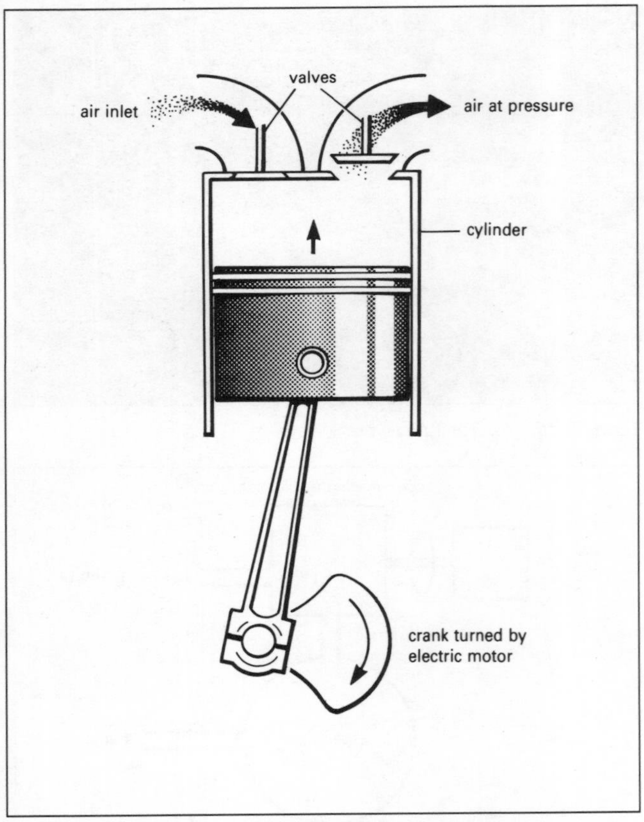

Figure 3.103 *Piston and valves of a single-acting reciprocating compressor*

Pneumatic Equipment Symbols

In designing pneumatic circuits it is inconvenient to draw pictures of all the items of pneumatic equipment to be used, so standard ISO symbols have been drawn up for this purpose. These are shown in Table 3.4. The two halves of the valve symbols show the routes for air flow in the non-operated (off) and operated (on) condition. The symbol is normally drawn showing the off state (Figure 3.104).

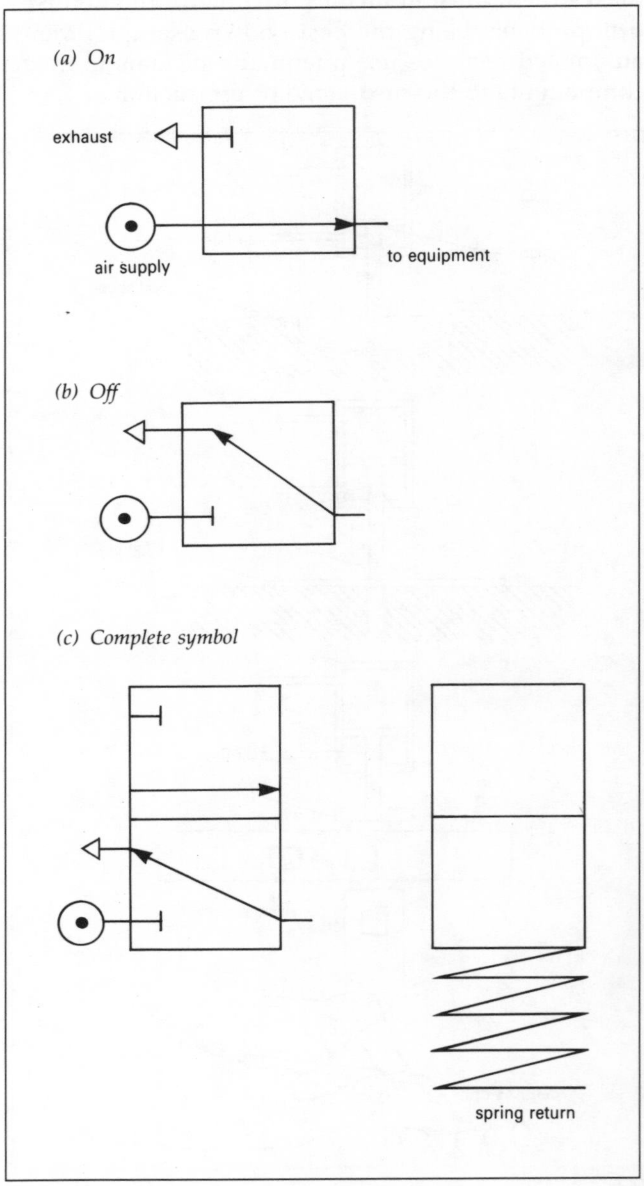

Figure 3.104 *The meaning of ISO valve symbol*

Table 3.4 Pneumatic Symbols

Equipment	*Symbol*
Air supply (compressor)	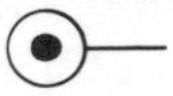
Exhaust	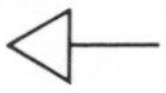
Single-acting cylinder, spring return	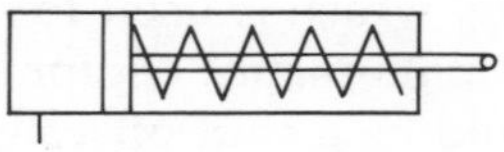
Double-acting cylinder	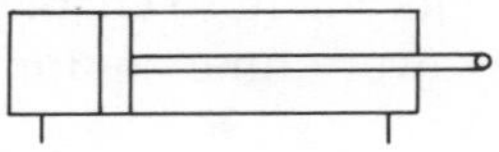
Main air line	
Control air line	
Air line junction	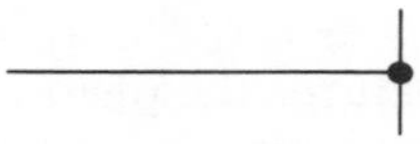
Air lines crossing without connecting	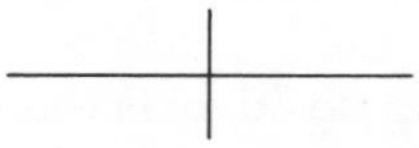
Ball valve (shut-off valve)	
3-port valve, air operated	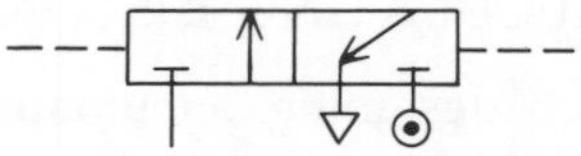
5-port valve, air operated	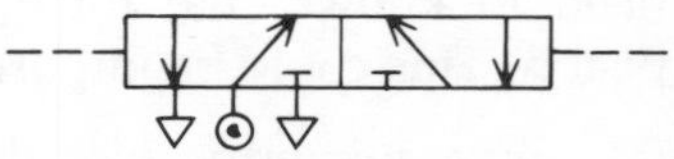
Push-button-operated 3-port valve	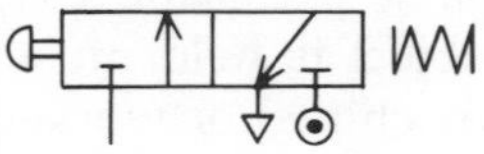
Lever-operated 3-port valve	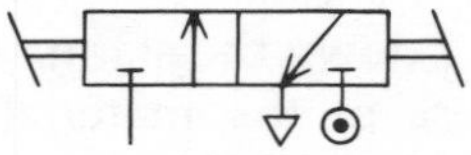
Plunger-operated 3-port valve	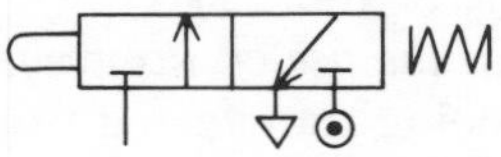
Roller-trip-operated 3-port valve	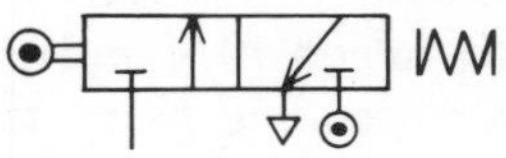
Diaphragm (pressure sensitive) 3-port valve	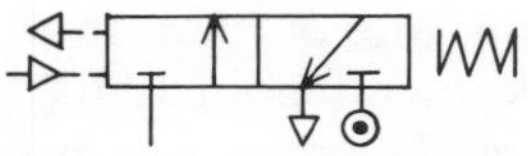

Table 3.4 Pneumatic Symbols (continued)

Equipment	*Symbol*
Solenoid-operated 3-port valve	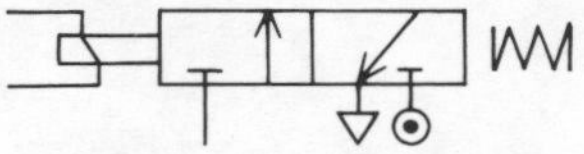
Switch-operated 5-port valve	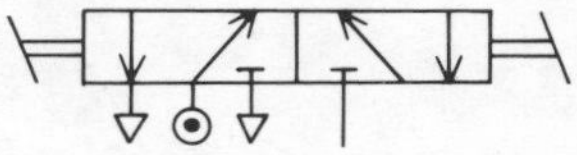
Shuttle valve	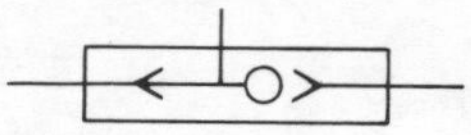
Reservoir	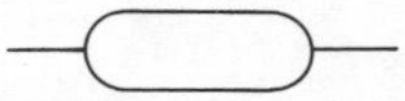
Flow regulator	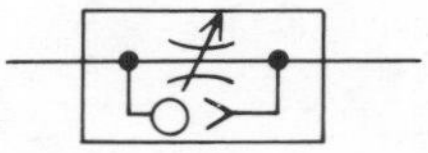
Restrictor	

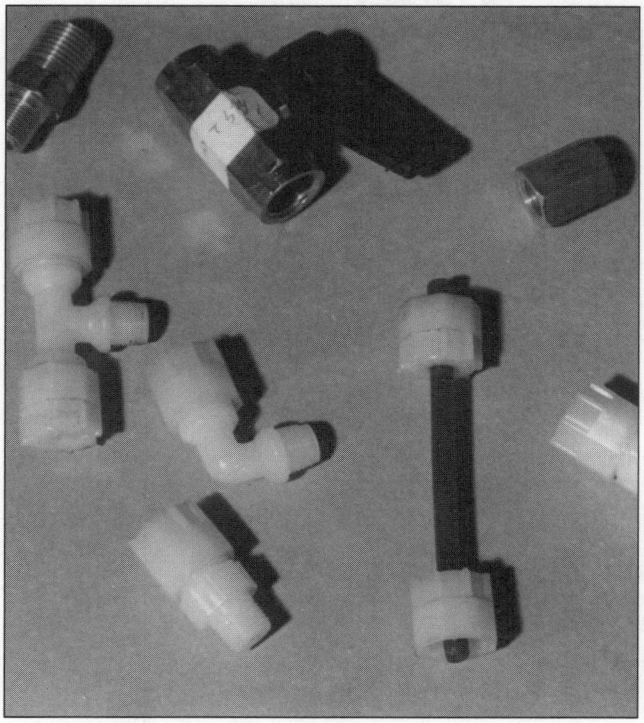

Figure 3.105 *Equipment for connecting pneumatic circuits*

Connecting Pneumatic Circuits

The basic pieces of equipment for connecting pneumatic circuits are shown in Figure 3.105. They include:

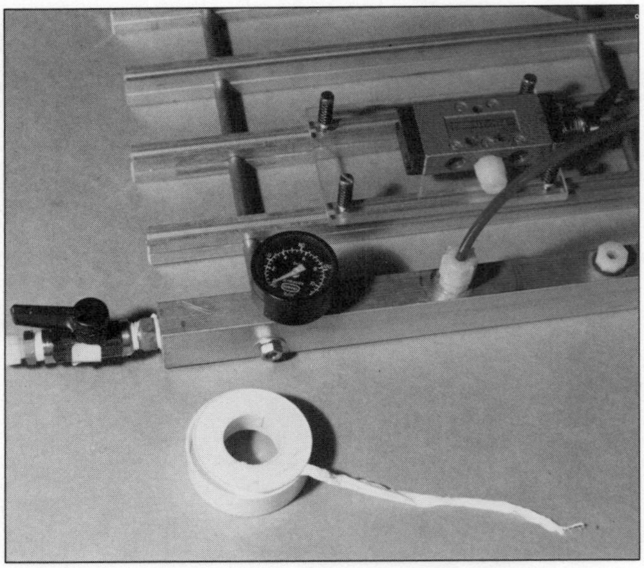

Figure 3.106 *PTFE tape, aluminium track and brackets*

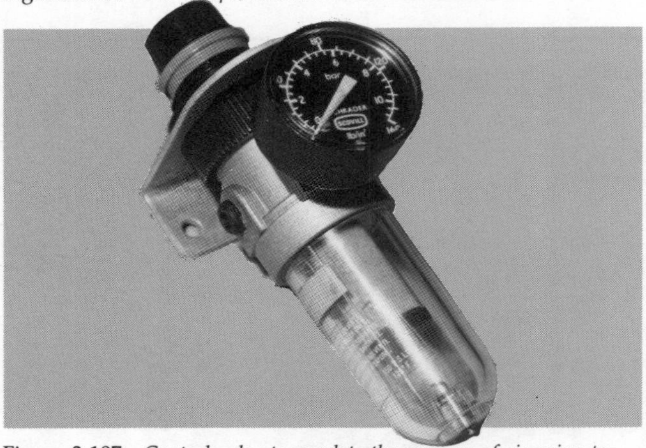

Figure 3.107 *Control valve to regulate the pressure of air going to pneumatic equipment*

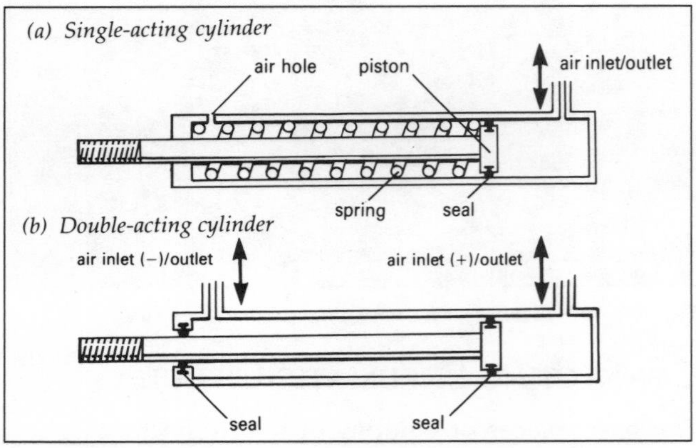

Figure 3.108 *Cylinders*

pipes; straight connectors; T-pieces; cylinder connections; right-angled bends; and ball valves to shut off air supply to small parts of the circuits. Other useful items include PTFE tape for sealing metal-to-metal connections and aluminium section and brackets for mounting pneumatic equipment (see Figure 3.106).

Air can be delivered down a pipe via a **control valve**, which is used to set the required pressure for the pneumatic equipment (Figure 3.107). There should be a shut-off valve between the control valve and equipment to enable the air supply to be shut off easily every time equipment needs to be adjusted.

Producing Movement with Cylinders

Movement in pneumatics is achieved using **cylinders**, which are of two types: single-acting and double-acting (see Figure 3.108). A single-acting cylinder produces a force only on the outward stroke. A spring returns the piston when the air is switched off. A double-acting cylinder produces a force on both strokes.

'Going positive' is the term for outward movement and 'going negative' the term for inward movement of the piston.

Calculating Piston Force

When designing pneumatic mechanisms, engineers need to know what force is to be delivered by a piston. This could be important in various situations:

(a) *on a pneumatic vice* the force with which an object is held must be known before it can be machined or worked (about 500–1000 N)
(b) *for a pneumatic stamping machine* the force pushing down the stamp will depend upon the hardness of the material being stamped (between 10 N and 500 N)
(c) *in the use of a conveyor belt* where containers are being transferred from one conveyor to another: the force to move the containers must be known (between 10 N and 1500 N)
(d) *for operating heavy vehicle brakes and clutches* as these need to be air assisted, the additional force on top of that from the pedals needs to be known (about 100 000 N)
(e) *for closing shop doors* the force to close the door must known (approximately 100–1000 N); excessive force could cause injury.

To calculate this force, the pressure of the air supply together with the piston area is needed for:

$$\text{pressure} = \frac{\text{force}}{\text{area}}$$

or

$$P = F/A$$

where pressure is measured in N/mm^2
force in newtons (N)
area in square millimetres (mm^2)

and it follows that

$$F = P \times A$$

Pistons are generally circular so:

$$\text{piston area} = \pi \times r^2 = \frac{\pi \times d^2}{4}$$

where r = radius of piston in millimetres
d = diameter of piston in millimetres

So the larger the pressure, the greater the force on the piston. Also, the larger the piston area, the greater the force.

Note that the standard unit of pressure in the SI system is the pascal (Pa) where:

$$1\ \text{Pa} = 1\ \text{N/m}^2$$

The cylinders in pneumatics are very small and it is easier to measure the area of them in square millimetres, for:

$$1\ \text{N/m}^2 \times 1\,000\,000\ \text{N/mm}^2$$

An alternative unit for pressure in pneumatics is the bar. Although not strictly accurate ($0.098\ \text{N/mm}^2 = 1$ bar), a usual conversion is:

$$1\ \text{N/mm}^2 = 10\ \text{bar}$$

Controlling Cylinders with Valves

Three-port valves and five-port valves are used to control the movement of cylinders. These can be either the spool or poppet type, as shown in Figure 3.109. The difference between poppet- and spool-operated valves is shown in Figure 3.110.

Note the different way in which air passes through the valves. This is important because poppet valves can only be connected in one way. The different construction of the spool valves allows them to be connected in any one of the three possible combinations, which is useful for pressure-sensitive circuits.

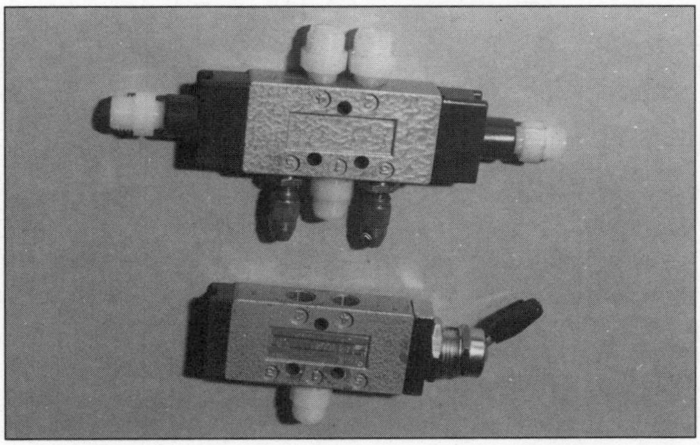

Figure 3.109 *(a) 3-port valves; (b) Two types of 5-port valve*

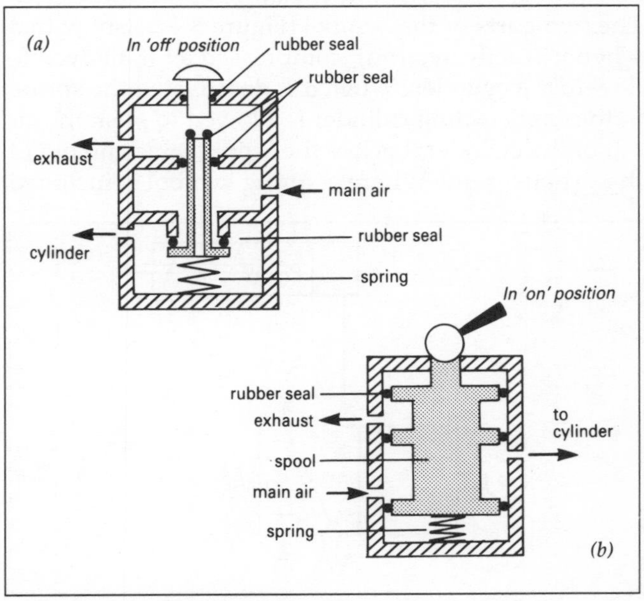

Figure 3.110 *(a) Inside a poppet valve; (b) Inside a spool valve*

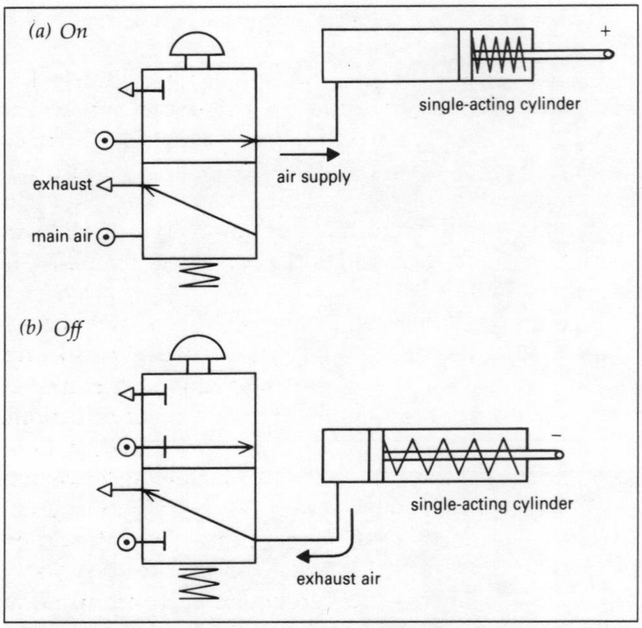

Figure 3.111 *A spring-return symbol on a push-button 3-port valve*

For a single-acting cylinder to work, compressed air must be introduced into the cylinder causing it to go positive. For the cylinder to return, or go negative, the air must be let out. This is the job of the 3-port valve.

Pneumatic components are usually represented by symbols when drawing pneumatic circuits. The symbols for valves show how the air lines are connected. The two parts of the symbol (Figure 3.111) show that when it is activated (on), compressed air is allowed to flow to the cylinder. When it is deactivated the spring in the single-acting cylinder is allowed to push the air out of the cylinder, back to the 3-port valve and out of the exhaust port. Where a spring symbol is included beneath a 3-port valve, it indicates that the valve will be reset by a spring (a 'spring return') after being activated (see Figure 3.111). Push-button, plunger and roller trip valves always do this whereas switch and solenoid valves will not.

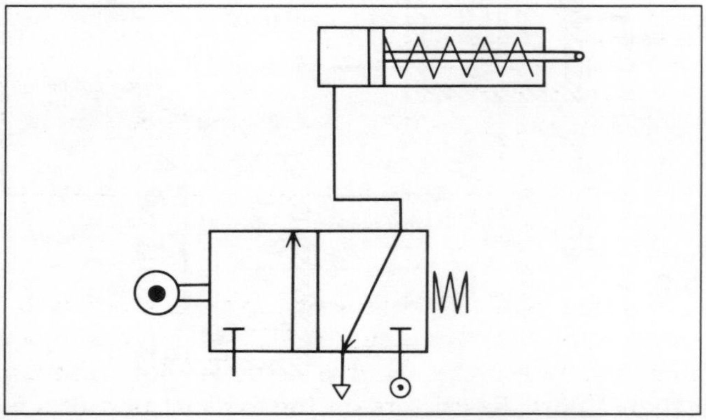

Figure 3.112 *A 3-port valve operating a single-acting cylinder*

Figure 3.112 shows a simple circuit in which a roller trip 3-port valve makes a single-acting cylinder go positive and illustrates how symbols are used.

If a double-acting cylinder replaces the single-acting one the circuit will not work. A double-acting cylinder needs compressed air to make the cylinder go negative. Another 3-port valve is needed and both must be spring-return types for the cylinder to work, otherwise air cannot escape through either of the 3-port valves (see Figure 3.113). However, both 3-port valves can be replaced by one 5-port valve. This allows air to pass into one part of the cylinder and, at the same time, allows air to pass out of the exhaust port from the other part of the cylinder (see Figure 3.114).

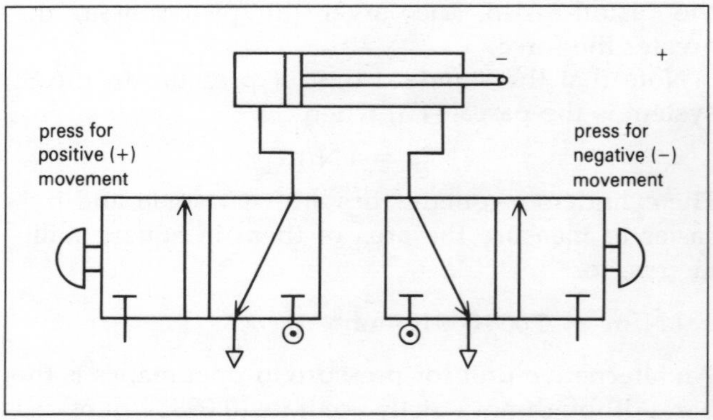

Figure 3.113 *Two spring-return 3-port valves operating a double-acting cylinder*

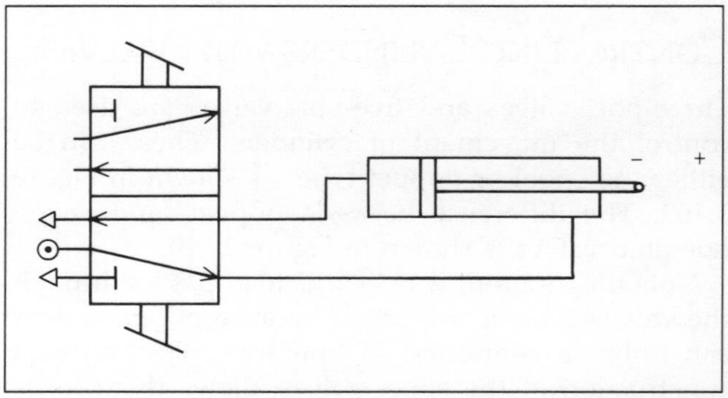

Figure 3.114 *Lever-operated 5-port valve operating a double-acting cylinder*

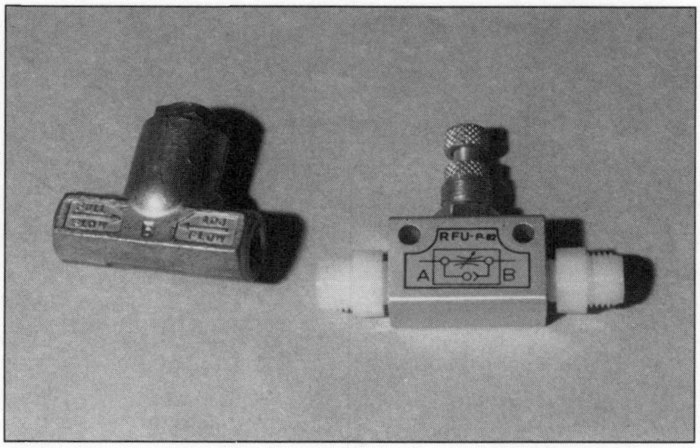

Figure 3.115 *A flow regulator*

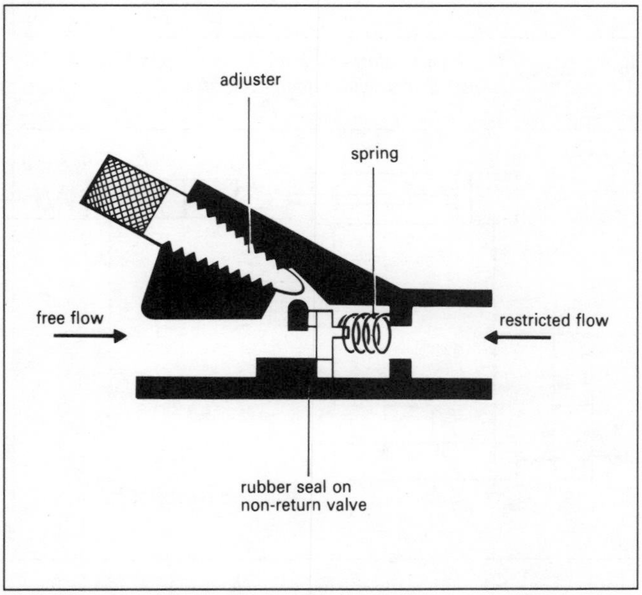

Figure 3.116 *Construction of a flow regulator*

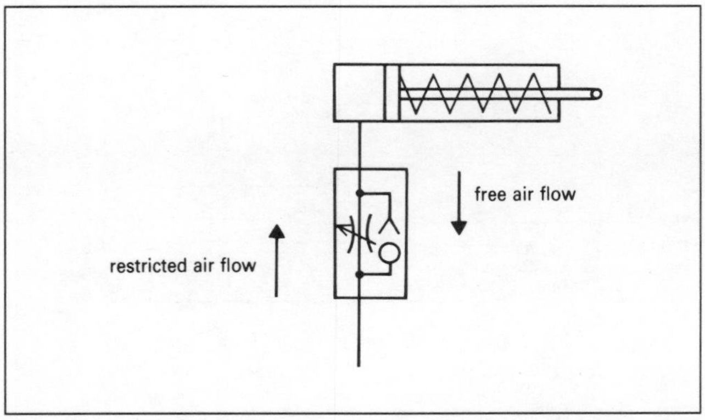

Figure 3.117 *A flow regulator governing the speed of outstroke of a single-acting cylinder*

Controlling Piston Speeds

If compressed air is introduced into a cylinder, the piston will move very quickly. This rapid movement is not always desirable and to vary the speed of piston travel, a **flow regulator** is introduced into the system (see Figure 3.115). This allows air to pass at a controlled rate in one direction and uncontrolled in the other. The construction of a flow regulator is shown in Figure 3.116.

The rate at which the flow regulator allows the air to pass can be varied, so that pressure builds up gradually behind the piston and the piston movement is smoother (see Figure 3.117). If both directions of piston movement need to be controlled, a flow regulator is required on both the supply and exhaust lines. For a single-acting cylinder, both flow regulators are included on the main air line. Care should be taken that they are mounted in opposite directions. Figure 3.118 shows flow regulators being used to control going positive and negative on single- and double-acting cylinders.

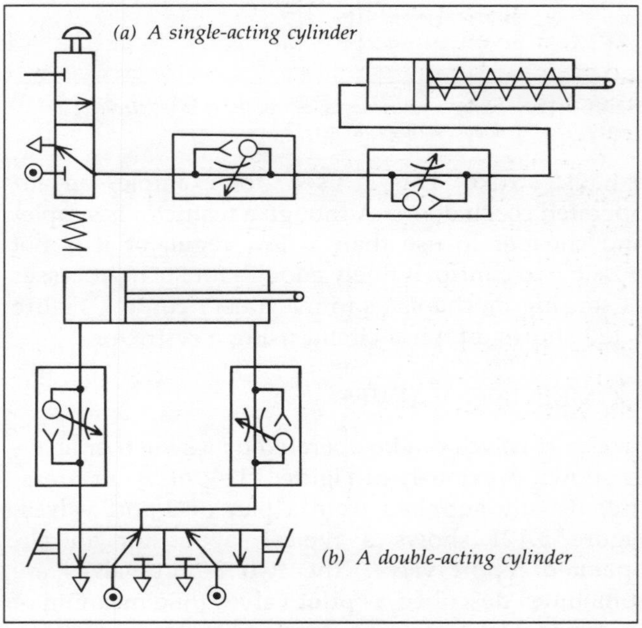

Figure 3.118 *Flow regulators controlling the stroke of a cylinder*

Another way of varying the piston speed is by using a restrictor (see Figure 3.119). This is simpler than a flow regulator and restricts air flow from an exhaust port. Restrictors on the exhaust port of a 5-port valve can be used to slow down motion on the

Figure 3.119 *A restrictor*

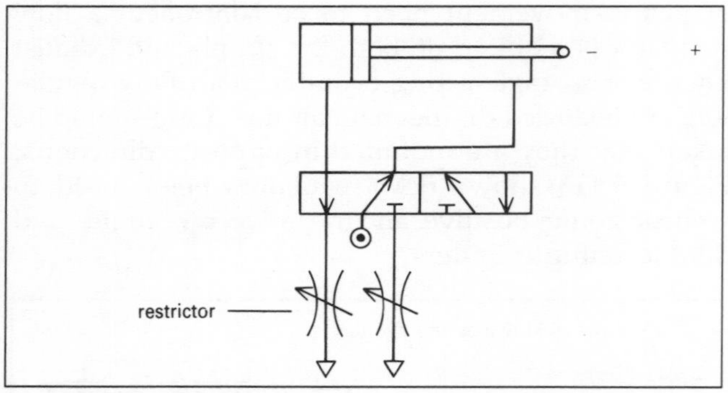

Figure 3.120 *Using a restrictor to control the exhaust stroke of a double-acting cylinder*

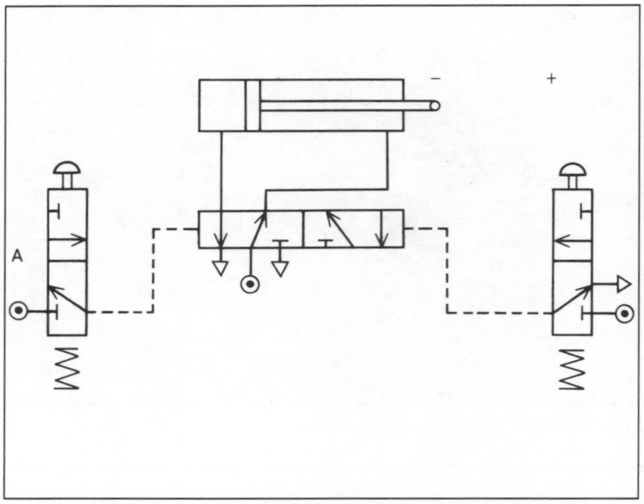

Figure 3.121 *Two 3-port valves operating a 5-port control valve connected to a double-acting cylinder*

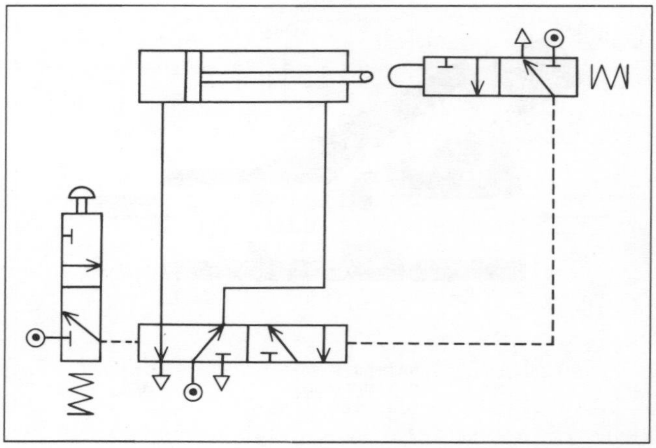

Figure 3.122 *Semi-automatic reset of a double-acting cylinder*

Figure 3.123 *A shuttle valve*

exhaust stroke. This is used, for example, on air-operated coach doors. Although a restrictor is simpler and cheaper to use than a flow regulator it is not possible to control it finely enough for such processes as sensing mechanisms in machinery control. Figure 3.120 shows a typical circuit using a restrictor.

Combining Valves

Five-port valves can be operated by a switch or lever, as shown previously in Figure 3.114, or by air pressure, usually supplied from a pair of 3-port valves. Figure 3.121 shows a typical layout for an air-operated 5-port valve. The two 3-port valves are sometimes described as **pilot valves** (one meaning of the word *pilot* is to act as starter to larger apparatus).

When pilot valve A is activated, it causes the 5-port valve to be activated, making the double-acting piston go positive. To make the double-acting piston go negative, the pilot 3-port valve B is activated. It is important that both 3-port valves are spring return types, such as push button or roller trip, or the circuit will not work; each pilot 3-port valve must return to

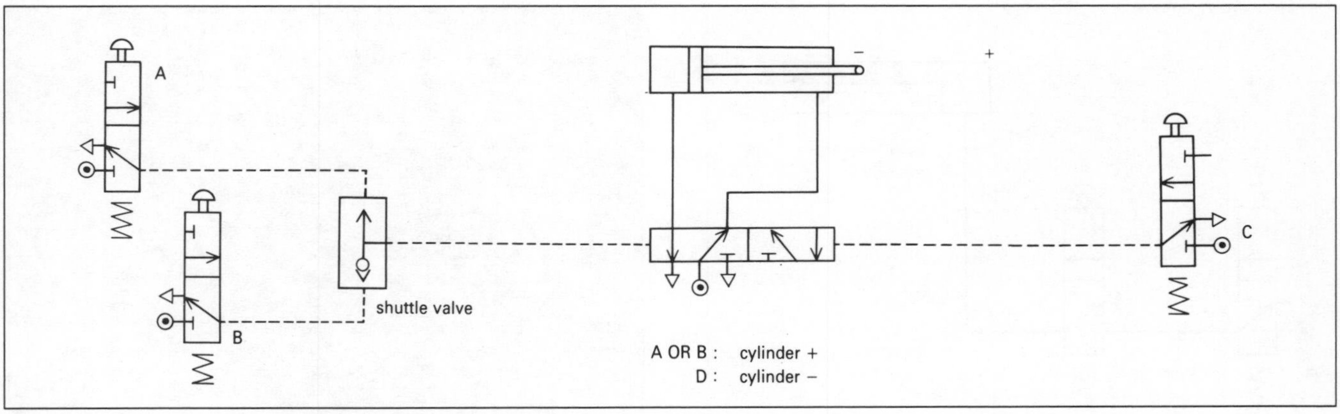

Figure 3.124 *Using a shuttle valve in the control of a piston*

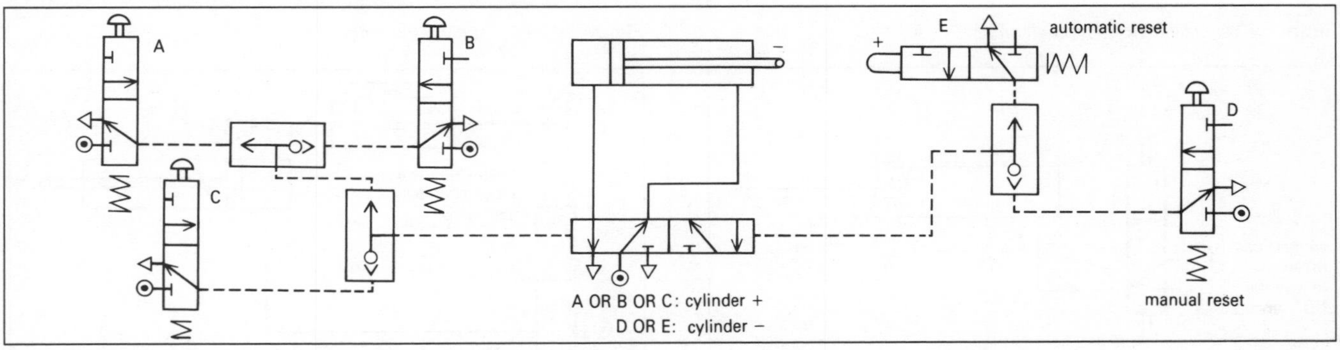

Figure 3.125 *3-port valves operating a 5-port control valve with both semi-automatic and manual reset*

its deactivated position. The pilot valves are connected to the 5-port control valve by a **control line**. This is distinct from the main air line which connects a valve to a cylinder. Figure 3.122 demonstrates how the circuit can be developed further by allowing the piston going positive to hit the reset valve B, making the cylinder go negative. This is a semi-automatic circuit.

The circuit can be modified further so that two 3-port pilot valves instead of one will cause the cylinder to go positive. This requires the use of a shuttle valve (see Figure 3.123). Figure 3.124 shows the use of the shuttle valve. Pilot valve A or B will make the piston go positive; pilot valve C will make the piston go negative. For every extra pilot valve, another shuttle valve is needed (Figure 3.125).

A fully **automatic circuit** can be achieved by arranging the double-acting cylinder to hit pilot valves on both its outward (+) and inward (−) movements, as in Figure 3.126, so that the double-acting cylinder reciprocates continuously.

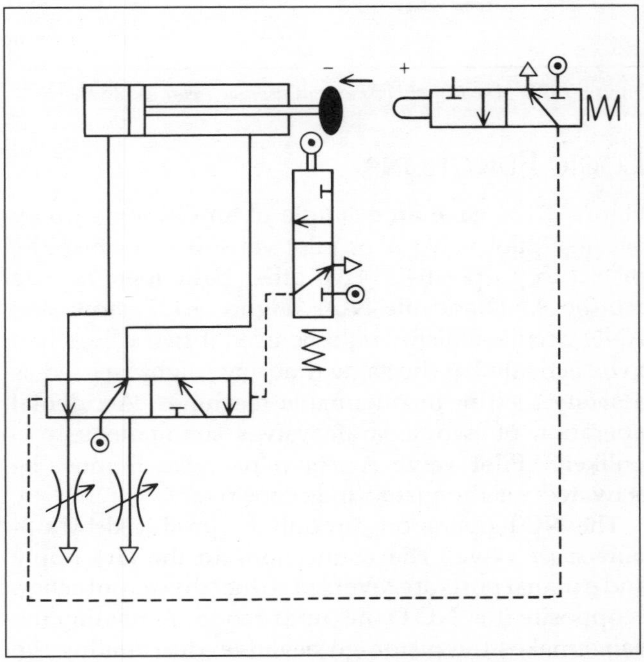

Figure 3.126 *Full automatic control giving reciprocating motion of a double-acting cylinder*

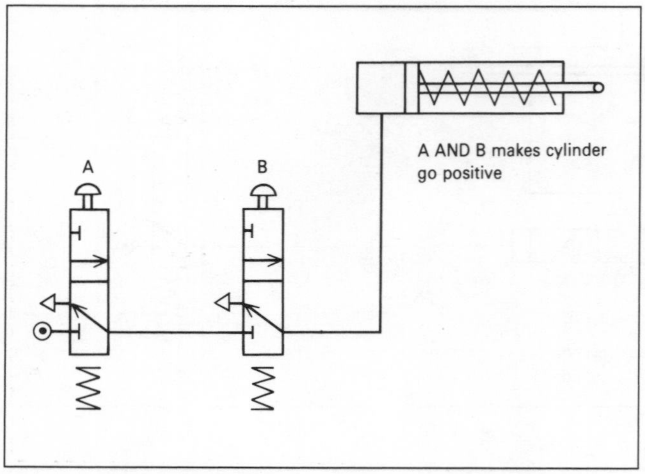

Figure 3.127 *The logical AND circuit*

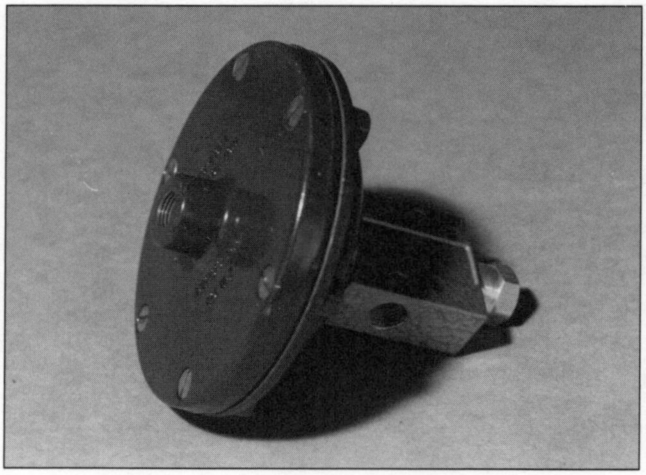
Figure 3.129 *A diaphragm valve*

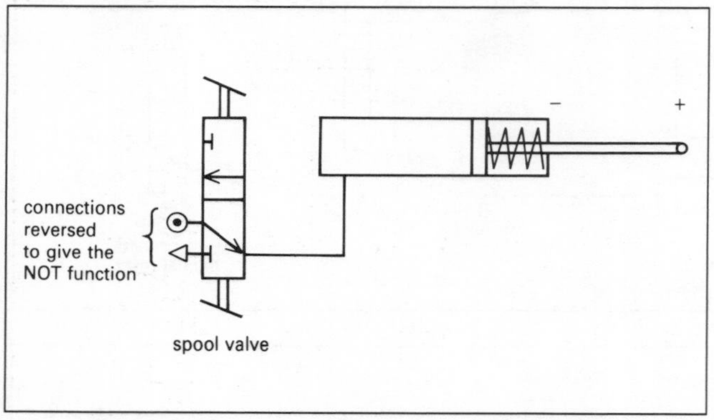

Figure 3.128 *The logical NOT circuit using a 3-port spool valve*

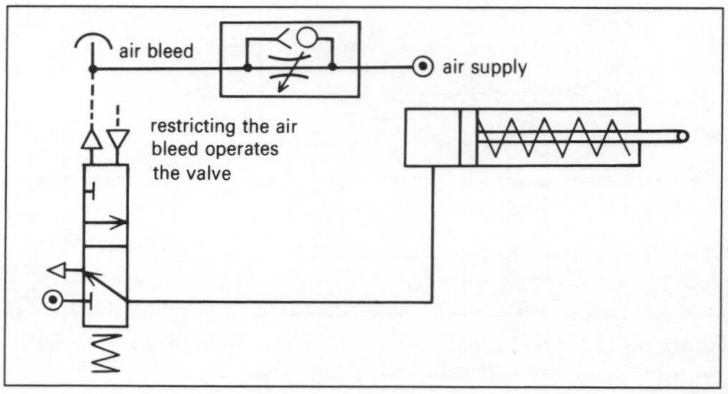

Figure 3.130 *An air-bleed circuit*

Logic Functions

Figure 3.124 gave an example of an OR logic circuit because pilot valve A or pilot valve B will cause the piston to go positive. Two other basic logic circuits are the AND and the NOT. Figure 3.127 shows the AND circuit, which would be used if two valves had to be activated at the same time and might be used as a safety feature in pneumatic machines. Accidental operation of two separate valves simultaneously is unlikely. Pilot valve A *and* pilot valve B must be activated for the piston to go positive.

The NOT operation can only be produced by a 3-port *spool* valve. The connections to the air supply and exhaust ports are reversed so that the output action is opposite (i.e. NOT) the input action. Activating the valve makes the piston go negative; deactivating the valve makes the piston go positive. The poppet valves do not allow the connections to be reversed.

Other Valves

A diaphragm valve is a 3-port valve operated by a change in air pressure (Figure 3.129).

There are the usual three connections – main air supply, exhaust and main air to the piston – as with all 3-port valves. In addition, there are two other connections. One is connected to the air supply, and the other to an open pipe, so that air is continuously bleeding away. This is an **air bleed system**, a typical layout of which is shown in Figure 3.130. If the rate of air bleed is reduced by an object near the end of the pipe, air pressure builds up quickly and the diaphragm valve is activated. The circuit is therefore very useful for detecting moving objects. However, such circuits waste a lot of compressed air even when the bleed air is reduced by including a flow regulator.

The diaphragm valve can also be used in a pressure-sensing circuit, the layout of which is shown in Figure 3.131.

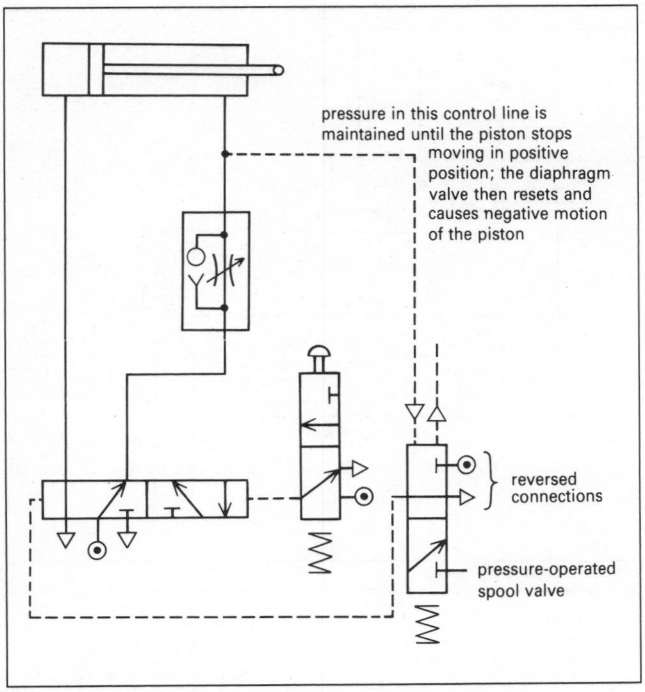

Figure 3.131 *A pressure-sensing circuit*

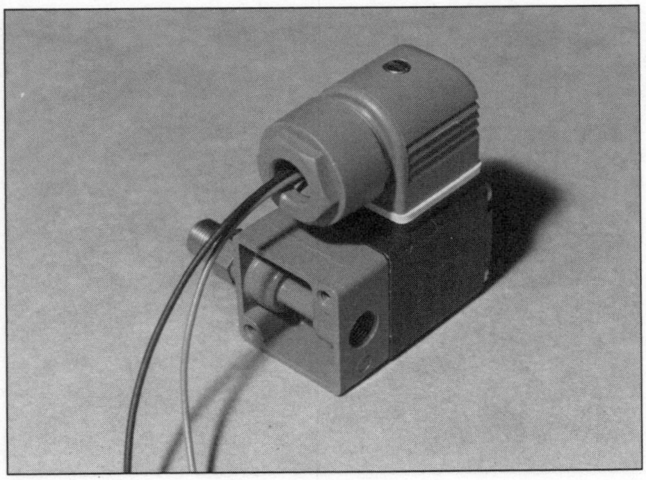

Figure 3.132 *A solenoid valve*

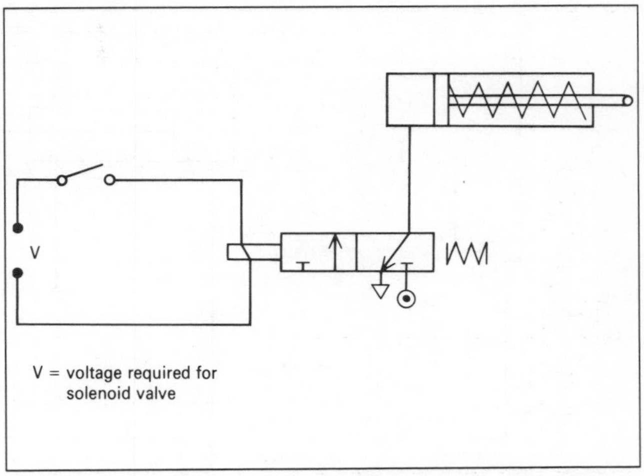

Figure 3.133 *A 3-port solenoid valve operating a single-acting cylinder*

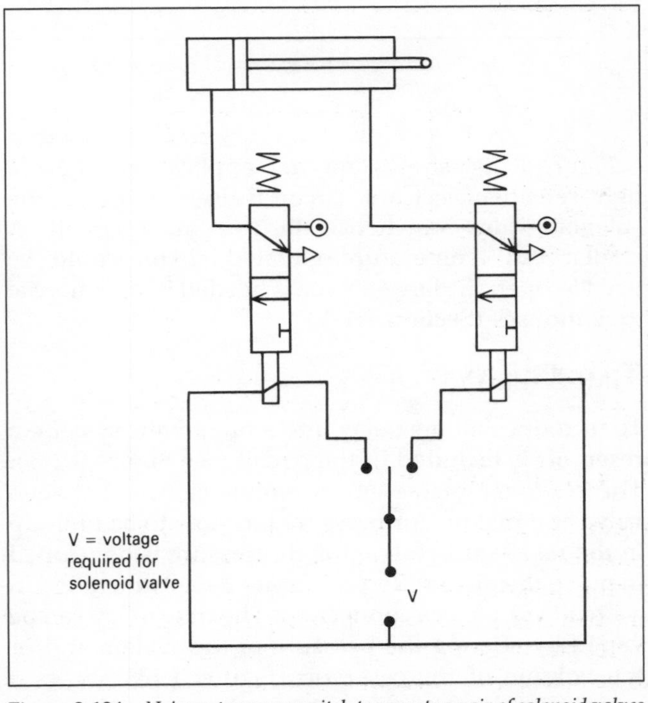

Figure 3.134 *Using a two-way switch to operate a pair of solenoid valves*

Any of the 3-port valves in previous circuit diagrams, with the exception of the diaphragm valves, could have been replaced by the solenoid valves. In Figure 3.134 a two-way switch is used to operate either of a pair of solenoid valves. The double-acting cylinder will then go both positive and negative from one switch. Automatic control of a pair of 3-port solenoid valves can be achieved using microswitches (see Figure 3.135).

The link between electrical systems and pneumatics is provided by the solenoid valve. Figure 3.132 shows a solenoid valve. It is operated by passing an electric current through a coil causing an iron bar inside the coil to move which activates the valve (Section 3:19). An electrical signal can be provided by a switch or an electronic circuit (see Figure 3.133).

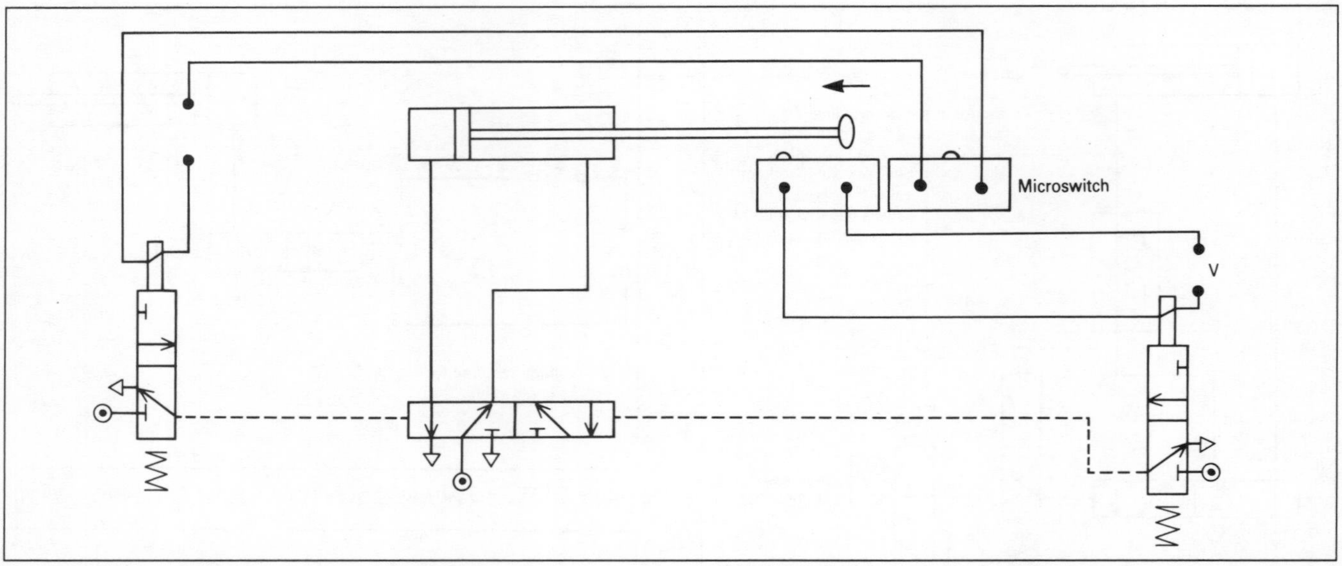

Figure 3.135 *Full automatic control of solenoid valves using microswitches*

Figure 3.136 shows another application where a light-sensitive electronic circuit is used to operate the solenoid valve and hence the pneumatic circuit. A similar but temperature-operated circuit could be used to open the large air vents needed in commercial greenhouses (Section 4:17).

Time Delays

To introduce a time delay into a pneumatic system, a **reservoir** is included in the circuit (see Figure 3.137). The reservoir increases the volume of air between valve and piston. Air pressure has now to be built up in the reservoir before enough pressure is developed to move the piston. Reservoirs are usually included in a circuit via T-piece connectors. The time delay can be varied by altering the pressure of the system and/or the volume of the reservoir. Figure 3.138 shows a simple circuit.

A flow regulator and a reservoir can be used to provide automatic reset of a double-acting piston. A 3-port valve operates a 5-port pressure-operated valve which makes a double-acting piston go positive (Figure 3.139). The air line making the piston go positive is connected, via a flow regulator and reservoir, to the second control input of the 5-port valve. After a time, set by the regulator and size of reservoir, enough pressure builds up to operate the 5-port valve and the piston goes negative.

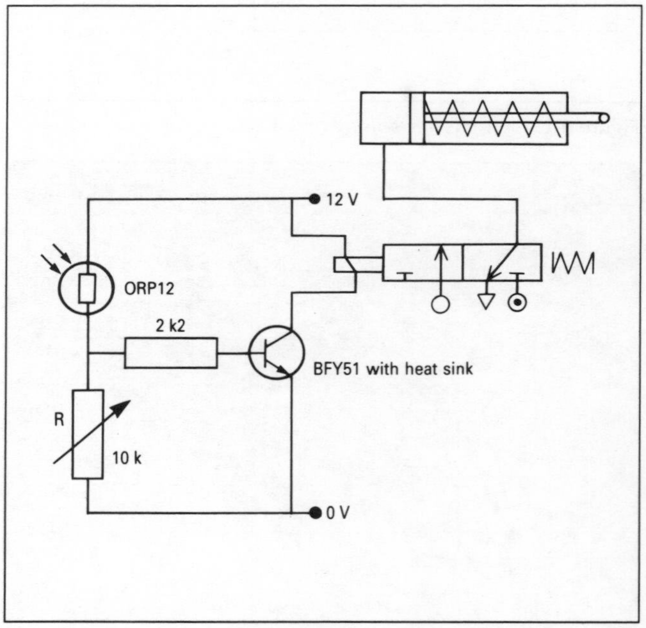

Figure 3.136 *A light-operated pneumatic circuit (see Figure 4.60 for use of relay if solenoid valve operating voltage is not suitable for direct connection)*

If the 3-port valve is replaced by a similar regulator and reservoir circuit connected to the second air line to the cylinder, a fully automatic reciprocating motion of the piston can then be produced. This could be used in the design of wear-testing machines used for carpets and fabrics. The rate of movement of the piston can be controlled with the flow regulators.

Pulse Circuits

Reservoirs can be used to give a pulse of compressed air to a circuit (see Figure 3.140). The 3-port valve in the diagram is connected differently from other circuits. The air supply is connected to the exhaust port, the reservoir to the cylinder port and the circuit to receive the pulse is connected to the main air port. Such connections are only possible with spool valves as the main air supply connected this way on a poppet valve would force the valve open continually. Reference to the valve constructions will show this (see Figure 3.110). The air stored in the reservoir can be used to operate a pressure operated valve but avoids the possibility of the pilot signal being held on.

Figure 3.137 *A reservoir*

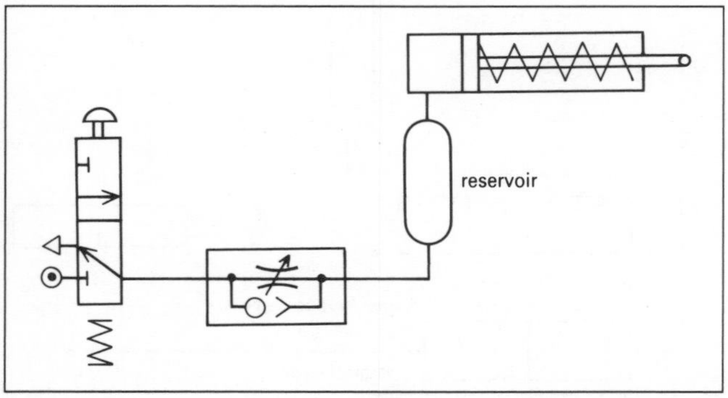

Figure 3.138 *Using a reservoir to introduce a time delay into a circuit*

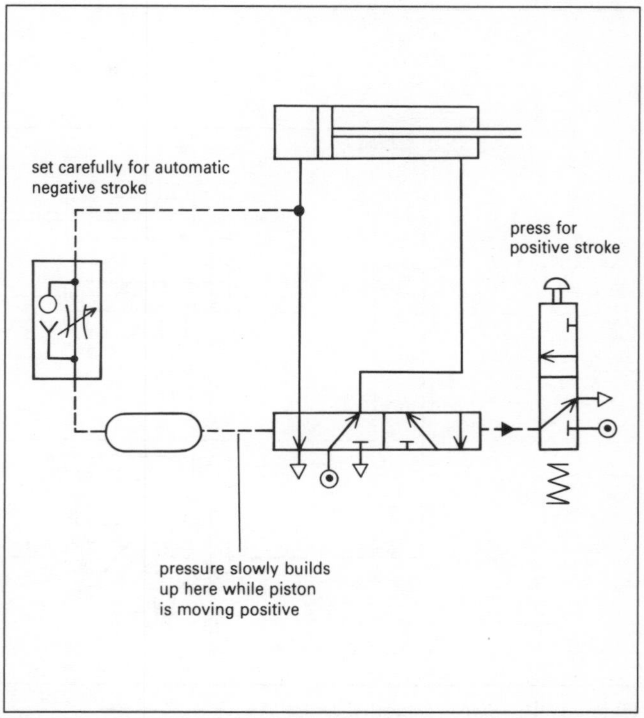

Figure 3.139 *Automatic reset using a flow regulator and a reservoir*

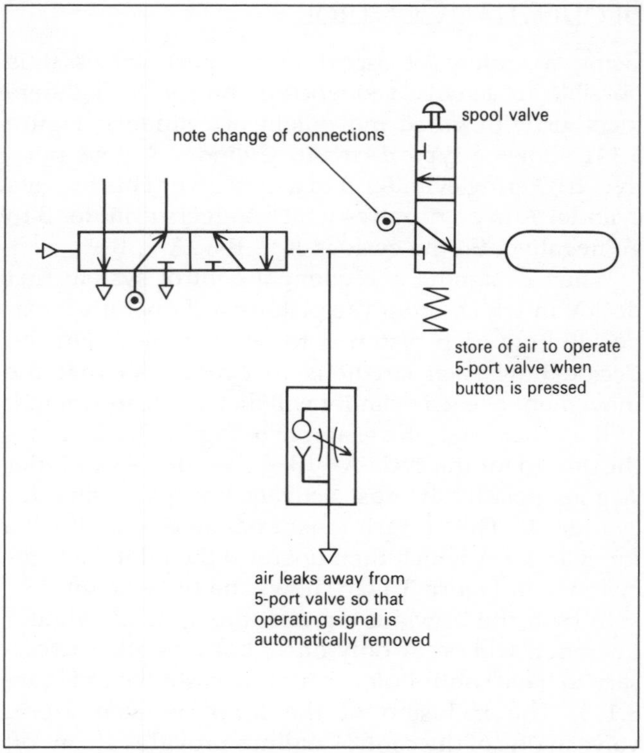

Figure 3.140 *Circuit for pulses of compressed air*

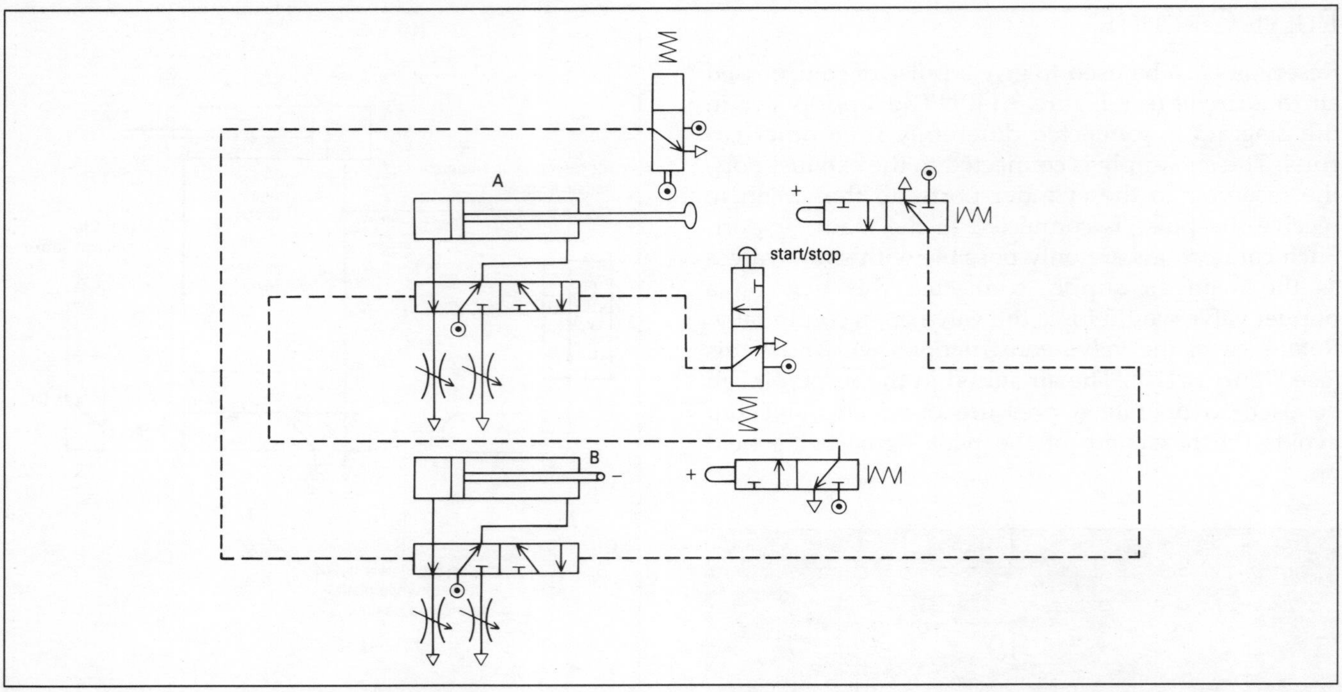

Figure 3.141 *Simple sequential control A+, B +, A−, B−*

SEQUENTIAL CONTROL

Using a variety of 3-port and 5-port valves it is possible to achieve sequencing control of cylinders together with timed movement of cylinders. Figure 3.141 shows a typical circuit. Cylinder A goes positive, triggering cylinder B to go positive. This triggers cylinder A to go negative which triggers cylinder B to go negative. So the cycle is A+, B+, A−, B−.

When designing a sequential control system first decide in which order the pistons will operate. Next, decide how each piston is to be controlled. Finally, decide how each circuit is to overlap so that the movement of each cylinder will dictate the movement of the other one. The example in Figure 3.142 shows the design for the cycle A+, B−, A−, B+. As cylinder A goes positive it must activate the reset valve for cylinder B. This in turn must operate the reset valve for cylinder A which then operates the pilot valve for cylinder B. Figure 3.142c shows the final circuit.

In both the previous circuits, the cycle of cylinder operation will occur only once, but it is often necessary to have continuous operation as shown in Figure 3.143. The inclusion of the lever-operated 3-port valve in one of the control air lines provides an on–off facility.

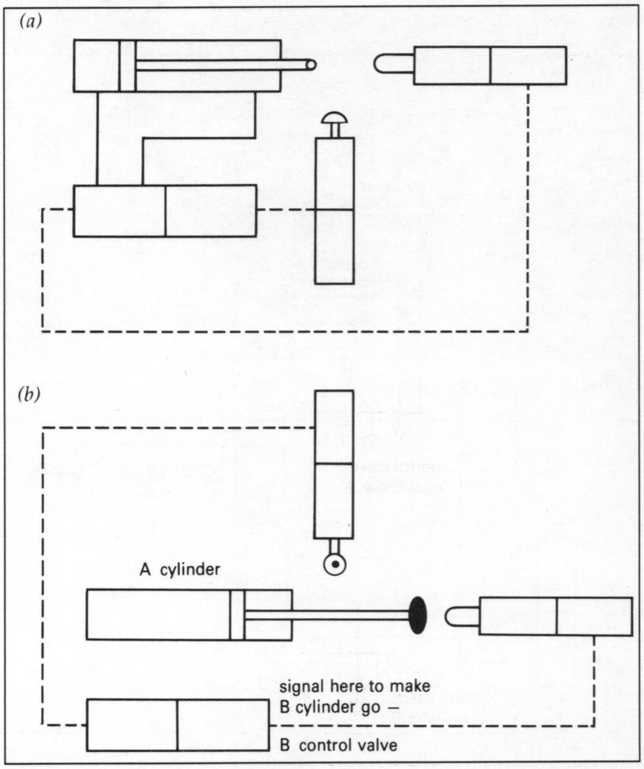

Figure 3.142 *(a) Controlling cylinder A; (b) Controlling cylinder B*

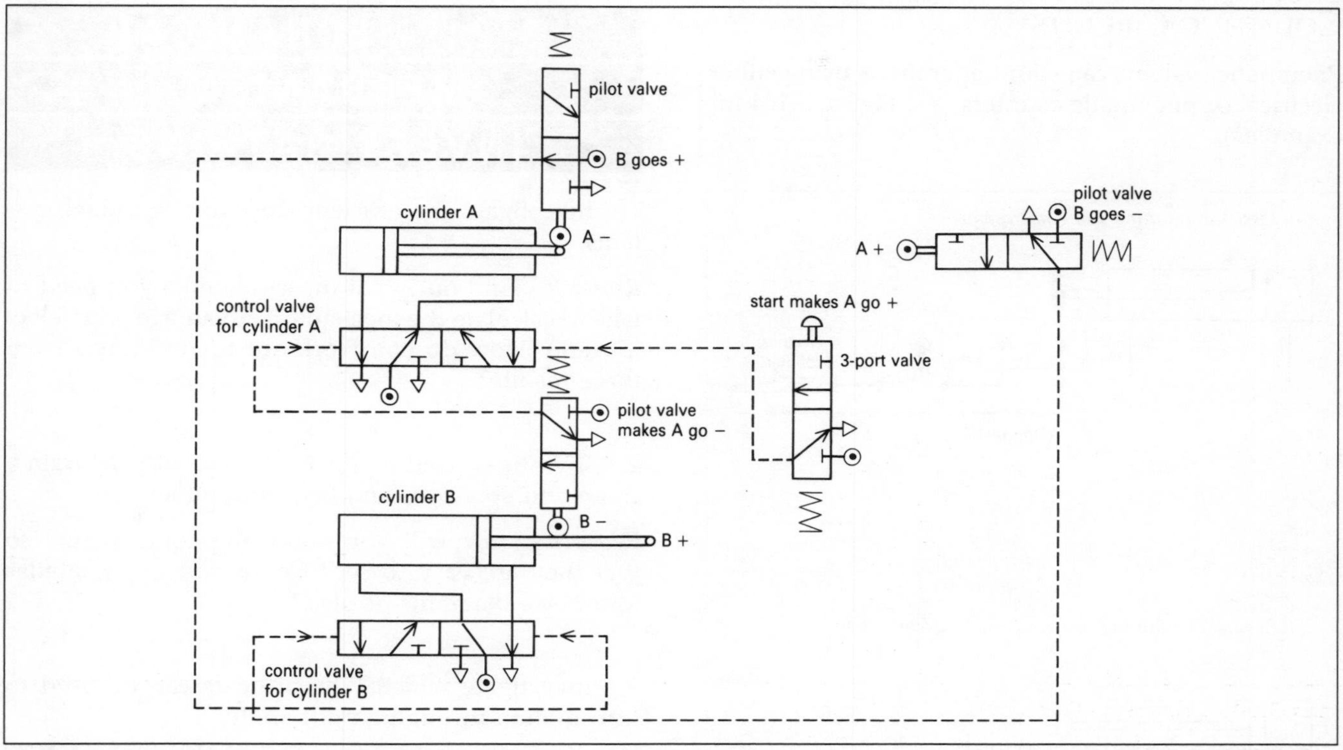

Figure 3.142 *(c) Sequential control A+, B−, A−, B+*

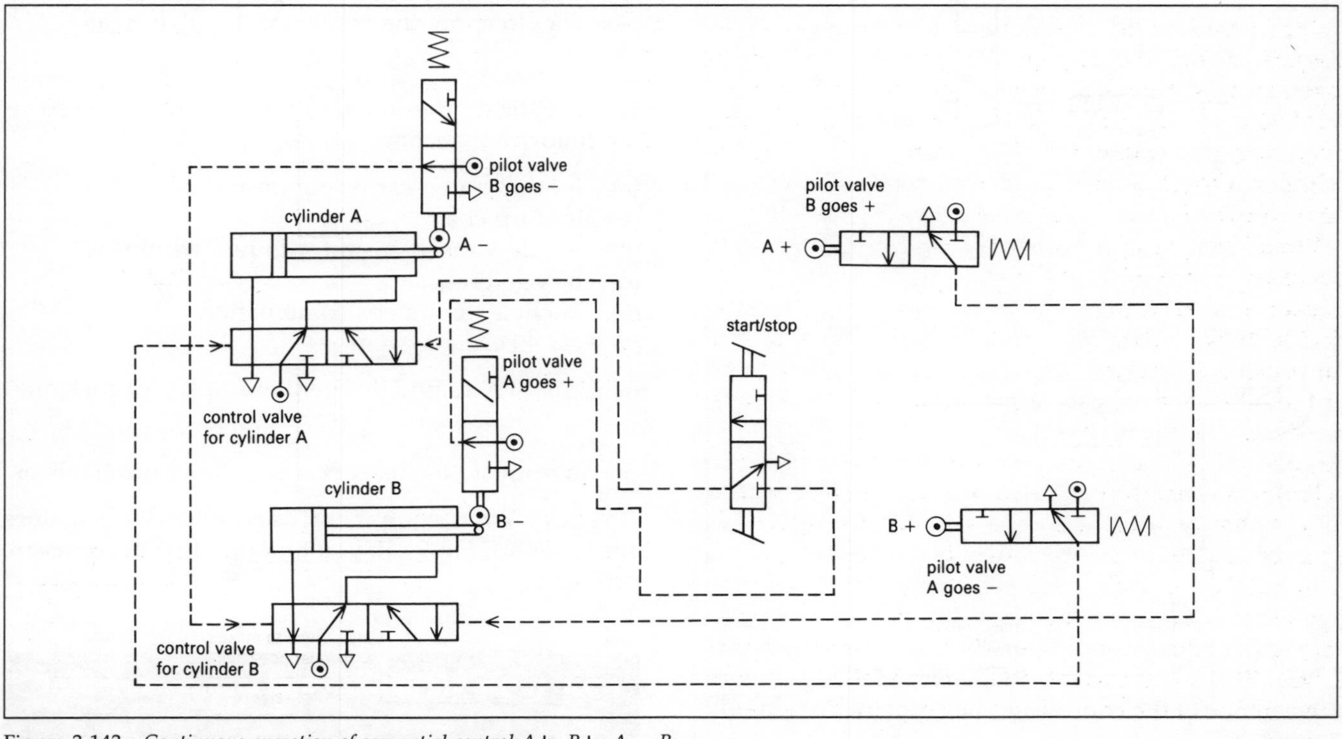

Figure 3.143 *Continuous operation of sequential control A+, B+, A−, B−*

Counting Circuits

Pneumatic systems can count operations using either electrical or pneumatic counters (see Figure 3.144 for examples).

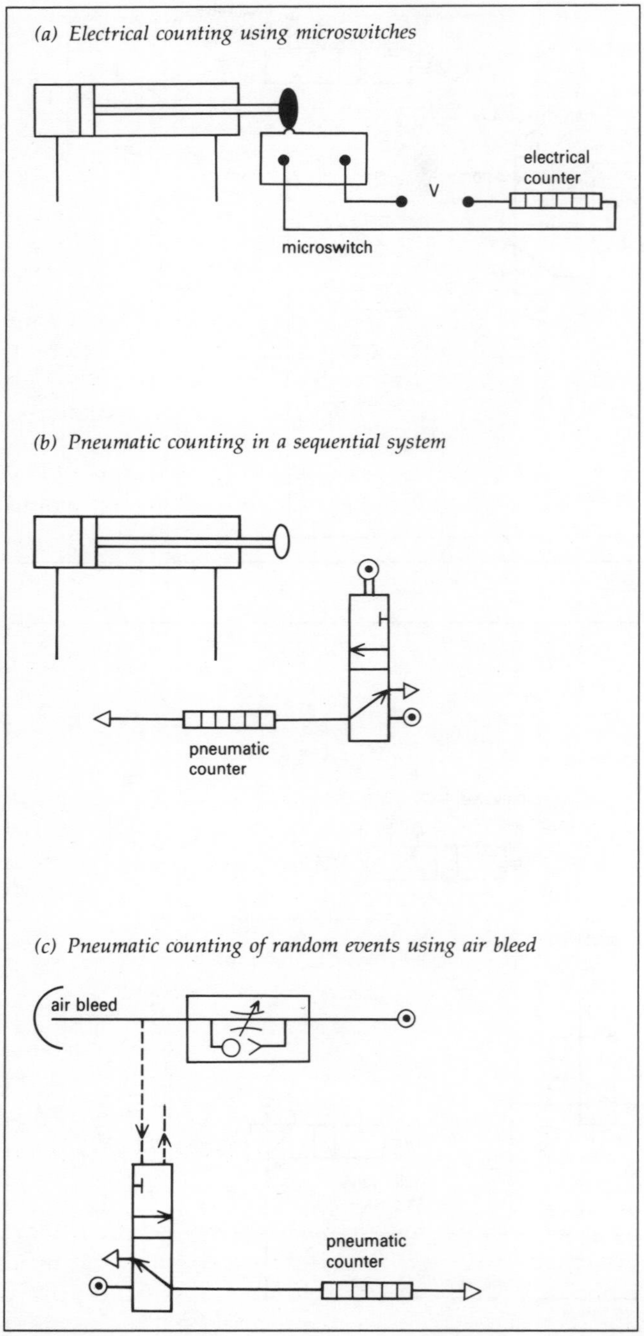

Figure 3.144 *Operating counters*

3:21 MECHANICAL MECHANISM INVESTIGATIONS

1. Investigate the efficiency of various pulley systems.

Research Find out what measurements you need to take to calculate the mechanical advantage and velocity ratio. How do you work out the efficiency from these results?

2. Investigate and compare the use of gear trains, chain and sprockets and belts and pulleys.

Research How will you show the comparisons so that they are easy to see? Could you use a tabular form? Are diagrams needed?

3. Investigate which type of gears can be used to turn motion through a right angle.

Research What is a right angle? Which type of gears can turn motion through a right angle? What is the best way to show the results of the investigation?

4. Investigate the linkages which could be used in the following mechanisms:

(a) foot-operated car tyre pump
(b) fold-up chair
(c) window mechanism for louvre windows
(d) bicycle brakes
(e) kitchen stool/steps combination
(f) car steering system.

Research Try to find different examples for each one.

5. Investigate the use of cams in timer mechanisms.

Research What equipment uses timers? What does the timer do? How can you find out how the cams are arranged?

Safety: Do not poke around in mains-operated equipment.

6. Investigate the use of ratchet and pawl mechanisms in clocks by building a model clock.

Research Clock makers have used ratchet and pawl mechanisms for hundreds of years. What part of the clock needs this mechanism? What is the time of swing of a pendulum 1 metre long? How is the motion of the ratchet altered to give an accurate time?

7. 'Couplings are an important part of many mechanisms.' Investigate the truth of this statement.

Research What is a coupling? Why are they needed? Are they essential to the operation of mechanisms? How will you illustrate the results of your investigations?

8. 'The crank and slider mechanism played an essential part in the industrial revolution.' Investigate this statement.

Research What was the industrial revolution? How does the crank and slider mechanism fit into the industrial revolution? How can you illustrate the results of the investigation?

9. Investigate different substances for lubrication properties.

Research What is meant by lubrication? What type of substances can be used? How are you going to compare them? What equipment will you need to carry out a simple experiment on various substances?

10. Investigate the efficiency of an electric motor in converting electrical energy to kinetic energy.

Research Mechanisms rely on changing one form of energy to another form of energy. No energy change can be completely efficient. You will need to find out how to measure the energy input to an electric motor and how to measure the kinetic energy of an object being moved by the motor.

11. Use plastic syringes to investigate the transmission of a force in pneumatic and hydraulic systems.

Research You will need to find out the difference between these two methods of transmitting forces. Are there any advantages of one system over the other system? What liquids can be used? What is meant by compressed air?

12. Investigate how 3-port and 5-port valves can be used to make a pneumatic piston move in and out continuously.

Research This mechanism can be used in an air controlled bell which could be used as a warning device in a pneumatic system. You will have to look up the different types of 3-port valves and decide which one would be easiest to use as the switching valve. Single-stroke or double-stroke pistons could be used. Which would be easiest to use? Which would do the job best?

13. Investigate how the force developed in a pneumatic cylinder depends on the air pressure and cross-sectional area of the cylinder.

Research What is meant by cross-sectional area and how is it calculated? How do you measure forces? You will need cylinders of various sizes and a method of changing and measuring the air pressure. You should end up with graphs to show your results. How will the axes be labelled?

14. Pneumatic systems are often used to open and close doors on coaches. Find out how this is done and build a model.

Research How is the door going to be operated? How many valves are needed? How is a shuttle valve used when combining valves? If the door moves too quickly it can cause injury. How can the speed of operation be controlled?

15. Pneumatic systems are often used to operate windscreen wipers which have two speed settings. Find out how this can be done and build a model.

Research You will need to link the movement of a piston with a mechanism to produce the circular motion of the wiper. How will you control the speed?

16. Investigate how the force produced by a solenoid depends on the number of turns of wire on the coil and the current passing through the coil.

Research You will need to set up an experiment to measure the force with which a soft iron bar is attracted into a solenoid. Two graphs will be needed to illustrate your results. Before you start you will need to consider carefully how a solenoid works, the number of turns of wire likely to be needed and how to take the necessary measurements.

4 electricity & electronics

The discovery of electricity has enabled society and industry to progress technologically faster than at any other time in its history. The ease with which electricity can be used to produce light, sound, heat and movement have made the quality of life much higher.

Electricity can be used in vastly different ways. For example, in industry, large quantities are used for the production of aluminium and alloy steels, but the current drawn by a microcomputer will be very small.

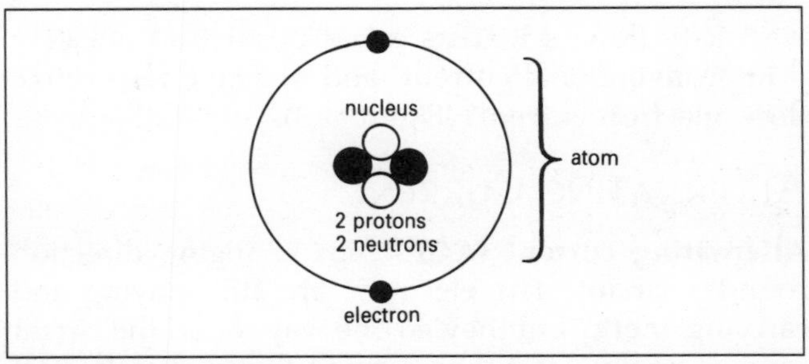

Figure 4.1 *An atom of helium*

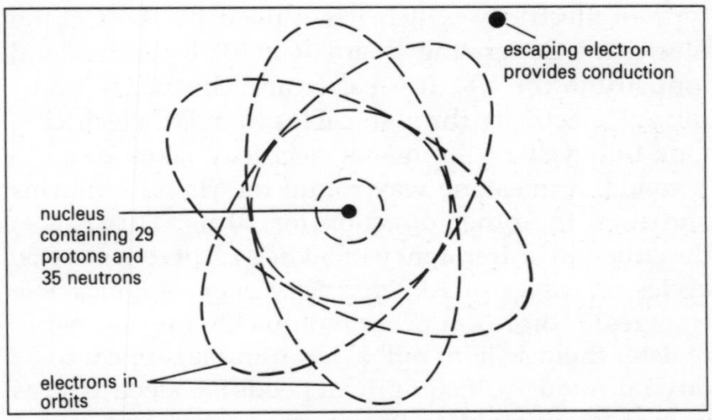

Figure 4.2 *Copper atoms with the outer electrons breaking away*

4:1 WHAT IS ELECTRICITY?

Electrons and Atoms

Scientists know from experiments and studies in physics that electricity is a flow of **electrons**. Electrons are negatively charged particles that are normally contained within the **atoms** which make up all substances. Figure 4.1 shows a helium atom which contains two electrons. The electrons can be thought of as orbiting the centre, or **nucleus**, of the atom.

Some atoms, however, have electrons which can easily break away from the positive, attractive forces of the nucleus of the atom (see Figure 4.2). Substances in which these 'free' electrons exist are conductors of electricity. The more easily the electrons break away, the better the substance is for conducting electricity. Electrons can be made to flow through a conductor if they are provided with a driving force. This is called the voltage or **electromotive force** (e.m.f.) and is measured in volts. Batteries (which scientists call **cells**) are often used to supply small and portable circuits.

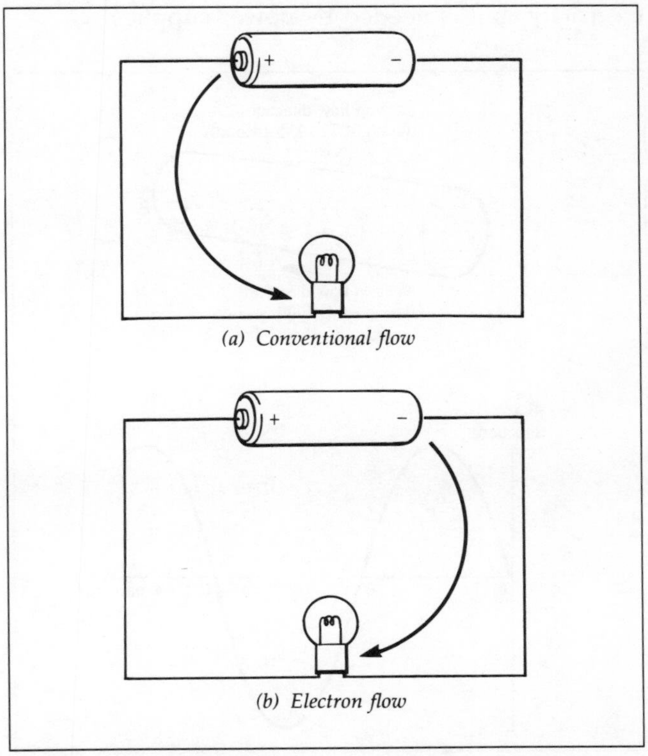

Figure 4.3 *Electrical current flow*

Direct Current

Electricity which always flows the same way in a circuit is called **direct current (DC)**. This is the type of electricity produced by a cell.

A cell has two terminals: the positive and the negative. Physicists in the nineteenth century thought that electricity flowed from the positive terminal to the negative terminal but further work showed that, in fact, electricity was a flow of electrons from the negative terminal to the positive. To distinguish between the two ways of looking at electricity flow, scientists called positive to negative flow 'conventional current' and negative to positive flow 'electron current' (Figure 4.3).

Alternating Current

Alternating current (AC) keeps changing direction round a circuit. The electrons are still moving and carrying energy but they go one way round the circuit for a short time and then stop and immediately start moving in the other direction (Figure 4.4). This is the type of electricity which is supplied by the Central Electricity Generating Board (CEGB) to homes and industry in the UK. It is easier and cheaper to transmit AC electricity through cables than DC electricity. One full cycle of the mains electricity takes 20 milliseconds; it goes one way round the circuit for 10 ms and then the other direction for 10 ms. This is also described by a **frequency** of 50 hertz; there will be 50 cycles or waves of AC electricity every second. The changes in direction occur too quickly for our eye to register them so light bulbs, for example, appear to be on continuously. If equipment needs DC electricity, as in such equipment as televisions, radios and record players, then the AC electricity is changed into DC electricity as it is needed by power supplies.

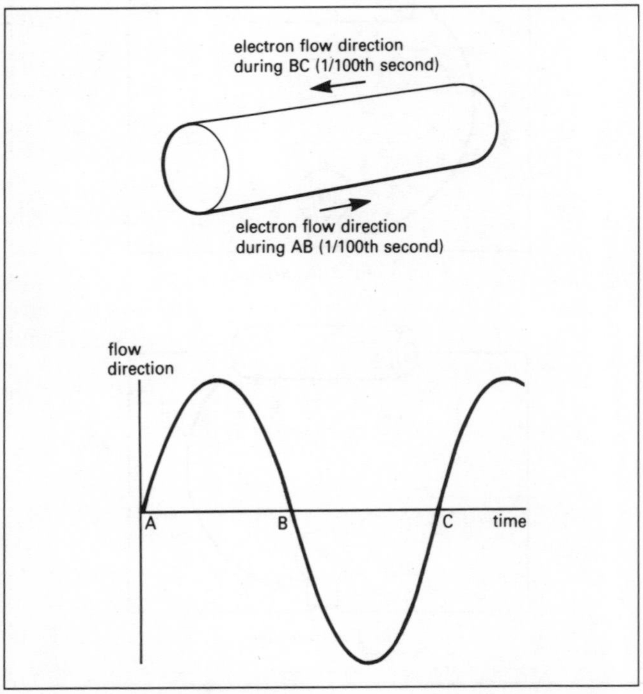

Figure 4.4 *Alternating current flow*

The variation of the alternating voltage with time is shown in Figure 4.5. The highest voltage reached is called the **peak voltage** which is about 340 V for mains electricity in Great Britain, Northern Ireland and many other countries. The effective voltage is less than the peak voltage because of the up and down nature of the electricity. The effective voltage, usually called the **root mean square (RMS)** voltage is the voltage which would provide the same effect as the equivalent direct voltage. A peak of 340 V provides an effective voltage of 240 V which is the normal value of the mains electricity in Great Britain (Figure 4.5).

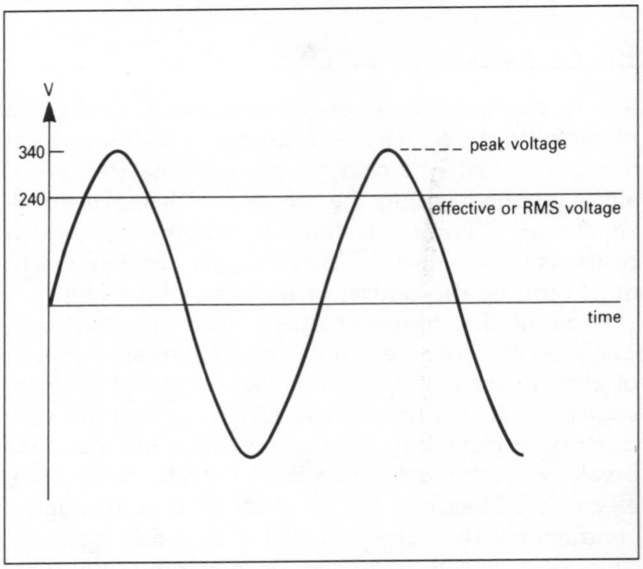

Figure 4.5 *Waveform of alternating current*

4:2 CIRCUITS

Types of Circuit

For electricity to flow, a complete **circuit** of conducting material must be made from one terminal of the power source to the other. Figure 4.6 gives examples of simple circuits.

Components can be connected into a circuit in two different ways: in series and in parallel. Series circuits contain components wired together one after the other; in parallel circuits the wire branches and connects components separately. In most cases, parallel circuits are part of series circuits. Figure 4.7 shows how they differ.

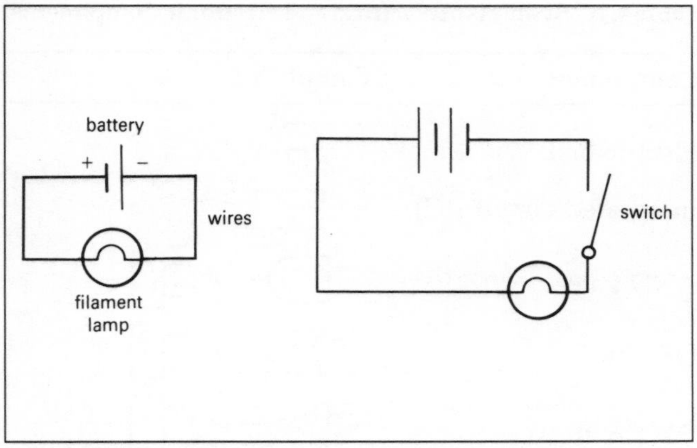

Figure 4.6 *Simple circuits*

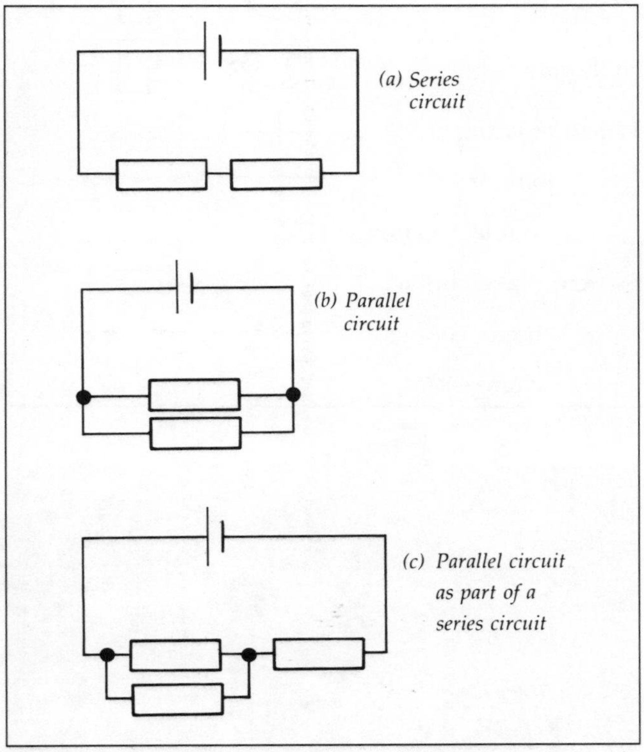

Figure 4.7 *Types of circuit*

Symbols

Circuit diagrams use symbols rather than actual pictures to show the parts used in the circuit. Table 4.1 shows the symbols for the most commonly used components. Figure 4.8 shows two more circuits which are identical except for layout. The first shows how electrical circuits are laid out and the second shows how electronic circuits are drawn.

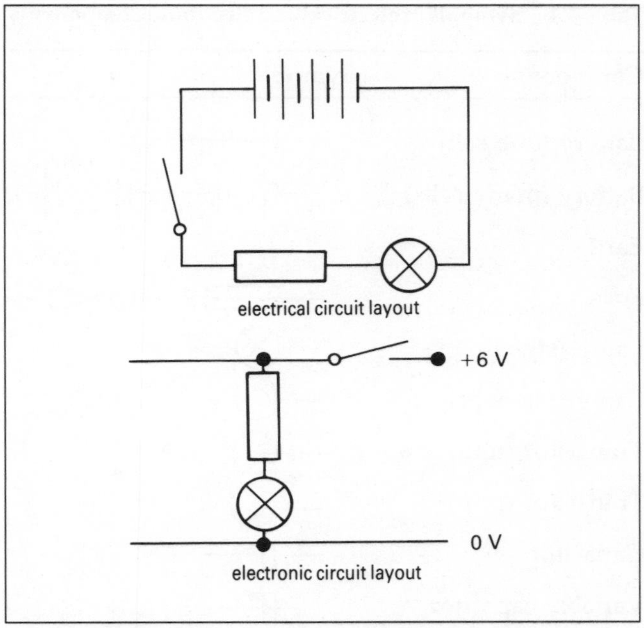

Figure 4.8 *Comparison of electrical and electronic circuits*

4:3 INTRODUCTION TO COMMON COMPONENTS

The components of electrical circuits have specific functions (see Table 4.1 for their symbols).

Resistors

A **resistor** limits the amount of current in a circuit by providing **resistance** to the flow. The resistance of a light-dependent resistor (LDR) increases or decreases depending on the amount of light falling on it. Similarly, the resistance of a thermistor will change with temperature. The resistance of **variable resistors** and pre-set variable resistors can be altered to suit the circuit. Figure 4.9 shows these types.

Capacitors

The **capacitor** is a device which stores electrical charge. As current flows to the capacitor in a circuit, charge builds up until the capacitor becomes fully charged. The current will then stop flowing until the capacitor loses some charge. As the charge builds up, so does the voltage across the capacitor and the capacitor becomes a miniature source of electricity. Figure 4.10 shows several different types of capacitor.

Table 4.1 Symbols of electrical and electronic Components

Component	Symbol
Battery (one cell)	
Battery (many cells)	or 12V
Earth	
Fuse	or
Lamp (signal)	
Lamp (filament)	
Transistor (npn)	
Transistor (pnp)	
Capacitor	
Variable capacitor	
Electrolytic capacitor	
Diode	or
Light-emitting diode (LED)	
Zener diode	
Resistor	
Variable resistor	
Preset variable resistor	
Light-dependent resistor (LDR)	
Thermistor	
Relay	
Reed relay	
Motor	
Generator	
Loudspeaker	
Microphone	
Earphone	

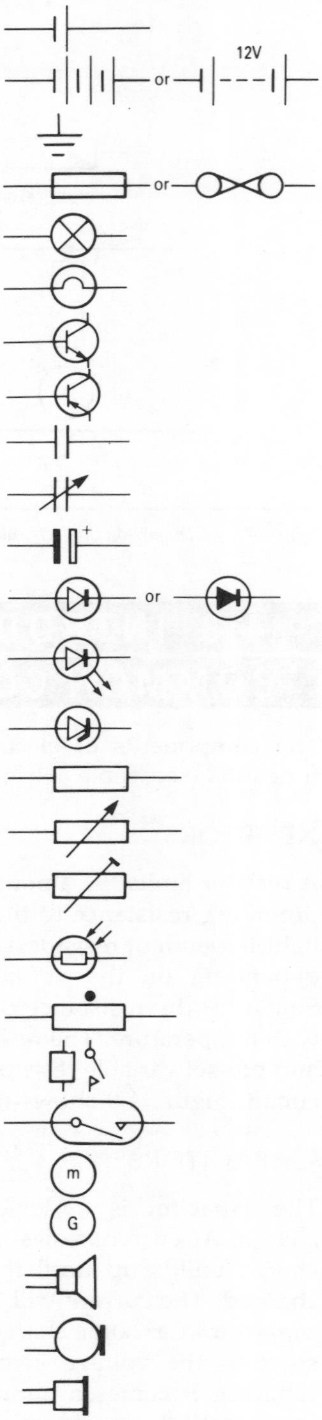

Table 4.1 Symbols of electrical and electronic Components

Component	Symbol
Electric bell	
Integrated circuit (IC)	
AND gate	or
OR gate	or
NOT gate	or
NAND gate	or
NOR gate	or
Wires: crossing	
joining	
double junction	
Switch: make contact	or
break contact	or
changeover	

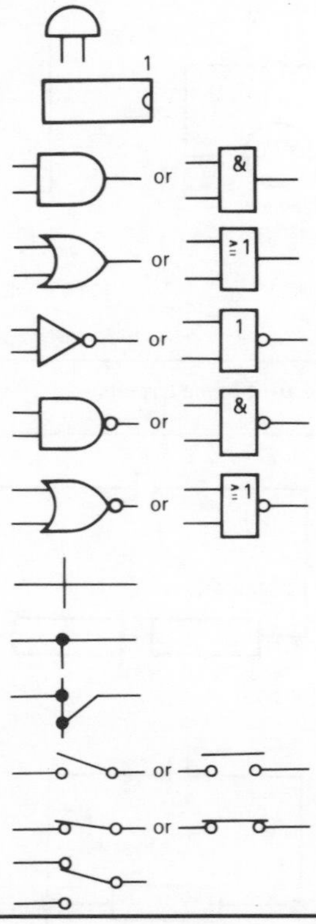

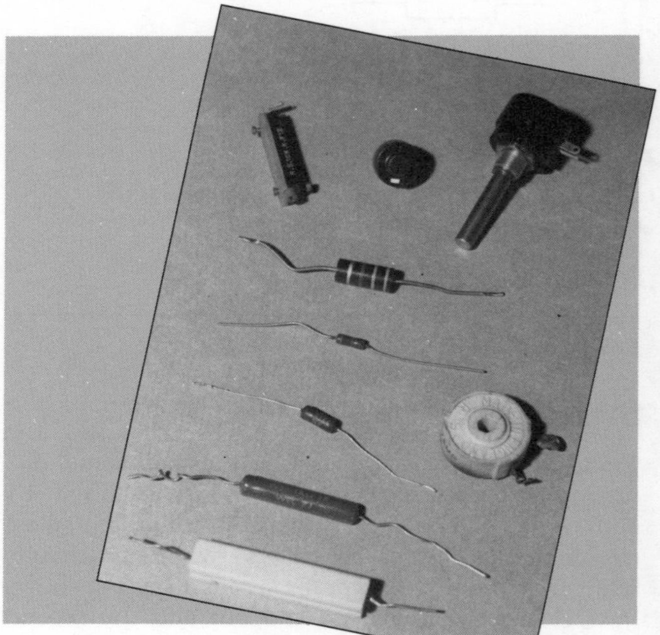

Figure 4.9 *Typical resistors*

Diodes

Diodes and light-emitting diodes (LED) will only allow current to flow in one direction. LEDs light up as current flows; red, green and yellow being the usual colours. Zener diodes (Section 4:15) can be used in power supplies to provide a fixed voltage.

Transistors

Transistors are devices which amplify (make bigger) electric currents. They are used in many electronic systems and are important components in, for example, computers, radios and televisions. A transistor is used as a switching and amplifying device; some typical transistors are shown in Figure 4.12.

Relays

The **relay** allows one circuit to switch another circuit at a different voltage. The reed relay is often used for low voltages (Figure 4.13).

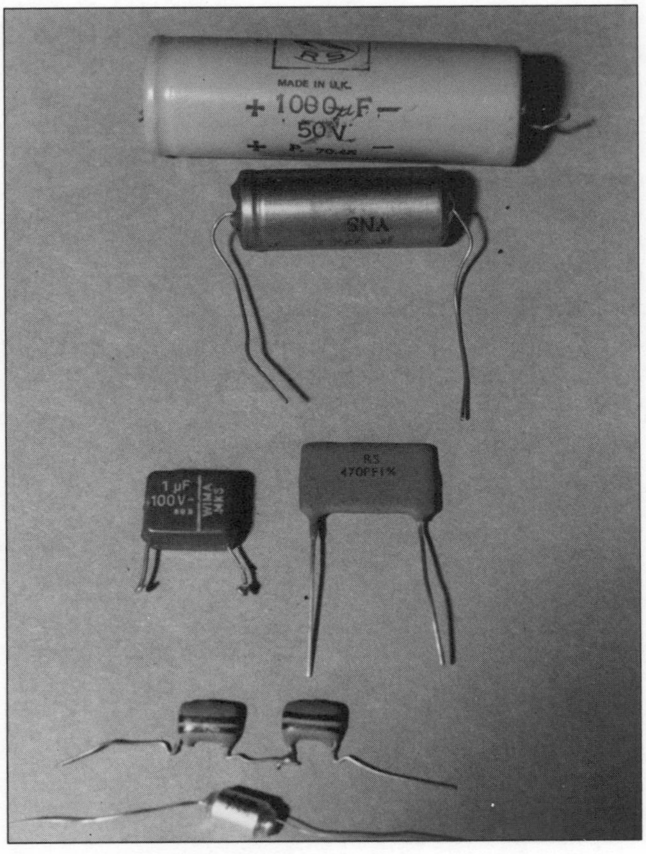

Figure 4.10 *Typical capacitors*

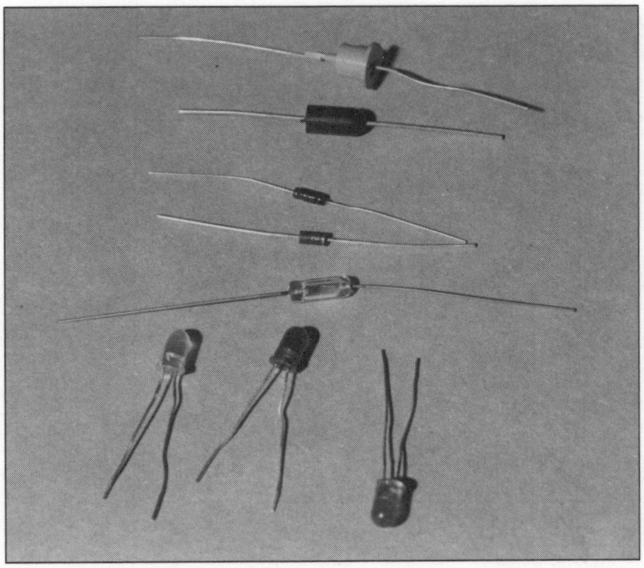

Figure 4.11 *Typical diodes*

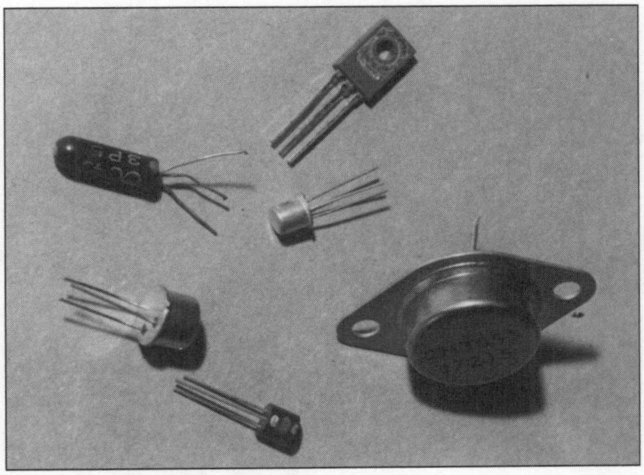

Figure 4.12 *Typical transistors*

Figure 4.13 *Typical relays*

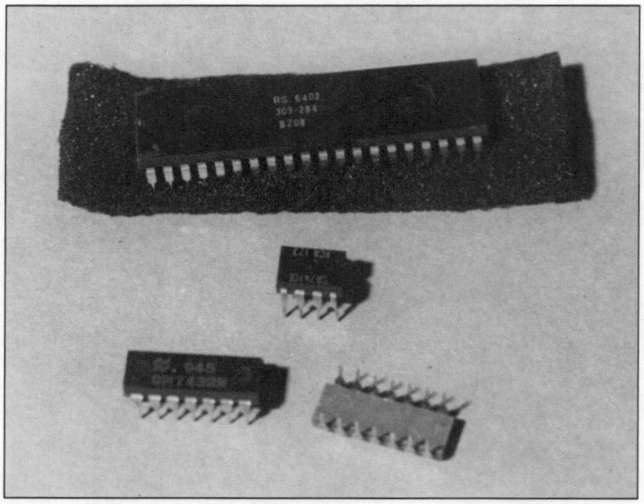

Figure 4.14 *Typical integrated circuits*

INTEGRATED CIRCUITS

Integrated circuits (ICs) contain large numbers of components, the arrangement of which will determine what an IC does. Some specialised ICs have decision-making functions and are known as **logic gates**. Figure 4.14 shows some typical examples.

TRANSFORMERS

Transformers are electromagnetic devices that can be used to increase or decrease the size of an alternating type of voltage. They are used by the CEGB in the transmission of electricity around the country and in power supplies which operate electrical and electronic equipment (Figure 4.15).

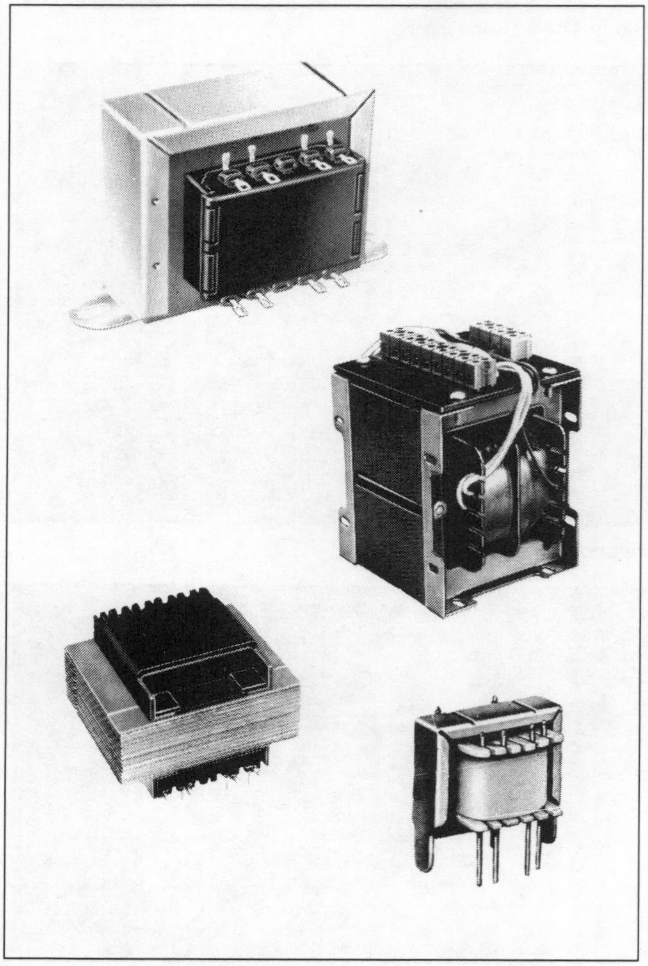

Figure 4.15 *Typical transformers*

4:4 MEASURING ELECTRICITY

The two properties of electricity that can be measured directly are the **current** (the flow of electricity) and the **voltage** (the force pushing the electricity through a conductor). Current is measured in amps (which is shortened to A) using an ammeter. Voltage is measured in volts (shortened to V) using a voltmeter. Ammeters are always connected into a circuit in series and voltmeters are always connected in parallel (see Figure 4.16).

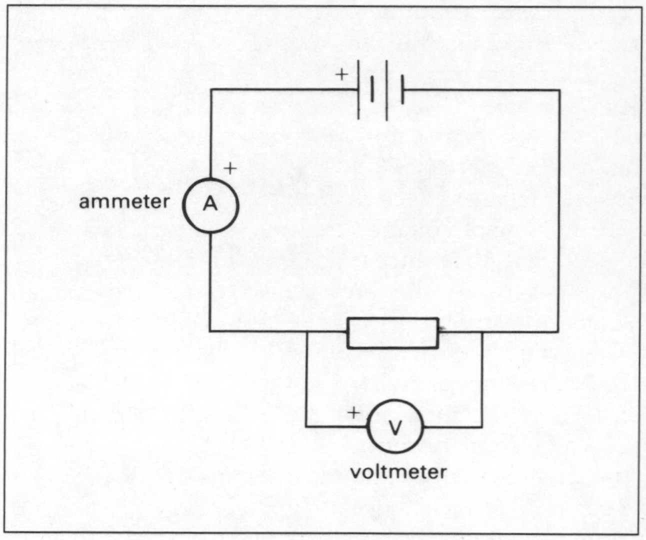

Figure 4.16 *Connecting voltmeters and ammeters in circuits*

Table 4.2 Ammeter readings from Figure 4.17(a)

Ammeter	*Reading (A)*
A_1	1
A_2	1
A_3	1
A_4	1

Table 4.3 Voltmeter readings from Figure 4.17(b)

Voltmeter	*Reading (V)*
V_1	0
V_2	1
V_3	2
V_4	3

Table 4.4 Ammeter readings from Figure 4.18

Ammeter	*Reading (A)*
A_1	1
A_2	0.5
A_3	0.5
A_4	1

Connecting an ammeter anywhere in a series circuit will show that the current is constant all the way round the circuit. Connecting a voltmeter across various parts of series circuit will show that the voltage drop across the various parts will change. This change depends on the resistance of different parts of the circuit (see Figure 4.17 and Table 4.2).

The change of voltage across a component is called the **potential difference (pd)**. The potential difference is a measure of the amount of electrical energy changed to another form of energy in the component.

The total voltage measured across the battery is called the electromotive force (e.m.f.). The e.m.f. is a measure of the total amount of energy available to push the electricity round the circuit.

In parallel circuits, adding the currents flowing in the separate branches of the parallel part will give the current flowing in the series part (see Figure 4.18 and Table 4.4).

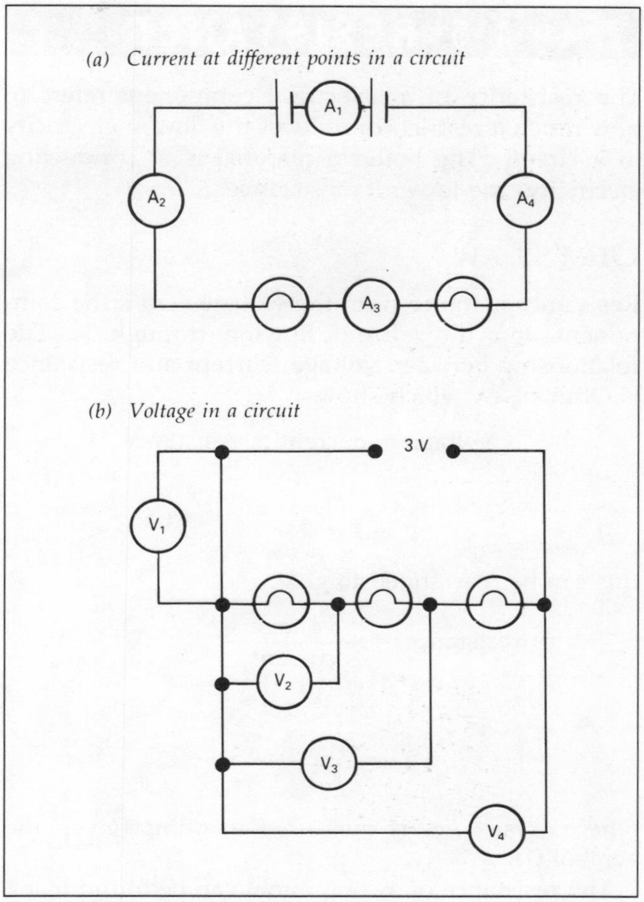

Figure 4.17 *Current and voltage in different parts of a circuit*

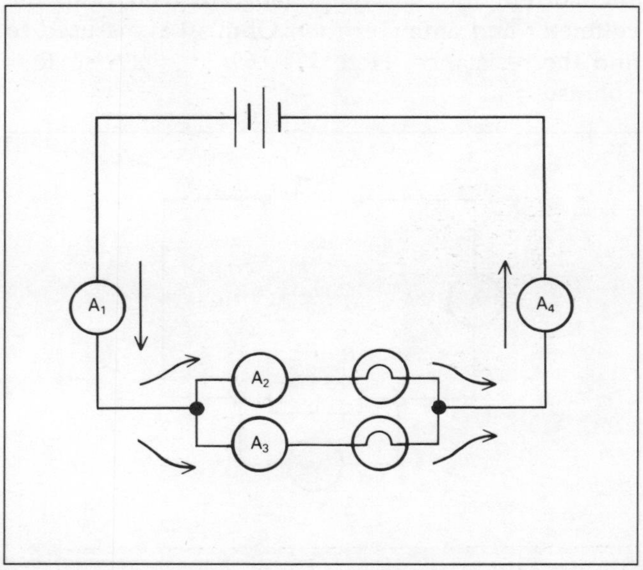

Figure 4.18 *Current flow in parallel circuits*

4:5 RESISTANCE

The resistance of an electrical component refers to how much it restricts or reduces the flow of electricity in a circuit. The better a material is at conducting electricity, the lower its resistance.

OHM'S LAW

Resistance is found from the voltage across the component and the current flowing through it. The relationship between voltage, current and resistance is Ohm's Law which shows:

$$\text{voltage} = \text{current} \times \text{resistance}$$

or

$$V = I \times R$$

this can be rearranged to give:

$$\text{resistance} = \frac{\text{voltage}}{\text{current}}$$

or

$$R = \frac{V}{I}$$

where resistance is measured in ohms (given the symbol Ω).

The resistance of a component can be found using the circuit shown in Figure 4.19. The values of voltage and current for the component are read from the voltmeter and ammeter then Ohm's Law is used to find the resistance. Here $V = 6\,\text{V}$, $I = 2\,\text{A}$ so $R = 3$ ohms.

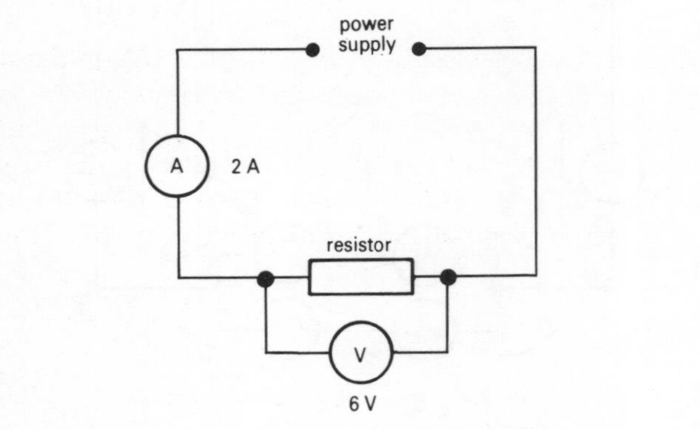

Figure 4.19 *Circuit to find the resistance of a component*

EFFECT OF TEMPERATURE

The effect of temperature upon resistance is important. For most materials which normally act as conductors, the resistance increases as the temperature increases. This is due to increased 'vibration' of atoms which reduces the flow of electrons. Figure 4.20 shows this effect on a light bulb as it warms up when the voltage across the bulb increases. The current is lower than would be expected for a component which obeys Ohm's Law. This effect is used in high temperature measurement. Platinum is used in these thermometers because of its high melting point and the linear change of resistance with temperature.

For the semiconductor materials, silicon, gallium and germanium, used in transistors, diodes and other electronic components, resistance decreases with a rise in temperature. The temperature rise causes electrons to be freed more easily from the atoms, increasing the 'sea' of electrons and so increasing the flow of electricity.

Care must be taken with the temperature of electronic components. If the temperature gets too high, a drop in resistance allows a greater current flow, leading to more component heating until a high enough temperature will cause the component to burn out. This is called **thermal runaway**. For this reason some components are fitted with heat sinks and circuit boards are mounted to enable excess heat to be removed by ventilation.

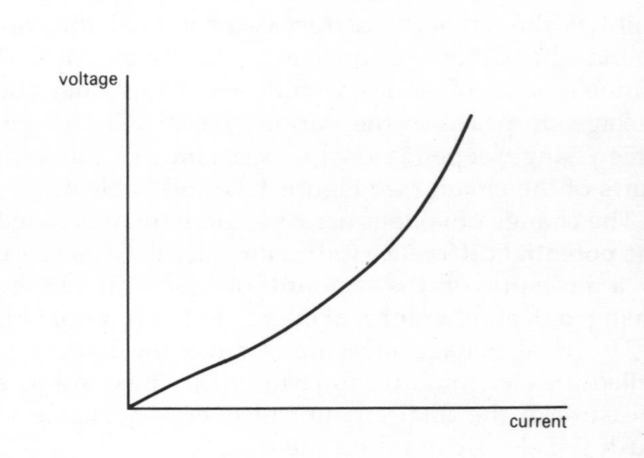

Figure 4.20 *Graph of current against voltage for a light bulb*

4:6 ELECTRICAL POWER RULES

Power is how much energy is converted into another form of energy every second. For example, if a light bulb has a power of 24 watts then 24 joules of electrical energy are being changed every second. Power is measured in watts and energy is measured in joules so:

$$24 \text{ watts} = 24 \text{ joules/second}$$

or

$$1 \text{ watt} = 1 \text{ joule/second}$$

To calculate electrical power, the relationship between voltage, current and power is used:

$$\text{power} = \text{voltage} \times \text{current}$$

or

$$P = V \times I$$

where power (P) is measured in watts, W
voltage (V) is measured in volts, V
current (I) is measured in amps, A

Electronic components, such as resistors, diodes and transistors, are always designed to withstand a certain power (amount of heating due to electrical energy being changed into heat energy). If the maximum power is exceeded then the component is likely to be ruined.

4:7 APPLYING OHM'S LAW AND THE POWER RULE TO CIRCUITS

The design of heater circuits is based on Ohm's Law and the power rule. In a 3 kW electric fire, the heating elements convert 3000 joules of electrical energy into heat energy every second. If mains voltage is 240 V then:

$$P = V \times I$$
$$3000 = 240 \times I$$
$$I = 12.5 \text{ A}$$

therefore the current flowing = 12.5 A. The resistance of the heater to allow this current to flow can be found from Ohm's Law:

$$V = I \times R$$
$$240 = 12.5 \times R$$
$$R = 19.2 \text{ ohms}$$

The resistance of the elements must be 19.2 ohms; the complete heater circuit is shown in Figure 4.21.

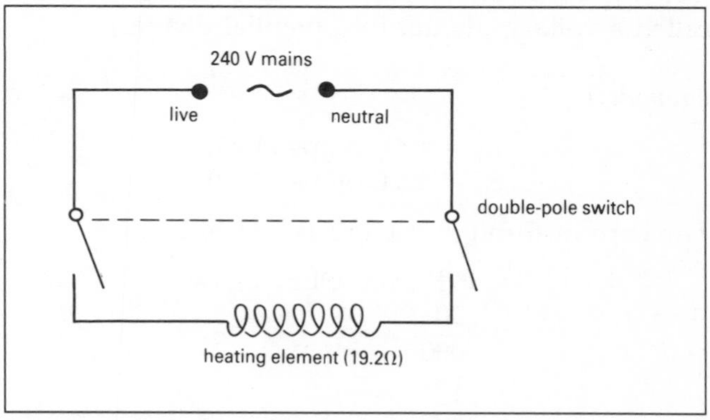

Figure 4.21 *Circuit for a 3 kW electric fire*

4:8 RESISTORS IN ELECTRONIC CIRCUITS

Resistors must be designed to withstand the heat they produce when electricity passes through them, otherwise they will fail. All resistors have a power rating which should not be exceeded when used in a circuit.

The cheapest type of resistors are the low-power types used for general applications. They are rated up to 1 W and are of a carbon composition.

Carbon film resistors can be obtained up to about 2 W. Metal oxide resistors are only available up to about 0.5 W but tend to be more stable. Wirewound resistors are used for higher heat dissipation, up to as much as 50 W in some circuits. These resistors can also be made to a better resistance accuracy than the other types mentioned above.

COMBINING RESISTORS

For resistors in series (see Figure 4.22) the total resistance is given by:

total resistance $R = R_1 + R_2$

For resistors in parallel (see Figure 4.23) the total resistance is found from:

$$\frac{1}{R} = \frac{1}{R_1} + \frac{1}{R_2}$$

Power Ratings

The choice of power rating will depend on the voltage across the resistor and the current through the resistor. Figure 4.22 shows a common type of series circuit called a voltage divider (or potential divider):

Example 1

$$R_1 = 1000 \text{ ohms } (1\,\text{k}0)$$
$$R_2 = 4000 \text{ ohms } (4\,\text{k}0)$$

The current through each resistor will be:

$$I = V/R \text{ from Ohm's Law}$$
$$= \frac{20}{5000}$$
$$= \frac{1}{250}$$
$$= 0.004\,\text{A}$$

For R_1 the voltage across is:

$$R_1 = 1/5\text{th of } 20\,\text{V}$$
$$= 4\,\text{V}$$

The power (or heat) given off will therefore be:

$$P = V \times I$$
$$= 4 \times 0.004$$
$$= 0.016\,\text{W}$$

For R_2 the power will be 4 times greater because there will be 16 V across R_2. 0.125 W carbon composition or metal oxide resistors would provide enough heat dissipation.

Example 2 Suppose our circuit required:

$$R_1 = 2 \text{ ohms}$$
$$R_2 = 8 \text{ ohms}$$

The voltage across each resistor would be the same as in Example 1 because the total voltage is shared between the resistors.

The current will be 500 times greater and so the power will be 500 times greater.

The power given off from R_1 will be 8 watts.

The power given off from R_2 will be 32 watts.

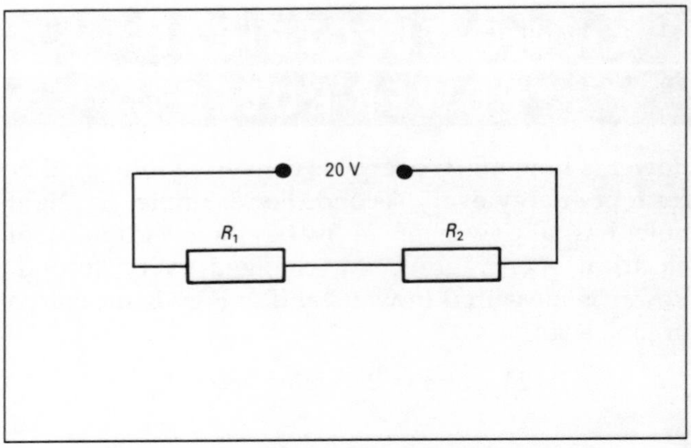

Figure 4.22 *Resistors in series: a voltage divider circuit*

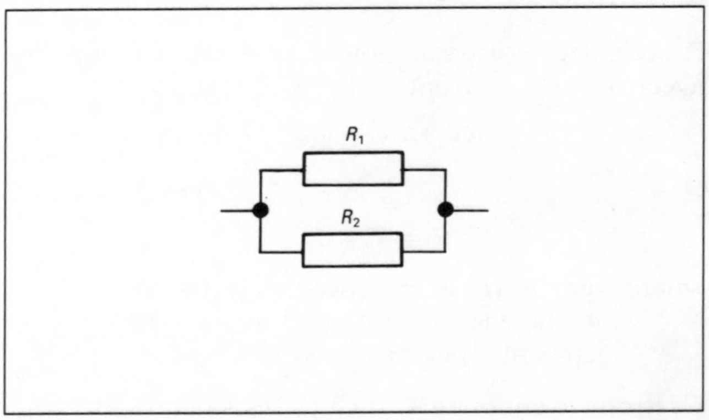

Figure 4.23 *Resistors in parallel*

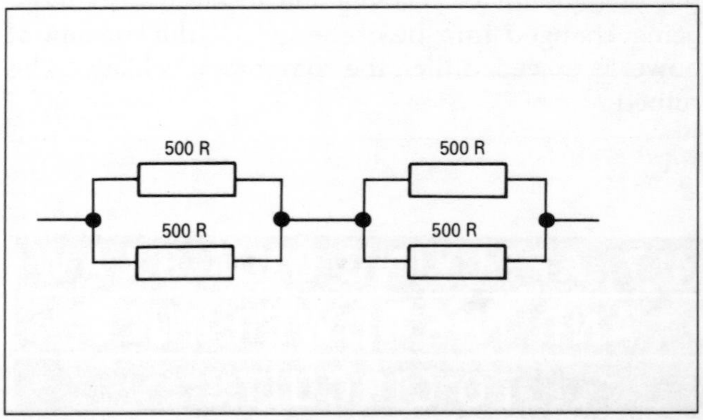

Figure 4.24 *Resistor combination to give increased power dissipation*

So wirewound resistors with very high power ratings would be needed.

Combinations of series and parallel resistors can be used to give increased power ratings. Figure 4.24 shows a typical combination, which has a total resistance of 500 ohms but with four times the power rating of the individual resistors.

Resistance Values and Tolerance

No resistor can be made to an exact resistance value. The amount by which a resistor can be higher or lower than its marked value is called the **tolerance**. It is normally given as a percentage. Coloured bands are normally used to mark the value and tolerance on resistors (Figure 4.25). Table 4.5 shows the code for these bands.

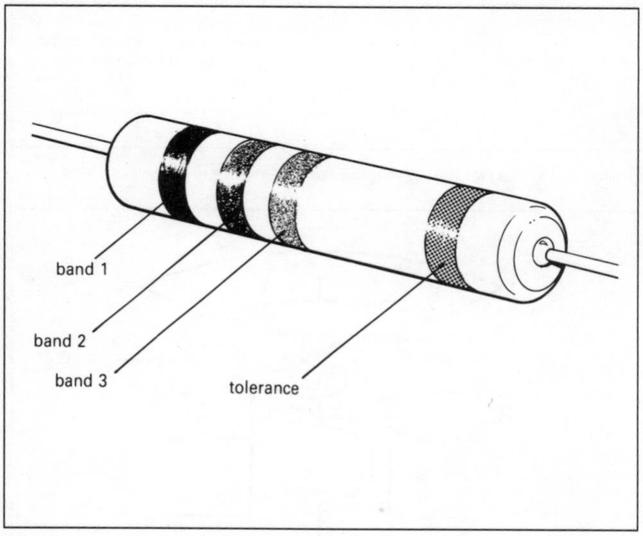

Figure 4.25 *Coloured bands on resistors*

Table 4.5 Resistor colour codes and tolerance

Colour	*Band 1*	*Band 2*	*Band 3*	*Band 4*
Black	0	0	× 1	Red 2%
Brown	1	1	× 10	Gold 5%
Red	2	2	× 100	Silver 10%
Orange	3	3	× 1 000	
Yellow	4	4	× 10 000	
Green	5	5	× 100 000	
Blue	6	6	× 1 000 000	
Violet	7	7	× 10 000 000	
Grey	8	8	× 100 000 000	
White	9	9	× 1 000 000 000	

So a resistor marked Brown Black Red Gold has a resistance of:

Brown	1		
Black		0	
Red			× 100 = 1000 ohms
Gold			± 50 ohms

For circuit diagrams, resistor values are written using a British Standard code shown in Table 4.6.

Table 4.6 Writing resistor values in circuit diagrams BS 1852 code

R39	means	0.39 ohms
2 R0	,,	2 ohms
2 k0	,,	2 000 ohms
2 k2	,,	2 200 ohms
39 k	,,	39 000 ohms
1 M0	,,	1 000 000 ohms

4:9 Effects of Electricity Passing Through a Conductor

When electricity passes through a conductor, it causes a magnetic and a heating effect.

Magnetic Effect

The magnetic field produced by electricity flowing in a conductor is shown in Figure 4.26. If a permanent magnet is brought close to the conductor, the magnetic field is distorted. The field lines will try and straighten, causing the wire to move (see Figure 4.27a). In an electric motor, electricity is passed into the coil via brushes and a commutator and the coil spins freely (Figure 4.27b).

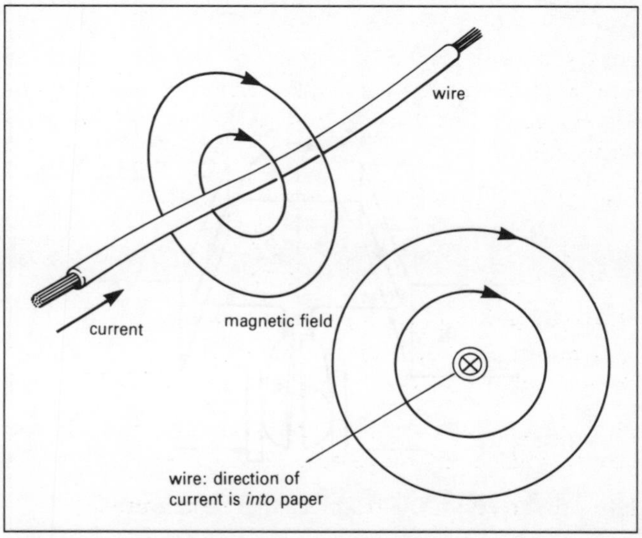

Figure 4.26 *Magnetic field produced by current flow*

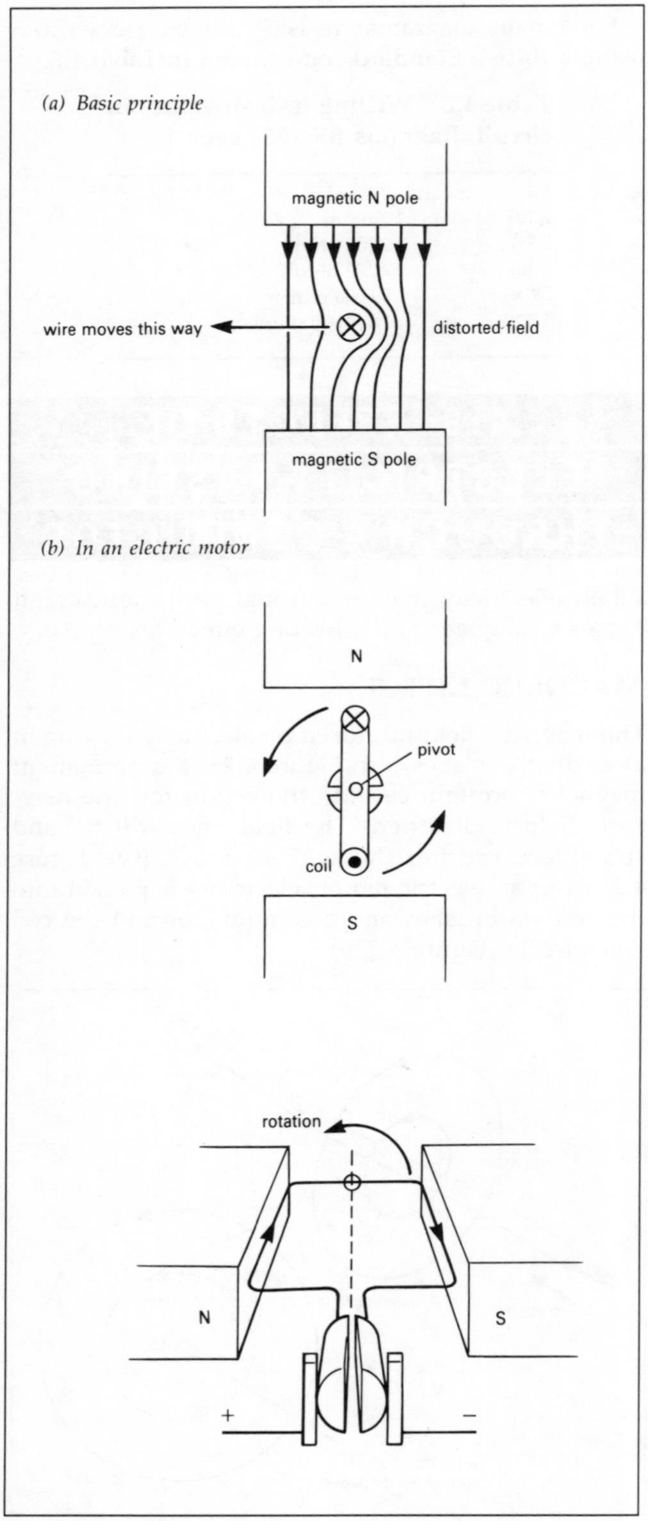

Figure 4.27 *Magnetic fields causing movement*

Heating Effect

The heating effect causes expansion of the wire as shown in Figure 4.28.

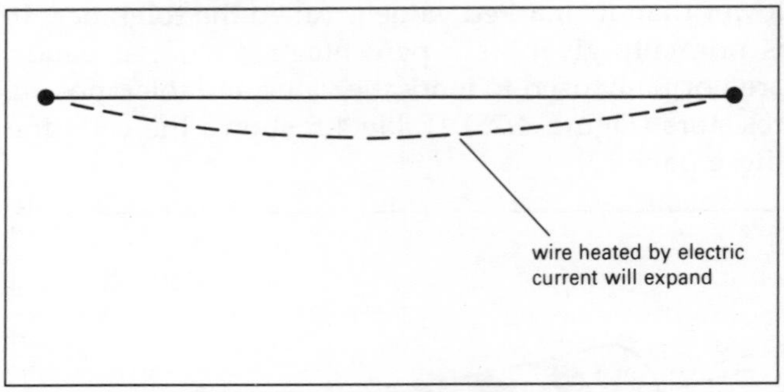

Figure 4.28 *Expansion of a wire due to heating*

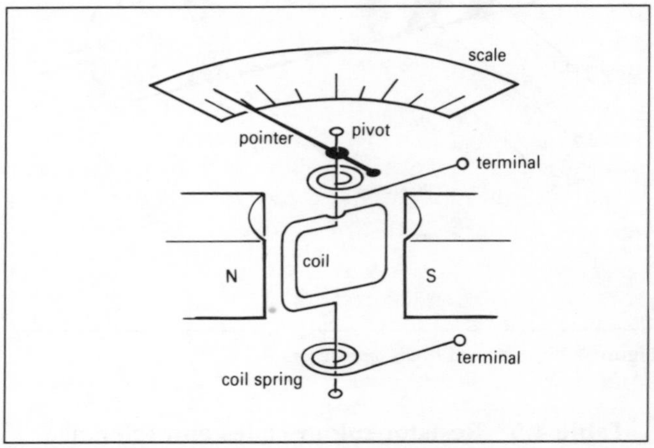

Figure 4.29 *Principle of a moving coil meter*

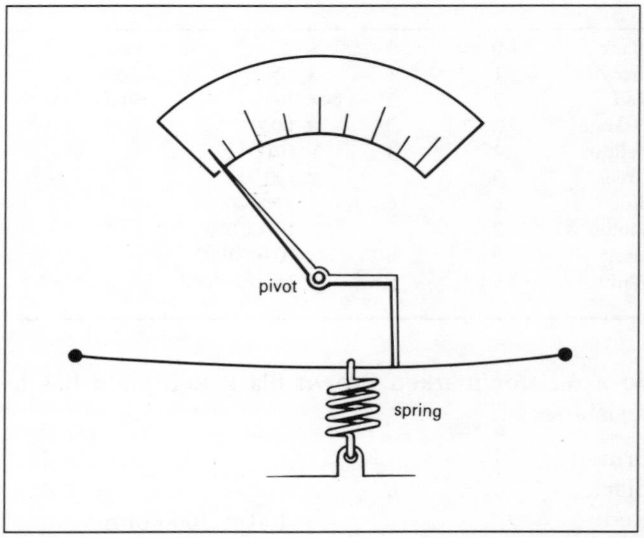

Figure 4.30 *A hot wire meter*

4:10 ELECTRICAL METERS

The measurement of electric current and potential difference relies on the effects of electricity passing through wires.

Moving Coil Meter

This meter uses the magnetic effect and is similar to a DC electric motor except that hair springs prevent the coil from rotating continuously. The springs apply a force to the coil equal but opposite to the force caused by the electricity passing through the wire (Figure 4.29). A coil of wire is wound on to an armature which revolves on a central spindle. Magnets are mounted around the coil. When an electric current passes through the coil, the distorted magnetic field causes the coil to turn on the spindle. The size of the electric current passing through the coil will determine the force with which the coil turns against the restraining hair springs. A pointer is mounted on the spindle and its movement is measured by a suitable scale (see Figure 4.29).

Hot Wire Meter

This uses the heating effect. The amount a wire expands can be measured using a system of pulleys and levers which moves a pointer across a scale (see Figure 4.30). This type of meter could be used to measure both AC and DC current. They are now rarely used because the moving coil meter is more robust and accurate. Diodes can be used to convert DC meters to AC meters.

Extending the Range of an Ammeter

Most meters are unsuitable for measuring the large range of electric currents which can vary from micro-amps to hundreds of amps. To extend the range of an ammeter, shunt resistors (see Figure 4.31) are placed across the terminals of the meter.

Low values of shunt resistors are chosen to allow a specific fraction of the current through the resistor. If the shunt resistor has 1/9th the resistance of the basic meter then 9/10ths of the current goes through the shunt and only 1/10th goes through the meter. The range of the meter is therefore extended by a factor of ten. At the same time the overall resistance of the meter is reduced to a much lower level which means that the ammeter has little effect on the flow of current. Ideally, the ammeter should have zero resistance but then no energy conversion could take place to make the pointer move.

Conversion of a Basic Meter to a Voltmeter

The basic meter could also be used as a voltmeter because the voltage (also called the potential difference) will cause a current to flow which then causes the pointer to move. The meter can therefore be calibrated in terms of volts instead of amperes. To extend the range of the voltmeter a resistance is connected in series with the basic meter (see Figure 4.32). If the series resistor, known as a multiplier resistor, has 9 times the resistance of the basic meter then 1/10th of the voltage will be measured by the meter. This will extend the range of a voltmeter by a factor of 10. The overall resistance of the meter will also be increased so it will have less effect on the circuit being measured.

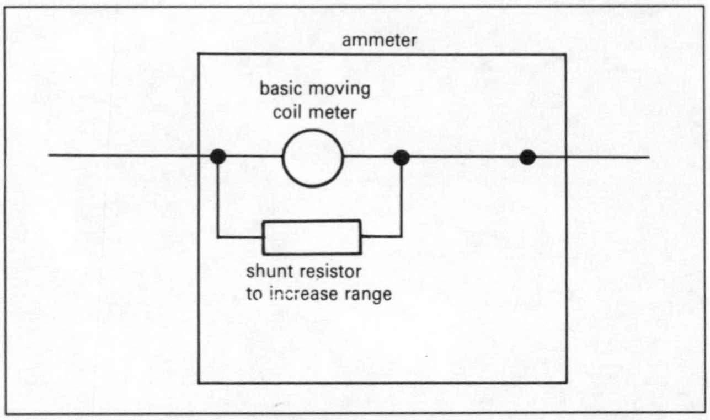

Figure 4.31 *Shunt resistors in parallel with meters to extend their range*

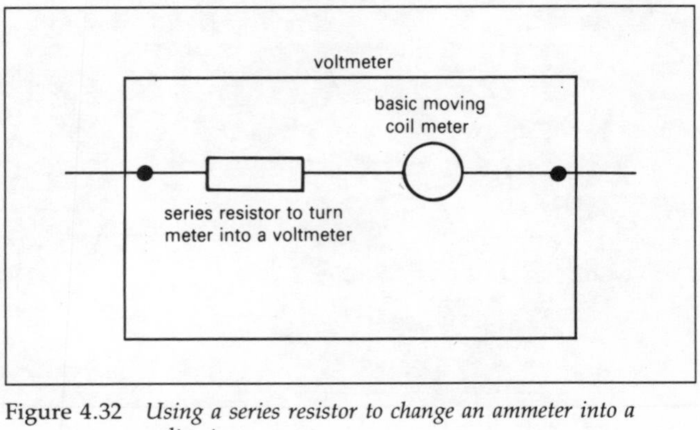

Figure 4.32 *Using a series resistor to change an ammeter into a voltmeter*

Figure 4.35 *Typical multimeters*

Resistance of Ammeters and Voltmeters

Ammeters measure the amount of current flowing round a circuit. They must therefore be connected *in series* (see Figure 4.33) with the rest of the circuit. An ammeter must have a very low resistance so that it does not alter the current when it is placed in the circuit.

Voltmeters measure voltage or the potential difference from one side of a component to the other side. They must therefore be connected *in parallel* with the components (Figure 4.34). The voltmeter must have as high a resistance as possible so that it does not alter the current passing through the component.

Multimeters

Multimeters combine the ammeter, voltmeter and ohmmeter. Typical types are shown in Figure 4.35.

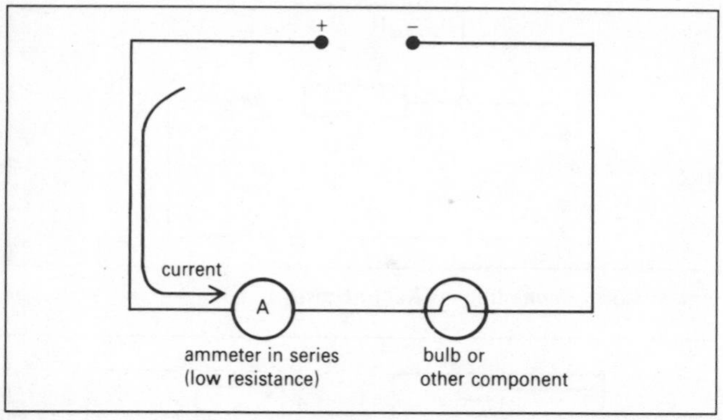

Figure 4.33 *An ammeter in a circuit*

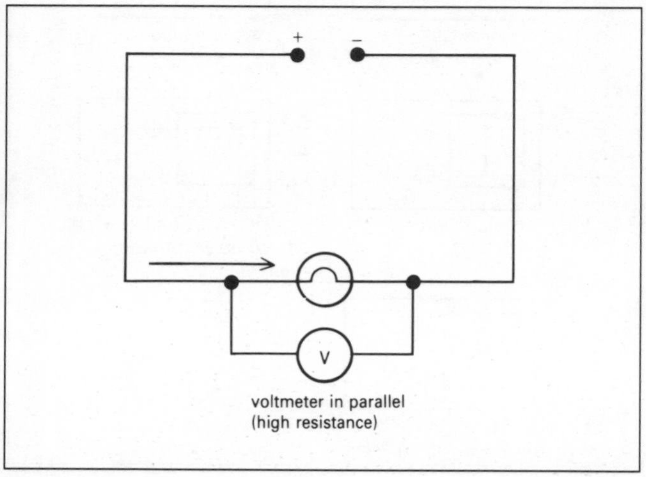

Figure 4.34 *A voltmeter in a circuit*

Digital meters use electronics to give a liquid crystal numerical display instead of a pointer moving across a scale. No moving parts are used and so they are generally more robust and easier to use once the various switching settings are understood. Some digital meters are auto-ranging which means that they switch themselves to the correct scaling factor for any input.

4:11 The Cathode Ray Oscilloscope

Basic System

The cathode ray oscilloscope (CRO) contains, like a television set, a cathode ray tube which has three main parts (Figure 4.36). The **electron gun** produces a beam of electrons. Electrons are released by heating the cathode and are then attracted by the positive charge on the anode. The grid is at a negative potential (voltage) with respect to the cathode and controls the number of electrons passing through its central hole from the cathode to anode; it is the brightness control. The anode is at a high positive potential (voltage) relative to the cathode and electrons are accelerated through the evacuated tube and focused into a narrow beam.

The vertical deflecting system is used to move the electron beam up and down by making the plates positive by connecting a voltage to the input terminals. These terminals are sometimes marked Y-input.

The horizontal deflecting system, usually called the timebase, is used to move the beam across the screen from left to right. When the beam reaches the right-hand edge it is quickly returned to the left to start its sweep again.

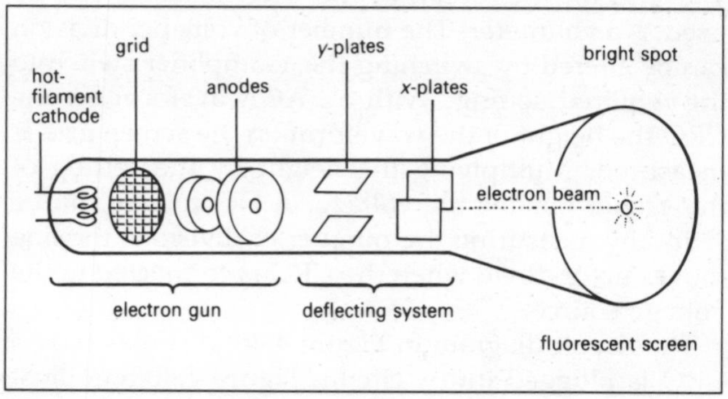

Figure 4.36 *Main parts of a cathode ray tube*

The fluorescent screen glows where the electron beam hits it. As the beam is swept across the screen a spot or line will appear depending on the speed of the sweep.

The CRO is used as a 'graph plotter' to show what an electrical signal looks like. The picture on the fluorescent screen is known as its waveform.

USING THE CRO TO SHOW A WAVEFORM

Before connecting a CRO in a circuit, the spot should be set in the centre. To do this, the timebase is turned off so that the dot is stationary. The *X* and *Y* shift are then used to centralise the spot. The brilliance and the focus controls are used to get the spot as sharp as possible. Figure 4.37 shows a typical CRO with these controls.

A CRO is connected in parallel with the part of a circuit being investigated (see Figure 4.38). The positive lead is plugged into the input terminal and the negative into the earth. The type of current going round the circuit should also be set. This will be either AC or DC. If there is a pd across the circuit, the spot will either appear as a vertical line for AC or just move up for DC.

To produce a true waveform, the timebase needs to be switched on. This will cause the dot to 'sweep' across the screen from left to right. The sweep speed of the spot will need to be about 10–20 ms per division for a wave of frequency 50 Hz and about 1 ms per division for a frequency of 1000 Hz. Figure 4.39 shows the expected appearance of the screen for various input voltages.

USING THE CRO AS A VOLTMETER

The grid on the screen of the CRO enables it to be used as a voltmeter. The number of volts per division can be altered by switching the *Y*-amplifier switch to the required setting. With an AC waveform on the CRO the height of the waveform on the screen grid is measured. Multiplying the height by the setting of the *Y* shift obtains the voltage. A DC voltage can be found by measuring the number of divisions the line moves up or down when the CRO is connected to the voltage source.

The circuit diagram in Figure 4.40(a) shows how a CRO is plugged into a circuit. Figure 4.40(b,c) illustrates the method of taking voltage readings.

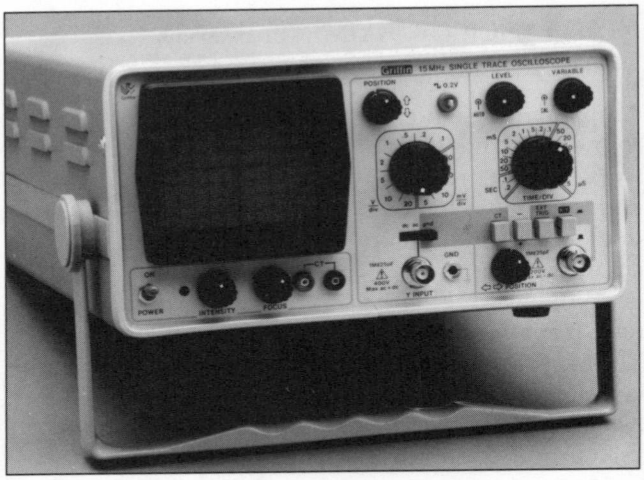

Figure 4.37 *A typical CRO*

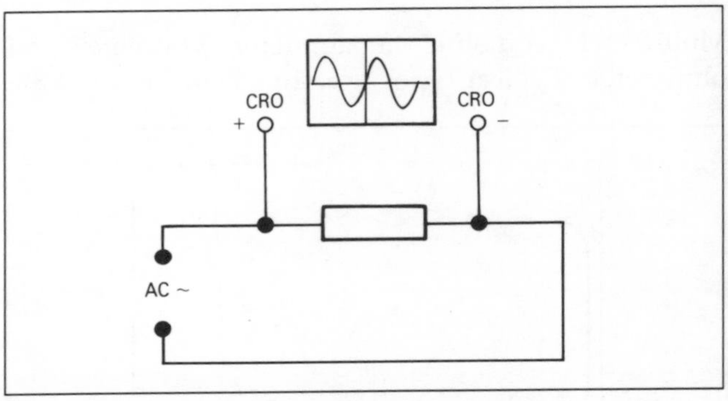

Figure 4.38 *Connecting a CRO in circuit*

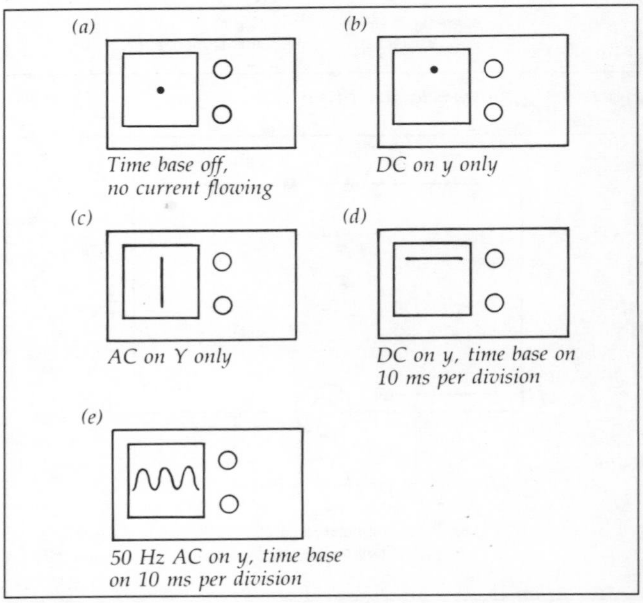

Figure 4.39 *Appearance of the CRO screen for various inputs*

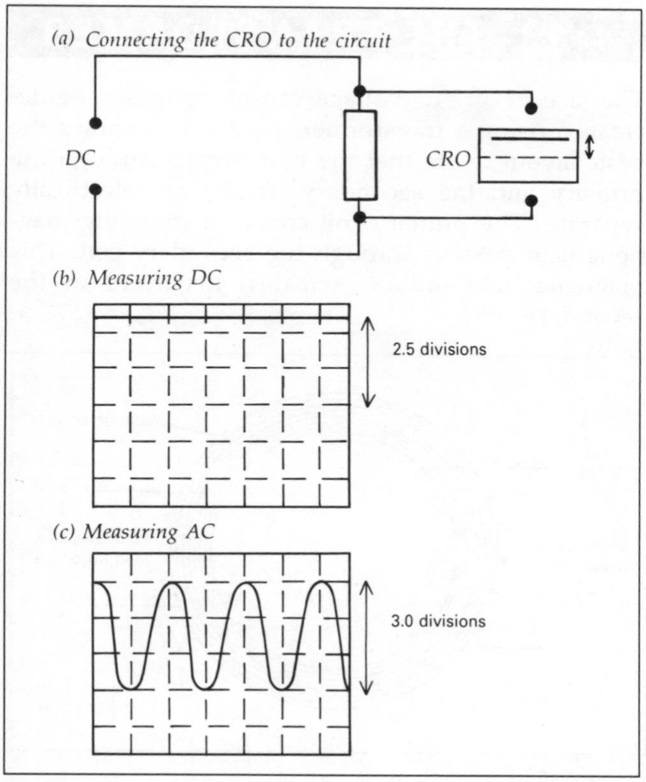

Figure 4.40 *Using a CRO as a voltmeter*

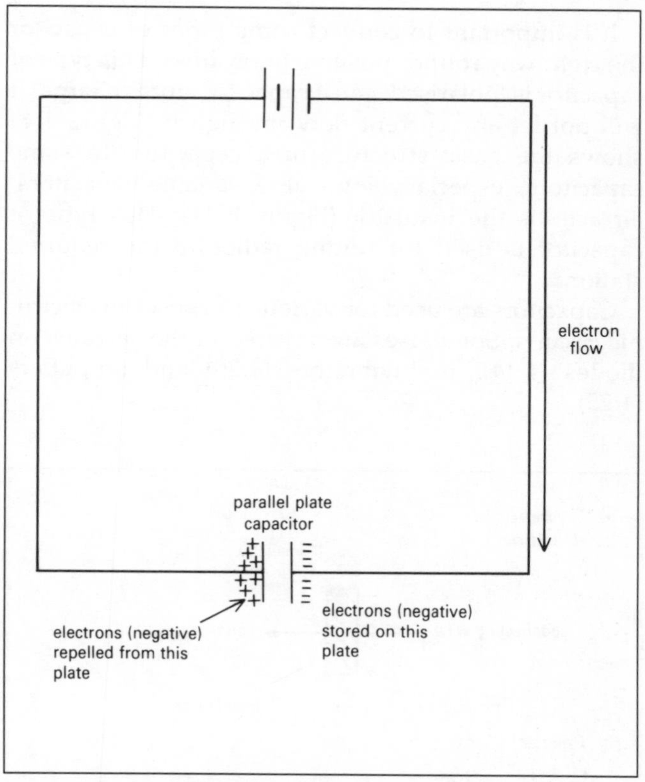

Figure 4.41 *Circuit to show a capacitor storing charge*

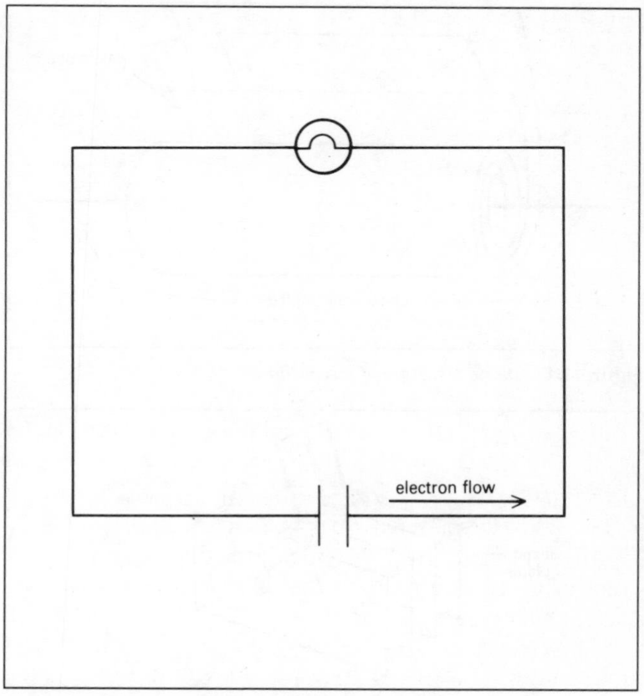

Figure 4.42 *Capacitor discharging through a light bulb*

4:12 CAPACITORS

Capacitors store small amounts of charge. The amount of charge stored is given by:

charge = capacitance × voltage across the capacitor

or

$$Q = C \times V$$

where charge (Q) is measured in coulombs
capacitance (C) is measured in farads
voltage (V) is measured in volts

A farad is a very large amount so the units usually used are:

microfarad $\mu F = 1/1\,000\,000\, F = 10^{-6} F$
nanofarad $nF = 10^{-9}$ F
picofarad $pF = 10^{-12}$ F

The circuit in Figure 4.41 shows how a capacitor stores charge. If the power supply is disconnected and a bulb put in its place, as in Figure 4.42, the capacitor will discharge through lighting the bulb.

It is important to connect some types of capacitor the right way round: positive to positive. This type of capacitor is 'polarised'. As a capacitor stores charge, it will not let any current flow through it. Figure 4.43 shows the basic structure of a capacitor. In some capacitors, especially low-value variable capacitors, air acts as the insulator (Figure 4.44). This type of capacitor is used for tuning radios to the required station.

Capacitors are used for various purposes in electronic circuits. Some uses are covered in the sections on diodes (4:14), multivibrators (4:20) and amplifiers (4:25).

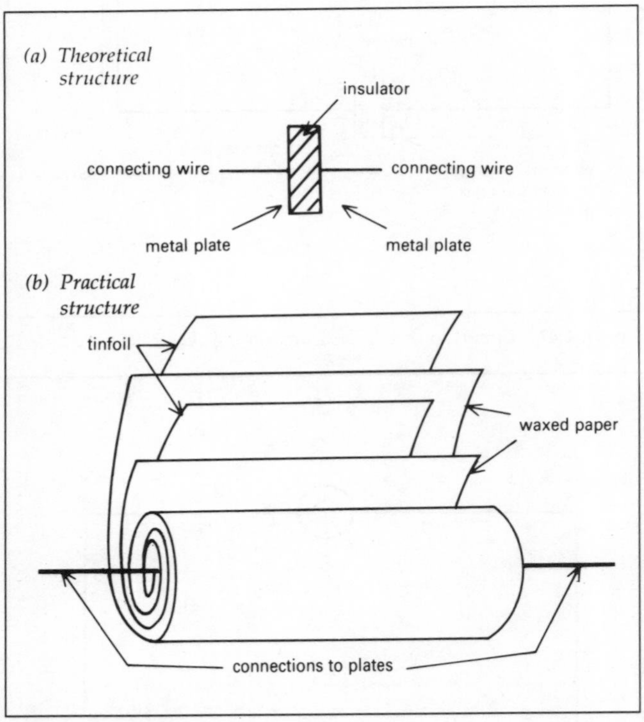

Figure 4.43 *Basic structure of a capacitor*

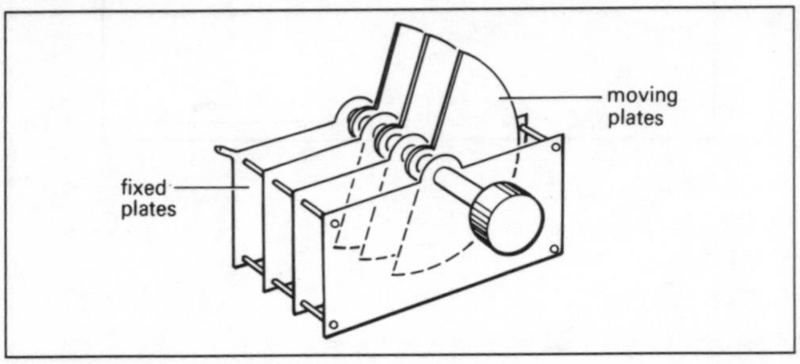

Figure 4.44 *Air-insulated capacitor*

4:13 THE TRANSFORMER

The size of an AC voltage can be increased or decreased using a **transformer**. Figure 4.45 shows the basic layout. Note that the two circuits through the primary and the secondary circuits are electrically separate. The primary coil creates a changing magnetic field passing through the secondary coil. This magnetic field induces (creates) a current in the secondary coil.

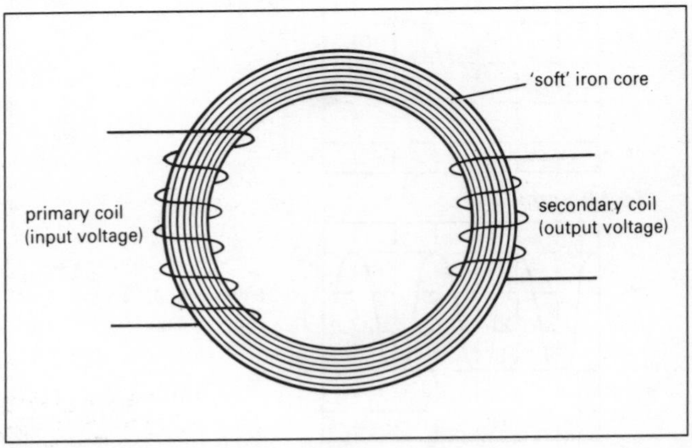

Figure 4.45 *Layout of a transformer*

The primary and secondary voltages are dependent on the number of turns of wire on each coil. If the secondary coil has half the number of turns of the primary coil then the secondary (or output) voltage is half the primary (or input) voltage. If the secondary coil has three times as many turns as the primary coil then the output voltage would be three times the input voltage. Obviously similar rules apply to other numbers of turns of wire on the coil. This can be summarised as:

$$\frac{\text{number of turns on primary coil}}{\text{number of turns on secondary coil}} = \frac{\text{primary or input voltage}}{\text{secondary or output voltage}}$$

or

$$\frac{N_p}{N_s} = \frac{V_p}{V_s}$$

A step-up transformer makes the output voltage greater than the input voltage, and a step-down transformer makes the output voltage smaller than the input voltage. If the transformer is 100% efficient then:

input power = output power

This means, in practical terms, that a doubling of voltage would give only half the current available in the output circuit. The first formula above can now be extended to:

$$\frac{N_p}{N_s} = \frac{V_p}{V_s} = \frac{I_s}{I_p}$$

where I_s is the secondary current (output)
I_p is the primary current (input)

both are measured in amps.

4:14 THE DIODE AND RECTIFICATION: CHANGING AC TO DC

There are many devices which can only use DC. These include televisions, calculators, computers and hi-fi systems. As only AC is available from the CEGB, a means of converting AC to DC is needed and this process is called **rectification**. Rectifying circuits contain diodes which only allow electricity to flow in one direction.

The circuit in Figure 4.46(a) shows a bulb lit by a battery, with an ammeter measuring the current. A CRO is plugged in either side of the bulb, to measure the voltage. The waveform is shown alongside the circuit. If the battery is replaced by an AC source (Figure 4.46b), the bulb will again light but the DC meter will show no current flowing because it cannot respond to AC current. (The pointer tries to move in opposite directions at a frequency of 50Hz.) If a diode is now inserted with the polarities as shown in Figure 4.46(c) the bulb will still light, although it will be a little dimmer, and the ammeter will give a reading. The diode has changed AC into a form of DC by cutting out the current flow in one direction.

Although the current in Figure 4.46(c) is a type of DC, it is not steady. The diode has just removed half of the wave, so this form is known as half-wave rectification. Some of the ripple effect can be smoothed out by placing a capacitor across the output of the circuit, in parallel with the bulb. Values of 100 to 1000 microfarad are normally suitable, depending on the current. Figure 4.46(d) shows the effect of the capacitor.

If the single diode is replaced with four diodes,

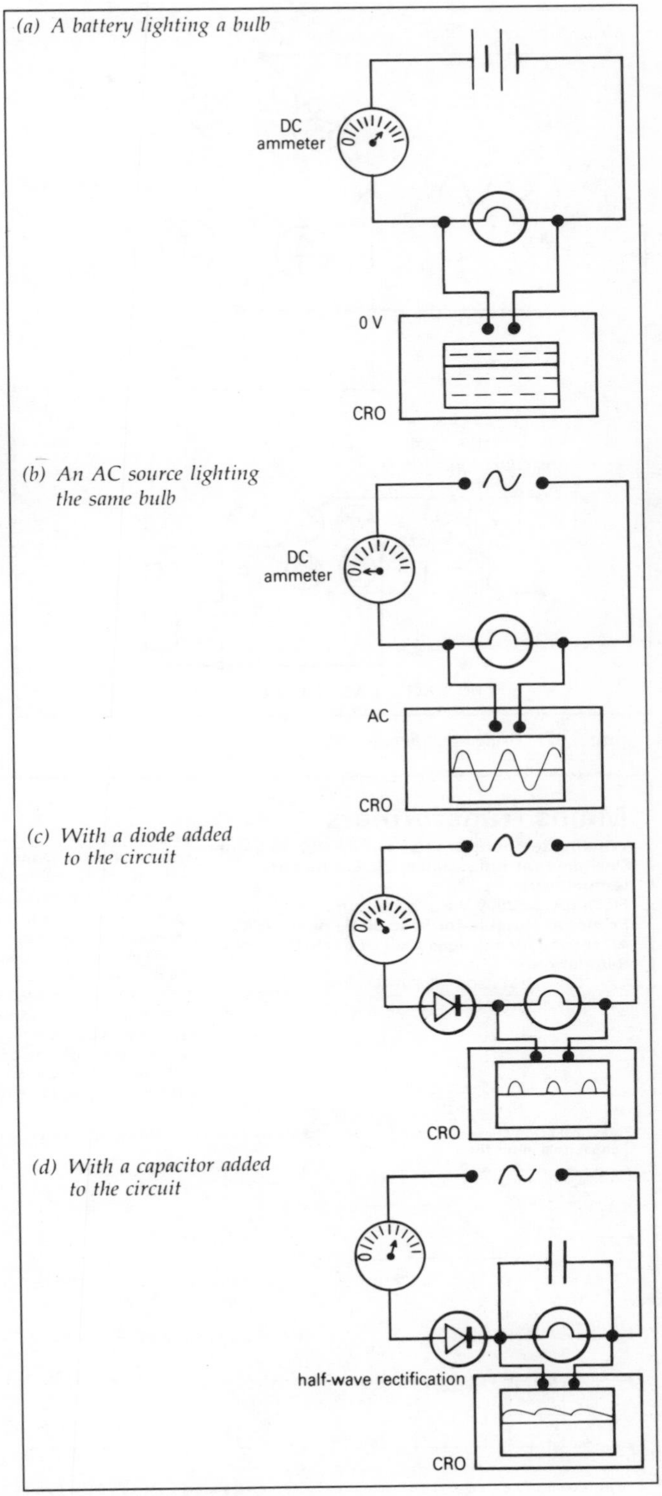

Figure 4.46 *Rectification*

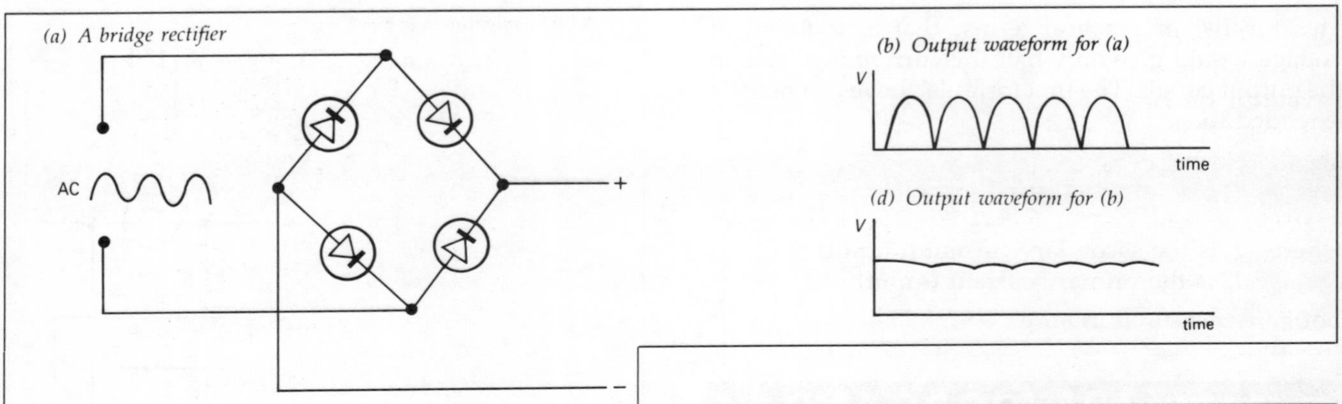

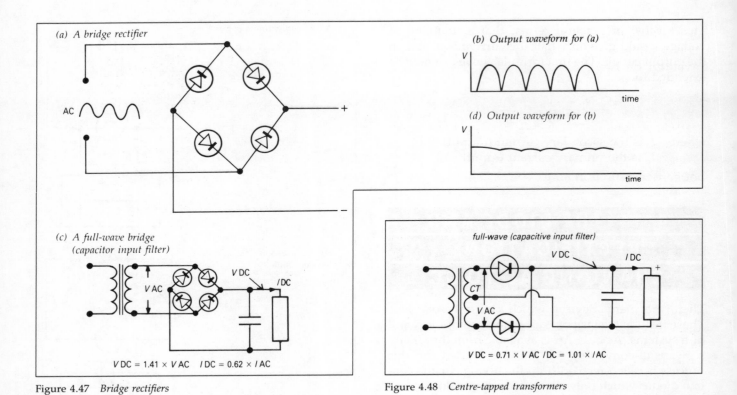

Figure 4.47 *Bridge rectifiers*

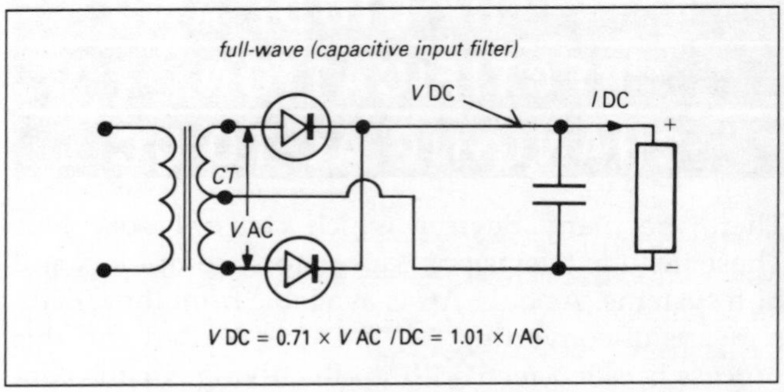

Figure 4.48 *Centre-tapped transformers*

Mains transformers

Winding temperature rise within CEE 15 limits.
Designed for full rating at 25 °C ambient temperature.
Flash tested 2000 V a.c. minimum.
Primaries suitable for 50 to 60 Hz operation.
All secondary voltages are FULL LOAD
Regulation =

$$\frac{\text{Off load voltage} - \text{full load voltage}}{\text{Off load voltage}} \times 100\%$$

transformer current ratings
When a transformer is used to supply any load other than a pure resistive one, it is necessary to derate its specified a.c. current rating to prevent overload. These current derating factors are shown below each circuit and relate the transformer a.c. current rating to the d.c. load current.
Note: Where a transformer has a VA rating, this is the product of the secondary a.c. voltage and the secondary a.c. current.

d.c. output voltage of circuits
Relationships between V d.c. and V a.c. shown below each rectifier circuit do not include losses.

The transformer's a.c. output voltage is specified at the full load current – off load, the voltage will rise in accordance with the regulation specified for that particular transformer.

rectifier ratings
For full-wave circuits, the average current per rectifier is 0·5 × I d.c. For half-wave circuits it equals I d.c. For all circuits each rectifier should have a V_{RRM} rating in excess of 1·4 × V a.c. except the half-wave capacitor input filter circuit which requires a rating in excess of 2·8 × V a.c.

Relationships and circuits shown below are intended as a guide and assume no circuit losses. For low d.c. voltages allowance should be made for the diode voltage drop.

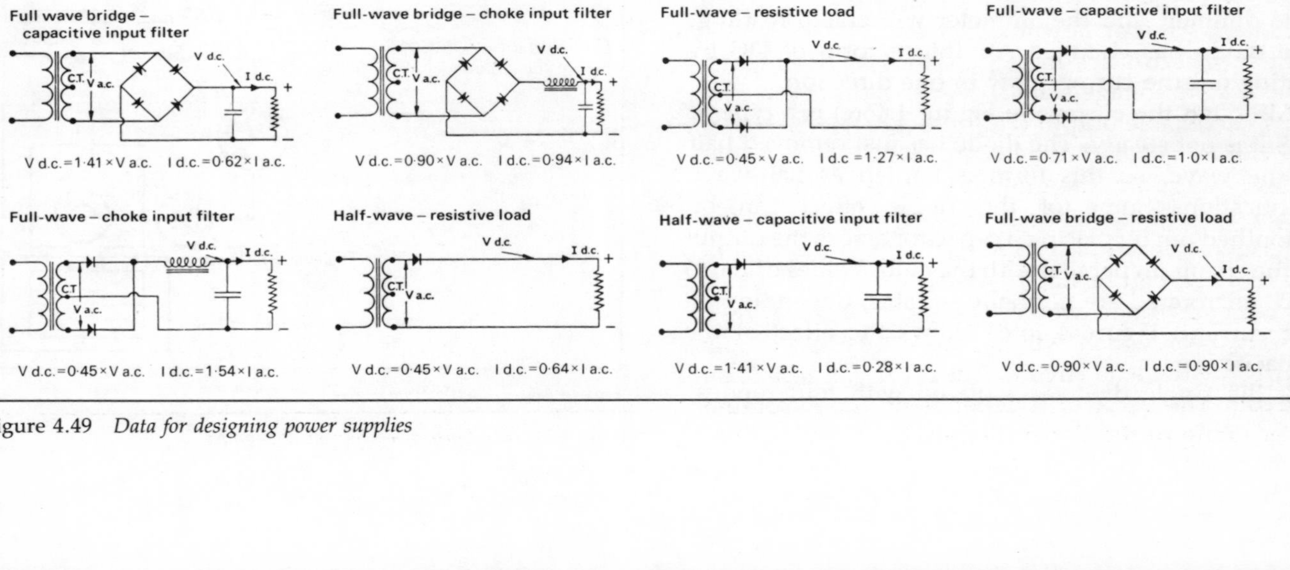

Figure 4.49 *Data for designing power supplies*

called a bridge rectifier (see Figure 4.47a) full-wave rectification is achieved. Figure 4.47(b) shows the waveform on the CRO, Using four diodes in this way ensures that all parts of the AC input are used and the electricity flow is always in the same direction. A closer approximation to true DC can be achieved by including a capacitor of about 100 to 1000 microfarad connected across the output (Figure 4.47c).

The capacitor stores and releases charge to give a smoothing effect to the rippled DC. The higher the current taken from the power supply, the bigger the capacitor needs to be to give sufficient smoothing. Capacitors up to 1 000 000 microfarads are commonly found in commercial power supplies. In Figure 4.48 centre-tapped transformers provide another method for a full-wave rectification.

When designing power supplies it is easiest to use data already produced and available. Figure 4.49 shows an extract from the RS catalogue. Notice that the voltage and current output depend on the type of circuit used. This type of information is available from reference books and other sources. An important skill in technology is the ability to search out and use this type of information within the design process to reduce the time and cost of development.

TO3

Monolithic voltage regulator intended for use as supplies for digital or linear integrated circuits. Internal fold-back overload and short-circuit protection. Case size TO3. Output voltage may be easily increased, e.g. the 5 V type can provide 6 V or 9 V, etc.

typical parameters	*5 V types*
Output current	1200 mA
Input voltage range	7–35 V
Load regulation	1%
Ripple rejection	70 dB
Output resistance	50 mΩ
Line regulation	0·1%
Output noise voltage (10 Hz–100 kHz)	0·04%
Short-circuit current	dependent on V_{in}
Suitable transformer	207–122 sec. in series

* A superimposed ripple of typically 10 mV pp at approximately 55 MHz may be present on the regulated output.

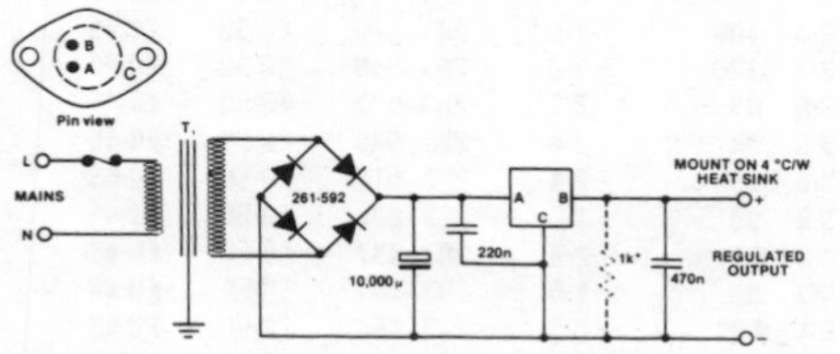

Figure 4.50 *(a) Typical voltage stabilisers*

4:15 VOLTAGE STABILISERS

It is often essential to make sure that the supply voltage to an electronic circuit is within a well-defined voltage range. If the voltage rises too high the circuit components might be ruined; a low voltage might result in inaccuracies in the circuit operation. Very sophisticated voltage stabilisers exist which can provide a very stable output (Figure 4.50). Simple stabilising can be carried out by components called Zener diodes which are designed to 'break down' at a specific reverse bias voltage without actually ruining the diode. An example circuit and current flow graph are shown in Figure 4.50(b) and 4.50(c).

The Zener diode would always be used with a series resistor which will dissipate any power not required by the load circuit. This is the simplest form of circuit. The value of R depends on the maximum power rating of the Zener diode.

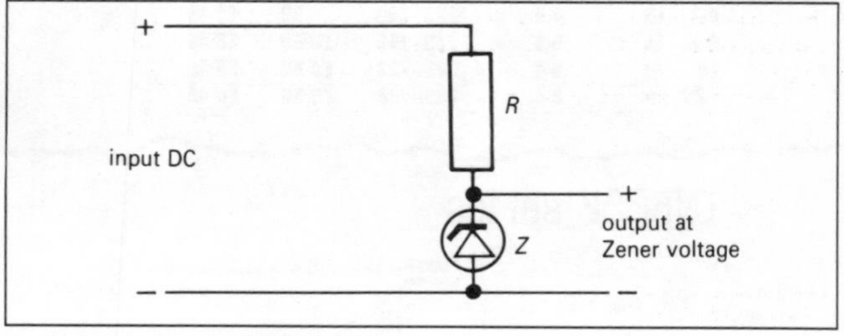

Figure 4.50 *(b) Using Zener diodes*

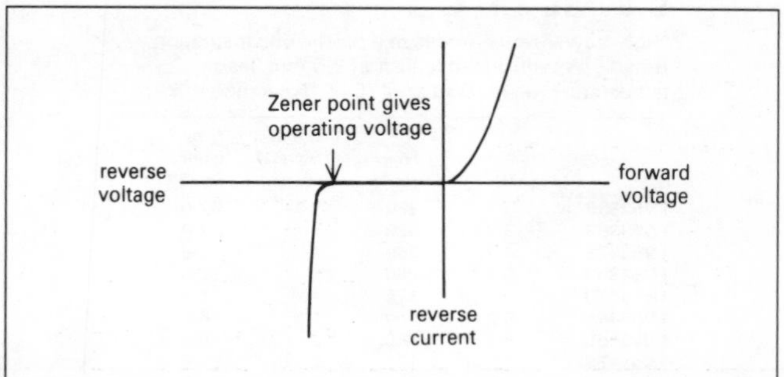

Figure 4.50 *(c) Zener diode current flow graph*

Table 4.7

BZX79 series

Supplied to RS by Mullard

500 mW

A range of silicon planar zener diodes intended for use as low voltage stabilizers or voltage references. DO-35 envelopes, ±5% tolerance.

technical specification	
Maximum power dissipation (If leads are kept at 50 °C at 8 mm from body)	500 mW
Non-repetitive peak reverse power dissipation	30 W (max.)
Maximum junction temp $V_Z < 3$ V	150 °C
$V_Z \geqslant 3$ V	200 °C
Thermal resistance from junction to tie point	0·30 °C/mW
θ_{JA} for p.c.b. mounting	
<50 mm² Cu 310 °C to 380 °C/W for 5 to 25 mm leads	
>100 mm² Cu 275 °C to 340 °C/W for 5 to 25 mm leads	

V_Z	slope res. (Ω) (max.)	temp. coeff. (mV/°C)	stock no.	price per pk 1–9	10+
2·4	100	−1·6	283–570	£0·50	£0·45
2·7	100	−2·0	283–586	£0·50	£0·45
3·0	95	−2·1	283–592	£0·50	£0·45
3·3	95	−2·4	283–609	£0·50	£0·45
3·6	90	−2·4	283–615	£0·50	£0·45
3·9	90	−2·5	283–621	£0·50	£0·45
4·3	90	−2·5	283–637	£0·50	£0·45
4·7	80	−1·4	283–643	£0·50	£0·45
5·1	60	−0·8	283–659	£0·50	£0·45
5·6	40	1·2	283–665	£0·50	£0·45
6·2	10	2·3	283–671	£0·50	£0·45
6·8	15	3·0	283–687	£0·50	£0·45
7·5	15	4·0	283–693	£0·50	£0·45
8·2	15	4·6	283–700	£0·50	£0·45
9·1	15	5·5	283–716	£0·50	£0·45
10	20	6·4	283–722	£0·50	£0·45
12	25	8·4	283–738	£0·50	£0·45

IN5333 series

L. 8·6 Dia. 3·5

Supplied to RS by Semitron

5 W at 25 °C

High-power zener diodes in a plastic encapsulation. Rated 5 W with a lead length of 9·5 mm, lead temperature maintained at ⩽75 °C. Tolerance ±5%.

type	V	I_{TEST} (mA)	slope res. (Ω) (max.)	temp. coeff. (mV/°C)
1N5333B	3·3	380	3	−2·0
1N5335B	3·9	320	2	−2·0
1N5337B	4·7	260	2	+1·5
1N5339B	5·6	220	1	+2·5
1N5342B	6·8	175	1	+5·0
1N5344B	8·2	150	1·5	+6·0
1N5346B	9·1	150	2	+6·0
1N5347B	10	125	2	+7·0
1N5349B	12	100	2·5	+10

Table 4.7 shows a typical list of Zener diodes with a 500 mW and 5 W rating (from the RS catalogue).

Example Suppose a 5 V output is wanted from a 9 V input. The nearest Zener voltage is 5.1 V. For a low current load, the 500 mW (0.5 W) Zener might be adequate:

$$\text{power} = V \times I$$
$$0.5 = 5.1 \times I$$
$$I = \frac{0.5}{5.1}$$
$$= 0.1\text{ A approx.}$$

Using $R = V/I$ and $V = 9 - 5.1 = 3.9$V

$$R = \frac{3.9}{0.1} = 39 \text{ ohms}$$

A 39 ohm resistor will therefore ensure that the Zener diode remains within its power rating when the external circuit is off or disconnected and all the current is passing through the Zener diode. Remember to choose a resistor of the correct power rating:

$$P = V \times I$$
$$= 3.9 \times 0.1$$
$$= 0.39\text{ W}$$

A resistor rated at 0.5 W or greater would be needed.

If the external circuit draws more than the designed maximum current then the voltage across the resistor will increase above 3.9 V and so the output will drop below 5.1 V. It is therefore necessary to specify the maximum output current when designing a power supply.

More complex stabilisers are available which ensure better protection than a single Zener diode. Suppliers often have sheets of example circuits: it is not always necessary to start from scratch in designing a power supply.

4:16 SAFETY

Safety is usually ensured by:

(a) using reliable components from a reputable supplier
(b) protection by fuses or other circuit breakers
(c) earthing all metal parts which can be touched
(d) visible indication of power on such as a neon indicator immediately after the mains switch.

Pupils should not normally be allowed to build mains-operated equipment. If such equipment is built it must have the full protection of earthing and fuses. Any wiring should be checked by a competent electrician if it is designed for direct connection to the mains. A fused plug should be fitted with a three-amp fuse for a power supply providing low voltage output. A fuse should also be connected in series with the output to protect internal components against short circuit or overload. Many power supplies obtainable in schools have a thermal circuit breaker on the output circuit.

Residual current circuit breakers (RCCB) are now very common for mains-operated equipment. An imbalance in the current between the live and neutral line, implying a leakage to earth, switches off the circuit within 30 milliseconds to protect against fatal electric shocks.

4:17 SWITCHES

Switching on a light or a television set is a simple manual process. Other switching processes can be remote or automatic. A washing machine control unit is an example of automatic switching to produce a complete wash cycle. Fire alarms and burglar alarms are automatic and can be connected directly to a fire station or police station to activate an alarm remotely.

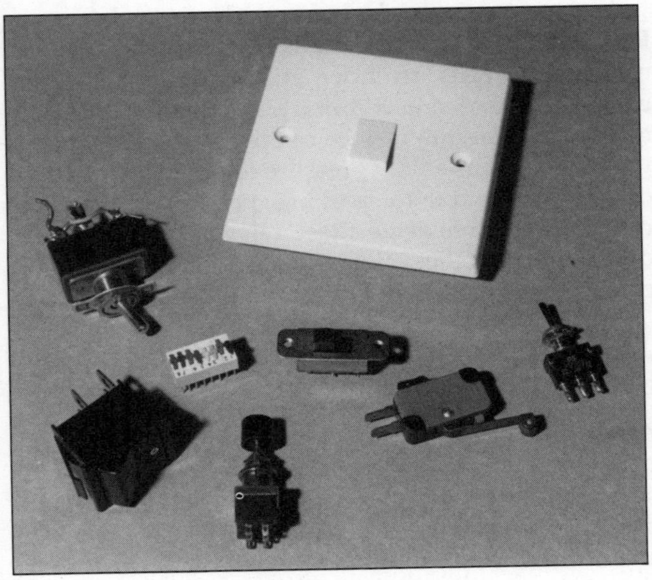

Figure 4.51 *Various switches*

There are three basic methods of switching which can be classified as:

(a) local (includes manual, microswitches and switches operated from a control panel)
(b) remote (switching that takes place away from a control centre)
(c) automatic (switching that occurs as a result of an action somewhere in the electrics of a device or mechanics of a machine).

LOCAL SWITCHING

Figure 4.51 shows some examples of the many switches that are available from suppliers. The specification of a switch will include:

(a) current-switching rating
(b) current-carrying rating
(c) voltage rating
(d) contact resistance
(e) action–momentary, alternate, latching
(f) contact configuration.

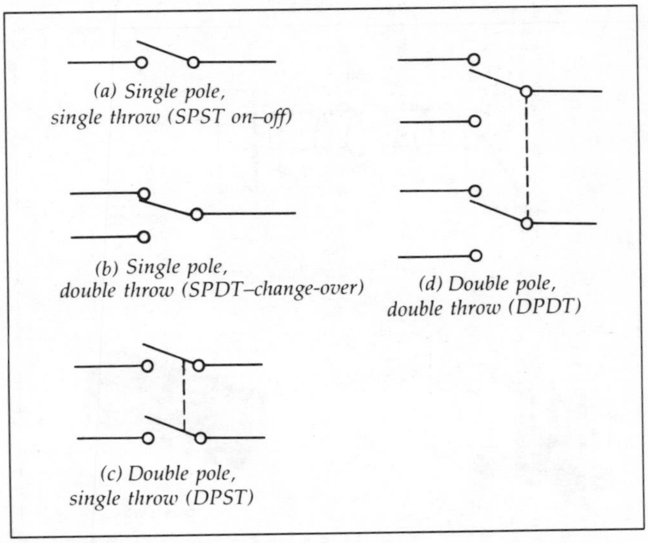

Figure 4.52 *Switch contact arrangements*

Figure 4.52 shows how the contacts are arranged in some typical examples.

Many other pole:throw combinations are possible and some switches, especially rotary types, can be built up to give any required multi-switching capability. Mains switches are sometimes double-pole types so that both live and neutral wires can be disconnected by the switch. The actual use will determine the complete switch specification.

Remote Switching

This type of switching involves one circuit (often a low power circuit) switching another circuit (often a high power or inaccessible circuit). The most common type of switch for this situation is a **relay** (see Figure 4.53).

The coil and soft iron core form an electromagnet when electric current flows through the coil circuit. Very low activating currents are required to pull the armature and move the contacts but very large voltages and currents can be switched at the contacts. The contacts are described in a similar way to ordinary switches, e.g. SPST (on–off), SPDT (change over).

When the current to the coil is switched off, the magnetic field collapses causing a **back e.m.f.** in the coil which can be many hundreds of volts. This back e.m.f. could damage components in the coil switching circuit so a diode is placed in parallel with the coil to allow the induced voltage to decay safely (Figure 4.54).

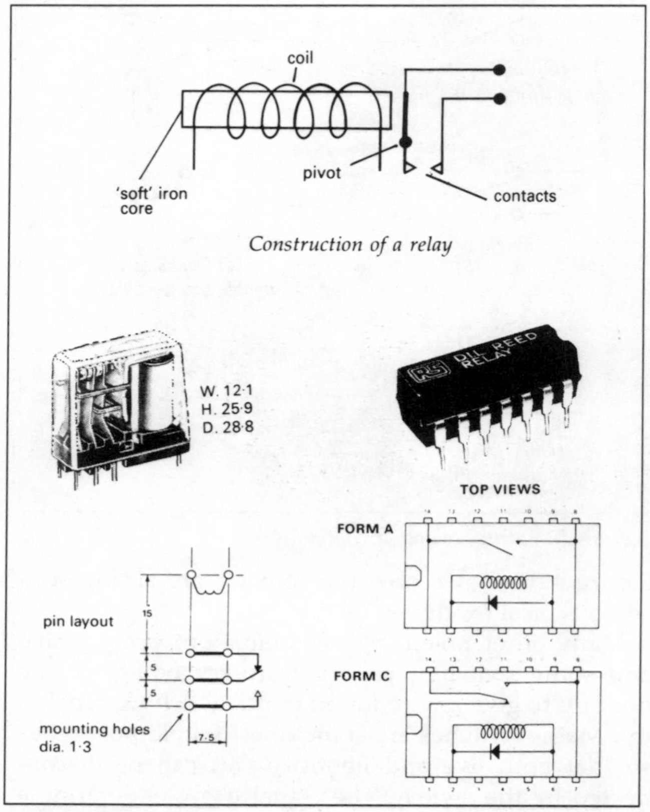

Figure 4.53 *Relays*

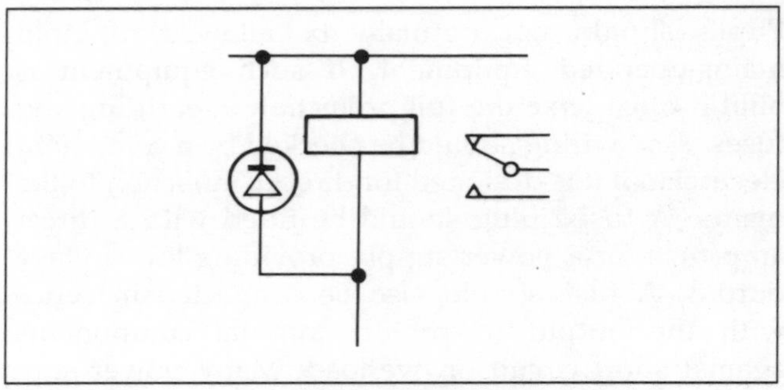

Figure 4.54 *Diode in parallel with a relay coil*

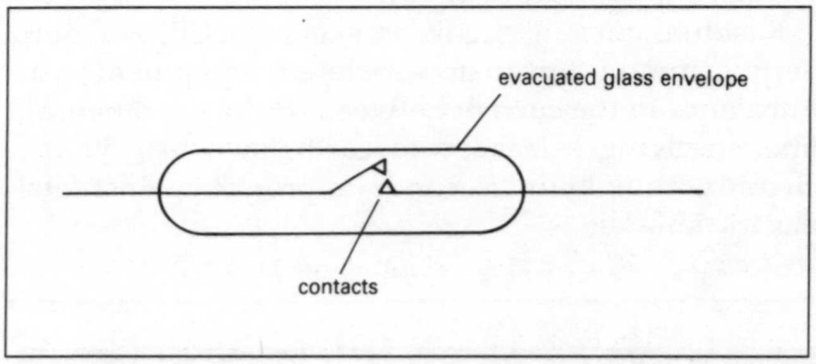

Figure 4.55 *Reed relay*

Many different types of relays are available and any designer would need to consider the requirements of the relay before deciding which one to use. A relay with contacts rated at a higher voltage and current than necessary might provide greater reliability at a slightly higher cost. The contact resistance, however, could also be higher which might cause problems in the secondary circuit.

Another type of relay, the reed relay, shown in Figure 4.55, is activated by a magnetic field which causes the 'reeds' to move and make or break the contacts. The reed and contacts are usually enclosed in a sealed glass tube which can be evacuated or filled with an inert gas at low pressure to prevent oxidation of the contacts due to sparking. Permanent magnets can be used to activate these relays. They are then called reed switches and are commonly used as door or window switches in burglar alarm systems.

Transistors and Automatic Switching

Automatic switching involves no intervention by people. The float switch in a washing machine ensures that water does not go above a certain level by switching off the water inlet valves. A float switch is also used in cars on brake master cylinders to warn the driver if the brake fluid is low. Automated industrial processes rely on automatic switches to measure, monitor and warn if anything goes wrong. Many automatic switches rely on a change in the electrical properties of a component in a circuit. Transistors are often used to detect this change and act as the switch.

THE TRANSISTOR

Transistors are devices with three terminals, the emitter (*e*), base (*b*) and collector (*c*). Figure 4.56 shows how a small **base** current allows a much larger current to flow from the **collector** to the **emitter**. This type of transistor is called an npn transistor. The npn describes the type of semiconductor used for the three parts of the transistor. Pnp types are also available, the current then passes the opposite way through the device.

The ratio between the collector and base currents is called the current gain, given the symbol h_{FE}. This is found from the formula:

$$\text{current gain } (h_{FE}) = \frac{\text{collector current}}{\text{base current}} = \frac{I_c}{I_b}$$

The current gain from Figure 4.56 is:

$$h_{FE} = \frac{I_c}{I_b} = \frac{50}{0.2} = 250$$

If the current is flowing from collector to emitter and from base to emitter, the emitter current can be found from:

$$\text{emitter current, } I_e = I_c + I_b$$

The size of current transistors can handle varies enormously, from a few milliamps up to many amps. It is important to know the maximum current any particular transistor can handle. Currents of 1–10 A are controlled by power transistors.

Transistors are sensitive to heat and will break down if not maintained within their operating temperature. When soldering them into circuits, a **heat sink** (see Figure 4.57a) should always be used. They might also get hot when operating and sometimes need to be mounted on large heat sinks to keep them cool (see Figure 4.57b).

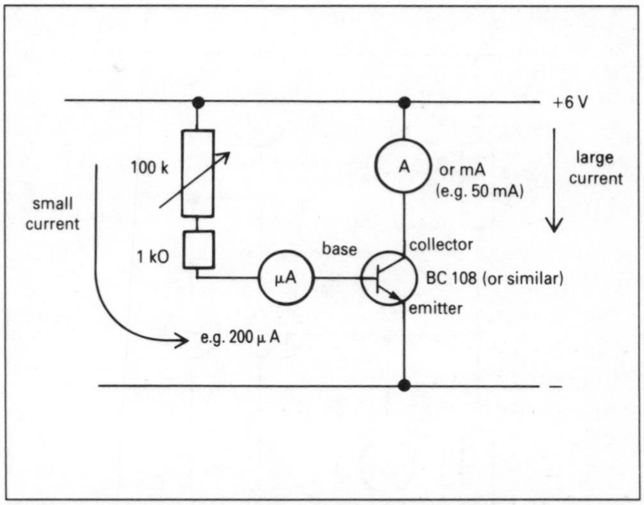

Figure 4.56 *Small base current allowing a much larger current to flow from collector to emitter*

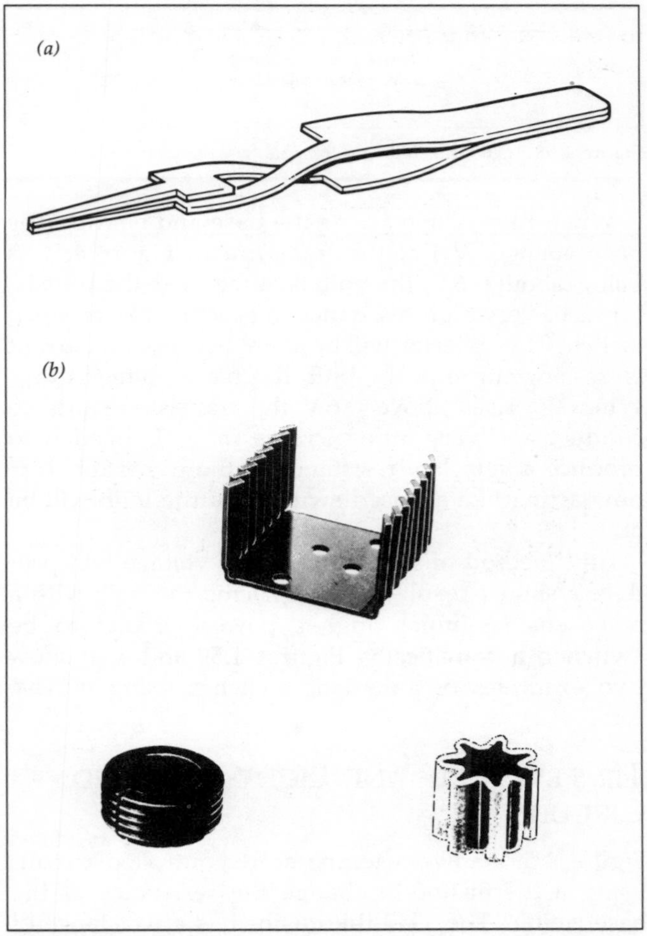

Figure 4.57 *Heat sinks*

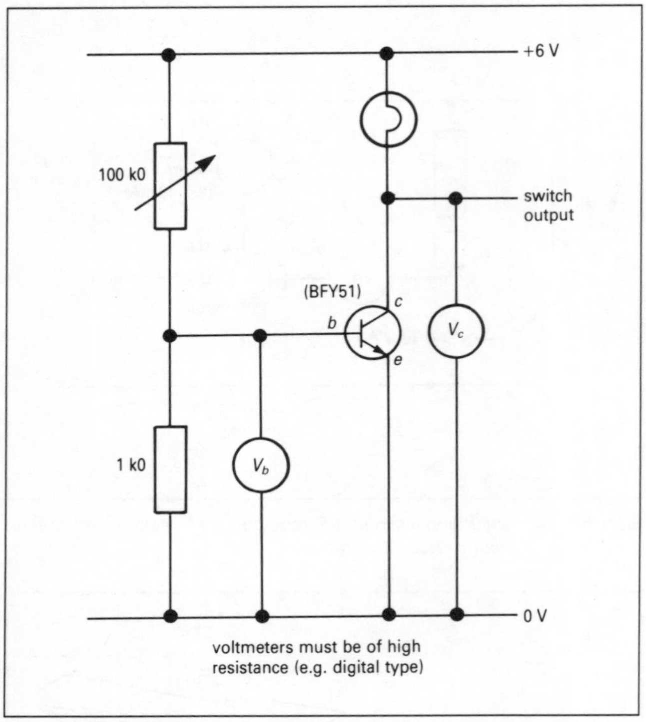

Figure 4.58 *Circuit including a transistor used as a switch*

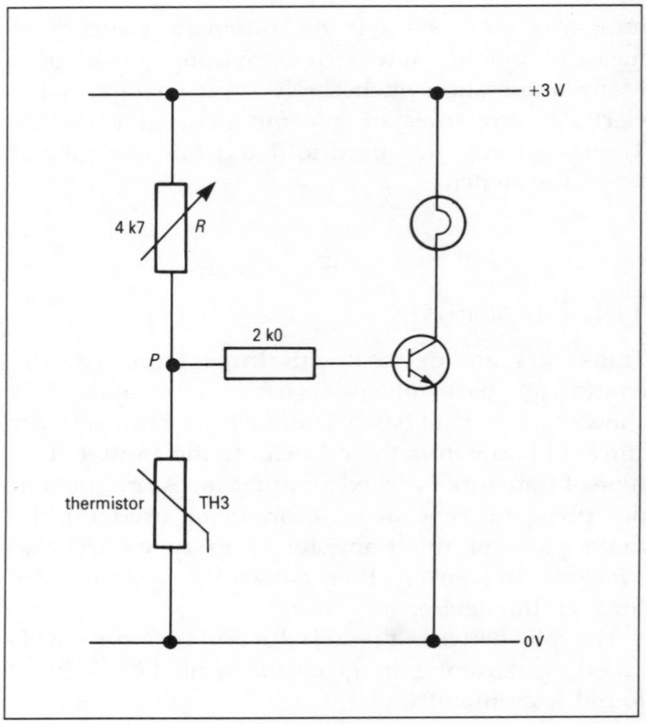

Figure 4.59 *Temperature-sensitive circuit*

When the voltage across the base and emitter (the base voltage, V_b) of the transistor in Figure 4.58 is below about 0.6 V, the bulb is off because the transistor has a very high resistance. It is acting like an open switch. The collector will be at 6 V because no current is passing through the bulb to give a voltage drop. When V_b rises above 0.6 V the transistor starts to conduct and very little increase in V_b is needed to produce a very low resistance in the transistor. It is now acting like a closed switch and the bulb will be on.

Any method of varying the base voltage will produce a similar result. Also, replacing the bulb with a relay enables much higher power circuits to be switched automatically. Figures 4.59 and 4.60 show two examples of automatic switches using transistors.

Temperature- and Light-operated Circuits

Figure 4.59 shows a temperature-controlled circuit, using a thermistor to change the resistance of the base circuit. The TH3 thermistor has a resistance of about 380 ohms at 25 °C and 28 ohms when hot.

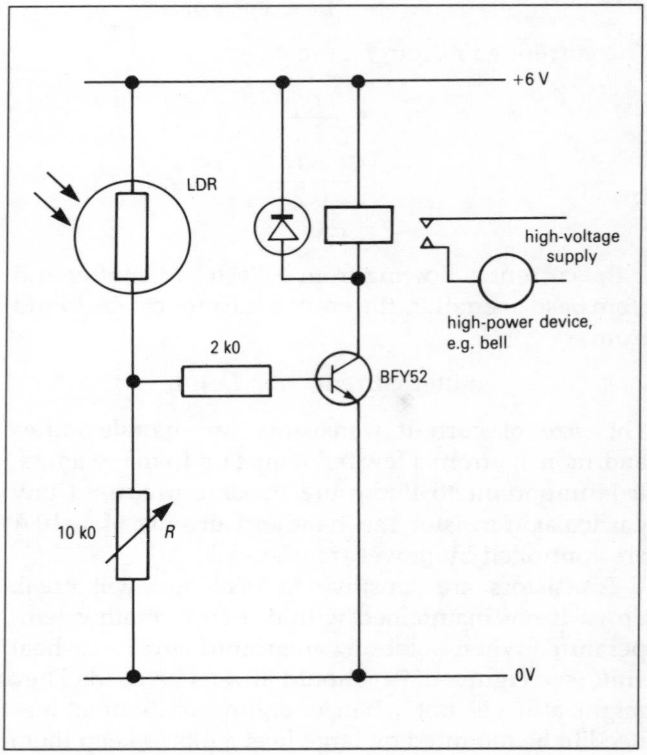

Figure 4.60 *Light-sensitive circuit*

At room temperature, point P in the circuit will be at about 1.5 V so the transistor is on. As the temperature increases the resistance of the thermistor falls, reducing the voltage at P and switching off the transistor. The drop of resistance due to a rise in temperature is called a negative temperature coefficient. The purpose of the variable resistor (used here in a potential divider) is to 'tune' the circuit to switch on at a specific temperature. The greater the resistance of the variable resistor, the lower the temperature to switch the circuit. The voltage divider is being used to **bias** the transistor to the correct voltage to work as required.

This type of circuit could be used as a thermostat to maintain a temperature. The bulb would be replaced by a relay to switch a heater and *R* would be a variable resistor to set the switching temperature.

Figure 4.60 is a light-controlled circuit using a light-dependent resistor (LDR) such as the ORP12. An ORP12 has a dark resistance of about 10 megohms and a light resistance around 100 ohms to 10 kilohms, depending on the light intensity. When light falls on the LDR, its resistance falls and so the voltage at P increases switching on the bulb. Again, a variable resistor is used to 'bias' the transistor.

The specification of the ORP12 is the type of information needed before a designer can choose an appropriate variable resistor *R*. This will decide the light level at which the circuit is switched. The relay is an interface device switching a high power circuit. Electric motors, solenoids, counters and buzzers could all be automatically controlled by this circuit via the relay.

Buffer Circuits

Modern industrial control processes often involve the use of computers. The control signals will originate from the computer's circuitry which will work at around 5 V to 12 V but only be able to provide a few milliamps of current. An **interface** is therefore needed to connect the computer to the device it is controlling.

This interface is generally known as a **buffer**. It often involves transistor switches and other components to provide electrical isolation of the computer from the controlled device in case of incorrect connections. Figure 4.61 shows a simple buffer circuit for use where the computer is close to the control element. The resistor in the base circuit provides extra protection to the computer circuits in case of an electrical fault in the external circuit, and ensures that the transistor base voltage is kept within specification limits.

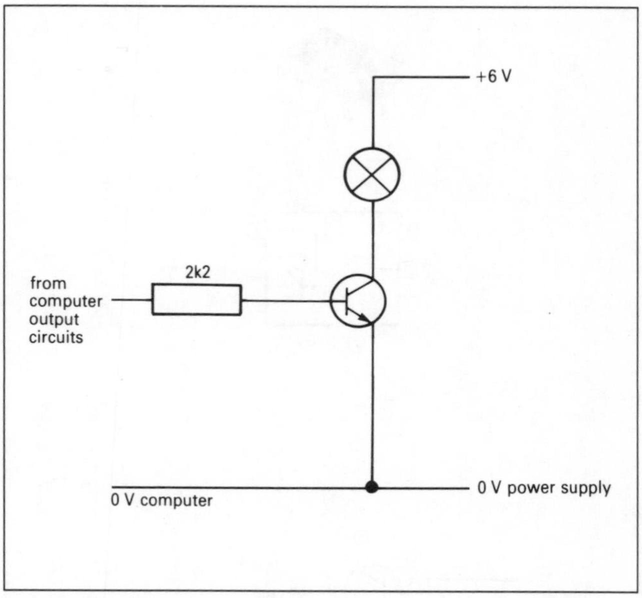

Figure 4.61 *Simple buffer circuit*

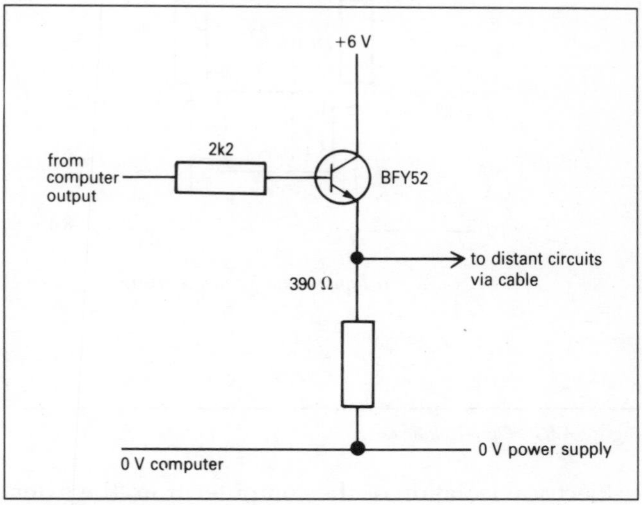

Figure 4.62 *Emitter follower circuit*

Figure 4.62 shows an alternative circuit, called an emitter follower. This is used to match the high-resistance, low-current computer circuit to cables for connection to distant control devices or circuits. This circuit gives high current gain with voltage gain of typically 0.95. It ensures good power transfer into the cable so that the signal reaches the remote devices.

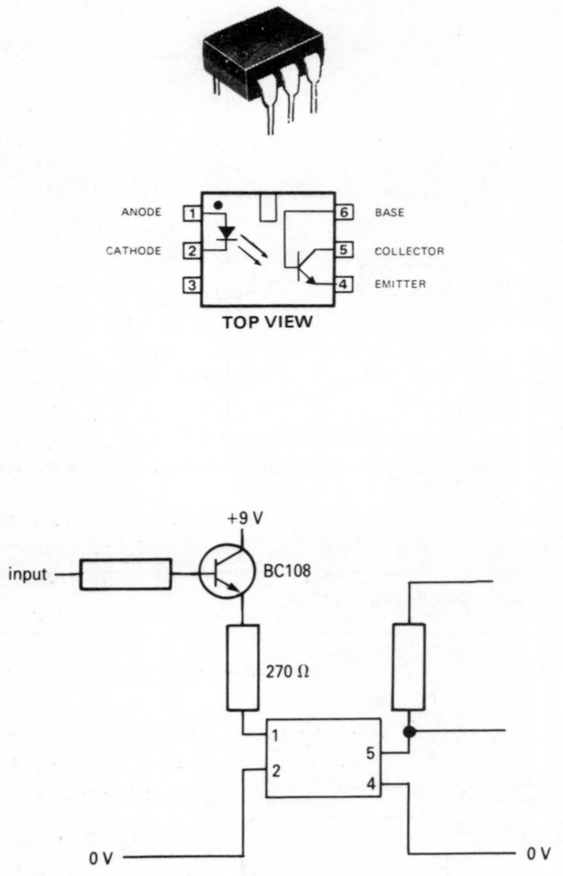

A typical opto-isolated circuit

Figure 4.63 *Opto-isolation*

Electrical isolation of the computer from the external circuits is sometimes desirable and opto-isolators have been designed specifically for this purpose. Opto-isolators can pass signals by light beams. The light is usually generated by a LED and is received by a light-sensitive transistor. The LED and transistor are contained within the same package, shown in Figure 4.63(a). Figure 4.63(b) shows a typical circuit using opto-isolation. This type of isolation is always needed in medical instrumentation, such as heart rate and breathing monitors, where connections are made to the body. In Figure 4.63(b), the power supplies of the input and output circuit are also separated to ensure complete isolation from mains equipment.

4:18 TRANSDUCERS

Many of the devices which are used in electronic circuits convert one form of energy into another form of energy. Such devices are called **transducers**. Those of interest here include electricity at either the start or end of the energy change.

The LDR and thermistor used in automatic switching circuits are transducers. Light energy is converted into the kinetic energy of electrons, giving more conduction electrons and hence higher currents and less resistance. The thermistor works in a similar way.

LEDs convert electrical energy into light energy. These diodes emit radiation of visible wavelengths when they are forward biased. They operate with currents of about 10 mA to 20 mA. LEDs should always be connected with the anode positive and manufacturer's specifications will usually have to be checked to recognise the anode and cathode. A series resistor should always be used to limit the current. The value of resistor can be calculated using Ohm's Law. There will always be about 2 V across the diode. Limiting the current to 10 mA will generally be safe but manufacturer's specifications should be consulted as some LEDs, especially green and yellow ones, might need currents as high as 40 mA.

standard 0·2 in l.e.d.

L. (Body) 8·6 Dia. 5·1 Lead pitch 0·1 in Leads 0·635 sq.
Cathode identified by 'flat' on body

For direct p.c.b. mounting or panel mounting using the black panel clip supplied with each diode. Clip suits a 6·35 mm (0·25 in) panel hole.

(quoted at 25 °C)	*red*	*green*	*yellow*	*red (wide angle)*	*units*
I_F max.	30	30	30	40	mA
I_F typ.	10	10	10	10	mA
V_R max.	3	3	3	3	V
P_D max.	100	115	115	115	mW
derate power	1·3	1·6	1·5	1·5	mW/°C
V_F at I_F typ.	2	2	2	2	V
intensity at I_F typ.	5	5	5	4	mcd
viewing angle	30	30	30	80	deg.
peak wavelength	635	565	585	635	nm

Figure 4.64 *LEDs: (a) Typical specification*

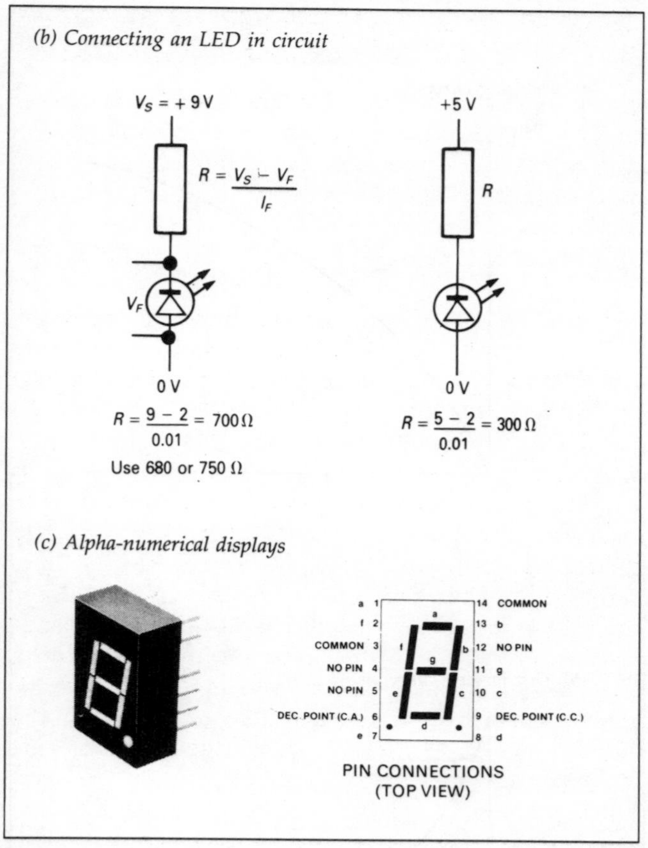

Figure 4.64 *(continued)*

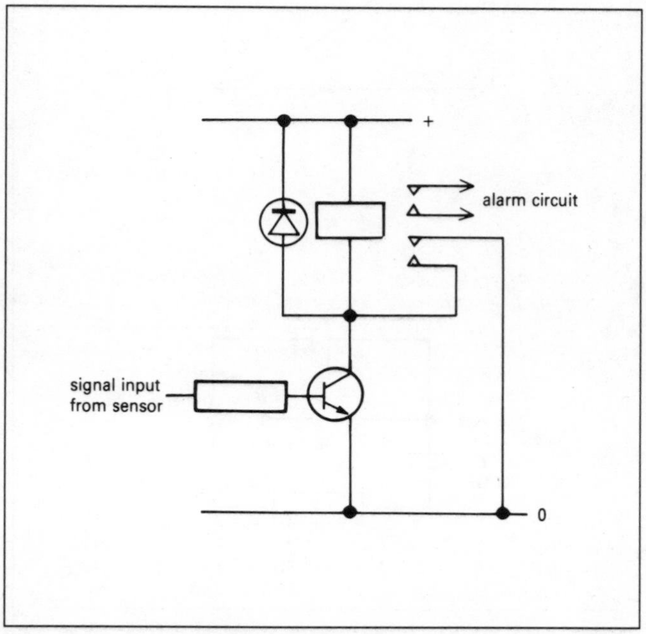

Figure 4.65 *Latching circuits using relays*

Figure 4.64(a) shows typical specifications for a LED commonly available in schools. Figure 4.64(b) shows the method of connection.

Alpha-numerical displays use many LEDs for displaying numbers or letters, depending on which LEDs are illuminated (Figure 4.64c). Liquid crystal displays have now superseded many LED displays because of the much lower current requirements (microamps instead of milliamps).

Some diodes emit radiation in the infra-red wavelength region and matched emitters and sensors can be used across distances of many metres. These are used in remote control application of the type seen in television controls. They are also used in some burglar alarm systems and in the control of model cars and boats. Other commonly used transducers include:

- loudspeakers (electrical energy to sound energy)
- microphones (sound energy to electrical energy)
- cathode ray tubes (electrical energy to light energy)
- photovoltaic cells (solar cells) (light energy into electrical energy)
- batteries (or cells) (chemical energy into electrical energy)
- electric motors (electrical energy to kinetic energy)
- generators (kinetic energy to electrical energy)
- solenoids (electrical energy to kinetic energy).

Ultrasonic emitters and sensors work at wavelengths of sound energy above normal hearing wavelengths but use the same overall energy changes as loudspeakers and microphones.

4:19 LATCHING CIRCUITS

Some circuits need to hold the output in a switched state when the switching influence has been removed. This is called latching. Burglar alarms using LDRs and fire alarms are examples of where this is necessary.

If a relay is used as the interface with the actual alarm then latching can be incorporated into the relay circuit. The relay contacts are used to complete a circuit in parallel with the transistor switch (see Figure 4.65). When the relay is energised by switching on, the transistor latching circuit connects the relay coil to zero volts in parallel with the transistor. Switching off the transistor will now have no effect on the relay and so the alarm will continue. The alarm would be reset by switching off the power supply to release the relay contacts.

4:20 DELAY AND TIMING CIRCUITS

Delay and timing circuits are common in electronic systems. Electronic clocks and timers, televisions, stereo radios and many other common devices all contain some form of delay or timing circuit. In most cases the delay, which can be a few microseconds to many seconds, is produced using capacitors.

ACTION OF A CAPACITOR

Delay and timing circuits use the charge or discharge of capacitors as a means of timing. Figure 4.66(a) shows how the charge builds up on a capacitor; Figure 4.66(b) shows the discharge curve and Figure 4.66(c) shows the circuit containing the capacitor. As the charge increases or decreases the voltage across the capacitor increases or decreases. This change in voltage can be used to switch transistors on and off at times which depend on the rate of change of voltage on the capacitor.

The rate of increase in the voltage depends on the value of the capacitance (C) and the series resistance (R). The value $C \times R$ is called the **time constant** of the circuit. C is measured in farads and R in ohms. The voltage will rise to 63% of its final voltage in one time constant and the capacitor will be fully charged after about 5 time constants. The time constant for the circuit in Figure 4.66(c) can be found from:

$$C \times R = 1000 \times 10^{-6} \times 10 \times 10^{3}$$
$$= 10 \text{ seconds}$$

It would therefore take 50 seconds to charge the capacitor.

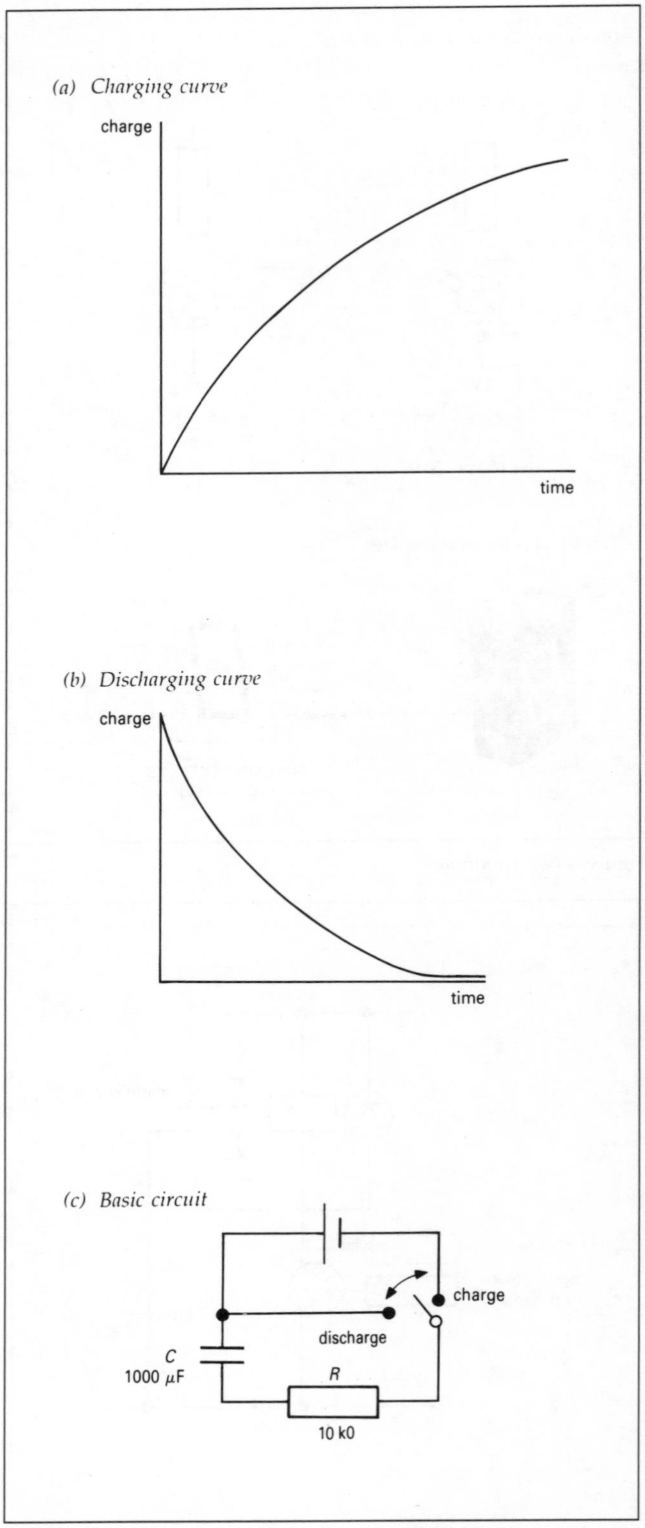

Figure 4.66 *Charging and discharging a capacitor*

SIMPLE TIME-DELAY CIRCUITS

Connecting the switch in Figure 4.67 to A discharges the capacitor completely. Connecting the switch to B allows the capacitor to charge up at a rate determined by the values of the resistor and the capacitor. When the voltage across the capacitor reaches about 0.6 V the transistor will switch on.

Figure 4.68 shows a better switching circuit. T_1 acts as an amplifier to switch on T_2 much faster. This type of transistor connection is called a Darlington driver or **Darlington pair**. The variable resistor in the timing circuit provides a method of varying the time between switching the switch and the bulb lighting. Replacing the bulb with a relay gives this circuit more flexibility.

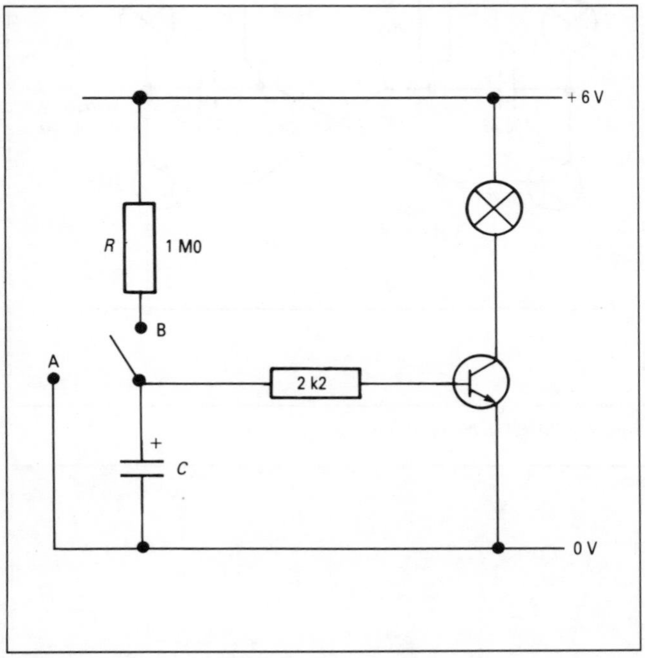

Figure 4.67 *A simple transistor time-delay circuit*

MULTIVIBRATOR CIRCUITS

The monostable **multivibrator** (Figure 4.69) has only one stable state, with T_1 off and T_2 on. The base of T_2 is held above 0.6 V by the resistor R_1. R_1 and C form the timing components. If the push switch S is momentarily pressed then the base of T_2 is connected to 0 V and the capacitor C is discharged. On releasing S, the capacitor will start to recharge through R_1 and the base voltage on T_2 will slowly increase. Eventually T_2 will switch on. The collector voltage on T_2 will fall and this reduces the base voltage on T_1 which will switch off. The circuit will then remain in this state until the switch S is again pressed.

A relay could be used to interface this circuit to mains-powered equipment such as photographic timers. Using relays with a combination of normally open and normally closed contacts makes this a very flexible circuit. The value of the capacitor and the resistor would depend on the application and R_1 would normally be a variable resistor. It is also possible to have various different resistors which can be switched in and out to provide more accurate and preset times. A rotary switch would normally be used.

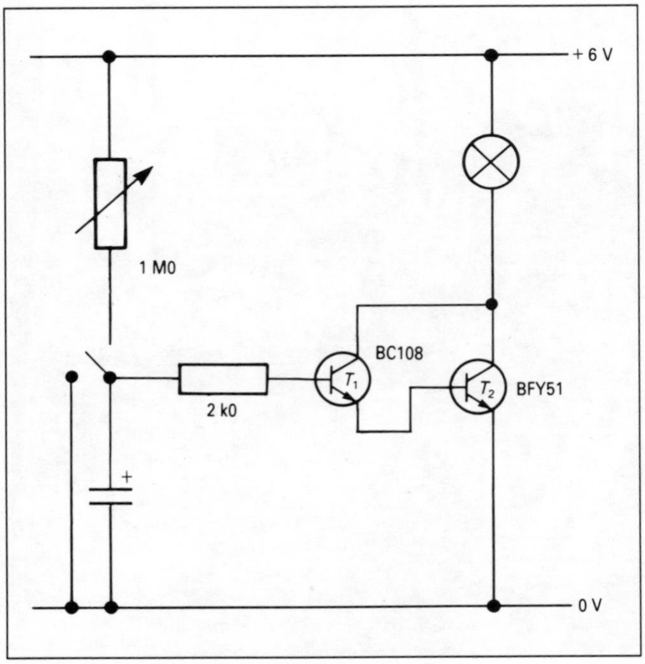

Figure 4.68 *Timing circuit with better switching action*

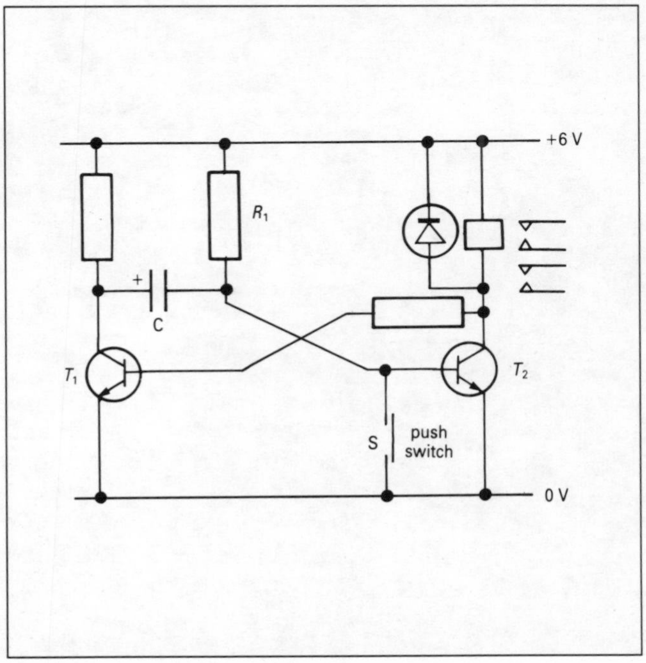

Figure 4.69 *Monostable multivibrator*

In astable multivibrators the transistors keep switching on and off continuously and will never be in a stable state. Figure 4.70 shows a typical circuit for the astable multivibrator. There are two sets of timing capacitor and resistor, R_1 and C_1 and R_2 and C_2.

If the timing components are the same value in each half of the circuit then each transistor will be on and off for equal time intervals. The rate at which the bulbs flash can be altered by using different values of R_1, C_1, R_2 and C_2 in the timing circuits. This type of circuit is often used in warning devices to attract attention. Figure 4.71 shows some typical applications. All the examples shown are warning systems in which the lights flash on and off. The switching rate can be set so that an audible warning device is produced by changing the value of the timing capacitor, C_1 and replacing one of the bulbs with a loudspeaker, as shown in Figure 4.72.

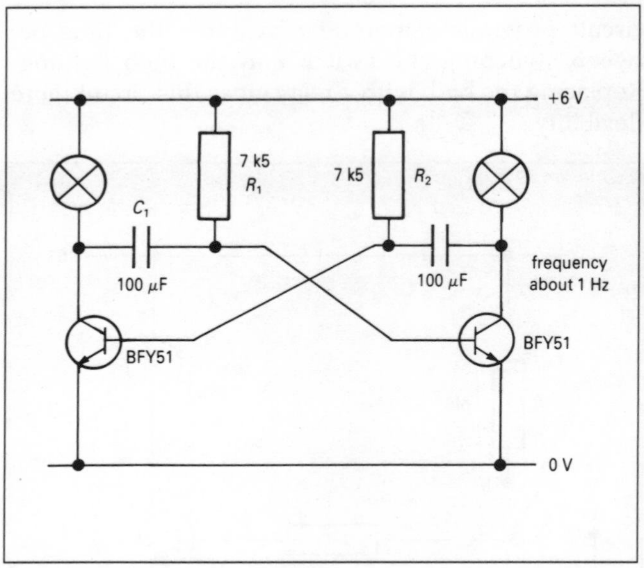

Figure 4.70 *Astable multivibrator*

Figure 4.71 *Examples of warning systems*

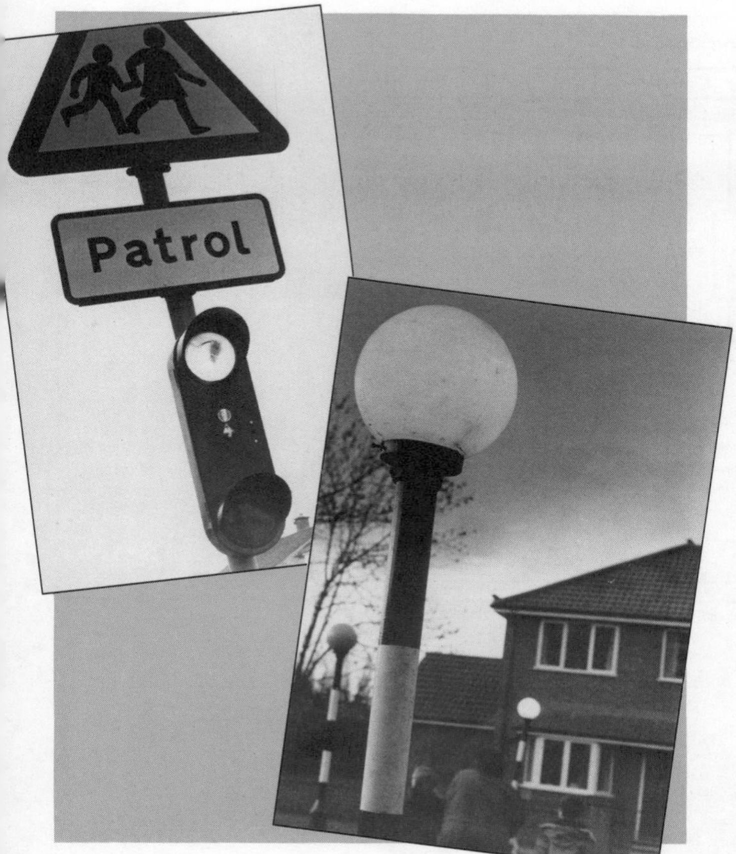

Figure 4.71 *(continued)*

Figure 4.73 shows how a practical timer and warning circuit can be produced by combining a timer circuit and an astable multivibrator. The switching on of the transistor in the timer circuit provides the power for the astable circuit to operate. *C* and *R* would be chosen to give the required timing delay.

A model flashing light system for use with model trains (Figure 4.74) could be made by replacing the bulbs in a slow astable circuit with red LEDs. A resistor should be in series with the LED.

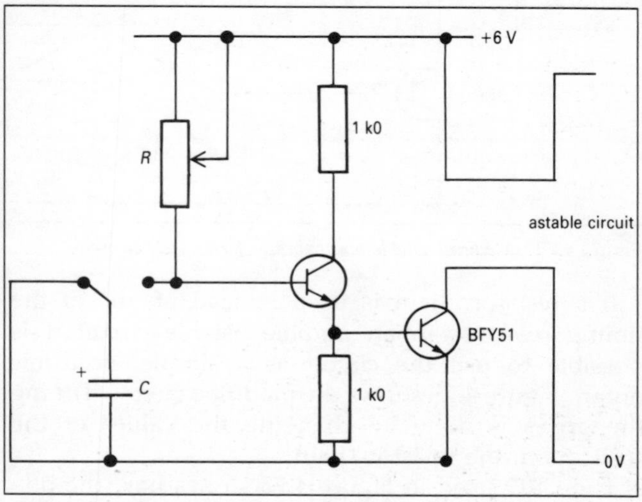

Figure 4.73 *Practical timer/warning circuit*

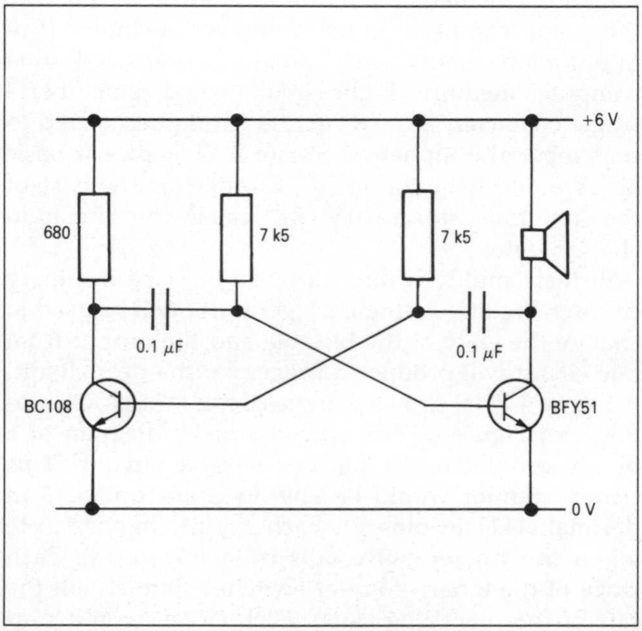

Figure 4.72 *Audio alarm using an astable multivibrator*

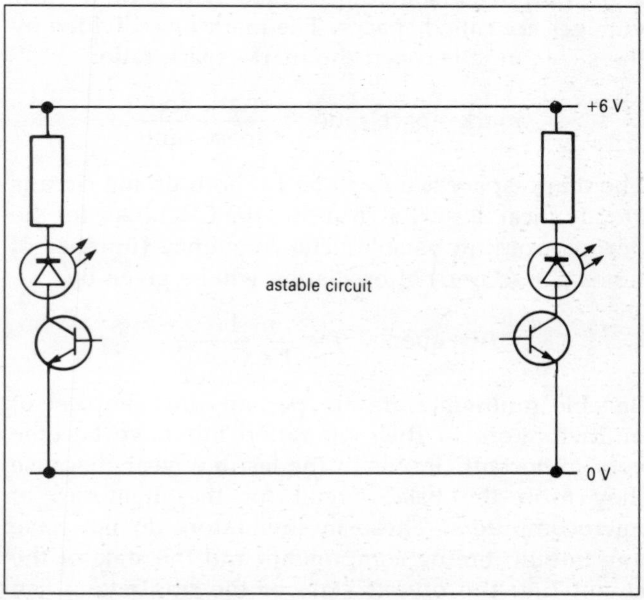

Figure 4.74 *Using LEDs for a model warning device*

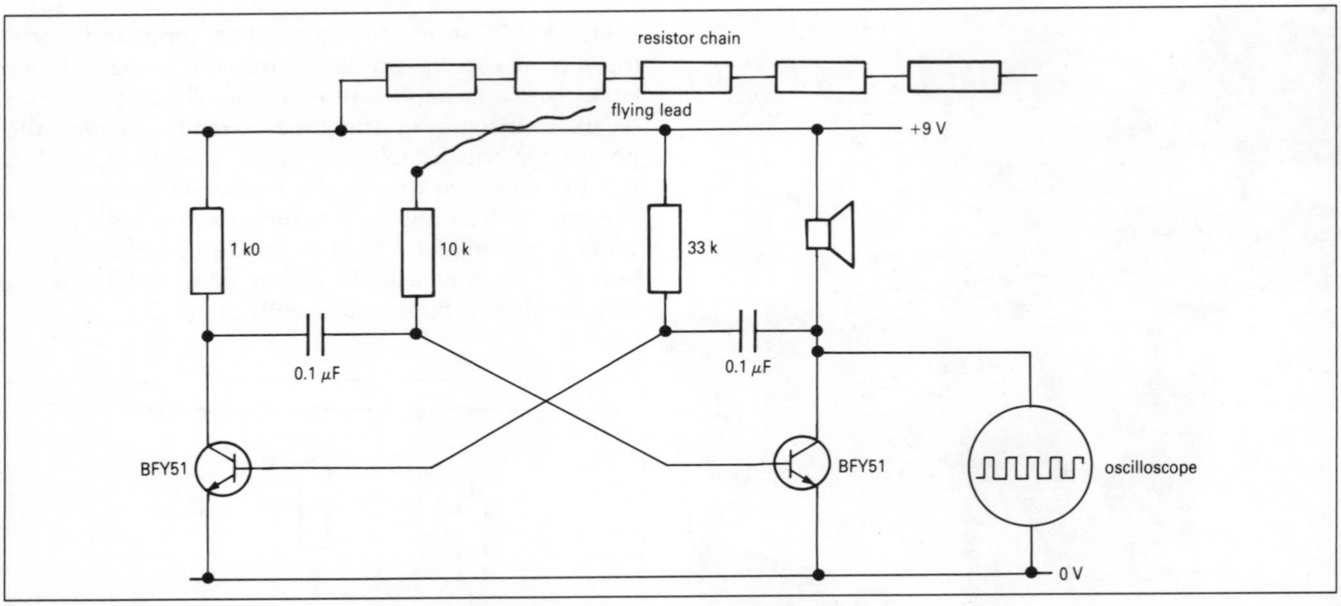

Figure 4.75 *Modified astable multivibrator for an electric organ*

If a resistor chain is used instead of one of the timing resistors in an audible astable circuit it is possible to use the circuit as a simple electronic organ. Figure 4.75 shows the modified circuit. Tuning the organ is done by changing the values of the resistors in the resistor chain.

The CRO used in Figure 4.75 shows how the on–off pulses vary for different notes. The high voltages at the output are sometimes called marks and the low voltages are called spaces. The mark time divided by the space time is called the **mark–space ratio:**

$$\text{mark–space ratio} = \frac{\text{mark time}}{\text{space time}}$$

The mark–space ratio will be 1 if both timing circuits are identical. Figure 4.76 shows the CRO trace for the output from an astable. The frequency (number of times per second) of oscillation will be given by:

$$\text{frequency, } f = \frac{1}{1.4\ C \times R}$$

Bistable multivibrators are perhaps the simplest of multivibrators in their operation but have become very important circuits in the last few years because they form the basic circuit for the memories of microcomputers. These multivibrators do not have any in-built timing components and the state of the circuit (i.e. the on–off state of the transistors) can only be changed by an external source.

The circuit will remain in the state

$$T_1 \text{ on, } T_2 \text{ off}$$

or

$$T_1 \text{ off, } T_2 \text{ on}$$

until it is switched by the external source. In this way the circuit can be used to 'remember' a single bit of information. Many such circuits are needed in a computer memory. Eight circuits could remember a single character, 26 × 8 circuits would be needed to remember the alphabet. Figure 4.77 shows a basic bistable multivibrator circuit. Connecting the base of the 'on' transistor to 0 V will cause the circuit to change state.

Bistable multivibrators can also be used in binary counter circuits. A single trigger pulse will be used to change the state of the bistable and the output from one circuit will produce a trigger for the next circuit.

Figure 4.78(a) shows a single circuit for this application and Figure 4.78(b) shows a block diagram of a binary counter involving four bistable circuits. This binary counter would be able to count up to 15 in decimal (1111 in binary). Each circuit changes state when the trigger pulse falls from 6 V to 0 V. Each stage of the binary counter switches state at half the rate of the preceding stage. Each circuit would start with T_1 off and T_2 on.

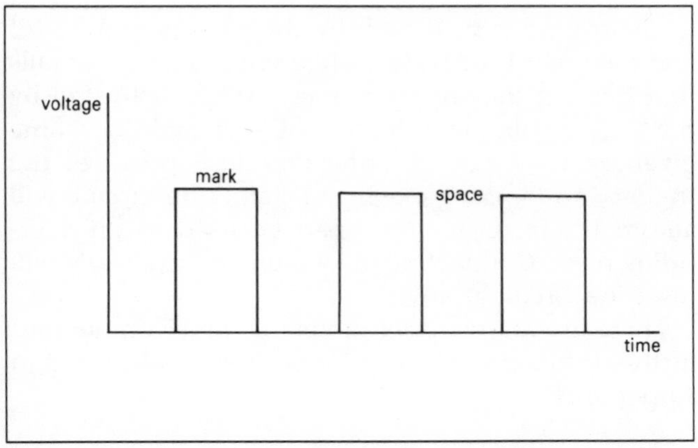

Figure 4.76 *Marks and space in the output from an astable multivibrator*

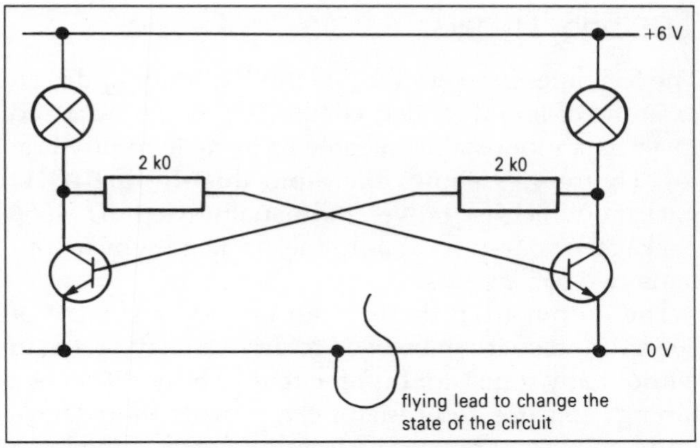

Figure 4.77 *Basic bistable multivibrator circuit*

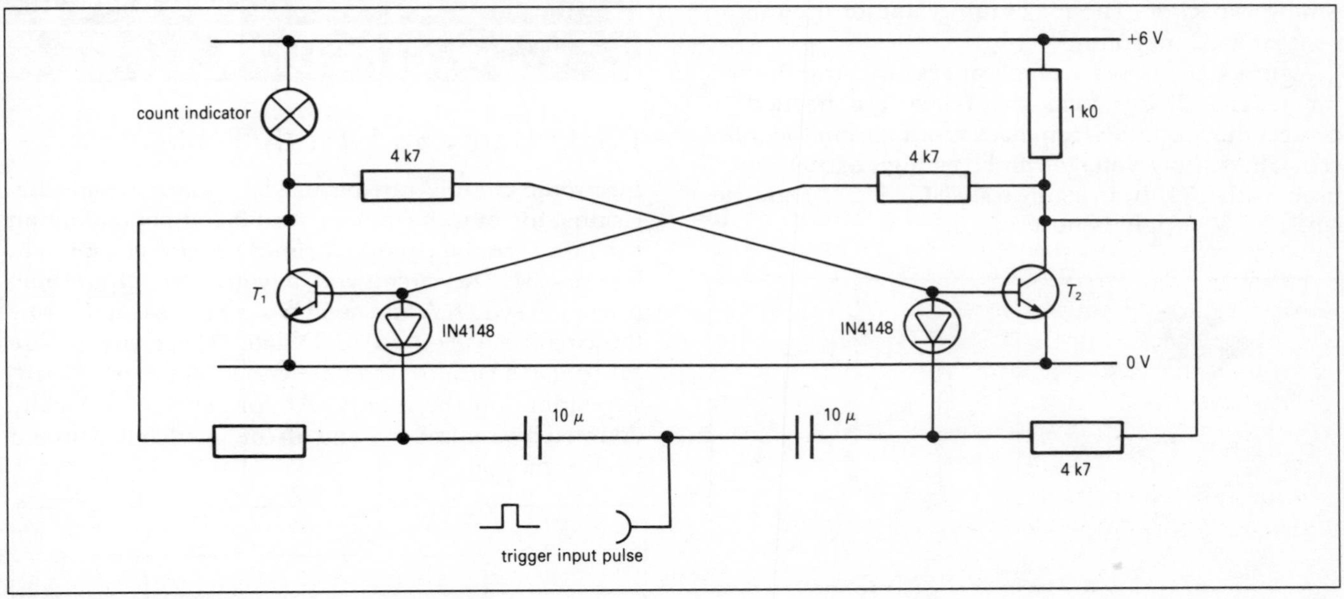

Figure 4.78 *Bistable multivibrators: (a) Single counter*

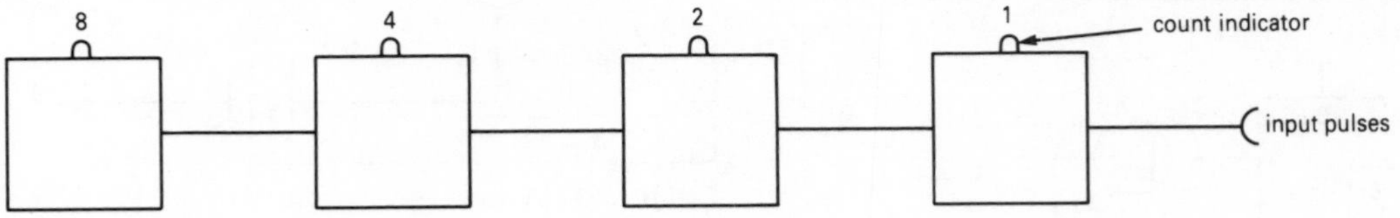

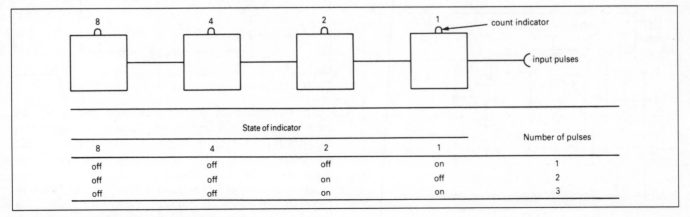

State of indicator				Number of pulses
8	4	2	1	
off	off	off	on	1
off	off	on	off	2
off	off	on	on	3

Figure 4.78 *(b) Block diagram for a binary counter*

The 555 Timer

The 555 timer is a very flexible multivibrator and is an example of an integrated circuit (IC). It can be wired to act as a monostable, astable or bistable multivibrator. Figure 4.79 shows the 8-pin **dual-in-line (DIL)** package which is the version usually used. The 556 package is a 14-pin dual-in-line package which contains two 555 circuits.

The output from the 555 can provide a current of 200 mA and so it can be used to drive a relay or a bulb without any transistor buffer circuit. The addition of a timing capacitor and resistor can provide time delays up to about one hour. The limiting factor is the leakage current of the internal components and external timing capacitor. The maximum value of the timing resistor is 20 megohm.

Figure 4.80 shows a practical circuit using the 555 timer. The diodes near the relays are needed to protect the 555 timer from back e.m.f.s from the relay coil. The supply voltage can be as high as 15 V but if used with TTL (transistor–transistor logic) logic circuits, a 5 V supply is needed.

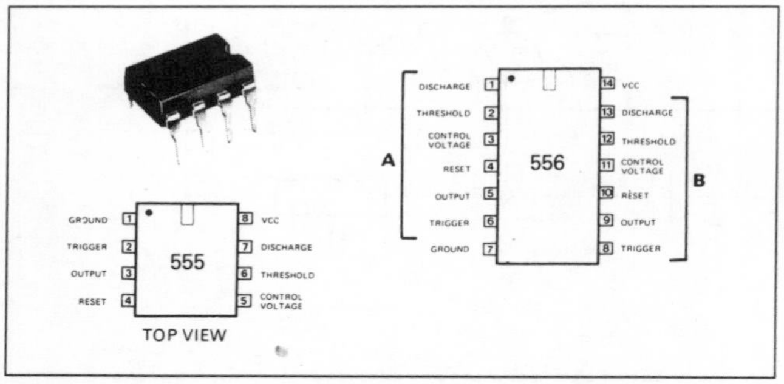

Figure 4.79 *A 555 timer and a 556 timer*

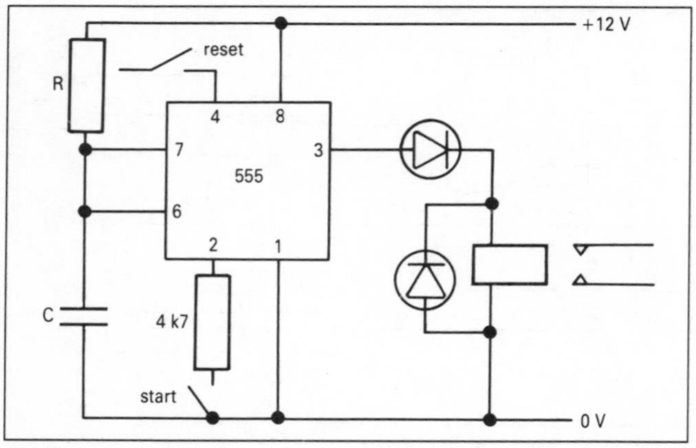

Figure 4.80 *A practical 555 timer circuit*

The trigger is held high by the 555 internal circuit and the timer is activated when the trigger input falls to a third of the supply voltage. When activated by the trigger going low the output goes high for a time given by $1.1 \times C \times R$. After this time, provided the trigger input has gone high again, the circuit will automatically reset. Pin 4 can be used as an overriding reset. Connecting pin 4 momentarily to 0 V will reset the circuit at any time.

There are many applications for the 555 timer and further information can be found from books listed in Appendix 7.

4:21 DECISION-MAKING CIRCUITS

Logic Gates and Truth Tables

Electronic circuits can be used to make simple decisions, the output from a circuit being dependent on the inputs to the circuit. A simple circuit is shown in Figure 4.81. This circuit will only give an output (bulb on) when switch A and switch B are on. In logic terms the circuit is called an AND gate. These circuits are called gates because they are either 'open' or 'closed' depending on the inputs. An 'on' switch is usually denoted by a number 1 and an 'off' switch is denoted by a number 0.

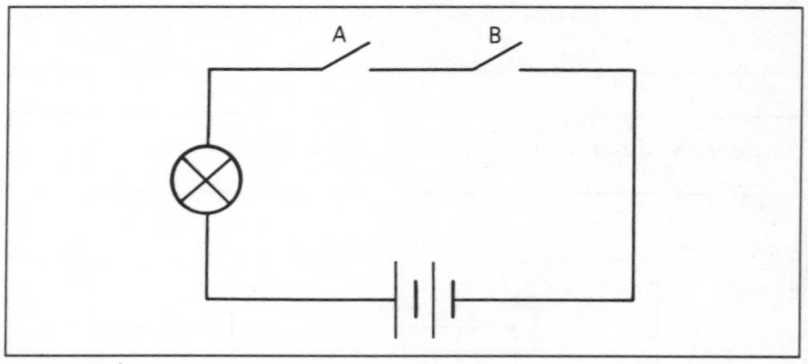

Figure 4.81 *A simple AND circuit*

The operation, or logical function, of the circuit can be written out in a **truth table**. The truth table for a two input AND circuit (Figure 4.81) is shown in Table 4.8. Both 'on' and 'off' terms and the more usual logic notation, 1 and 0, are given.

Another simple logic circuit is an OR gate. This will have the switches in parallel. Figure 4.82 shows a simple OR gate and its truth table.

Table 4.8 Truth table for an AND circuit

Switch A	*Switch B*	*Bulb*	*A*	*B*	*Output*
off	off	off	0	0	0
off	on	off	0	1	0
on	off	off	1	0	0
on	on	on	1	1	1

These simple circuits are very limited in their applications because they need someone to operate the switches. Practical logic circuits use electronic components such as transistors as the switches. These can then be operated by voltages being switched on and off by other electronic circuits. The basis of these circuits is the transistor being operated in the switch mode. Diodes are used where necessary to provide isolation of the inputs.

The operating voltages are usually taken to be greater than 3 V for a logical 1 and less than 0.8 V for a logical 0. This is, however,usually simplified to high and low voltages and for transistor circuits 5 V and 0 V are used.

On–off logic circuits are called digital circuits. The on–off voltages from a digital circuit are called **digital voltages**. Continuously variable voltages, like the variable output from an LDR, are called **analogue voltages**. Figure 4.83 shows how the two types of voltage would appear on an oscilloscope or graph.

Other logic gates which are used in decision-making circuits are the NOT gate, NAND gate and NOR gate. Figure 4.84 summarises the truth table of

(a)

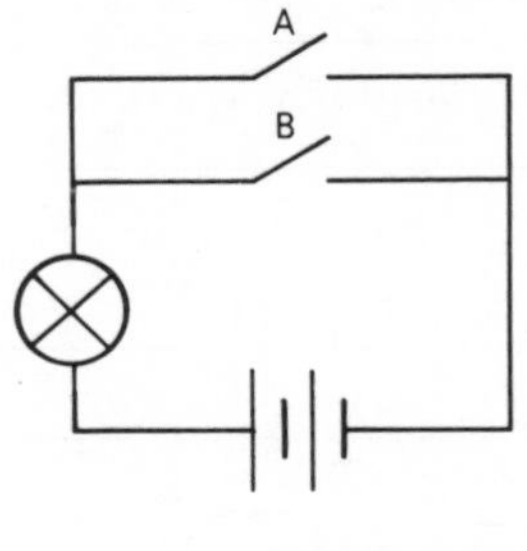

(b)

A	B	Output
0	0	0
0	1	1
1	0	1
1	1	1

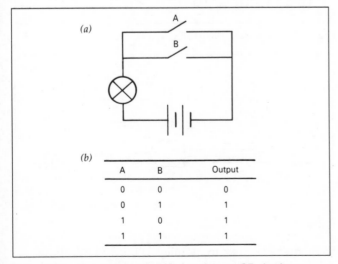

Figure 4.82 *Circuit and truth table for a 2-input OR circuit*

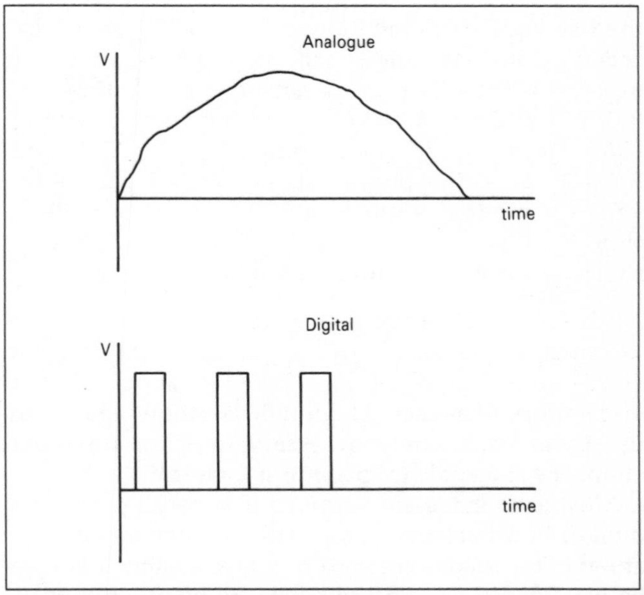

Figure 4.83 *Analogue and digital signals*

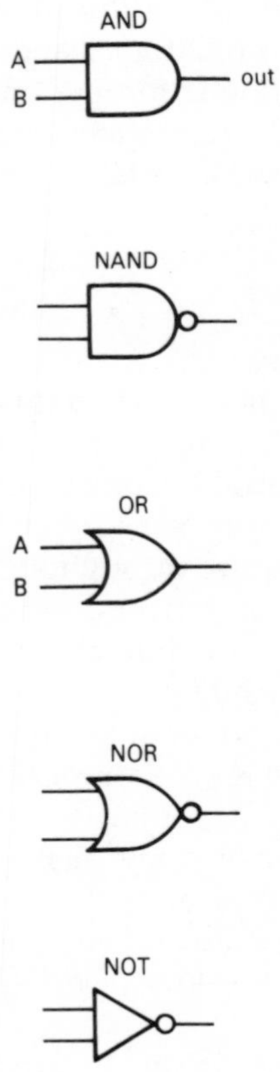

AND

A	B	Out
0	0	0
0	1	0
1	0	0
1	1	1

NAND

A	B	Out
0	0	1
0	1	1
1	0	1
1	1	0

OR

A	B	Out
0	0	0
0	1	1
1	0	1
1	1	1

NOR

A	B	Out
0	0	1
0	1	0
1	0	0
1	1	0

NOT

In	Out
1	0
0	1

Figure 4.84 *Summary of logic gates*

the five logic gates mentioned. The NOT gate is also called an inverter and it will always have only one input. All the other gates can have any number of inputs but 2-input, 4-input and sometimes 8-input gates are most common. Comparing the AND and NAND gates, the output of the NAND gate is inverted compared with the AND. NAND is really a shortened way of writing NOT AND. NOR is a shortened way of writing NOT OR.

Practical Logic Gates

The important aspect of logic gates is knowing how to use them. It is rarely necessary to know anything about the internal structure of a logic gate.

Most logic gates are supplied in a package called a dual-in-line package (DIL). The circuits themselves are about a millimetre across but, to enable a DIL to be used easily, connections have to be much bigger. The connections are brought out of the plastic package in two parallel rows, hence the name DIL. The number of connections will depend on the number and type of gate but 14- and 16-pin DIL packages are the most common. One connection is for 5 V, one to 0 V and the others are used for the logic gates. Figure 4.85 shows some standard DIL packages taken from a supplier's data sheet.

Combining Logic Gates

Most practical decision-making circuits will require a combination of logic gates. An example of this is a control system for a modern central heating system. Having more than one temperature sensor can ensure better control of the temperature throughout the house. A system might have four sensors, with all four registering a low temperature before the boiler was switched on. So a 4-input AND gate would be needed. The only other requirement would be for the sensors to give a logical 1 (5 V) when the temperature was low (see Figure 4.86).

A more complicated arrangement may allow the boiler to switch on when any one or both of two upstairs rooms are low in temperature and any one or both of two downstairs rooms are low (see Figure 4.87).

It is quite easy to simulate these circuits by arranging for the inputs to be switched manually. Any inputs of TTL circuits left disconnected will auto-

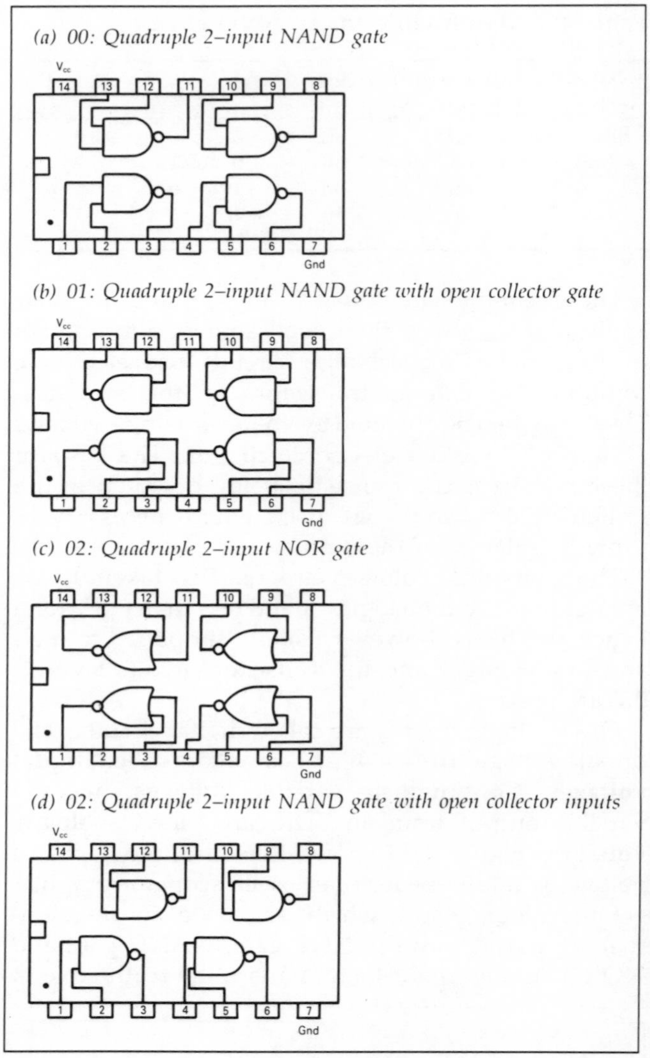

Figure 4.85 *Standard DIL packages of TTL circuits*

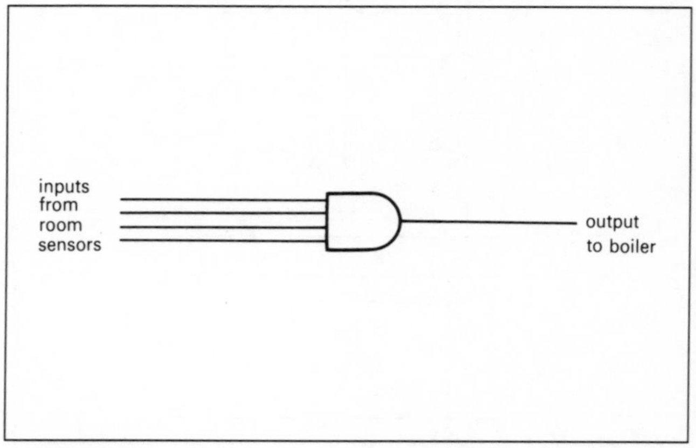

Figure 4.86 *AND gate control of heating boiler*

matically go high so it is often necessary to connect them through 1 kilohm resistors to 0 V. The various methods of input connections are shown in Figure 4.88.

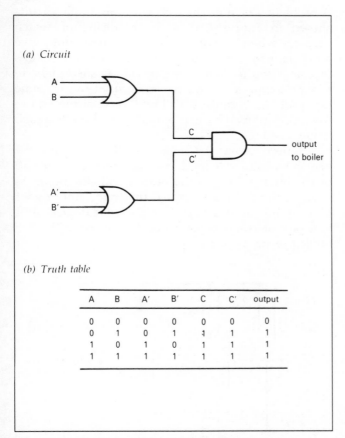

(a) Circuit

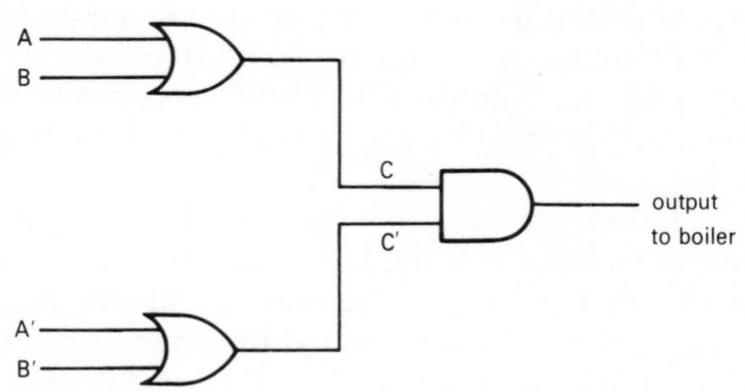

(b) Truth table

A	B	A′	B′	C	C′	output
0	0	0	0	0	0	0
0	1	0	1	1	1	1
1	0	1	0	1	1	1
1	1	1	1	1	1	1

Figure 4.87 *Combining AND and OR gates for boiler*

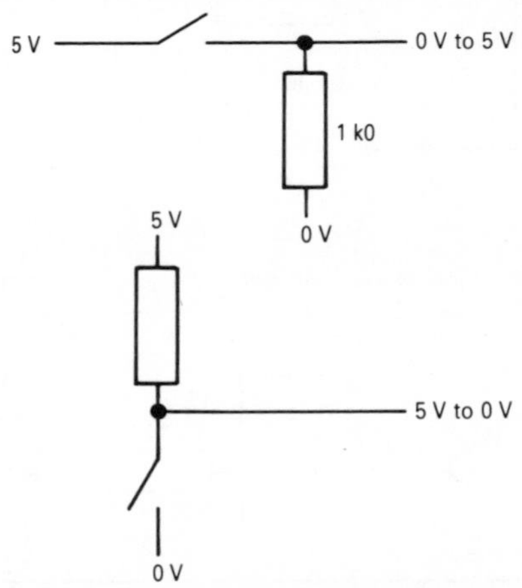

Figure 4.88 *Switching the inputs to TTL circuits*

NAND gates can be combined to give any other logical function. This can often be used to reduce the number of types of TTL circuits needed on a circuit board which enables easier maintenance and simpler stock requirements. Figure 4.89 shows some of these combinations.

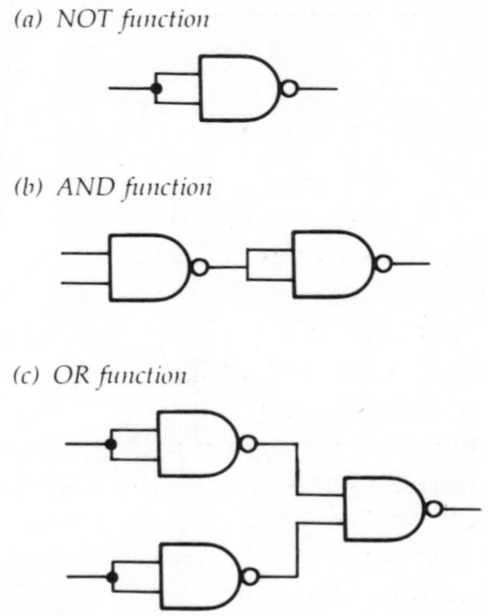

Figure 4.89 *Combining NAND gates*

TTL and CMOS Logic Circuits

Figure 4.85 shows circuits called TTL circuits (transistor–transistor logic circuits). They are designed to work within quite small voltage tolerance range and the specifications will give a working voltage of 4.75–5.25 V.

Another type of circuit available is known as a CMOS circuit (complementary metal-oxide-semiconductor logic). These circuits work within a much wider voltage range of about 3–15 V but they are very easily damaged by static charges. Even static charges from the body are enough to damage the circuits inside the DIL package and so they may not be very practical for experimentation in a school laboratory. However, the voltage range does mean that the power supply is not critical and the logic states are much less likely to change through noise on the mains. The basic logic functions are the same whichever type of circuit is used.

There are various rules to be followed when using TTL type circuits. In general, each output can be connected to 10 TTL inputs. This is called the fan-out.

Each output can accept (or 'sink') a current of about 10 mA in its low state but, according to the specifications, can only provide a current of about 0.5 mA when in its high state. This means that a buffer transistor is normally required when driving a relay or lamp. Figure 4.90 shows some example circuits from a TTL output.

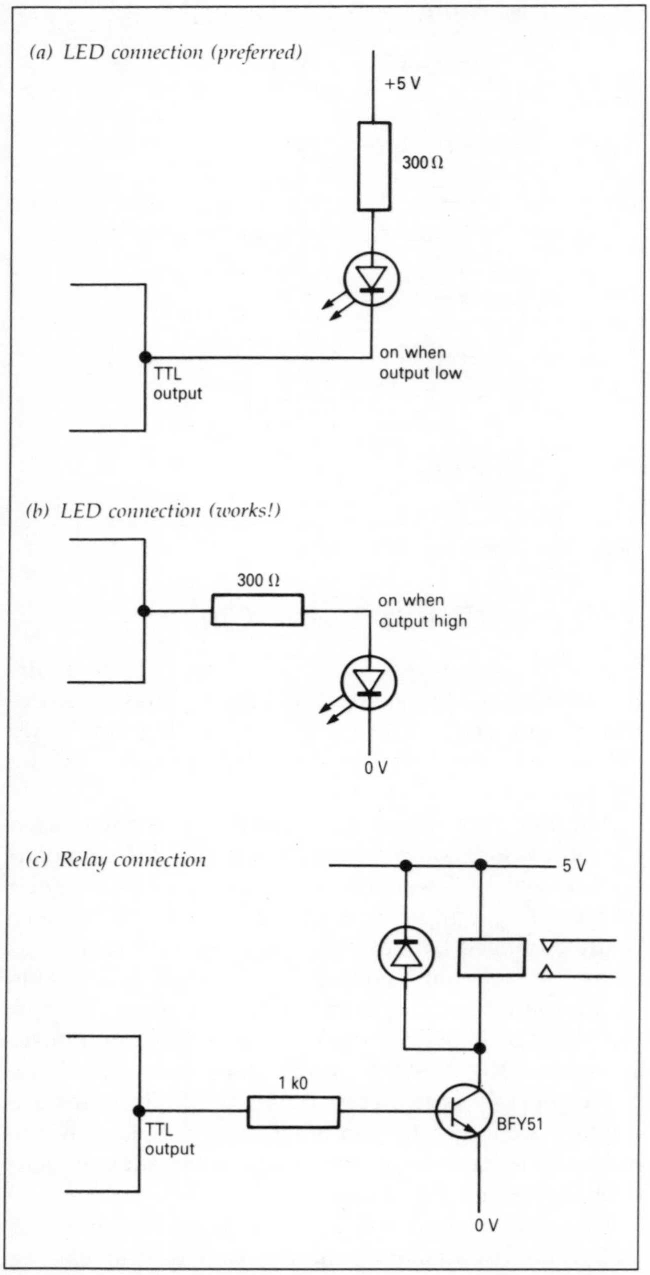

Figure 4.90 *Example TTL circuits*

4:22 SWITCH DEBOUNCING

A problem which might arise with the simple circuits shown in Figure 4.90 is the bouncing of switch contacts when a switch is closed. This would give more than one input pulse to the logic circuit. Circuits that are used to count are particularly susceptible to this problem. A 555 timer can be used to overcome this problem because it will only reset at the end of the timed interval if the input has gone back to a high value (see Figure 4.91).

A time of about 0.2 seconds will ensure that the switch has settled to its closed position before the end of the interval and so the output will stay high. As soon as the switch is opened the trigger input goes high so the output will go to a low value (logical 0). A low output could be obtained by inverting the 555 output using a NOT gate.

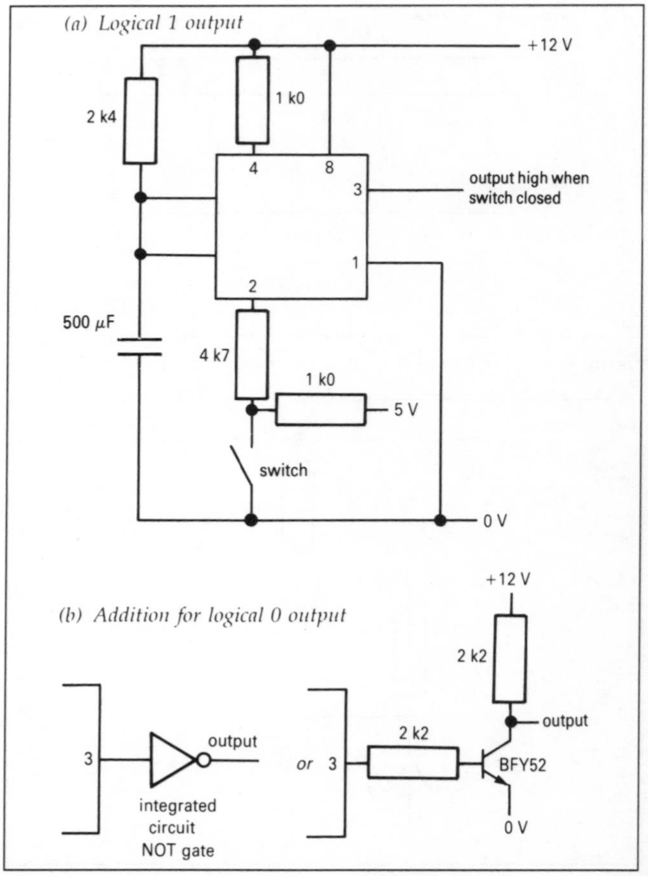

Figure 4.91 *Using a 555 timer to debounce a switch*

4:23 PULSE SHAPING: THE SCHMITT TRIGGER

If switch contacts are being opened and closed quickly then it is better to use a special circuit called a **Schmitt trigger**, shown in Figure 4.92. This is specially designed to 'clean' irregular or slowly varying pulses. Some TTL logic circuits can be obtained with the Schmitt trigger input stage already built into them. For example, the TTL 7413 is described as a 'Dual 4-input NAND gate with Schmitt trigger input stages'.

The Schmitt trigger produces fast switching because the switch on and off levels are different and the input stage has transistors connected in such a way that the switching from one state to the other state is very fast. Figure 4.93 shows a Schmitt trigger being used as a 'cleaner' for a telephone dial contact so that the pulses can be counted. Figure 4.94 shows how the slowly varying input such as that from a thermistor can be interfaced to TTL logic type circuits.

4:24 COMPUTER CONTROL

USER PORTS

Using computers to control the environment is a process which combines many of the aspects of electricity and electronics described previously in this chapter. The computer itself is built around logic

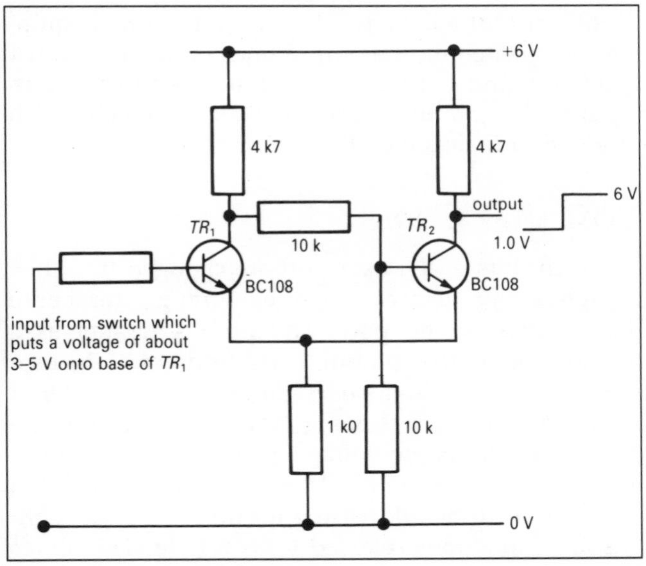

Figure 4.92 *Circuit for Schmitt trigger*

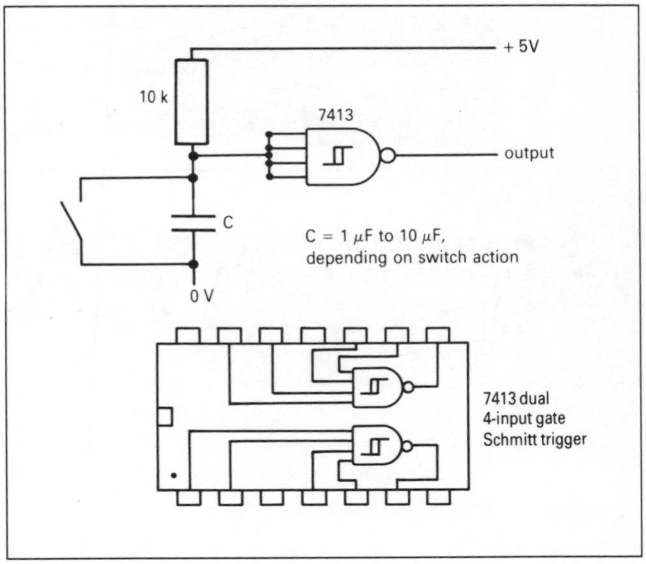

Figure 4.93 *Switch pulse cleaner*

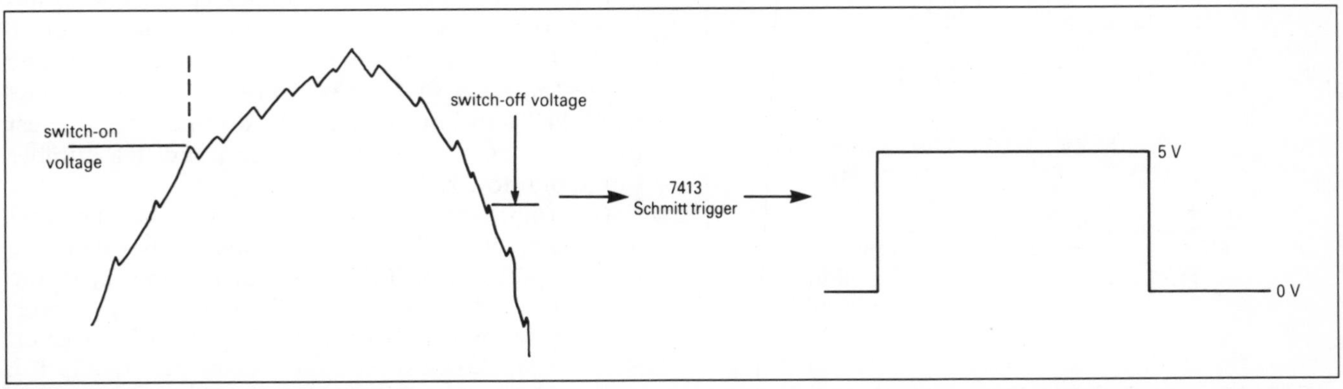

Figure 4.94 *Input and output for a Schmitt trigger interface*

circuits. The link to the 'outside world' is through connections which can be switched between logical 1 and logical 0 (5 V and 0 V) depending on the decision-making process set up within the computer. The connections from the computer to the outside are often called the **user port** or **parallel ports**. Most user ports relevant to technology in schools will have 8 lines which can be programmed as either inputs or outputs. Each of the 8 lines can carry one 'bit' of information. Figure 4.95 shows some user ports on some computers available in schools.

To be able to read information from the port or write data out to the port, it is necessary to use the commands which the computer understands. The commands are part of the computer language. Most computers in schools use **BASIC** and the exact format of the command used to get information in and out of the computer will depend on the computer and the form of BASIC which is in use. It is not possible to cover all forms here and the manual with the computer will need to be consulted. The format is, however, similar for most computers and will probably consist of PEEK and POKE or IN and OUT.

Poke or Out will be used to control external equipment by switching the output lines between logical 1 and 0 or 0 and 1. Peek or In will be used to sense an input to the computer from an external switch which produces a logical 0 or 1.

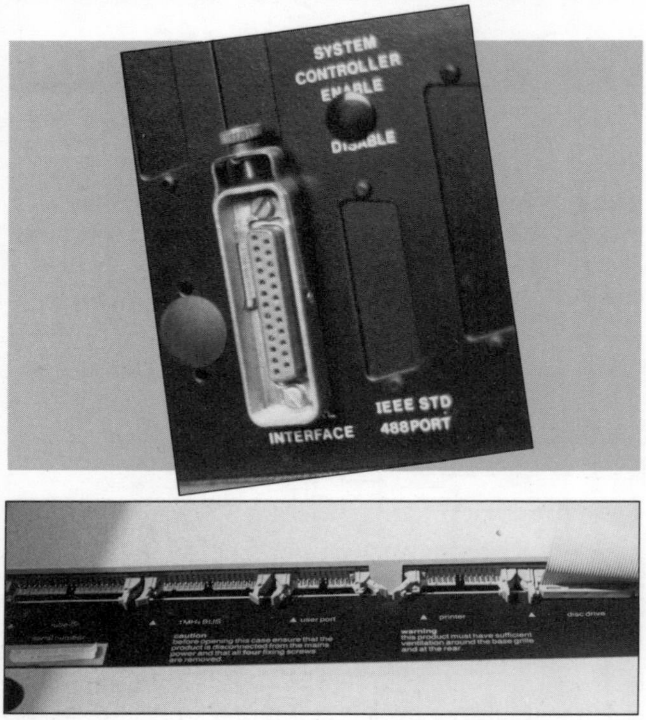

Figure 4.95 *User ports available on computers in schools*

Number	State of output lines							
0	L	L	L	L	L	L	L	L
1	L	L	L	L	L	L	L	H
3	L	L	L	L	L	L	H	H
5	L	L	L	L	L	H	L	H
8	L	L	L	L	H	L	L	L
128	H	L	L	L	L	L	L	L
255	H	H	H	H	H	H	H	H

7	6	5	4	3	2	1	0	computer output lines
128	64	32	16	8	4	2	1	number which will make the output line 'high'

Figure 4.96 *Writing to a user port (H = high, L = low)*

Computer Codes

The eight bits of the user port are changed from low to high or high to low voltages by writing a number to the **address** of the port. The port is treated as a memory slot in the computer. The address of the user port will be given in the user guide of the computer or interface unit which is being used. Interface units are often used to prevent damage to the computer if incorrect voltages are used. Most computers used in schools use 16-bit addressing for the memory. (Eight bits are sometimes referred to as a **byte**. Two bytes grouped together produce a word of sixteen bits.)

The highest number which can be obtained, and hence the highest number address, is therefore 1111111111111111 in binary or 65535 in decimal. The highest number that can be represented by eight bits is 11111111 in binary or 255 in decimal. The lowest number is zero so eight bits correspond to a number range of 0 to 255.

The right-hand bit is sometimes called the least significant bit (LSB). The left-most bit is called the most significant bit (MSB). Writing a one (1) to the user port will make the LSB go to a high level. Writing 128 will make the MSB go to a high level. Figure 4.96 shows some examples of the state of the user port for different numbers written to the port.

Table 4.9

LSD	MSD	0 000	1 001	2 010	3 011	4 100	5 101	6 110	7 111
0	0000	NUL	DLE	SP	0	@	P		p
1	0001	SOH	DC1	!	1	A	Q	a	q
2	0010	STX	DC2	″	2	B	R	b	r
3	0011	ETX	DC3	#	3	C	S	c	s
4	0100	EOT	DC4	$	4	D	T	d	t
5	0101	ENQ	NAK	%	5	E	U	e	u
6	0110	ACK	SYN	&	6	F	V	f	v
7	0111	BEL	ETB	′	7	G	W	g	w
8	1000	BS	CAN	(	8	H	X	h	x
9	1001	HT	EM	)	9	I	Y	i	y
A	1010	LF	SUB	°	:	J	Z	j	z
B	1011	VT	ESC	+	;	K	[	k	{
C	1100	FF	FS	,	<	L	\	l	|
D	1101	CR	GS	–	=	M	]	m	}
E	1110	SO	RS	•	>	N	↑	n	~
F	1111	SI	VS	/	?	O	←	o	DEL

Table 4.9 shows the code normally used to represent characters stored in eight-bit memories. This is the American Standard Code for Information Interchange (**ASCII**).

The ASCII table enables letters, spaces, speech marks and other symbols to be represented by a binary number. The letter A is represented by the decimal number 65 which is 1000001 in binary. The number 1 is represented by 0110001. A space is represented by 0100000. Everything which you need to store must have an ASCII code otherwise it will not be understood by the computer.

Hexadecimal numbers, or Hex for short, are numbers to base 16 rather than base 10 (decimal) or base 2 (binary). Hex needs 16 symbols which are shown in Table 4.10.

Table 4.10 Hex numbers

Decimal	*Hexadecimal*
0	0
1	1
2	2
3	3
4	4
5	5
6	6
7	7
8	8
9	9
10	A
11	B
12	C
13	D
14	E
15	F

The Hex notation is often used as a shorthand for binary. For example:

1111	becomes F
10000	becomes 10
11110	becomes 1E
11111111	becomes FF.

The binary coded decimal (BCD) code is often used in electronic counting circuits for either input or output. In BCD, each decimal digit of a number is converted to its binary equivalent.

Decimal	2 is 0010 in BCD
	8 becomes 1000
and	28 would be written as 0010 1000.

Counter integrated circuits, such as the 7493, count input pulses and provide outputs in BCD format. Figure 4.97 shows how the 7493 counters can be used to give a 0 to 99 counter. The 7493s will reset to 0 after 9 and the next higher counter (ten's counter) will count 1 when the line labelled D (eight's line) is reset. This system can be extended for counters giving readings above 99. The 7447 IC is a circuit which changes the BCD to the correct format for the LEDs of the numerical display.

Computer Output Signals

The output port can only provide a current of about 5 mA. It is always necessary, therefore, to provide some form of buffer circuit to switch external circuits.

This buffer would usually take the form of a transistor switch, either a single transistor or a Darlington driver circuit. Possible circuits are shown in Figure 4.98(a)–(c).

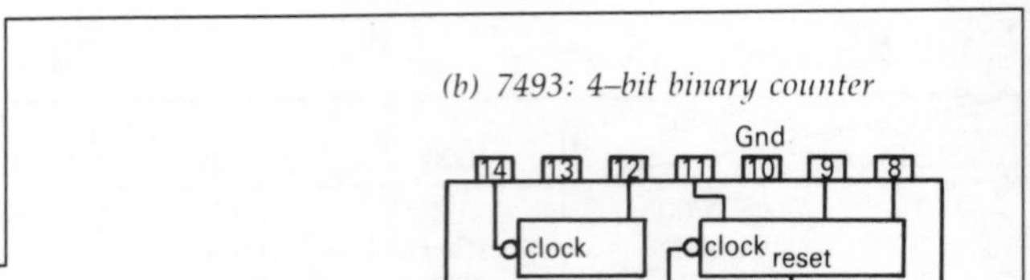
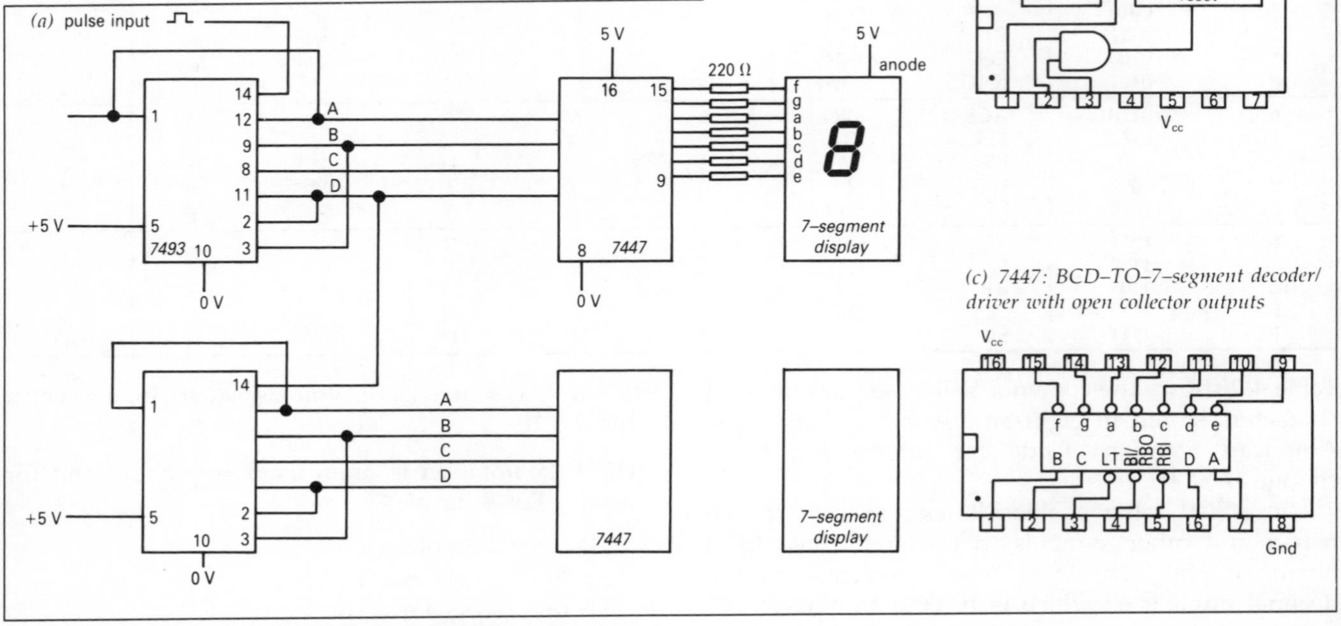

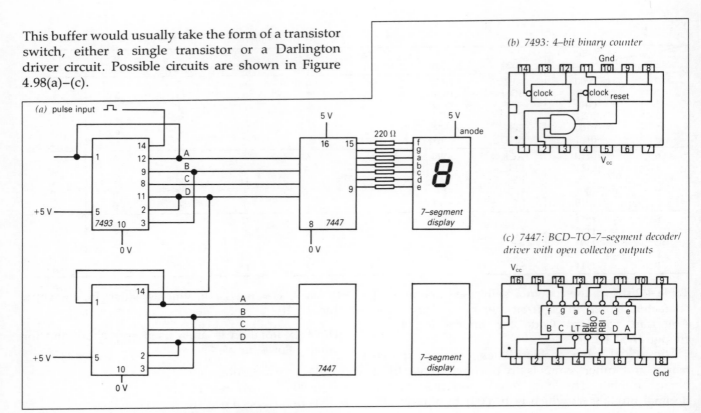

Figure 4.97 *0–99 counter using binary coded decimal counters*

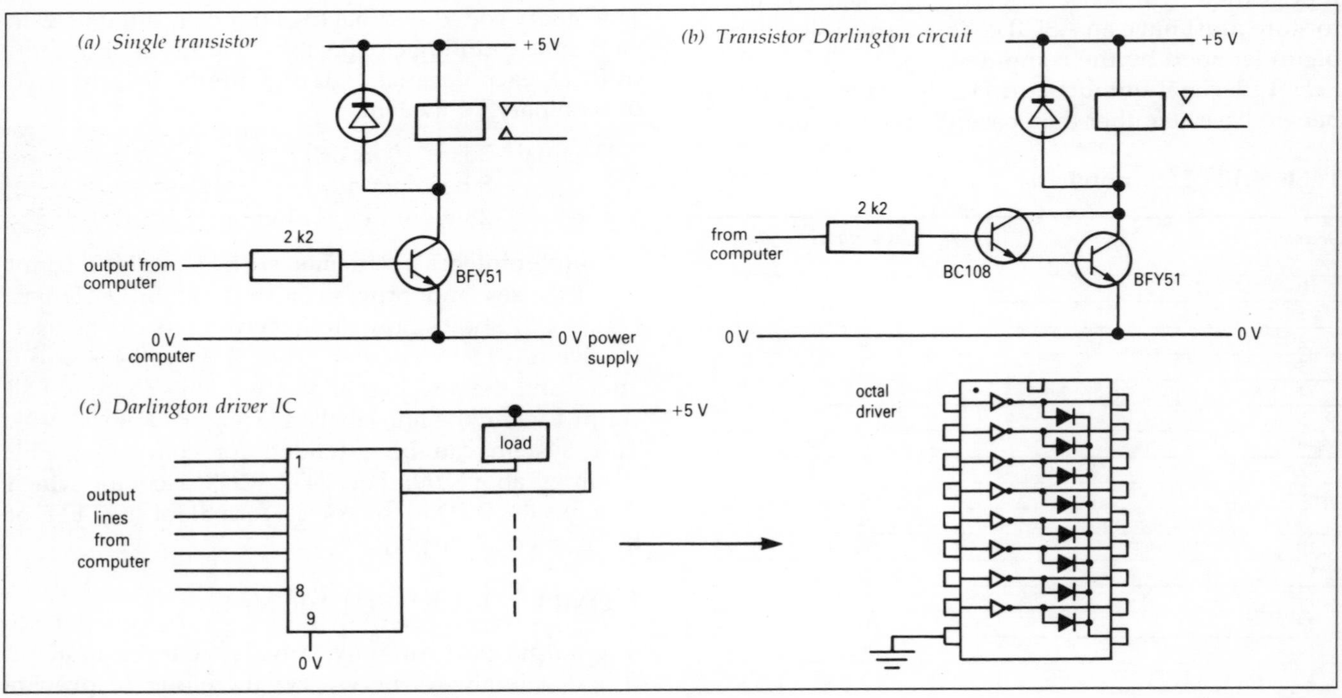

Figure 4.98 *Output buffer circuits for computer control*

The Darlington driver (Figure 4.98c) shown is an integrated circuit package designed to switch relays or solenoid type devices. The protection diodes and input resistors are included in the integrated circuit. This Darlington driver IC has 8 inputs leading to 8 outputs (RS stock number 303-422) so it is convenient for control from an 8-bit port. Each output can sink about 0.5 A so it can operate a variety of relays.

In some applications it is wise to isolate the computer output from the external devices to prevent accidental damage to the computer. This is usually done using opto-couplers. (A typical circuit is shown in Figure 4.63.) Commercially available computer interfaces would use this type of isolation and voltages up to 4 kV could be applied to the external circuit without damage to the computer.

INPUT SIGNALS

Input circuits are used to sense the state of the system being controlled. This might be a switch indicating a set position or a more complicated circuit sensing a 'variable' which is being controlled. The inputs of a user port can only sense a high voltage or a low voltage so a simple input circuit would be needed (Figure 4.99).

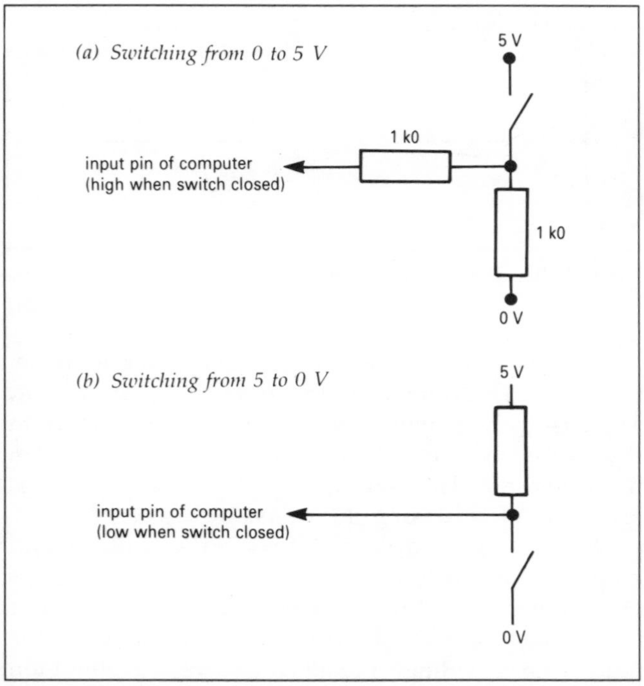

Figure 4.99 *Input circuits*

Light or temperature levels can provide an input if a Schmitt trigger or high-gain amplifier is used to switch the output at a specific voltage level. The LDR and thermistor could be used to produce a voltage variation. Figure 4.100 shows the LDR circuit which allows the computer to act according to its programing. The variable resistor adjusts the switching level.

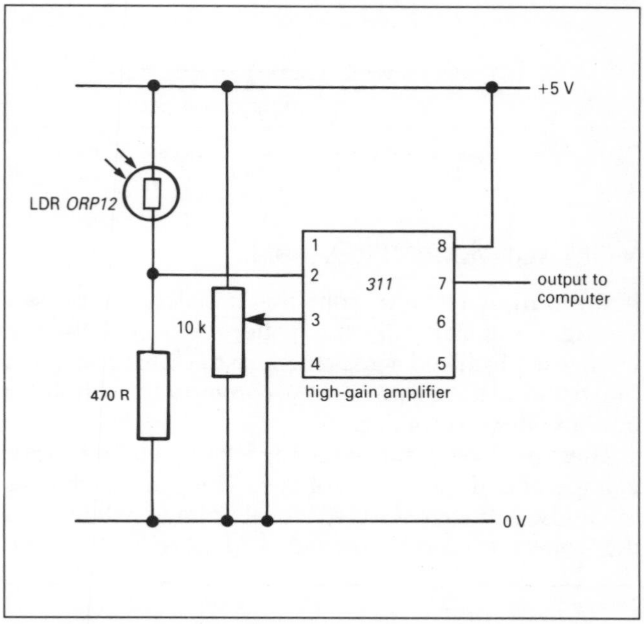

Figure 4.100 *An LDR circuit linked to computer user input port*

4:25 THE TRANSISTOR AS AN AMPLIFIER

CURRENT AMPLIFICATION

In a transistor, a very small base current can produce a much larger current between the collector and emitter. More control over the input and DC voltages on the terminals of the transistor can give an output current which is a constant multiple of the input current. The transistor will then be operating as a linear amplifier. Figure 4.101 shows that the collector current is about 200 times bigger than the base current. This is the basic function of an amplifier. It is a device which produces an output larger than the input. The DC current gain, h_{FE}, is given by I_c/I_b. The full current flow through the transistor is given by $I_e = I_c + I_b$.

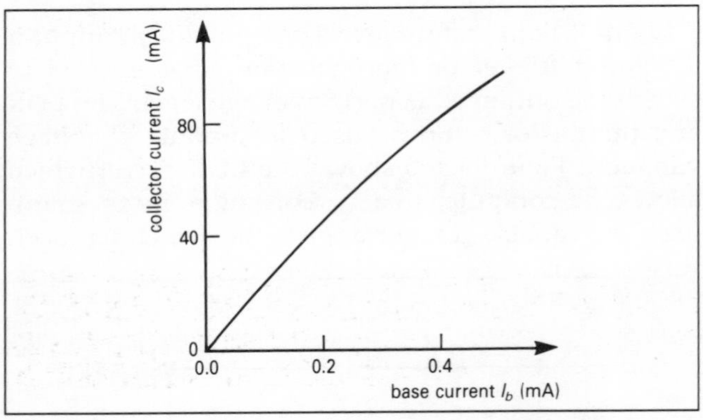

Figure 4.101 *Base-collector current characteristics for a BC 107 transistor*

VOLTAGE AMPLIFICATION

If the output current from the transistor is passed through a resistor in the collector circuit then a voltage is produced across the resistor. This resistor is called the load resistor and it converts the amplifier into a voltage amplifier.

There will be a **phase change** between the input voltage and the output voltage. This means that as the input voltage rises the output voltage will fall. As the collector current increases (Figure 4.102), the voltage drop across the resistor will increase. This has the effect of reducing the voltage at the collector, which reduces the voltage at the output from the amplifier.

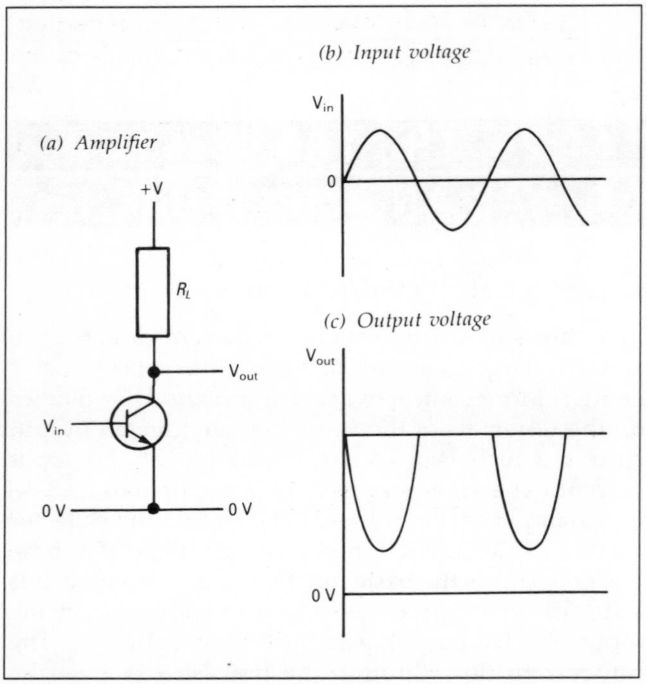

Figure 4.102 *Voltage amplifier using a load resistor*

Ohm's Law can be used to determine the size of the voltage drop across the load resistor. Using $V = I \times R$, it can be seen that changing the value of R will alter the voltage across the resistor. The maximum voltage change at the output is set by the supply voltage. The output will swing above and below the static DC voltage on the collector. Figure 4.103 shows a simple amplifier.

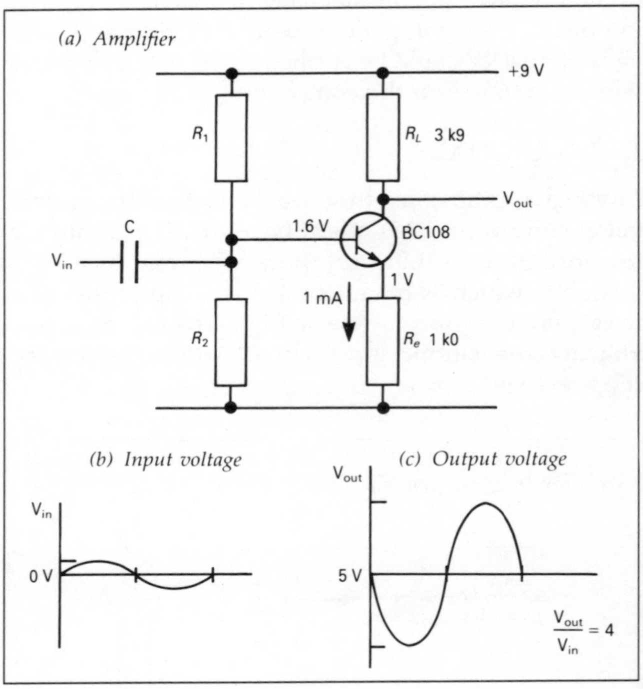

Figure 4.103 *Transistor as an amplifier*

The emitter resistor and potential divider are to set the correct DC voltage at the emitter of the transistor. The base voltage will then be about 0.6 V higher than the emitter because of the junction characteristics of the transistor. The setting of the correct DC voltage levels is called **biasing** the transistor.

The biasing is designed to set the voltage and amplification factors and maintain these settings when the temperature changes. The potential divider in the base circuit should be set up to give the required base voltage and allow a current of about ten times the expected base current to flow through the divider. The BC108 transistor gives a current gain of about 300. In the circuit of Figure 4.103(a) this will give a base current of about 3.3 microamps to give a collector current of 1 milliamp. The voltage across R_1 is about 7.4 V (9 − 1.6). Using Ohm's Law, with a current of 33 microamps through R_1 gives:

$$R_1 = \frac{7.4}{33\times10^{-6}} = 224\,000 \text{ ohms}$$

This will give a resistor value of about 220 k for R_1.

The voltage across R_2 is about 1.6 V so the value of

$$R_2 = \frac{1.6}{7.4} \times 220\text{ k} = 47\text{ k ohms}$$

The voltage gain for this type of amplifier is given approximately by R_L/R_e

voltage gain = 3.9/1.0 which is approximately 4

The input and output would be as shown in Figure 4.103(b). A CRO could be used to measure the input and output voltages to find the exact gain given by the amplifier.

The capacitor on the input is called a DC blocking capacitor. It is used to prevent external DC voltages affecting the bias levels of the amplifier. The AC signal passes through the capacitor. If the voltage swing becomes too high then clipping occurs, as can be seen in Figure. 4.104. This is caused by trying to send the output voltage above and below the supply voltages.

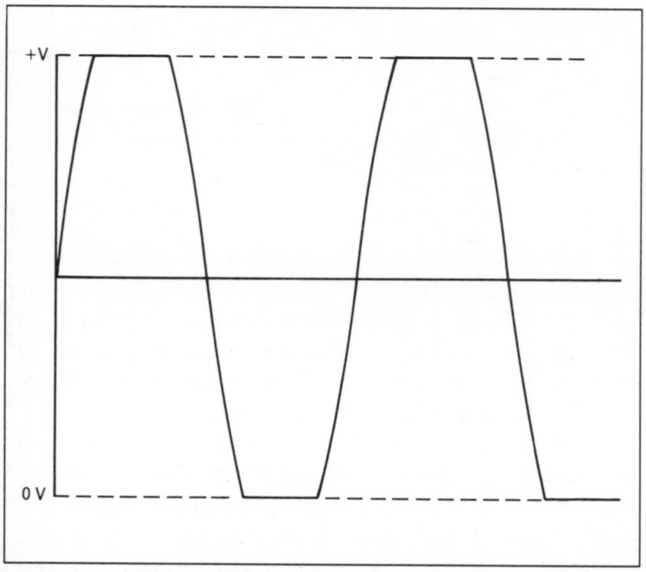

Figure 4.104 *Clipping in amplifier circuits*

As the input voltage gets higher, the clipped waves would become even squarer. This can be used to produce a simple clock pulse circuit for logic gate work. A small 50 Hz voltage from a laboratory power supply would give a clock with pulses square enough to operate TTL circuits.

4:26 OPERATIONAL AMPLIFIERS

Operational amplifiers were originally used as high-gain amplifiers operating on DC voltages. These were used in analogue computers for mathematical operations. High-gain amplifiers are now used in many applications without any reference to mathematical operations but the name has remained the same. Operational amplifiers are usually called op amps.

Op amps are integrated circuits and can be bought in various packages. A common op amp is the 741 in an 8-pin or 14-pin dual-in-line package. They can also be bought in a metal can format (TO-5) similar to transistors but with eight connecting wires. The 8-pin DIL package has connections, as shown in Figure 4.105. If the inverting input is made slightly more positive than the non-inverting input, then the output will become more negative. If the non-inverting input is more positive then the output will become more positive.

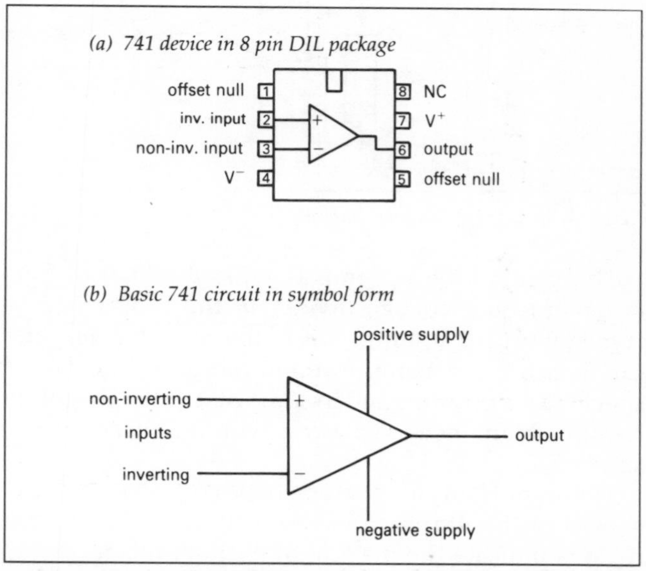

Figure 4.105 *Op amp IC packages*

The 741 will work with supply voltages in the range ± 3 V to ± 15 V. The 741 will operate from a single power supply (e.g. 6–30 V) but extra components are needed in the circuit. The output can be set to zero with zero input by connecting a variable resistor between pins 1 and 5 and adjusting the resistor, which is shown in Figure 4.106(a), until the output is correctly set. This is called the output offset. Figure 4.106(a) shows a simple circuit which could be used to investigate the basic DC properties of the op amp. Fig. 4.106(b) would be used to investigate the AC properties.

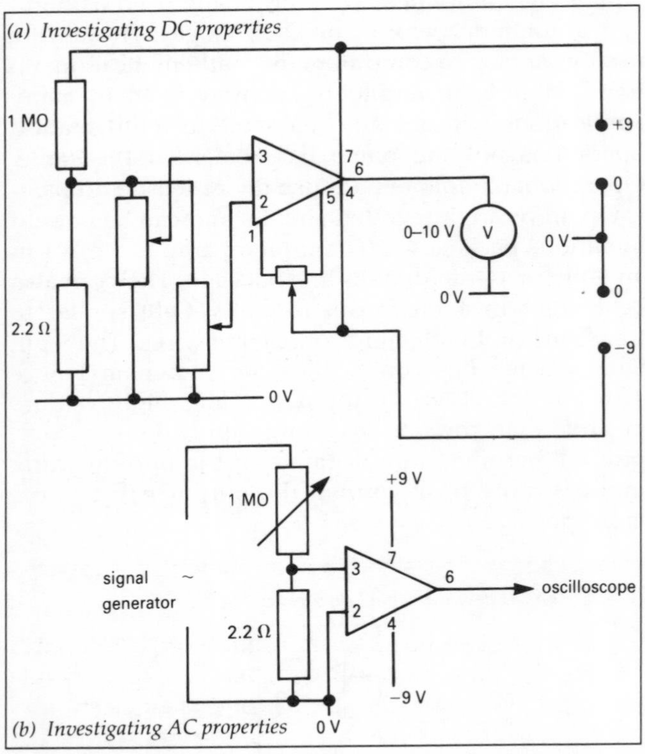

Figure 4.106 *The operational amplifier*

The gain of the op amp is typically 200 000. The rather unequal voltage divider in the input circuits (1 megohm to 2.2 ohm) reflects this possible amplification factor. A maximum amplification factor is rarely specified for op amps and in some cases the 1 megohm resistor might need replacing with a 2 megohm resistor.

The input/output characteristics of the 741 are shown in the graph of Figure 4.107. The horizontal regions indicate the maximum output voltage swing due to the supply voltage.

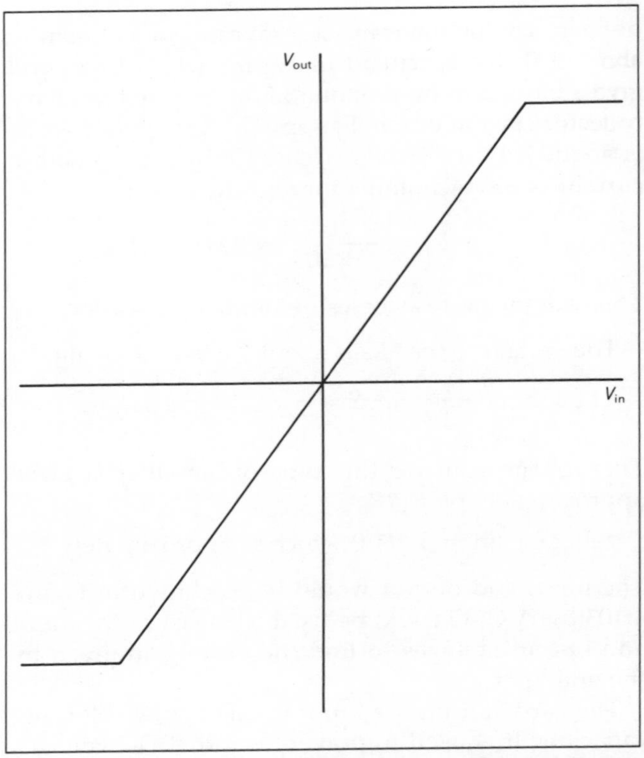

Figure 4.107 *Input/output characteristics of the 741 op amp package*

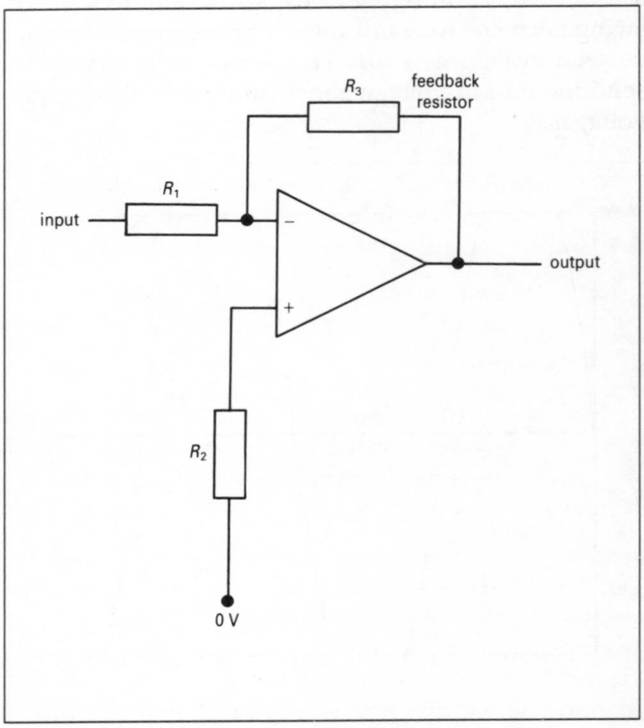

Figure 4.108 *Feedback in op amp circuit design*

The open loop gain is very high but amplifiers rarely use such high amplification factors. The gain can be controlled by providing a **feedback path** from the output to the input. This then gives a closed loop gain which provides the op amps with many more applications in AC and DC amplifier circuits. The op amp can be the basis of audio amplifiers, electronic ammeters and voltmeters, audio mixers, pre-amplifiers, Schmitt triggers and astable multivibrator circuits. The basic feedback circuit is quite easy to arrange, as shown in Figure 4.108. The voltage gain is given by R_3/R_1. Typical values for R_3 are 50 kilohms and 1 kilohms for R_1, giving a gain of 50 times.

4:27 ELECTRICITY AND ELECTRONICS INVESTIGATIONS

1. Make a list of common electrical appliances. For each one list the different electrical and electronic devices and components they contain.

Research What is an electrical appliance? What do we mean by devices and components? Some components are listed in Section 4:3. What other common components are there in everyday use in the home and school?

2. Use an electric circuit to investigate whether a material is a good conductor of electricity. Tabulate your results for different materials.

Research What is a circuit? You will need to make up your own definition of 'good conductor' and 'bad conductor' (insulator).

3. Investigate the colour coding on resistors which shows the resistance value and the tolerance. Compare the values with measured values using an ohmmeter.

Research Look up the colour code in section 4.8. Your results will include:
  nominal value (given by the coloured bands)
  tolerance (given by the last coloured band)
  actual value (measured with ohmeter)
How do you use an ohmmeter? Are all the measured values within the stated tolerance?

4. Use an ohmmeter or a voltmeter/ammeter circuit to investigate the effects of connecting resistors in series and parallel.

Research Use of ohmmeters and/or voltmeters and ammeters. How is the resistance calculated from voltage and current? What are series and parallel circuits?

5. (a) Design and carry out an experiment which could be used to show that a wire wound resistor obeys Ohm's Law. (b) Design and carry out an experiment which could be used to investigate whether a light bulb obeys Ohm's Law.

Research Ohm's Law is a basic law of electricity. What does it tell us? What result will you expect for a resistor obeying the law? What is the difference between wire wound resistors and other resistors? What affect does temperature have on resistance of a wire?

6. Investigate the flow of electricity through a semiconductor diode for DC and AC electricity.

Research What is a semiconductor diode? What is DC and AC? Diodes will burn out easily if they are inserted into circuits without some series resistance so you should use a light bulb in series with the diode. An ammeter and cathode ray oscilloscope will help to find out what is happening in the circuit.

7. Investigate the structure and action of a capacitor.

Research How is the capacitor made up? Electricity cannot pass through a capacitor but is a very useful component. What is the purpose of it in an electronic circuit?

8. Design and build a circuit to demonstrate the charge storage properties of a capacitor.

Research How are capacitors charged up? What can you use to show that electric charge has been stored?

9. Build and investigate a half-wave rectifier and a full-wave rectifier. Use an oscilloscope to compare the output from each circuit with and without the use of a smoothing capacitor. Discuss the use of such circuits.

Research Look up the rectifier circuits in Section 4.14. Make sure that you know the maximum current for the diode you are using and keep below this current by selecting a suitable resistor. What power of resistor will you need? (Section 4:7)

10. Use the circuit shown in Figure 4.109 to investigate the operation of the transistor as a switch.

Research Some voltmeters have a resistance low enough to affect this circuit. You will need to use a high resistance voltmeter, such as an electronic multimeter type, to measure the voltages between A and B as the resistance is varied. Do the same between C and D. What is happening to the current into the base as the base voltage is increased? How does this affect the collector current? Can you recognise the different terminals of the transistor? The size of the current in the base and collector circuits will give you more information.

11. Transducers can be used to provide a variable input to a transistor switch circuit. Investigate which transducers can be used in this way.

Research Types of transducers and their characteristics. Connecting transducers into transistor circuits.

12. Investigate the use of relays so that low-voltage, low-power circuits can be used to switch high-voltage appliances.

Research What is a relay and how does it work? What happens to the magnetic energy in the coil when the coil circuit is switched off? How does this affect the operation of relays from transistor circuits?

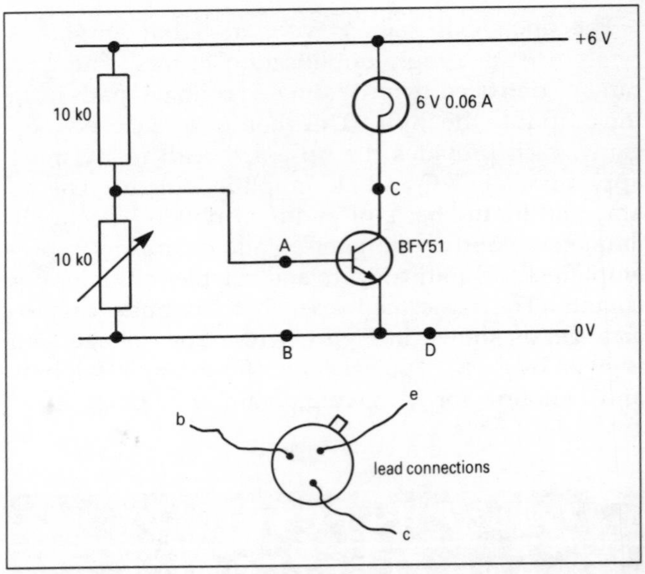

Figure 4.109 *Investigating the operation of a transistor*

13. Investigate the open loop gain and closed loop gain of a 741 operational amplifier.

Research What is an operational amplifier? How is it wired up? What is meant by *gain*? How can you use a CRO to measure the gain?

14. Use integrated circuits to investigate the operation of the AND and OR logic circuits.

Research What are logic circuits? What does AND mean? What does OR mean? How would you use a voltmeter to work out the truth table for integrated circuit versions of the AND and OR?

appendix 1

SAFETY IN THE LABORATORY AND WORKSHOP

The importance of safety in technology cannot be understated. Activities in science rooms and the craft workshops together with activities specific to the technology room all mean special care and thought should be taken.

ELECTRICITY

A safe *maximum working voltage is 12 volts.* Most equipment should operate up to this maximum. Any higher voltages, especially mains *should be under supervision only.*

MACHINES

1. **Whenever a machine is being used, goggles must be worn**. This includes vertical drilling machines, hand-held power drills, lathes and milling machines.

2. **For grinding machines, special grade goggles must be worn**. Ordinary goggles will *not* do as they do not totally cover the eyes and are likely to spot burn where red-hot pieces of metal and grinding wheel fly off.

3. **Before using any machine, the correct operating procedure should be known.** It is easy to overload smaller machines so, before using a machine, get your teacher, tutor or supervisor to check it after you set it up. This is especially important for lathes and milling machines where the right tool, tool angle and so on are vital.

PNEUMATICS

1. A special problem exists which is specific to pneumatics. Compressed air, if allowed to play on any breaks in the skin (cuts, grazes) or any opening in the body, can cause embolisms. These are bubbles in the blood. If a bubble makes its way to the brain, it will explode causing brain damage and possibly death.

   On no account should compressed air be used unless the pipes are connected to equipment.

2. All joints are prone to leaks, so make sure the rubber '0' rings are in place for pipe fittings; and where metal/metal joints are used, PTFE tape should be wrapped around the thread to make the joint seal properly.

3. Compressed air should not be used to get swarf and bits off machines. Not only is the compressed air a danger but the bits could cause injury to unprotected eyes.

a p p e n d i x 2

CIRCUIT BOARD CONSTRUCTION METHODS

There are four methods which can be used to construct electronic circuits:

(a) prototype systems
(b) matrix board
(c) veroboard
(d) printed circuit board.

The method used will depend on the stage of the design, the number of circuits to be produced and the production method.

PROTOTYPE SYSTEMS

It is possible that you have already used a form of prototyping system in basic electricity work. Prototype systems allow the electronic components to be plugged in and out without any soldering. Figure A.1 shows some available prototype systems. More complex systems do not have the components fixed to special holders. The wires of the components are connected by pushing them into spring connectors. The spring connectors are connected together by metal strips so that components can be easily joined together.

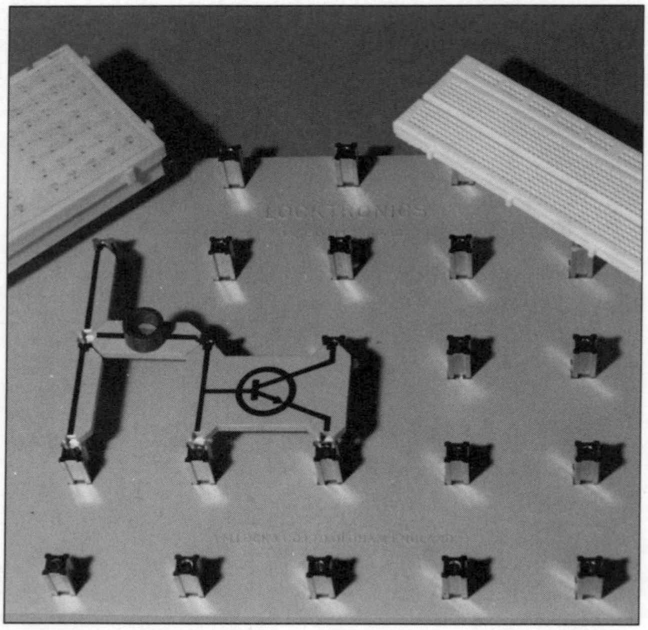

Figure A.1 *Prototype systems*

MATRIX BOARD

Matrix board (Figure A.2) is a mica board with holes drilled to form a regular grid. Special pins can be fitted into the holes where connections are required and components and connecting wires can be soldered on to the pins. The advantage of this board is that the pins can be inserted in the same pattern as the circuit diagram. The step from circuit diagram to layout design and on to building the circuit is quite straightforward.

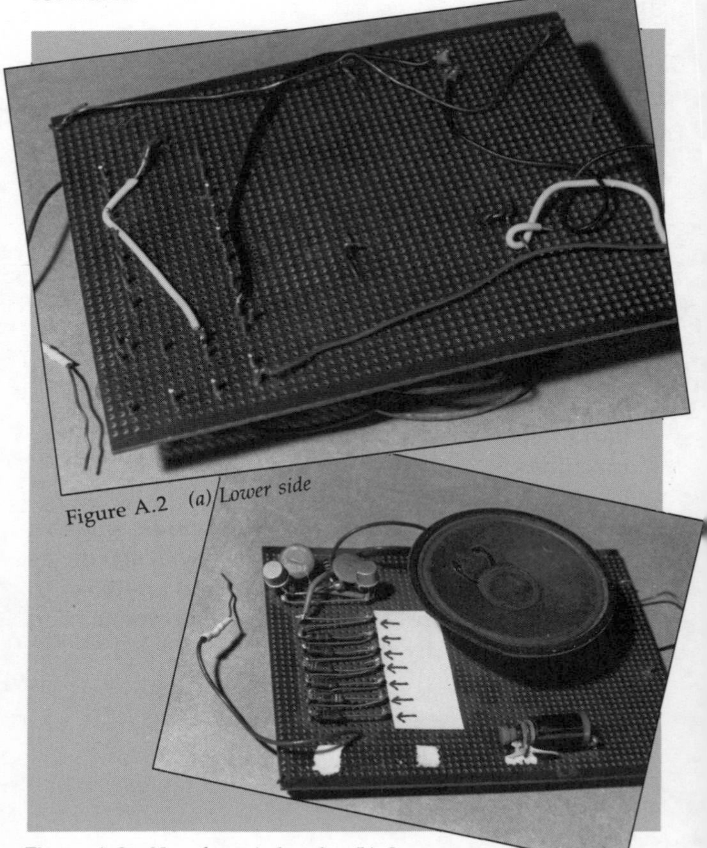

Figure A.2 (a) *Lower side*

Figure A.2 *Use of matrix board:* (b) *Components on upper side*

VEROBOARD

This is a type of matrix board but copper strips are fixed on to one side of the board connecting lines of holes. Figure A.3 shows this type of board being used. The transfer from circuit design to layout design is more complicated than with ordinary matrix board because of the fixed position of the copper strips. The copper strips are often cut to provide separation of the component connections along one line of holes. The components are fixed to the opposite side to the copper strips and this must be remembered when transferring the layout on to the veroboard. Veroboard would be used for a more permanent test circuit or where only a few circuits are to be built.

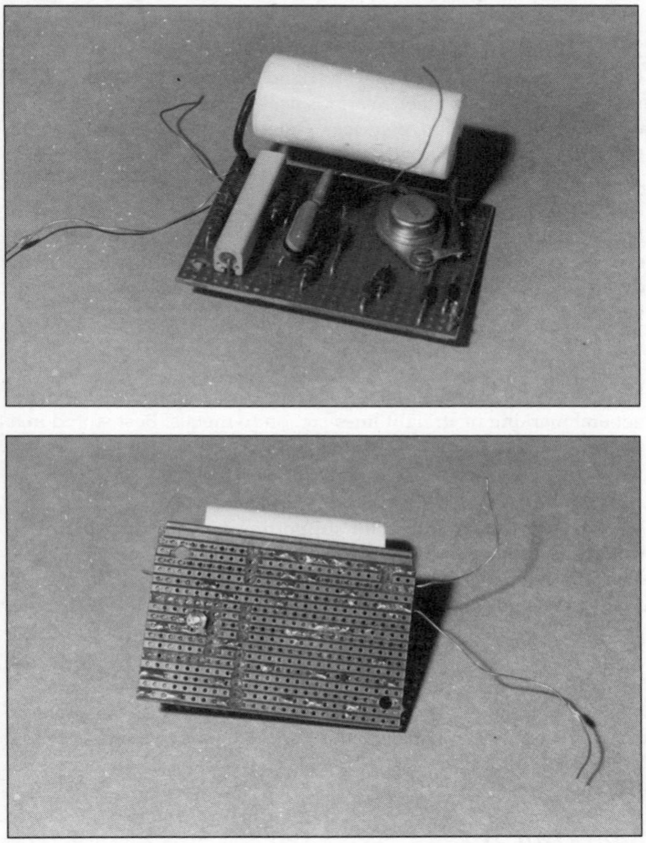

Figure A.3 *Use of veroboard: (a) Component side (b) Lower side*

Printed Circuit Board

This method of circuit construction is used for the final version of a circuit and is suitable for mass production. The complete theory of printed circuit design in a commercial environment is beyond the scope of this book. However, there are simple methods of printed circuit production which can be carried out successfully in a school environment with very little equipment.

The boards are made of an epoxy resin material completely covered on one or both sides with copper. The circuit is produced in the copper by covering up the copper that is required for the circuit and removing the rest of the copper by the use of chemicals. A solution of ferric chloride (iron III chloride) is usually used to remove the copper. This process is called 'etching'. Materials that are not removed by the etching chemicals are used to prevent the copper being removed from the circuit areas. This can be done in two ways. The quickest way is to use an etch-resistant ink pen to draw the pattern of the circuit on to the copper. The copper should be cleaned thoroughly before marking the circuit. Very fine steel wool will provide a clean surface. It is also possible to buy etch-resist transfers of the various patterns normally found in printed circuit boards. These transfers will take longer to lay out but will generally give a better result.

Once the circuit has been drawn on to the copper, remembering that the components will be fitted on to the side away from the copper tracks, the board can be put into a tray of ferric chloride. The type of tray used in photography is quite satisfactory. The tray should be rocked gently to keep fresh ferric chloride in contact with the board but ferric chloride is corrosive, so spills or splashes should be avoided. If you do get any of the chemical on you wash it off quickly with lots of cold water.

There are other methods for producing printed circuit boards. A photographic process is often used and many thousands of identical boards can be made for mass-produced equipment. More detail will be found in the specialist books listed in Appendix 7.

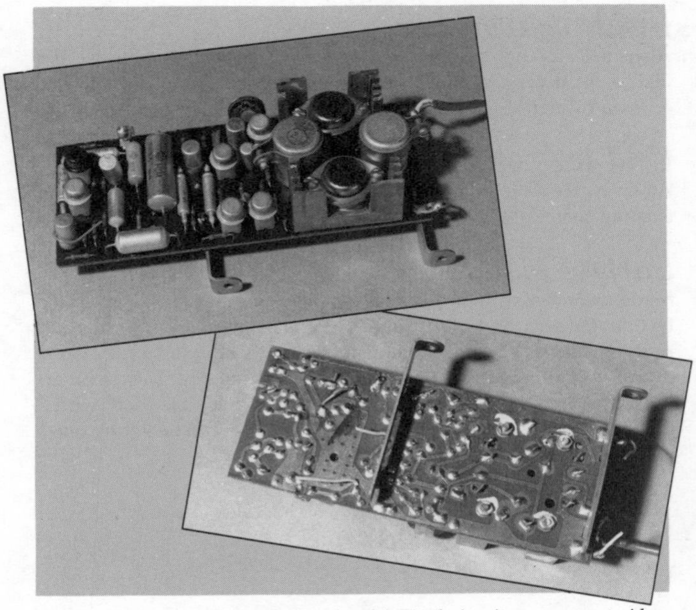

Figure A.4 *Printed circuit board: (a) Final circuit, component side (b) Final circuit, lower side*

appendix 3

MARKING-OUT TOOLS

Table A.1 Marking-out tools associated with technology

Tool/Description and use

Steel rule
The rustless steel these are made from is brittle and snaps easily, especially when dropped or bent. They are best stored vertically and used carefully if they are to give consistent measurements over any length of time.

Centre punch
Made from high carbon steel hardened and tempered, they are designed for rough treatment for marking the start of drilled holes. However, only the top is designed to be hit with a hammer. The point should be especially hard and ground to a point to enable a good start for any hole. Best stored vertically in racks with the point protected.

Dividers
Made from high carbon steel left soft and used for accurate marking of arcs and circles. The points of dividers must be sharp or they will not scribe an accurate line. They are best stored with the points closed together vertically in racks with the points covered.

Outside calipers
Made of mild steel (rustless) and used to find the thickness of plates and the diameter of bars of materials; the thin section of the caliper arms are particularly prone to bending and distortion so should be stored when not in use supported from the top.

Inside calipers
Also made of rustless mild steel, these are used to measure the inside diameters of holes and tubes; for care and storage see outside calipers.

Odd leg calipers
Again made from rustless mild steel; they mark lines parallel to existing material sides; for care and storage, see *outside calipers*.

Surface plate
Made from cast iron and very accurately ground flat. It is used for testing flatness and right angles, bends and marking out with scribing block and angle plate. It is very heavy and brittle so if dropped or hit, it will shatter. Hot objects should not be scribed on the plate. Store on a flat surface, preferably where it is used, with a wooden cover over the surface. The surface should be lightly oiled and kept free of dirt.

Scribing block
Made from mild steel or cast iron and ground flat (block scriber made of high carbon steel). Various uses for marking the centres of circles and heights above surface plate. Store in a cupboard with the scriber vertical, curved point down.

Vee block
Made from mild steel ground flat and square. Used for marking out centres for drilling and turning. Should be stored in a cupboard. Often used with clamps which should be stored in a cupboard vertically.

Scriber
Made from high carbon steel hardened and tempered. Used for general marking of straight lines etc. on to metals. Best stored in a vertical position in racks with the point covered.

Angle plate
Made of cast iron and used for supporting and checking pieces of work at a right angle to the surface plate. Heat and knocks could damage the plate so should be handled carefully. Store in a cupboard when not in use.

Try square
Made from rustless steel and used for checking, measuring and marking right angles on work as well as testing for the squareness of work. Very easily damaged and knocked out of square so needs to be handled carefully. Store in a rack so that the blade cannot be distorted.

Marking ink
Usually a thick copper sulphate solution with other additives. Used for painting the surface of metal prior to marking out. A bottle which is not easily knocked over and with a brush fitted in the lid is a good idea. Mounting on a large flat piece of wood may help. Store in a cupboard when not in use.

appendix 4

DRAWING AND GRAPHIC COMMUNICATION

It is said that 'A drawing is worth a thousand words'. Ideas are communicated more easily and quickly with a drawing than with a description.

Design Sketches

The guidelines for good design sketches are:

(a) clarity—ideas should be immediately obvious
(b) good detail—where a specific detail cannot be shown on the main sketch, a separate detail is a good idea complete with reference to the main sketch
(c) presentation—it should be obvious how the designer's ideas have developed from first stages to final designs
(d) reasoning—every stage of the design process should be shown indicating the decision taken at each stage and why it was taken.

Working Drawing

The rules of graphic communication are quite strict. They are far too detailed for this book. Appendix 7 contains books (possibly available at school) which will give this detail. However, technology is more concerned with the presentation of ideas on paper and only the working drawing should be accurately drawn and carefully dimensioned. The general layout of a drawing page is shown in Figure A.5.

The diagram shows an A3-sized drawing board. Other sizes of paper are:

A1 840 mm × 594 mm
A2 594 mm × 420 mm
A3 420 mm × 297 mm
A4 297 mm × 210 mm

The presentation of working drawing depends on clarity. The usual method for lines is shown in Figure A.6. Figure A.7 gives an example of how each of these lines is used and how drawings are dimensioned.

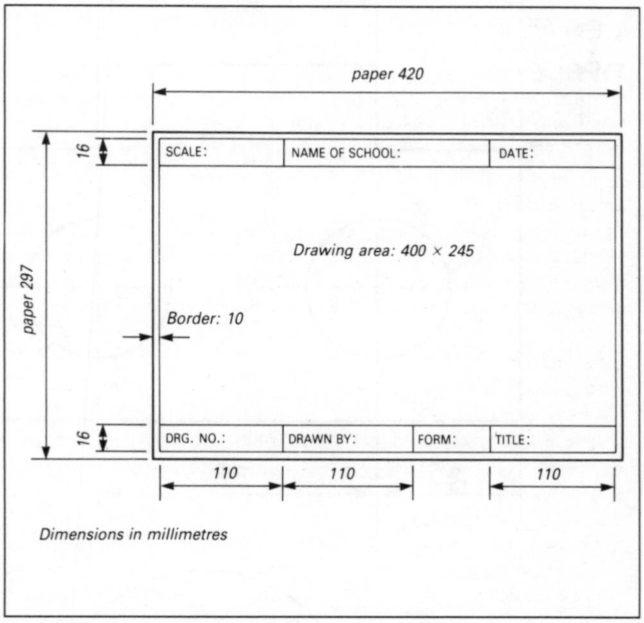

Figure A.5 *General layout of a drawing page*

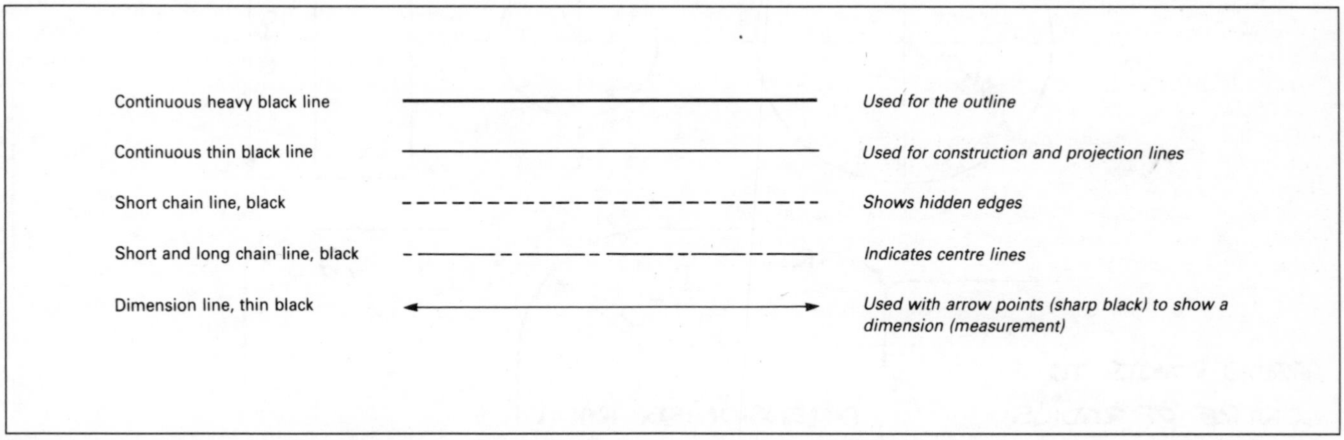

Figure A.6 *Convention for drawing lines (BS308)*

METHODS OF DRAWING

Figures A.8, A.9 and A.10 show various methods of drawing. Sectional drawings may occasionally be required. Appendix 7 lists references to further sources of information.

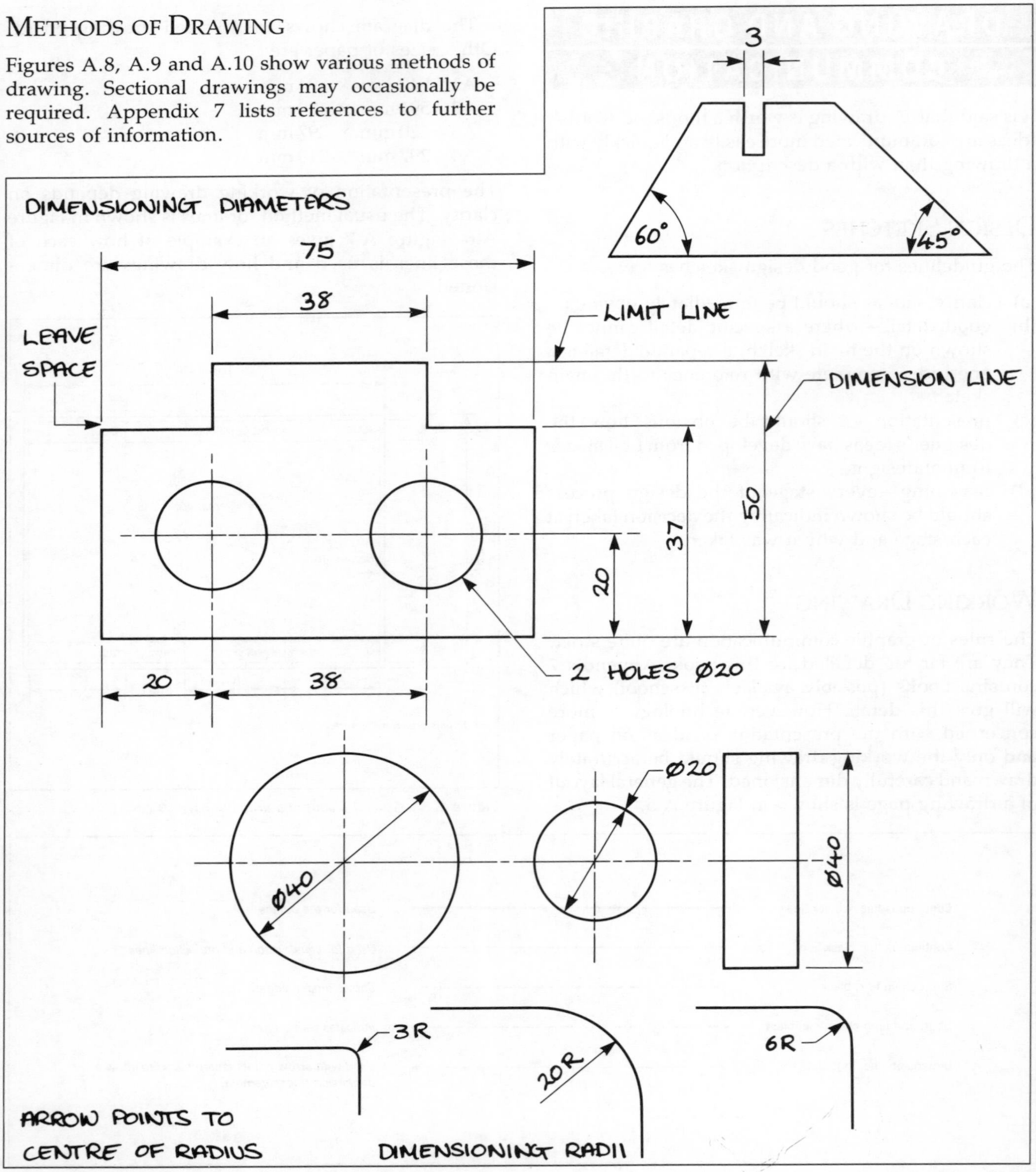

Figure A.7 *Line and dimension conventions*

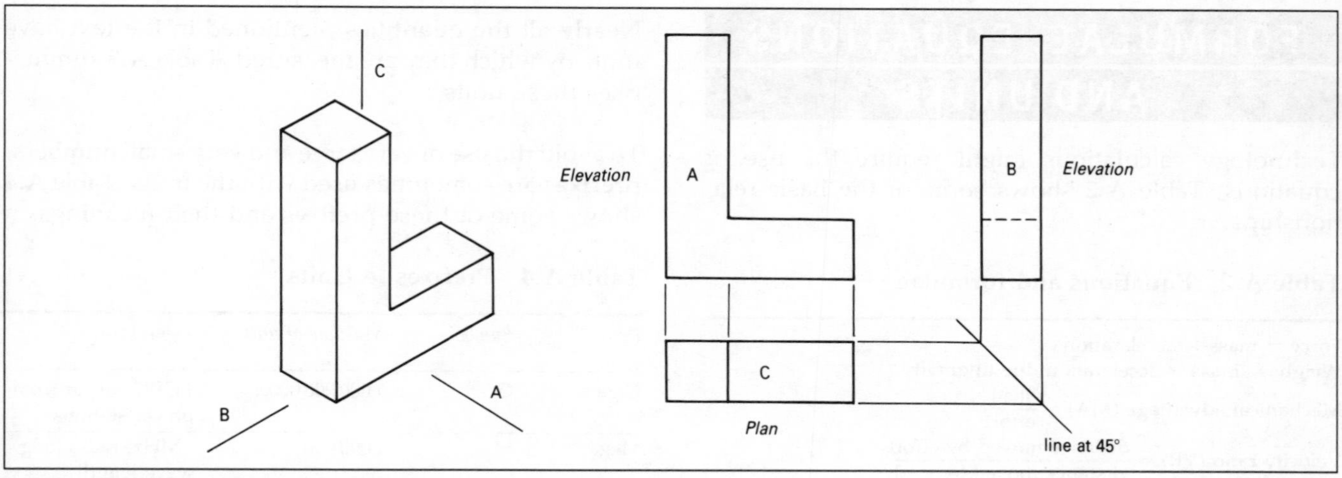

Figure A.8 *Orthographic projection (1st angle)*

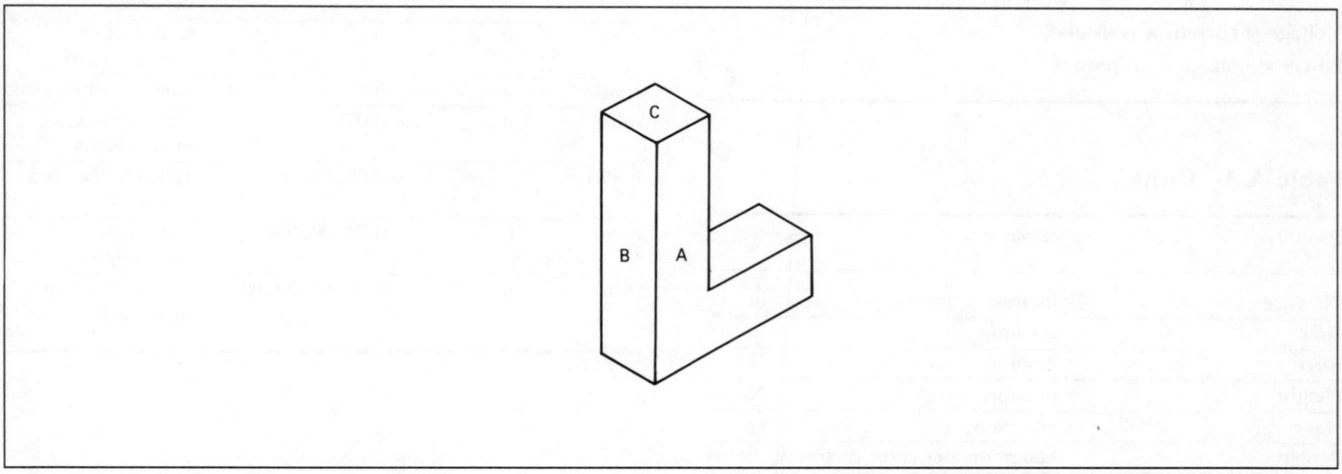

Figure A.9 *Isometric projection*

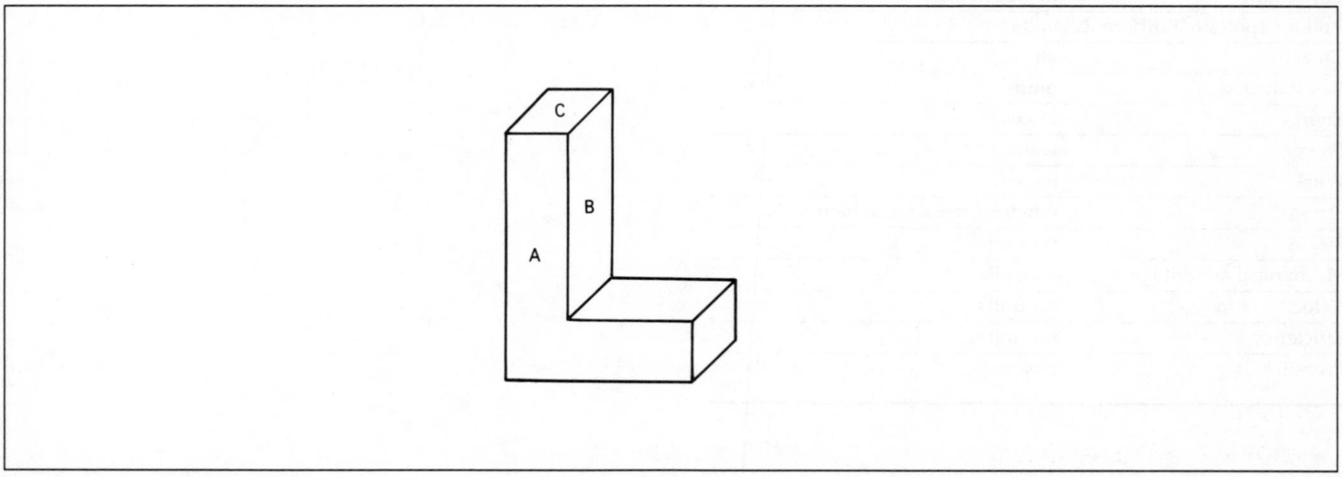

Figure A.10 *Oblique projection*

appendix 5

FORMULAE, EQUATIONS AND UNITS

Technology calculations might require the use of equations. Table A.2 shows some of the basic relationships.

Table A.2 Equations and formulae

Force = mass × acceleration

Weight = mass × acceleration due to gravity

$$\text{Mechanical advantage (MA)} = \frac{\text{load}}{\text{effort}}$$

$$\text{Velocity ratio (VR)} = \frac{\text{distance moved by effort}}{\text{distance moved by load}}$$

$$\text{Efficiency} = \frac{\text{MA}}{\text{VR}} \times 100 = \frac{\text{work out}}{\text{work in}} \times 100\%$$

Voltage = current × resistance

Power = voltage × current

Table A.3 Units

Quantity	*Name of unit*	*Symbol*
Distance	metres	m
Time	seconds	s
Force	newton	N
Weight	newton	N
Mass	kilogram	kg
Density	kilograms per cubic metre	kg/m^3
Volume	cubic metres	m^3
Capacitance	microfarads	μF
Voltage (potential difference)	volts	V
Current	amps	A
Resistance	ohms	Ω
Energy	joules	J
Power	watts	W
Work	joules	J
Stress	newtons per square metre	N/m^2
Strain	no units	–
Mechanical advantage	no units	–
Velocity ratio	no units	–
Efficiency	no units	–
Pressure	pascals	Pa

Nearly all the quantities mentioned in the text have units by which they are measured. Table A.3 summarises these units.

To avoid the use of very large and very small numbers, **prefixes** are sometimes used with the units. Table A.4 shows some of these prefixes and their meanings.

Table A.4 Prefixes to Units

Prefix	*Symbol*	*Multiple of unit*	*Typical use*
Giga	G	1 000 000 000	1 GW, output from power stations
Mega	M	1 000 000	1 MHz, radio long wave length
kilo	k	1000	1 km, long distances
deci	d	0.1	1 dB, sound measurement
centi	c	0.01	1 cm, small lengths
milli	m	0.001	1 ms, very short time periods
micro		0.000 001	1 μF, charge on a capacitor
nano	n	0.000 000 001	1 nm, light wavelength
pico	p	0.000 000 000 001	1 pF, very small capacitors

appendix 6

USEFUL ADDRESSES

GCSE Examining Group Addresses

London and East Anglia Group
LEAG
East Anglian Examinations Board
'The Lindens'
Lexden Road
Colchester CO3 3RL

Midland Examining Group
MEG
The Local Examination Syndicate
1 Hills Road
Cambridge CB1 2EU

Northern Examining Association
NEA
Joint Matriculation Board
Manchester M15 6EU

Northern Ireland Schools Examination Council
NISEC
Examination Office
Beechill House
Beechill Road
Belfast BT8 4RS

Southern Examining Group
SEG
Stag Hill House
Guildford
Surrey GU2 5XJ

Welsh Joint Education Committee
WJEC
245 Western Avenue
Cardiff CF5 2YX

Tools, Components and Materials

Tools, materials
Arkon Tools
21–23 Cherry Tree Rise
Buckhurst Hill
Essex IG9 6ET

Lathes
CNC Lathes Boxford Ltd
Wheatly
Halifax
West Yorkshire HX3 5AF

Information on gas
British Gas Education Service
PO Box 46
Hounslow
Middlesex TW4 6NF

Information on oil-based products (plastics)
British Petroleum Education Service
PO Box 5
Wetherby
West Yorkshire LS23 6YY

Electronic components, tools
Cirkit Holding Ltd
Park Lane
Broxbourne
Hertfordshire EN10 7NQ

Robotics and computer-controlled lathes
Colne Robotics Ltd
Beaufort Road
Off Richmond Road
East Twickenham
Middlesex TW1 2PQ

Extensive range of technology supplies
Commotion Technology Supplies
241 Green Street
Enfield
Middlesex EN3 7SJ

Vacuum forming, strip heaters, injection moulders, plastic working machines
C.R. Clarke & Co.
(Vacuum and Plastic Forming Machines)
Unit 3 Betws Industrial Park
Ammanford
Dyfed SA18 2LS

Computer interface and control equipment
Deltronics
91 Heol-y-Parc
Cafneithin
Llanelli
Dyfed SA14 7DL

Pneumatic equipment, Fischertechnik, Meccano and other technology equipment
Economatics
Education Division
4 Orgreave Crescent
Dove House Industrial Estate
Handsworth
Sheffield S13 9NQ
Tel. 0742 690801

Computer interfaces and control equipment
Educational Electronics
30 Lake Street
Leighton Buzzard
Bedfordshire
LU7 8RX

Plastics samples, teaching aids
Education Service of the Plastics Industry
University of Technology
Loughborough
Leicestershire LE11 3TU

Information on electricity generation and transmission
Electricity Council
30 Millbank
London SW1P 4RD

Full range of metalworking machines from small to large
Emco
E.M.E. Ltd
131 Holyhead Road
Handsworth
Birmingham B21 0BE

Model-making supplies, plastic sheeting, tools
Ema Model Supplies Ltd
58–60 The Centre
Feltham
Middlesex TW13 4BH

Electronic components, tools, test equipment
Farnell Electronic Components Ltd
Canal Road
Leeds LS12 2TU

Fischertechnik kits for model making
Fischer Technik
Artur Fischer (UK) Ltd
Fischer House
25 Newton Road
Marlow
Buckinghamshire SL7 1JT

General science and technology equipment
Griffin and George Ltd
Bishop Meadow Road
Loughborough
Leicestershire LE11 0RG

Electronic components
JPR Electronics Ltd
Unit M
Kingsway Industrial Estate
Kingsway
Luton
Bedfordshire LU1 1LP

Circuit board equipment tools, test equipment
Kelan Circuits Ltd
Farnell Technology Park
Boroughbridge
North Yorkshire YO5 9UY

Legotechnic for model making and demonstrating mechanisms
Lego UK Ltd
Education Division
Ruthin Road
Wrexham
Clwyd LL13 7TQ

Electronics on large size electronic circuit building
A.M. Lock
Neville Street
Middleton Road
Oldham
Lancashire 0L9 6LF

Electronic components
Maplin Electronic Supplies Ltd
PO Box 3
Rayleigh
Essex SS6 8LR
Tel. 0702 552911

Microelectronics circuit boards
Omega Electronics
12 Oxhill Road
Middle Tysoe
Warwickshire CV35 0SX

Science and technology teaching equipment
Philip Harris Ltd
Lynn Lane
Shenstone
Lichfield
Staffordshire WS14 0EE

Electronic components, tools, test equipment
RS Components
PO Box 99
Corby
Northamptonshire NN17 9RS
Tel. 0536 201201

Plastic wheels, propellors, balsa wood
Solarbo Ltd
Commerce Way
Lancing
Sussex BN15 8TE

Mini pliers, side cutters, plastic tube, wire, motors etc.
Southern Science & Technology Forum
The University
Southampton SO9 5NH

Printed circuit production, general technology equipment
Testbed Technology Ltd
PO Box 70
Clarendon Road
Blackburn
Lancashire BB1 9TD

Extensive range of technology equipment
Technology Teaching Systems Ltd
Penmore House
Hasland Road,
Hasland
Chesterfield S41 0SJ

Computer equipment
Watford Electronics
Jessa House
250 Lower High Street
Watford WD1 2AN
Tel. 0923 37774

Surplus nuts, bolts, nails, metal offcuts
K.M. Whiston Ltd
New Mills
Stockport SK12 4PT

Technology teaching equipment
Nottingham Educational Supplies
17 Ludlow Hill Road
West Bridgford
Nottingham NG2 6HP

Test equipment, power supplies, computer interfaces, microelectronic teaching systems
Unilab Ltd
Clarendon Road
Blackburn
Lancashire BB1 9TA

Components, plastic construction kits, pneumatics equipment
Vento Solenoids Ltd
43 Burners Lane
Kiln Farm
Milton Keynes
Buckinghamshire MK11 3HA

appendix 7

FURTHER READING AND REFERENCES

Barker, B.G. *Foundation Electronics*, Nelson, 1981

Barlex D. & Kimbell, R. *CDT Projects and Approaches*, Macmillan Education, 1986

BP Education Service, *Microelectronics—Practical Approaches for Schools and Colleges*, Tecmedia, 1981

British Standards Institution, *Graphical symbols for use in schools*, BSI Education, 1986

Dance, J. B. *Op Amps, Their Principles and Applications*, Newne's Technical Book, 1982

Duncan, T. *Success in Electronics*, John Murray, 1983

Fair, D. & Kenny, M. *Design graphics*, Hodder & Stoughton, 1988

Gordon, J.E. *Structures (or Why Things Don't Fall Down)*, Penguin, 1978

Gordon, J.E. *The New Science of Strong Materials (or Why You Don't Fall Through the Floor)*, Penguin, 1976

Hall, G. *Design and Plastics*, Hodder and Stoughton, 1988

Hughes, M.J. & Colwell, M.A. *Printed Circuit Assembly*, Newne's Technical Books, 1977

Jones, M.H. *A Practical Introduction to Electronic Circuits*, Cambridge University Press, 1977

Kaye, G. & Laby, T. *Tables of Physical and Chemical Constants*, Longman, 1986

Parr, E.A. *IC 555 Projects*, Babani Publishing, 1978

Penfold, R.A., *How to design and make your own PCB's*, Babani Publishing, 1983

Schools Council, *Modular Courses in Technology:* Mechanisms, Pneumatics, Electronics; Structures, Materials, Problem Solving, Oliver & Boyd, 1980

Thomas, G.H. *Metalwork Technology*, John Murray, 1972

Periodicals:

Educational Computing, Redwood Publishing

Electronic Systems News, I.E.E., Savoy Place, London WC2 0BL

School Technology, Trent International Centre for School Technology

Examination Board Literature:

Many publications such as coursework memoranda and teachers' guides. Contact your GCSE Examination Group.

Further information on most aspects of technology in schools can be obtained from the Trent International Centre for School Technology, Trent Polytechnic, Burton Street, Nottingham (Previously NCST).

appendix 8

KEY WORDS

This is a list of all the words highlighted in their major position in the text together with their meanings and section numbers of main entry.

A

Active axis (2:16) the axis of a strain gauge which is placed along the expected axis of strain when testing structures.

Additives (3:18) chemicals which are added in small quantities to change the properties of particular mixes of chemicals.

Address (4:24) a number which refers to a single store in a computer's memory.

Air bleed system (3:20) in pneumatics, a type of circuit which continually leaks air out of a tube. Blocking the tube causes a pressure-sensitive valve to operate.

Alloy (2:15) a composition of two or more metals mixed or chemically combined with properties different from the separate metals.

Alternating current (AC) (4:1) electricity which keeps changing direction of flow. The positive and negative terminals keep changing. This usually happens rapidly (mains electricity alternates 50 times a second or 50Hz).

Alternator (3:19) a generator of alternating current (AC) electricity.

Amplify (4:3) usually associated with waves and electronics, means to make a signal or wave bigger.

Analogue voltage (4:21) this is a voltage which changes continuously and is usually caused by a 'physical' change applied to an electronic component, such as a change in the temperature of a thermistor.

ASCII (4:24) American Standard Code for Information Interchange; the standard binary codes used by computers.

Atom (4:1) made up from electrons, protons and neutrons. Each element (or pure substance) is made up of atoms which are all the same and the smallest part of an element which can exist alone.

Automatic circuit (3:20) circuits that operate continually without operator intervention.

Axial load (3:8) a load along a shaft or axle.

B

Back e.m.f. (4:17) the voltage created when a magnetic field collapses. This would happen when a relay or a motor is turned off.

Base (4:17) one of the three connections of a transistor.

BASIC (4:24) a high-level computer programming language, which is 'user friendly' or easier to use.

Bearing (3:8) used where a moving surface is supported by a non-moving surface. There are three types: flat, journal and thrust.

Biasing (4:25) used to set the operating voltages of electronic devices such as transistors and diodes.

Brake (3:16) a mechanism to stop or slow a moving object such as a motor vehicle.

Buffer (4:17) a small electronic circuit connected between a computer and another piece of electronic circuitry enabling the computer to operate the circuit. Provides some electrical protection for the computer.

Bush (3:8) a simple form of bearing used to absorb small movement, reduce friction and reduce wear of metal components.

Byte (4:24) made up of eight bits of binary information. Used in computer codes.

C

Cam (3:10) a mechanism to convert circular motion to linear motion. The resulting linear motion depends on the shape of the cam.

Cam follower (3:10) the object which is in contact with a cam as it rotates. It responds to the shape of the cam.

Capacitor (4:3) an electronic device which stores small amounts of electrical charge.

Cell (4:1) a source of low voltage, direct current

electricity. Cells are often joined in series to give batteries.

Centre of gravity (2:3) the point through which the weight of an object acts.

Circuit (electronic) (4:2) a circuit made up from electronic components which works by connecting to the positive and negative terminals of a power supply.

Circuit (pneumatic) (3:20) an arrangement of components which use compressed air to produce controlled movement.

Clutch (3:15) the mechanism through which the power of an engine or motor is transferred to the driving shaft. The clutch disconnects the power unit from the drive shaft to allow the changing of gears or stopping the drive shaft.

Collector (4:17) one of the connections of a transistor.

Compression moulding (2:15) a means of moulding plastics, especially thermosetting plastics. The ingredients of the plastic are squashed into a mould and then heated.

Compressor (3:20) a machine which produces compressed air for use in pneumatics.

Conduction (2:17) heat transfer within a solid due to energy transfer between molecules and atoms.

Control line (3:20) in pneumatics, a compressed air line which connects pilot and control valves.

Control valve (3:20) a valve used to control a pneumatic cylinder.

Convection (2:17) heat transfer which occurs within a liquid or a gas, either of which expands when heated, becomes less dense, and rises above the colder more dense part of the liquid or gas.

Crank and slider (3:14) a mechanism for converting linear motion to circular motion. A common example is a piston and cylinder.

Current (4:4) electrical current is a flow of electrons in a conductor. Measured in amps (A).

Cylinder (3:20) when compressed air is introduced, the piston inside the cylinder will move. There are two types of cylinder—single acting and double acting.

D

Darlington pair (4:20) a pair of transistors connected so that the emitter of one is connected to the base of the other. The combination gives high current gain.

Digital voltage (4:21) a voltage which is either on or off, usually shown as 1 or 0. It is used in computer systems and digital control systems.

Diode (4:3) an electronic component which only allows electricity to flow in one direction.

Direct current (DC) (4:1) electricity which always goes round the circuit in the same direction, conventionally from positive to negative.

Distance magnifier (3:1) a machine which takes an input force or effort and increases the distance over which it can act also reducing the size of the force. Many types of levers are distance magnifiers.

Driven shaft (3:7) where gears are enmeshed, the driven gear is mounted on this shaft from which comes the output motion of the machine.

Driving shaft (3:7) the enmeshed gear on the input side of a machine is mounted on this shaft.

Dual-in-line (DIL) package (4:21) integrated circuits are packaged in this form for ease and connection into circuits.

Dynamic force (2:7) force which acts as the result of a moving object or load.

Dynamo (3:19) an electricity generator producing DC only.

E

Efficiency (3:7) when one form of energy is converted to another, the fraction of energy successfully converted and not lost or wasted gives the efficiency of the energy conversion. Expressed as a percentage, it has no units.

Electric motor (3:19) it converts electricity to rotary motion.

Electromagnetic waves (2:17) a family of transverse waves which, depending on frequency and wavelength, will have a variety of properties, ranging from gamma rays to radio waves. An effective method of transferring energy from one place to another.

Electromotive force (e.m.f.) (4:1) the force which pushes electrons around an electric circuit to give an electric current.

Electron (4:1) a very small particle (the smallest in an atom) which carries a negative charge. It orbits around the central nucleus of the atom and is almost massless.

Electron gun (4:11) the device at the back of all cathode ray tubes which produces a 'cloud' of electrons by heating a negatively charged filament. This cloud is focused on to a beam by an anode towards which the electrons fly at high speed.

Emitter (4:17) one of the three connections on a transistor. On an npn transistor, the emitter is connected to the ground rail.

F

Factor of safety (2:14) how much stronger a material is compared to the load it is being asked to carry. If the load to be carried is 100 N and the material can handle 200 N before breaking, the factor of safety is 2. A factor of safety of 4 is more usual.

Feedback path (4:26) when part of the output from an electronic circuit is fed back into the input of the circuit, this is called feedback. The part of the circuit through which feedback flows is the feedback path.

Flow regulator (3:20) in pneumatics, this device controls the flow of air through the pipes so that pressure changes can be varied.

Force (2:4, 3:1) when a force is applied to an object its direction of travel or its speed will alter. Measured in newtons (N).

Force magnifier (3:1) usually applied to machines, where a machine has a larger output force compared with the input force.

Frequency (4:1) used to describe waveforms. It is the number of waves passing a chosen point every second. Measured in hertz (Hz) or cycles per second.

Friction (3:7) the force which opposes motion when two surfaces are rubbing together.

Fulcrum (2:6) the pivot point of a lever around which the load and effort move.

G

Gears (3:17) circular discs with teeth on. There are many different types such as pinion, spur, bevel, mitre, helical.

Gear ratio (3:17) where gears are meshing, the ratio of the teeth on one gear to the teeth on another gear. Used to calculate turning speeds.

Gravity (2:4) the force which pulls towards the centre of the earth.

H

Heat sink (4:17) a piece of metal attached to certain electronic components, such as power transistors, which generate heat. The materials chosen are good conductors of heat and help to keep the electronic components cool by conducting heat away from the component.

I

Interface (4:17) an electronic 'box of tricks' designed to be run by a computer to enable the control of electric motors and the interpretation of analogue readings from instruments.

Integrated circuits (IC) (4:3) miniaturised electronic circuits enclosed in a small plastic case. Many thousands of components are built into a very small space, usually less than a centimetre square.

K

Kinetic energy (3:3) the energy of moving objects. Measured in joules.

L

Lever (3:5) a simple machine with three easily recognisable parts: the effort, load and pivot. Scissors and the see-saw are common examples.

Linkages (3:6) these result from combining several levers to obtain a desired motion

Logic gate (4.3) an electronic decision-making circuit. AND, OR, NOT, NAND and NOR are typical examples.

Lubricant (3:18) a fluid which helps to reduce friction between two surfaces.

Lubricator (3:18) where regular lubrication is needed and manual application is inconvenient, a lubricator will continually feed a measured amount of lubricant between the surfaces in contact.

M

Mark–space ratio (4:20) the ratio of the on-time to off-time. Associated with wave forms especially square waves.

Mass (2:4) the amount of substance there is of an object. Measured in kilograms (kg).

Mechanical advantage (MA) (3:7) the ratio of load and effort applied to a machine. It has no units.

Mechanism (3:1) a device which produces useful force and motion to do a particular job.

Modulus of elasticity (2:13) sometimes called Young's Modulus. A measure of elasticity of a material. Measured in newtons per square metre.

Moment of force (2:6, 3:4) the turning force calculated by multiplying a force by the distance of the force from the fulcrum.

Multivibrator (4:20) a special class of electronic circuits. There are three types: monostable, bistable and astable.

N

Newton (2:4) the unit of force and weight.

Nucleus (4:1) the centre of an atom. It contains most of the mass of an atom consisting of protons and neutrons.

P

Parallel ports (4:24) the output port from a computer which normally has eight signal lines which can be used for computer control.

Particle composite (2:15) a material which is made up by combining particles. A common example is concrete.

Passive axis (2:16) the axis at right angles to the active axis (see above) of a strain gauge. There would be no measurable change along the passive axis.

Peak voltage (4:1) the maximum voltage at the top of an AC voltage. For 240 volt AC (RMS, root mean square, voltage) the peak voltage is about 315 volts.

Phase change (4:25) the relative position of input and output waves from a circuit. If the input is at maximum when the output is at minimum, as in a single transistor amplifier, then the phase change is 180 degrees.

Pilot valves (3:20) in pneumatics, a pilot valve operates another (air operated) valve via a control air line.

Pivot (3:5) see fulcrum.

Plastics (2:15) a class of materials based upon the carbon–carbon chain of atoms. There are three types: thermoplastics, thermosets and elastomers.

Pneumatics (3:20) using compressed air to operate mechanisms.

Pneumatic valve (3:20) valve which allows compressed air to enter and leave a pneumatic device.

Polariscope (2:16) device used to check for strain patterns in models of structural components. Uses polarised light.

Potential difference (PD) (4:4) voltage (or electrical force) across two points in an electrical circuit. Measured in volts (V).

Potential energy (3:3) energy stored in an object due to its position or condition. Provides an ability to do work.

Power (3:3, 4:6) amount of energy converted or transferred by a mechanism per second. Measured in watts (W).

Pulley (3:7) wheel over which a string or belt will run enabling small efforts to lift large loads.

R

Radial load (3:8) load applied at right angles to an axle or shaft.

Radiation (2:17) form of heat energy that travels in the form of electromagnetic waves. Can travel through a vacuum.

Reciprocating motion (3:2) motion which goes

backwards and forwards. A pendulum and a piston in a cylinder are typical examples.

Rectification (4:14) the process of changing alternating current to direct current.

Relay (4:17) electromagnetic device which allows one circuit to switch another (usually at a different voltage or current flow) whilst keeping the circuits electrically separate.

Reservoir (3:20) in pneumatics, stores air for a short time putting a time delay into pneumatic circuits.

Resistance (4:3) electrical resistance restricts electrical current (electron flow) in a conductor. Measured in ohms.

Resistor (4:3) device with a measured amount of electrical resistance.

Resultant force (2:9) total force occurring as a result of two or more forces being added together.

Root mean square (RMS) (4:1) method used to find the effective voltage of an AC voltage. The RMS voltage gives the same effect as a DC voltage of the same value.

S

Scalar (2:9) quantity having size only, e.g. temperature, mass, density, viscosity, electrical resistance.

Schmitt trigger (4:23) electronic circuit which will send an output signal (or voltage) only when the input to the circuit reaches a certain voltage level.

Screw thread (3:13) helical pattern on a steel rod which, depending on the screw form, can be used for many different purposes, e.g. bolts, car jacks, lathe lead screws.

Soft iron (3:19) iron which does not retain magnetism. Used as the core of transformers and other electromagnetic devices.

Solenoid (3:19) a closely wound coil of wire. When a current flows through the coil it acts like a magnet. The magnetic field is often concentrated in the centre by winding the coil round a soft iron core.

Sprocket and chain (3:7) mechanism to transfer rotary motion from one place to another. A bicycle uses this arrangement.

Static force (2:7) force due to the weight of a structure and the stationary forces on the structure (opposite of dynamic).

Strain (2:12) change in length of an object in relation to its original length when placed under load. Sometimes given as a percentage.

Stress (2:12) force per unit cross-sectional area of an object. Measured in newtons per square metre or similar unit, such as N/mn^2.

Strut (2:7) part of a structure which is always in compression.

T

Thermal runaway (4:5) result of electrical flow through an electrical component. The heating effect of the flow decreases the resistance of the component allowing more flow and so more heating. Often leads to failure of the component.

Thermoplastic (2:15) type of plastic which is hard when cool yet soft when hot. As a result, it can be formed and reformed many times.

Thermoset (2:15) type of plastic which, when first made, is soft. Once hardened, it cannot be softened by heat.

Tie (2:7) part of a structure which is always in tension.

Time constant (4:20) property of a capacitor/resistor combination which can be used in timing.

Tolerance (4:8) used to give the accuracy to which something is made. In this case it is referring to the value of a resistor.

Torque (3:4) turning force usually of an axle or rotating arm. Measured in newton metres. Also see moment of force.

Transducer (4:18) a device which changes one form of energy to another form of energy. Often described as either input or output transducers.

Transformer (4:3) a device which changes the voltage of electricity. Only works with AC electricity.

Transistor (4:3) electronic semiconductor device with three connections, base, emitter and collector. When a voltage of 0.6 V appears across the base/

emitter connections, a current will flow from the collector to the emitter.

Truth table (4:21) list of logic gate functions, usually shown as 1 for 'on' or conducting and 0 for 'off'.

Turning force (2:6) see torque.

U

Universal joints (3:9) used on connections between rotating shafts when the shafts are not in line with each other.

User port (4:24) usually a parallel port of a computer used for control purposes. Digital signals can pass to or from the computer.

V

Variable resistor (4:3) electronic component with a changeable amount of electrical resistance.

Vector (2:9) quantity with size *and* direction, e.g. force, weight, velocity.

Velocity ratio (3:7) property of a mechanism or machine; the distance moved by the effort divided by the distance moved by the load. Also called the gear ratio when using gears.

Viscosity (3:18) thickness of a fluid. It can be determined by the time it takes an object to fall down through a vertical column of the fluid.

W

Weight (2:4) force with which gravity pulls on a mass. Measured in newtons. A mass of one kilogram has a weight of about 10 newtons.

Work (3:3) done whenever a force moves; given by the size of the force multiplied by the distance the force moves. It is a measure of the energy converted and has units of joules.

index